2017 U.S. INDUSTRY & MARKET OUTLOOK

NATIONAL EDITION

The 2017 U.S. Industry & Market Outlook report is the leading annual publication that describes over 100 major U.S. industries and 500+ minor industries. Published each year in October, the Outlook report provides the most current and accurate estimates of the size of the largest manufacutring, retail, wholesale and services industries in the United States.

With over 250 pages, the National edition of the 2017 U.S. Industry & Market Outlook features:

- 2017 establishments, employment and sales totals for each industry
- 2018 forecast establishments, employment and sales totals
- 5-year trend establishments and sales totals
- Industry financial ratios such as sales per employees, sales per establishment and employees per establishment
- 2017 establishments and sales totals for 500+ minor industries
- Industry definitions and descriptions

The 2017 U.S. Industry & Market Outlook report is available in the Barnes Reports' online subscription service.

The Outlook report is available for purchase in either PDF, spreadsheet (Excel) or print format edition.

The 2017 U.S. Industry & Market Outlook report is an essential reference tool for industry researchers, market analysts, CEOs and leading industry executives.

2017 U.S. Industry & Market Outlook

2017 U.S. INDUSTRY & MARKET OUTLOOK

TABLE OF CONTENTS

INDUSTRY	PAGE NUMBER
Construction	
Single-Family Housing Construction Industry	7
Electrical Contractors Industry	9
Plumbing & Heating & A/C Contractors	11
Carpentry Contractors Industry	13
Manufacturing	
Breakfast Cereal Manufacturing Industry	15
Frozen Food Manufacturing Industry	17
Cookie Cracker & Pasta Mfg. Industry	19
Snack Food Manufacturing Industry	21
Soft-Drink Manufacturing Industry	23
Breweries & Beer-Making Industry	25
Wineries & Wine-Making Industry	27
Distilleries & Alcohol-Making Industry	29
Men's & Boys' Apparel Mfg. Industry	31
Women's & Girls' Apparel Mfg. Industry	33
Paper Mills Industry	35
Printing Industry	37
Petroleum Refineries Industry	39
Petrochemical Manufacturing Industry	41
Pharmaceutical Preparation Mfg. Industry	43
Electronic Computer Manufacturing Industry	45
Telephone Equipment Mfg. Industry	47
Radio/TV Broadcast Equipment Industry	49
Audio & Visual Equipment Mfg. Industry	51
Semi-Conductor & Electronic Components Mfg.	53
Software Reproducing Industry	55
Major Appliance Manufacturing Industry	57
Automobile & Motor Vehicle Mfg. Industry	59
Heavy Duty Truck Mfg.	61
Automobile Gas Engine & Engine Parts Mfg.	63
Aircraft Manufacturing Industry	65
Kitchen Cabinet & Countertop Mfg. Industry	67
Household & Institutional Furniture Mfg.	69
Office Furniture Manufacturing Industry	71
Medical Equipment & Supplies Mfg. Industry	73
Sign Manufacturing	75

TABLE OF CONTENTS

INDUSTRY   **PAGE NUMBER**

Wholesales
Automobile & Other Vehicles Wholesale   77
Motor Vehicle Parts & Supplies Wholesales   79
Furniture Wholesale Industry   81
Home Furnishings Wholesale Industry   83
Office Equipment Wholesales Industry   85
Computer & Equipment Wholesale Industry   87
Hardware Wholesale Industry   89
Printing & Writing Paper Wholesales   91
Men's & Boys' Clothing Wholesales Industry   93
Women's & Children's Clothing Wholesale   95
General-Line Grocery Wholesale Industry   97
Beer & Ale Wholesale Industry   99
Wine & Alcoholic Beverages Wholesales   101
Book/Periodical/Newspaper Wholesales   103

Retail
New Car Dealers Industry   105
Furniture Stores Industry   107
Appliance/TV/Electronics Stores Industry   109
Computer & Software Stores Industry   111
Home Centers Industry   113
Hardware Stores Industry   115
Grocery Stores Industry   117
Beer & Wine & Liquor Stores Industry   119
Pharmacies & Drug Stores Industry   121
Gas Stations with Convenience Stores   123
Men's Clothing Stores Industry   125
Women's Clothing Stores Industry   127
Family Clothing Stores Industry   129
Book Stores Retailing Industry   131
Department Stores Industry   133
Warehouse Clubs & Superstores Industry   135
Office Supplies & Stationery Stores Industry   137
Electronic Shopping & Mail Order Houses   139

TABLE OF CONTENTS

INDUSTRY   **PAGE NUMBER**

Transportation & Warehouse
Scheduled Air Transportation Industry   141
Local Freight Trucking Industry   143
Freight Trucking Long Distance Industry   145
General Warehousing & Storage Industry   147

Information
Newspaper Publishing Industry   149
Periodical Publishing Industry   151
Book Publishing Industry   153
Database & Directory Publishing Industry   155
Software Publishing Industry   157
Motion Pictures & Video Production Industry   159
Music Publishing Industry   161
Radio Broadcasting Industry   163
Television Broadcasting Services Industry   165
Cable Television Networks Industry   167
Wired Telecommunications Carriers Industry   169
Wireless Telecommunications Carriers   171
Data Processing Services Industry   173

Finance & Insurance
Commercial Banking Industry   175
Mortgage & Non-Mortgage Loan Brokers   177
Investment Banking & Securities Dealing   179
Securities Brokerage Industry   181
Life Insurance Carriers Industry   183
Health & Medical Insurance Carriers   185
Property & Casualty Insurance Carriers   187
Insurance Agencies & Brokerages Industry   189

Real Estate
Offices of Real Estate Agents & Brokers   191
Real Estate Property Managers Industry   193

Professional Services
Offices of Lawyers Industry   195
Offices of Certified Public Accountants   197
Architectural Services Industry   199
Engineering Services Industry   201
Interior Design Services Industry   203
Graphic Designs Services Industry   205
Computer Systems Designs Services Industry   207

TABLE OF CONTENTS

INDUSTRY   **PAGE NUMBER**

Professional Services
Management Consulting Services Industry   209
Advertising Agencies Industry   211
Public Relations Agencies Industry   213
Direct Mail Advertising Industry   215
Marketing Research & Public Opinion Polling   217
Veterinary Services   219
Telemarketing Services Industry   221
Security Guards & Patrol Services Industry   223

Educational Services
Colleges & Universities Industry   225
Exam Preparation & Tutoring Industry   227
Educational Support Services Industry   229

Health Care Services
Offices of Physicians Industry   231
Offices of Dentists Industry   233
Medical Laboratories Industry   235
Home Health Care Services Industry   237
Medical & Surgical Hospitals Industry   239
Nursing Care Facilities Industry   241
Community Care Facilities for the Elderly   243

Arts & Recreation
Musical Groups & artists Industry   245
Spectator Sports Industry   247
Agents & Managers for Artists & Athletes   249
Golf Courses & Country Clubs Industry   251
Fitness & Recreational Sports Centers   253

Accomodation & Food
Hotels & Motels Industry   255
Full-Service Restaurants Industry   257
Fast Food Restaurants Industry   259
Drinking Places & Bars Industry   261

Appendix: Definitions & Terms   263

SINGLE-FAMILY HOUSING CONSTRUCTION INDUSTRY (NAICS 236115)

NAICS 236115: Single-Family Housing Construction. This industry comprises establishments primarily responsible for the entire construction (i.e., new work, additions, alterations, and repairs) of single family residential housing units (e.g., single family detached houses, town houses, or row houses where each housing unit is separated by a ground-to-roof wall and where no housing units are constructed above or below). This industry includes establishments responsible for additions and alterations to mobile homes and on-site assembly of modular and prefabricated houses. Establishments identified as single family construction management firms are also included in this industry.

INDUSTRY ESTABLISHMENTS, SALES & EMPLOYMENT TRENDS

	Year					Percent Chg. Year-to-Year			
	2014	2015	2016	2017	2018	14-15	15-16	16-17	17-18
Establishments	104,885	107,769	110,814	113,488	114,872	2.7%	2.8%	2.4%	1.2%
Sales ($Millions)	64,922	68,714	72,581	76,234	78,947	5.8%	5.6%	5.0%	3.6%
Employment	268,555	275,940	283,735	290,583	294,127	2.7%	2.8%	2.4%	1.2%
Sales ($M)/Estab.	0.62	0.64	0.65	0.67	0.69	3.0%	2.7%	2.6%	2.3%
Sales ($)/Emp.	241,747	249,017	255,804	262,349	268,411	3.0%	2.7%	2.6%	2.3%

3-YEAR TREND – ESTIMATED NUMBER OF ESTABLISHMENTS

Year	Employee Size of Establishment									Total
	1-4 Emps.	5-9 Emps.	10-19 Emps.	20-49 Emps.	50-99 Emps.	100-249 Emps.	250-499 Emps.	>500 Emps.	Non-Employer	Employ-ment
2016	43,543	7,165	2,576	915	129	38	4	1	56,443	110,814
2017	44,594	7,338	2,638	937	132	39	4	1	57,805	113,488
2018	45,137	7,428	2,670	948	134	39	4	1	58,510	114,872

3-YEAR TREND – ESTIMATED INDUSTRY SALES ($MILLIONS)

Year	Employee Size of Establishment									Total
	1-4 Emps.	5-9 Emps.	10-19 Emps.	20-49 Emps.	50-99 Emps.	100-249 Emps.	250-499 Emps.	>500 Emps.	Non-Employer	Employ-ment
2016	27,184.2	11,757.7	10,629.0	9,993.3	3,094.7	2,461.2	921.7	426.4	6,112.4	72,580.7
2017	28,552.7	12,349.6	11,164.1	10,496.4	3,250.5	2,585.1	968.1	447.7	6,420.1	76,234.4
2018	29,568.7	12,789.1	11,561.3	10,869.9	3,366.2	2,677.1	1,002.6	463.6	6,648.6	78,947.1

3-YEAR TREND – ESTIMATED NUMBER OF EMPLOYEES

Year	Employee Size of Establishment									Total
	1-4 Emps.	5-9 Emps.	10-19 Emps.	20-49 Emps.	50-99 Emps.	100-249 Emps.	250-499 Emps.	>500 Emps.	Non-Employer	Employ-ment
2016	108,857	41,559	35,031	27,540	7,656	4,796	1,229	624	56,443	283,735
2017	111,484	42,562	35,877	28,205	7,841	4,912	1,259	639	57,805	290,583
2018	112,844	43,081	36,314	28,549	7,937	4,972	1,274	647	58,510	294,127

SINGLE-FAMILY HOUSING CONSTRUCTION INDUSTRY (NAICS 236115)

SUB-INDUSTRIES – 2017 ESTIMATED INDUSTRY SALES, ESTABLISHMENTS & EMPLOYMENT

Sub-Industries	Cate-gory*	Establish-ments	Sales ($Mill)	Employ-ment
Single-family housing construction	Major1	68,277	37,757.6	159,875
Single-family home remodeling, additions, and repairs	Minor1	4,105	2,962.8	12,108
General remodeling, single-family houses	Minor2	19,609	11,367.0	47,140
Mobile home repair, on site	Minor2	199	139.8	545
Patio and deck construction and repair	Minor2	546	354.9	1,677
Repairing fire damage, single-family houses	Minor2	253	543.1	2,865
New construction, single-family houses	Minor2	20,370	22,876.8	65,598
Prefabricated single-family house erection	Minor2	74	140.5	499
Townhouse construction	Minor2	55	92.0	278

*Category-Major categories (Major1) are more general descriptions for companies that self-selected to capture the many functions they perform in the industry. Minor categories (Minor1, Minor2) are more specific for companies that have more detailed functions (Minor1 is a larger category than Minor2). Minor categories figures (sales, etc.) can be aggregated to larger minor categories (Minor2 sums to Minor1) and major categories overall figures.

ELECTRICAL CONTRACTORS INDUSTRY
NAICS 23821

NAICS 23821: Electrical Contractors . This industry comprises establishments primarily engaged in one or more of the following: (1) performing electrical work at the site (e.g., installing wiring); (2) servicing electrical equipment at the site; and (3) the combined activity of selling and installing electrical equipment. The electrical work performed includes new work, additions, alterations, and maintenance and repairs.

INDUSTRY ESTABLISHMENTS, SALES & EMPLOYMENT TRENDS

	Year					Percent Chg. Year-to-Year			
	2014	2015	2016	2017	2018	14-15	15-16	16-17	17-18
Establishments	121,924	125,643	131,105	137,513	144,220	3.1%	4.3%	4.9%	4.9%
Sales ($Millions)	120,229	133,119	148,200	165,014	182,800	10.7%	11.3%	11.3%	10.8%
Employment	754,534	777,552	811,351	851,010	892,514	3.1%	4.3%	4.9%	4.9%
Sales ($M)/Estab.	0.99	1.06	1.13	1.20	1.27	7.4%	6.7%	6.2%	5.6%
Sales ($)/Emp.	159,343	171,203	182,658	193,904	204,815	7.4%	6.7%	6.2%	5.6%

3-YEAR TREND — ESTIMATED NUMBER OF ESTABLISHMENTS

Year	Employee Size of Establishment									Total
	1-4 Emps.	5-9 Emps.	10-19 Emps.	20-49 Emps.	50-99 Emps.	100-249 Emps.	250-499 Emps.	>500 Emps.	Non-Employer	Employ-ment
2016	46,276	13,556	7,997	5,100	1,673	808	169	69	55,458	131,105
2017	48,537	14,219	8,388	5,349	1,755	847	177	72	58,168	137,513
2018	50,905	14,912	8,797	5,610	1,841	888	186	76	61,005	144,220

3-YEAR TREND — ESTIMATED INDUSTRY SALES ($MILLIONS)

Year	Employee Size of Establishment									Total
	1-4 Emps.	5-9 Emps.	10-19 Emps.	20-49 Emps.	50-99 Emps.	100-249 Emps.	250-499 Emps.	>500 Emps.	Non-Employer	Employ-ment
2016	13,823.8	10,643.9	15,789.9	26,654.3	19,221.8	25,004.1	17,618.1	14,925.2	4,518.7	148,199.7
2017	15,414.1	11,868.4	17,606.4	29,720.7	21,433.1	27,880.7	19,644.9	16,407.7	5,038.6	165,014.3
2018	17,098.6	13,165.4	19,530.4	32,968.7	23,775.3	30,927.5	21,791.7	17,953.2	5,589.2	182,800.1

3-YEAR TREND — ESTIMATED NUMBER OF EMPLOYEES

Year	Employee Size of Establishment									Total
	1-4 Emps.	5-9 Emps.	10-19 Emps.	20-49 Emps.	50-99 Emps.	100-249 Emps.	250-499 Emps.	>500 Emps.	Non-Employer	Employ-ment
2016	115,689	78,627	108,759	153,515	99,386	101,832	49,110	48,976	55,458	811,351
2017	121,344	82,470	114,075	161,018	104,244	106,810	51,511	51,370	58,168	851,010
2018	127,262	86,492	119,639	168,871	109,328	112,019	54,023	53,875	61,005	892,514

ELECTRICAL CONTRACTORS INDUSTRY
NAICS 23821

SUB-INDUSTRIES – 2017 ESTIMATED INDUSTRY
SALES, ESTABLISHMENTS & EMPLOYMENT

Sub-Industries	Category*	Establish-ments	Sales ($Mill)	Employ-ment
Electrical work	Major1	82,492	58,855.7	357,553
Electric power systems contractors	Minor1	961	8,831.1	9,071
Cogeneration specialization	Minor2	32	45.7	823
Computer power conditioning	Minor2	32	32.0	140
Standby or emergency power specialization	Minor2	65	73.1	537
Switchgear and related devices installation	Minor2	35	139.8	485
Electronic controls installation	Minor1	1,160	1,626.3	8,504
Computerized controls installation	Minor2	145	782.4	2,221
Energy management controls	Minor2	725	2,311.1	6,836
Environmental system control installation	Minor2	192	1,202.1	2,036
Communications specialization	Minor1	2,016	3,728.3	19,664
Cable television installation	Minor2	727	1,226.2	8,962
Fiber optic cable installation	Minor2	806	1,563.3	8,401
Sound equipment specialization	Minor2	4,570	1,299.4	9,181
Telephone and telephone equipment installation	Minor2	2,386	3,557.3	19,696
Voice, data, and video wiring contractor	Minor2	633	1,116.8	6,253
Safety and security specialization	Minor1	1,595	1,535.5	12,145
Access control systems specialization	Minor2	258	466.3	2,125
Closed circuit television installation	Minor2	123	169.5	1,052
Fire detection and burglar alarm systems specialization	Minor2	3,254	3,731.9	27,322
Banking machine installation and service	Minor2	108	194.1	974
Computer installation	Minor2	794	739.8	4,388
General electrical contractor	Minor2	33,621	70,399.2	336,542
Lighting contractor	Minor2	784	1,387.6	6,097

*Category-Major categories (Major1) are more general descriptions for companies that self-selected to capture the many functions they perform in the industry. Minor categories (Minor1, Minor2) are more specific for companies that have more detailed functions (Minor1 is a larger category than Minor2). Minor categories figures (sales, etc.) can be aggregated to larger minor categories (Minor2 sums to Minor1) and major categories overall figures.

PLUMBING & HEATING & A/C CONTRACTORS NAICS 23822

NAICS 23822: Plumbing & Heating & A/C Contractors. This industry comprises establishments primarily engaged in one or more of the following: (1) installing plumbing, heating, and air-conditioning equipment; (2) servicing plumbing, heating, and air-conditioning equipment; and (3) the combined activity of selling and installing plumbing, heating, and air-conditioning equipment. The plumbing, heating, and air-conditioning work performed includes new work, additions, alterations, and maintenance and repairs.

INDUSTRY ESTABLISHMENTS, SALES & EMPLOYMENT TRENDS

	Year					Percent Chg. Year-to-Year			
	2014	2015	2016	2017	2018	14-15	15-16	16-17	17-18
Establishments	138,421	143,729	151,167	159,881	169,081	3.8%	5.2%	5.8%	5.8%
Sales ($Millions)	151,595	166,194	183,643	203,380	224,381	9.6%	10.5%	10.7%	10.3%
Employment	915,047	950,132	999,303	1,056,911	1,117,725	3.8%	5.2%	5.8%	5.8%
Sales ($M)/Estab.	1.10	1.16	1.21	1.27	1.33	5.6%	5.1%	4.7%	4.3%
Sales ($)/Emp.	165,669	174,916	183,771	192,428	200,748	5.6%	5.1%	4.7%	4.3%

3-YEAR TREND – ESTIMATED NUMBER OF ESTABLISHMENTS

Year	Employee Size of Establishment									Total
	1-4 Emps.	5-9 Emps.	10-19 Emps.	20-49 Emps.	50-99 Emps.	100-249 Emps.	250-499 Emps.	>500 Emps.	Non-Employer	Employ-ment
2016	62,737	19,232	11,983	6,986	1,968	837	174	51	47,200	151,167
2017	66,353	20,340	12,674	7,389	2,081	885	184	54	49,921	159,881
2018	70,171	21,511	13,403	7,814	2,201	936	194	57	52,793	169,081

3-YEAR TREND – ESTIMATED INDUSTRY SALES ($MILLIONS)

Year	Employee Size of Establishment									Total
	1-4 Emps.	5-9 Emps.	10-19 Emps.	20-49 Emps.	50-99 Emps.	100-249 Emps.	250-499 Emps.	>500 Emps.	Non-Employer	Employ-ment
2016	19,524.5	15,730.9	24,649.7	38,036.3	23,552.9	26,984.1	18,878.3	11,754.9	4,531.0	183,642.6
2017	21,648.4	17,442.2	27,331.3	42,174.0	26,115.1	29,919.5	20,931.9	12,793.2	5,023.9	203,379.5
2018	23,910.6	19,264.8	30,187.2	46,581.0	28,844.0	33,045.9	23,119.2	13,879.3	5,548.9	224,381.1

3-YEAR TREND – ESTIMATED NUMBER OF EMPLOYEES

Year	Employee Size of Establishment									Total
	1-4 Emps.	5-9 Emps.	10-19 Emps.	20-49 Emps.	50-99 Emps.	100-249 Emps.	250-499 Emps.	>500 Emps.	Non-Employer	Employ-ment
2016	156,842	111,543	162,974	210,279	116,895	105,487	50,512	37,572	47,200	999,303
2017	165,883	117,973	172,369	222,402	123,634	111,568	53,424	39,738	49,921	1,056,911
2018	175,428	124,761	182,287	235,199	130,747	117,987	56,498	42,024	52,793	1,117,725

PLUMBING & HEATING & A/C CONTRACTORS
NAICS 23822

SUB-INDUSTRIES — 2017 ESTIMATED INDUSTRY SALES, ESTABLISHMENTS & EMPLOYMENT

Sub-Industries	Cate-gory*	Establish-ments	Sales ($Mill)	Employ-ment
Plumbing, heating, air-conditioning	Major1	21,658	26,427.1	139,504
Boiler and furnace contractors	Minor1	401	590.7	3,124
Boiler maintenance contractor	Minor2	158	2,631.9	1,915
Boiler setting contractor	Minor2	37	100.6	423
Heating systems repair and maintenance	Minor2	2,014	1,452.3	9,442
Hydronics heating contractor	Minor2	119	119.8	850
Plumbing contractors	Minor1	55,448	51,528.2	306,249
Septic system construction	Minor2	2,928	1,716.5	11,839
Sprinkler contractors	Minor1	1,634	1,569.1	11,429
Fire sprinkler system installation	Minor2	1,814	5,979.5	35,330
Irrigation sprinkler system installation	Minor2	1,622	2,055.4	12,206
Heating and air conditioning contractors	Minor1	28,244	38,334.6	159,225
Mechanical contractor	Minor2	10,990	29,593.7	134,376
Process piping contractor	Minor2	135	669.2	3,016
Solar energy contractor	Minor2	1,422	3,012.7	9,398
Ventilation and duct work contractor	Minor2	798	1,984.8	9,960
Warm air heating and air conditioning contractor	Minor2	27,234	32,270.8	190,140
Refrigeration contractor	Minor2	3,226	3,342.6	18,487

*Category-Major categories (Major1) are more general descriptions for companies that self-selected to capture the many functions they perform in the industry. Minor categories (Minor1, Minor2) are more specific for companies that have more detailed functions (Minor1 is a larger category than Minor2). Minor categories figures (sales, etc.) can be aggregated to larger minor categories (Minor2 sums to Minor1) and major categories overall figures.

CARPENTRY CONTRACTORS INDUSTRY
NAICS 23835

NAICS 23835: Carpentry Contractors. This industry comprises establishments primarily engaged in framing, carpentry, and finishing work. The carpentry work performed includes new work, additions, alterations, and maintenance and repairs. Activities performed by establishments in this industry range from the installation of doors and windows to paneling, steel framing work, and ship joinery.

INDUSTRY ESTABLISHMENTS, SALES & EMPLOYMENT TRENDS

	Year					Percent Chg. Year-to-Year			
	2014	2015	2016	2017	2018	14-15	15-16	16-17	17-18
Establishments	75,149	74,223	73,919	75,688	77,492	-1.2%	-0.4%	2.4%	2.4%
Sales ($Millions)	21,596	22,792	24,113	26,116	28,154	5.5%	5.8%	8.3%	7.8%
Employment	182,046	179,804	179,065	183,352	187,722	-1.2%	-0.4%	2.4%	2.4%
Sales ($M)/Estab.	0.29	0.31	0.33	0.35	0.36	6.9%	6.2%	5.8%	5.3%
Sales ($)/Emp.	118,629	126,763	134,659	142,436	149,976	6.9%	6.2%	5.8%	5.3%

3-YEAR TREND – ESTIMATED NUMBER OF ESTABLISHMENTS

Year	Employee Size of Establishment									Total
	1-4 Emps.	5-9 Emps.	10-19 Emps.	20-49 Emps.	50-99 Emps.	100-249 Emps.	250-499 Emps.	>500 Emps.	Non-Employer	Employ-ment
2016	19,404	3,573	1,676	749	142	50	5	0	48,321	73,919
2017	19,869	3,658	1,716	766	145	51	5	0	49,478	75,688
2018	20,342	3,745	1,757	785	148	53	5	0	50,657	77,492

3-YEAR TREND – ESTIMATED INDUSTRY SALES ($MILLIONS)

Year	Employee Size of Establishment									Total
	1-4 Emps.	5-9 Emps.	10-19 Emps.	20-49 Emps.	50-99 Emps.	100-249 Emps.	250-499 Emps.	>500 Emps.	Non-Employer	Employ-ment
2016	6,167.3	2,984.4	3,521.1	4,162.2	1,731.3	1,652.6	546.1	5.7	3,342.1	24,112.7
2017	6,679.6	3,232.4	3,813.6	4,508.0	1,875.1	1,789.9	591.4	6.1	3,619.7	26,115.9
2018	7,200.9	3,484.6	4,111.2	4,859.8	2,021.5	1,929.6	637.6	6.4	3,902.2	28,153.8

3-YEAR TREND – ESTIMATED NUMBER OF EMPLOYEES

Year	Employee Size of Establishment									Total
	1-4 Emps.	5-9 Emps.	10-19 Emps.	20-49 Emps.	50-99 Emps.	100-249 Emps.	250-499 Emps.	>500 Emps.	Non-Employer	Employ-ment
2016	48,510	20,721	22,795	22,531	8,414	6,326	1,431	18	48,321	179,065
2017	49,671	21,217	23,341	23,070	8,615	6,477	1,465	18	49,478	183,352
2018	50,855	21,722	23,897	23,620	8,820	6,632	1,500	19	50,657	187,722

CARPENTRY CONTRACTORS INDUSTRY
NAICS 23835

SUB-INDUSTRIES — 2017 ESTIMATED INDUSTRY
SALES, ESTABLISHMENTS & EMPLOYMENT

Sub-Industries	Cate-gory*	Establish-ments	Sales ($Mill)	Employ-ment
Carpentry work	Major1	44,006	8,596.4	75,727
Cabinet and finish carpentry	Minor1	8,279	2,705.5	19,562
Cabinet building and installation	Minor2	5,670	2,164.9	16,117
Finish and trim carpentry	Minor2	3,157	989.2	7,903
Window and door installation and erection	Minor1	2,186	1,049.8	7,139
Garage door, installation or erection	Minor2	3,228	1,284.4	9,210
Window and door (prefabricated) installation	Minor2	2,942	2,418.6	12,693
Framing contractor	Minor2	5,732	6,024.4	29,170
Lightweight steel framing (metal stud) installation	Minor2	240	327.8	2,262
Ship joinery	Minor2	41	69.3	171
Store fixture installation	Minor2	208	485.5	3,398

*Category-Major categories (Major1) are more general descriptions for companies that self-selected to capture the many functions they perform in the industry. Minor categories (Minor1, Minor2) are more specific for companies that have more detailed functions (Minor1 is a larger category than Minor2). Minor categories figures (sales, etc.) can be aggregated to larger minor categories (Minor2 sums to Minor1) and major categories overall figures.

BREAKFAST CEREAL MANUFACTURING INDUSTRY
NAICS 31123

NAICS 31123: Breakfast Cereal Manufacturing. This industry comprises establishments primarily responsible for manufacturing cereal breakfast foods and related preparations, except breakfast bars. Establishments primarily engaged in manufacturing granola bars and other types of breakfast bars are classified in 2064.

INDUSTRY ESTABLISHMENTS, SALES & EMPLOYMENT TRENDS

	Year					Percent Chg. Year-to-Year			
	2014	2015	2016	2017	2018	14-15	15-16	16-17	17-18
Establishments	98	94	90	92	94	-4.2%	-3.9%	1.8%	2.0%
Sales ($Millions)	10,798	10,848	10,892	11,549	12,230	0.5%	0.4%	6.0%	5.9%
Employment	11,439	10,957	10,531	10,719	10,932	-4.2%	-3.9%	1.8%	2.0%
Sales ($M)/Estab.	110.36	115.75	120.92	125.97	130.80	4.9%	4.5%	4.2%	3.8%
Sales ($)/Emp.	943,959	990,053	1,034,261	1,077,464	1,118,776	4.9%	4.5%	4.2%	3.8%

3-YEAR TREND – ESTIMATED NUMBER OF ESTABLISHMENTS

Year	Employee Size of Establishment									Total
	1-4 Emps.	5-9 Emps.	10-19 Emps.	20-49 Emps.	50-99 Emps.	100-249 Emps.	250-499 Emps.	>500 Emps.	Non-Employer	Employ-ment
2016	21	5	7	1	7	15	11	8	15	90
2017	22	5	7	1	7	15	11	8	15	92
2018	22	5	8	1	8	15	11	9	15	94

3-YEAR TREND – ESTIMATED INDUSTRY SALES ($MILLIONS)

Year	Employee Size of Establishment									Total
	1-4 Emps.	5-9 Emps.	10-19 Emps.	20-49 Emps.	50-99 Emps.	100-249 Emps.	250-499 Emps.	>500 Emps.	Non-Employer	Employ-ment
2016	20.9	11.9	48.0	15.9	279.3	1,505.4	3,805.4	5,203.4	1.9	10,892.1
2017	22.1	12.6	50.9	16.8	296.1	1,596.2	4,035.0	5,517.1	2.0	11,549.0
2018	23.4	13.4	53.9	17.8	313.6	1,690.4	4,273.1	5,842.5	2.1	12,230.3

3-YEAR TREND – ESTIMATED NUMBER OF EMPLOYEES

Year	Employee Size of Establishment									Total
	1-4 Emps.	5-9 Emps.	10-19 Emps.	20-49 Emps.	50-99 Emps.	100-249 Emps.	250-499 Emps.	>500 Emps.	Non-Employer	Employ-ment
2016	53	27	100	28	437	1,857	3,214	4,800	15	10,531
2017	54	27	102	28	445	1,891	3,271	4,886	15	10,719
2018	55	28	104	29	454	1,928	3,336	4,983	15	10,932

BREAKFAST CEREAL MANUFACTURING INDUSTRY
NAICS 31123

SUB-INDUSTRIES – 2017 ESTIMATED INDUSTRY SALES, ESTABLISHMENTS & EMPLOYMENT

Sub-Industries	Category*	Establish-ments	Sales ($Mill)	Employ-ment
Cereal breakfast foods	Major1	61	6,251.8	8,549
Coffee substitutes, made from grain	Minor2	4	0.6	27
Corn flakes: prepared as cereal breakfast food	Minor2	2	0.2	38
Corn, hulled: prepared as cereal breakfast food	Minor2	0	0.0	1
Granola and muesli, except bars and clusters	Minor2	5	1.0	137
Hominy grits: prepared as cereal breakfast food	Minor2	0	0.0	3
Infants' foods, cereal type	Minor2	6	2.0	84
Oatmeal: prepared as cereal breakfast food	Minor2	1	0.4	8
Rice: prepared as cereal breakfast food	Minor2	7	0.3	653
Soy: prepared as cereal breakfast food	Minor2	0	0.1	3
Wheat flakes: prepared as cereal breakfast food	Minor2	4	5,292.6	1,216

*Category-Major categories (Major1) are more general descriptions for companies that self-selected to capture the many functions they perform in the industry. Minor categories (Minor1, Minor2) are more specific for companies that have more detailed functions (Minor1 is a larger category than Minor2). Minor categories figures (sales, etc.) can be aggregated to larger minor categories (Minor2 sums to Minor1) and major categories overall figures.

FROZEN FOOD MANUFACTURING INDUSTRY
NAICS 31141

NAICS 31141: Frozen Food Manufacturing. This industry comprises establishments primarily manufacturing frozen bakery products, except bread and bread-type rolls. Establishments primarily engaged in manufacturing frozen bread and bread-type rolls are classified in 2051.

INDUSTRY ESTABLISHMENTS, SALES & EMPLOYMENT TRENDS

	Year					Percent Chg. Year-to-Year			
	2014	2015	2016	2017	2018	14-15	15-16	16-17	17-18
Establishments	1,429	1,439	1,458	1,473	1,491	0.7%	1.3%	1.0%	1.2%
Sales ($Millions)	28,772	30,065	31,475	32,812	34,167	4.5%	4.7%	4.2%	4.1%
Employment	75,405	75,907	76,906	77,708	78,679	0.7%	1.3%	1.0%	1.2%
Sales ($M)/Estab.	20.13	20.90	21.59	22.28	22.91	3.8%	3.3%	3.2%	2.8%
Sales ($)/Emp.	381,575	396,073	409,271	422,248	434,255	3.8%	3.3%	3.2%	2.8%

3-YEAR TREND — ESTIMATED NUMBER OF ESTABLISHMENTS

Year	Employee Size of Establishment									Total
	1-4 Emps.	5-9 Emps.	10-19 Emps.	20-49 Emps.	50-99 Emps.	100-249 Emps.	250-499 Emps.	>500 Emps.	Non-Employer	Employ-ment
2016	116	70	89	143	85	118	59	43	734	1,458
2017	117	71	90	144	86	120	60	43	742	1,473
2018	119	72	91	146	87	121	61	44	751	1,491

3-YEAR TREND — ESTIMATED INDUSTRY SALES ($MILLIONS)

Year	Employee Size of Establishment									Total
	1-4 Emps.	5-9 Emps.	10-19 Emps.	20-49 Emps.	50-99 Emps.	100-249 Emps.	250-499 Emps.	>500 Emps.	Non-Employer	Employ-ment
2016	50.1	79.7	252.6	1,075.8	1,402.0	5,281.1	8,899.9	14,381.5	52.8	31,475.4
2017	52.3	83.2	263.8	1,123.7	1,464.5	5,516.2	9,296.1	14,957.0	55.1	32,811.9
2018	54.6	86.8	275.4	1,172.9	1,528.5	5,757.4	9,702.6	15,531.0	57.5	34,166.7

3-YEAR TREND — ESTIMATED NUMBER OF EMPLOYEES

Year	Employee Size of Establishment									Total
	1-4 Emps.	5-9 Emps.	10-19 Emps.	20-49 Emps.	50-99 Emps.	100-249 Emps.	250-499 Emps.	>500 Emps.	Non-Employer	Employ-ment
2016	291	408	1,207	4,298	5,028	14,919	17,208	32,813	734	76,906
2017	294	412	1,219	4,343	5,081	15,074	17,388	33,155	742	77,708
2018	297	418	1,235	4,397	5,144	15,263	17,605	33,569	751	78,679

FROZEN FOOD MANUFACTURING INDUSTRY
NAICS 31141

SUB-INDUSTRIES — 2017 ESTIMATED INDUSTRY SALES, ESTABLISHMENTS & EMPLOYMENT

Sub-Industries	Cate-gory*	Establish-ments	Sales ($Mill)	Employ-ment
Frozen fruits and vegetables	Major1	220	2,662.9	5,133
Frozen fruits and vegetables	Minor1	42	1,040.7	4,314
Citrus pulp, dried	Minor2	15	30.6	43
Fruits, quick frozen and cold pack (frozen)	Minor2	90	3,173.0	6,773
Potato products, quick frozen and cold pack	Minor2	57	451.2	5,140
Vegetables, quick frozen & cold pack, excl. potato produc	Minor2	97	5,232.8	10,559
Fruit juices	Minor1	170	3,827.1	4,275
Fruit juices, frozen	Minor2	20	81.6	997
Frozen specialties, nec	Major1	382	7,025.2	21,483
Breakfasts, frozen and packaged	Minor2	25	2,157.9	783
Dinners, frozen and packaged	Minor2	42	2,508.2	5,127
Ethnic foods, nec, frozen	Minor2	105	1,233.2	4,618
Lunches, frozen and packaged	Minor2	7	109.9	138
Pizza, frozen	Minor2	133	2,636.7	6,637
Snacks, incl. onion rings, cheese sticks, etc.	Minor2	46	225.3	882
Spaghetti and meatballs, frozen	Minor2	1	2.7	6
Waffles, frozen	Minor2	20	412.2	332
Whipped topping, frozen	Minor2	1	0.6	468

*Category-Major categories (Major1) are more general descriptions for companies that self-selected to capture the many functions they perform in the industry. Minor categories (Minor1, Minor2) are more specific for companies that have more detailed functions (Minor1 is a larger category than Minor2). Minor categories figures (sales, etc.) can be aggregated to larger minor categories (Minor2 sums to Minor1) and major categories overall figures.

COOKIE CRACKER & PASTA MFG. INDUSTRY
NAICS 31182

NAICS 31182: Cookie Cracker & Pasta Mfg. This industry comprises establishments primarily manufacturing fresh cookies, crackers, pretzels, and similar `dry' bakery products. Establishments primarily engaged in producing other fresh bakery products are classified in 2051.

INDUSTRY ESTABLISHMENTS, SALES & EMPLOYMENT TRENDS

	Year					Percent Chg. Year-to-Year			
	2014	2015	2016	2017	2018	14-15	15-16	16-17	17-18
Establishments	1,547	1,581	1,625	1,652	1,682	2.2%	2.8%	1.6%	1.8%
Sales ($Millions)	21,599	23,227	25,017	26,568	28,169	7.5%	7.7%	6.2%	6.0%
Employment	47,256	48,278	49,635	50,439	51,360	2.2%	2.8%	1.6%	1.8%
Sales ($M)/Estab.	13.96	14.69	15.39	16.09	16.75	5.3%	4.8%	4.5%	4.1%
Sales ($)/Emp.	457,072	481,106	504,020	526,741	548,465	5.3%	4.8%	4.5%	4.1%

3-YEAR TREND — ESTIMATED NUMBER OF ESTABLISHMENTS

Year	Employee Size of Establishment									Total
	1-4 Emps.	5-9 Emps.	10-19 Emps.	20-49 Emps.	50-99 Emps.	100-249 Emps.	250-499 Emps.	>500 Emps.	Non-Employer	Employ-ment
2016	244	145	123	161	67	84	40	23	739	1,625
2017	248	147	125	163	68	85	41	23	751	1,652
2018	252	150	127	166	70	87	41	24	765	1,682

3-YEAR TREND — ESTIMATED INDUSTRY SALES ($MILLIONS)

Year	Employee Size of Establishment									Total
	1-4 Emps.	5-9 Emps.	10-19 Emps.	20-49 Emps.	50-99 Emps.	100-249 Emps.	250-499 Emps.	>500 Emps.	Non-Employer	Employ-ment
2016	134.7	210.6	449.0	1,554.1	1,429.1	4,814.4	7,707.7	8,664.8	52.8	25,017.3
2017	143.2	223.8	477.2	1,651.8	1,518.9	5,117.1	8,192.2	9,187.7	56.1	26,568.1
2018	151.9	237.5	506.4	1,753.0	1,611.9	5,430.3	8,693.8	9,724.6	59.6	28,169.0

3-YEAR TREND — ESTIMATED NUMBER OF EMPLOYEES

Year	Employee Size of Establishment									Total
	1-4 Emps.	5-9 Emps.	10-19 Emps.	20-49 Emps.	50-99 Emps.	100-249 Emps.	250-499 Emps.	>500 Emps.	Non-Employer	Employ-ment
2016	609	841	1,671	4,837	3,993	10,596	11,611	14,738	739	49,635
2017	619	854	1,698	4,915	4,058	10,767	11,799	14,977	751	50,439
2018	630	870	1,729	5,005	4,132	10,964	12,014	15,250	765	51,360

SUB-INDUSTRIES — 2017 ESTIMATED INDUSTRY SALES, ESTABLISHMENTS & EMPLOYMENT

Sub-Industries	Category*	Establish-ments	Sales ($Mill)	Employ-ment
Cookies and crackers	Major1	261	1,400.4	7,192
Bakery products, dry	Minor2	192	1,996.0	2,823
Biscuits, dry	Minor2	19	6.7	3,892
Communion wafers	Minor2	3	43.1	70
Cones, ice cream	Minor2	54	106.3	1,294
Cookies	Minor2	513	15,904.6	19,405
Cracker meal and crumbs	Minor2	4	75.4	144
Crackers, dry, nec	Minor2	25	372.8	834
Matzoths	Minor2	4	0.7	102
Pretzels	Minor2	229	1,231.5	4,379
Rice cakes	Minor2	16	12.1	35
Rusk, machine made	Minor2	1	0.7	3
Soda crackers	Minor2	1	100.9	169
Sugar wafers	Minor2	1	6.7	16
Prepared flour mixes and doughs	Major1	115	1,451.4	4,440
Flours and flour mixes, from purchased flour	Minor1	18	270.1	1,126
Biscuit mixes, prepared: from purchased flour	Minor2	2	73.7	46
Blended flour: from purchased flour	Minor2	7	160.3	113
Bread and bread type roll mixes: from purchased flour	Minor2	27	20.2	831
Cake mixes, prepared: from purchased flour	Minor2	22	232.5	332
Doughnut mixes, prepared: from purchased flour	Minor2	20	226.7	547
Farina, except cereal breakfast food: from purchased flou	Minor2	4	8.7	30
Pancake mixes, prepared: from purchased flour	Minor2	22	59.2	89
Pizza mixes: from purchased flour	Minor2	7	121.3	102
Doughs and batters, from purchased flour	Minor1	9	221.0	421
Biscuit dough, prepared: from purchased flour	Minor2	13	1,712.8	486
Doughs, frozen or refrigerated: from purchased flour	Minor2	27	306.2	937
Pancake batter, frozen or refrigerated: from purchased flo	Minor2	4	24.6	32
Pizza doughs, prepared: from purchased flour	Minor2	29	421.7	547

*Category-Major categories (Major1) are more general descriptions for companies that self-selected to capture the many functions they perform in the industry. Minor categories (Minor1, Minor2) are more specific for companies that have more detailed functions (Minor1 is a larger category than Minor2). Minor categories figures (sales, etc.) can be aggregated to larger minor categories (Minor2 sums to Minor1) and major categories overall figures.

SNACK FOOD MANUFACTURING INDUSTRY
NAICS 31191

NAICS 31191: Snack Food Manufacturing. This industry comprises establishments primarily responsible for manufacturing potato chips, corn chips, and similar snacks. Pretzels and crackers are classified in 2052; candy covered popcorn is classified in 2064; salted, roasted, cooked or canned nuts and seeds are classified in 2068; and packaged unpopped popcorn is classified in 2099.

INDUSTRY ESTABLISHMENTS, SALES & EMPLOYMENT TRENDS

	Year					Percent Chg. Year-to-Year			
	2014	2015	2016	2017	2018	14-15	15-16	16-17	17-18
Establishments	6,573	6,693	6,859	6,992	7,143	1.8%	2.5%	1.9%	2.2%
Sales ($Millions)	34,636	37,138	39,870	42,470	45,159	7.2%	7.4%	6.5%	6.3%
Employment	52,046	52,997	54,311	55,366	56,558	1.8%	2.5%	1.9%	2.2%
Sales ($M)/Estab.	5.27	5.55	5.81	6.07	6.32	5.3%	4.8%	4.5%	4.1%
Sales ($)/Emp.	665,486	700,757	734,114	767,079	798,462	5.3%	4.8%	4.5%	4.1%

3-YEAR TREND – ESTIMATED NUMBER OF ESTABLISHMENTS

Year	Employee Size of Establishment									Total
	1-4 Emps.	5-9 Emps.	10-19 Emps.	20-49 Emps.	50-99 Emps.	100-249 Emps.	250-499 Emps.	>500 Emps.	Non-Employer	Employ-ment
2016	165	96	96	100	75	76	46	22	6,183	6,859
2017	168	98	98	102	77	78	47	22	6,303	6,992
2018	172	100	100	104	78	79	48	23	6,439	7,143

3-YEAR TREND – ESTIMATED INDUSTRY SALES ($MILLIONS)

Year	Employee Size of Establishment									Total
	1-4 Emps.	5-9 Emps.	10-19 Emps.	20-49 Emps.	50-99 Emps.	100-249 Emps.	250-499 Emps.	>500 Emps.	Non-Employer	Employ-ment
2016	142.5	218.1	548.4	1,514.6	2,497.1	6,823.5	13,861.9	13,761.1	503.2	39,870.2
2017	152.1	232.7	585.3	1,616.5	2,665.0	7,282.4	14,794.3	14,604.9	537.0	42,470.2
2018	162.0	248.0	623.6	1,722.4	2,839.7	7,759.7	15,763.9	15,467.7	572.2	45,159.2

3-YEAR TREND – ESTIMATED NUMBER OF EMPLOYEES

Year	Employee Size of Establishment									Total
	1-4 Emps.	5-9 Emps.	10-19 Emps.	20-49 Emps.	50-99 Emps.	100-249 Emps.	250-499 Emps.	>500 Emps.	Non-Employer	Employ-ment
2016	412	557	1,306	3,015	4,463	9,606	13,357	15,413	6,183	54,311
2017	420	568	1,331	3,074	4,550	9,793	13,616	15,712	6,303	55,366
2018	429	580	1,360	3,140	4,648	10,003	13,909	16,050	6,439	56,558

SNACK FOOD MANUFACTURING INDUSTRY
NAICS 31191

SUB-INDUSTRIES – 2017 ESTIMATED INDUSTRY SALES, ESTABLISHMENTS & EMPLOYMENT

Sub-Industries	Category*	Establish-ments	Sales ($Mill)	Employ-ment
Potato chips and similar snacks	Major1	3,387	41,894.5	33,275
Potato chips and other potato-based snacks	Minor1	1,119	385.6	8,333
Potato sticks	Minor2	31	1.9	47
Corn chips and other corn-based snacks	Minor1	420	22.7	5,149
Popcorn, already popped (except candy covered)	Minor2	497	15.4	550
Tortilla chips	Minor2	1,057	139.7	6,025
Cheese curls and puffs	Minor2	93	1.3	1,035
Onion fries	Minor2	47	0.4	14
Pork rinds	Minor2	342	8.8	938

*Category-Major categories (Major1) are more general descriptions for companies that self-selected to capture the many functions they perform in the industry. Minor categories (Minor1, Minor2) are more specific for companies that have more detailed functions (Minor1 is a larger category than Minor2). Minor categories figures (sales, etc.) can be aggregated to larger minor categories (Minor2 sums to Minor1) and major categories overall figures.

Soft Drink Mfg.
(NAICS 312111)

NAICS 312111: Soft Drink Manufacturing
This U.S. industry comprises establishments primarily engaged in establishments primarily engaged in manufacturing soft drinks and carbonated waters. Fruit and vegetable juices are classified in 2032-2038; fruit syrups for flavoring are classified in 2087; and nonalcoholic cider is classified in 2099. Bottling natural spring waters is classified in 5149.

Industry Establishments, Sales & Employment Trends

	Year					Percent Chg. Year-to-Year			
	2014	2015	2016	2017	2018	14-15	15-16	16-17	17-18
Establishments	580	554	526	505	484	-4.6%	-4.9%	-4.0%	-4.3%
Sales ($Millions)	31,778	33,115	34,075	35,179	35,975	4.2%	2.9%	3.2%	2.3%
Employment	42,750	40,795	38,779	37,231	35,633	-4.6%	-4.9%	-4.0%	-4.3%
Sales ($M)/Estab.	54.77	59.81	64.75	69.62	74.39	9.2%	8.2%	7.5%	6.8%
Sales ($)/Emp.	743,333	811,756	878,696	944,893	1,009,606	9.2%	8.2%	7.5%	6.8%

3-Year Trend — Estimated Number of Establishments

Year	Employee Size of Establishment									Total Employ-ment
	1-4 Emps.	5-9 Emps.	10-19 Emps.	20-49 Emps.	50-99 Emps.	100-249 Emps.	250-499 Emps.	>500 Emps.	Non-Employer	
2016	73	37	36	48	70	128	39	8	87	526
2017	70	36	35	46	67	123	37	8	84	505
2018	67	34	33	44	64	118	36	8	80	484

3-Year Trend — Estimated Industry Sales ($Millions)

Year	Employee Size of Establishment									Total Employ-ment
	1-4 Emps.	5-9 Emps.	10-19 Emps.	20-49 Emps.	50-99 Emps.	100-249 Emps.	250-499 Emps.	>500 Emps.	Non-Employer	
2016	68.6	92.4	226.8	795.4	2,540.1	12,536.5	12,885.8	4,917.2	12.0	34,074.8
2017	70.8	95.4	234.1	821.1	2,622.4	12,942.6	13,303.2	5,077.0	12.3	35,179.1
2018	72.4	97.6	239.4	839.7	2,681.7	13,235.2	13,604.0	5,192.3	12.6	35,975.1

3-Year Trend — Estimated Number of Employees

Year	Employee Size of Establishment									Total Employ-ment
	1-4 Emps.	5-9 Emps.	10-19 Emps.	20-49 Emps.	50-99 Emps.	100-249 Emps.	250-499 Emps.	>500 Emps.	Non-Employer	
2016	181	216	493	1,447	4,149	16,128	11,347	4,730	87	38,779
2017	174	207	474	1,389	3,983	15,485	10,894	4,541	84	37,231
2018	167	198	453	1,330	3,812	14,820	10,426	4,346	80	35,633

SOFT DRINK MFG.
(NAICS 312111)

SUB-INDUSTRIES – 2017 ESTIMATED INDUSTRY
SALES, ESTABLISHMENTS & EMPLOYMENT

Sub-Industries	Cate-gory*	Establish-ments	Sales ($Mill)	Employ-ment
Bottled and canned soft drinks	Major1	199	25,613.7	12,815
Iced tea and fruit drinks, bottled and canned	Minor1	7	253.5	285
Fruit drinks (less than 100% juice): packaged in cans, etc	Minor2	9	98.2	221
Lemonade: packaged in cans, bottles, etc.	Minor2	2	30.7	15
Tea, iced: packaged in cans, bottles, etc.	Minor2	3	92.4	42
Pasteurized and mineral waters, bottled and canned	Minor1	13	41.1	329
Mineral water, carbonated: packaged in cans, bottles, etc	Minor2	20	248.9	545
Water, natural: packaged in cans, bottles, etc.	Minor2	45	248.3	939
Carbonated soft drinks, bottled and canned	Minor1	38	259.2	4,905
Carbonated beverages, nonalcoholic: pkged. in cans, bot	Minor2	53	3,950.3	4,377
Soft drinks: packaged in cans, bottles, etc.	Minor2	115	4,342.8	12,757

*Category-Major categories (Major1) are more general descriptions for companies that self-selected to capture the many
functions they perform in the industry. Minor categories (Minor1, Minor2) are more specific for companies that have more detailed
functions (Minor1 is a larger category than Minor2). Minor categories figures (sales, etc.) can be aggregated to larger minor categories
(Minor2 sums to Minor1) and major categories overall figures.

BREWERIES & BEER-MAKING INDUSTRY
NAICS 31212

NAICS 31212: Breweries. This industry comprises establishments primarily engaged in brewing beer, ale, malt liquors, and nonalcoholic beer.

INDUSTRY ESTABLISHMENTS, SALES & EMPLOYMENT TRENDS

	Year					Percent Chg. Year-to-Year			
	2014	2015	2016	2017	2018	14-15	15-16	16-17	17-18
Establishments	2,092	2,245	2,367	2,519	2,678	7.3%	5.5%	6.4%	6.3%
Sales ($Millions)	26,212	28,836	31,121	33,823	36,650	10.0%	7.9%	8.7%	8.4%
Employment	36,350	39,007	41,139	43,770	46,532	7.3%	5.5%	6.4%	6.3%
Sales ($M)/Estab.	12.53	12.85	13.15	13.43	13.69	2.5%	2.3%	2.2%	1.9%
Sales ($)/Emp.	721,102	739,259	756,474	772,751	787,643	2.5%	2.3%	2.2%	1.9%

3-YEAR TREND — ESTIMATED NUMBER OF ESTABLISHMENTS

Year	Employee Size of Establishment									Total
	1-4 Emps.	5-9 Emps.	10-19 Emps.	20-49 Emps.	50-99 Emps.	100-249 Emps.	250-499 Emps.	>500 Emps.	Non-Employer	Employ-ment
2016	999	360	266	205	70	43	8	24	392	2,367
2017	1,063	383	283	218	75	46	8	25	418	2,519
2018	1,130	407	301	232	79	49	9	27	444	2,678

3-YEAR TREND — ESTIMATED INDUSTRY SALES ($MILLIONS)

Year	Employee Size of Establishment									Total
	1-4 Emps.	5-9 Emps.	10-19 Emps.	20-49 Emps.	50-99 Emps.	100-249 Emps.	250-499 Emps.	>500 Emps.	Non-Employer	Employ-ment
2016	947.9	897.3	1,667.5	3,399.4	2,559.7	4,228.3	2,625.2	14,747.4	48.0	31,120.8
2017	1,032.5	977.3	1,816.2	3,702.5	2,787.9	4,605.3	2,859.3	15,990.0	52.3	33,823.2
2018	1,121.0	1,061.1	1,971.9	4,020.0	3,026.9	5,000.2	3,104.5	17,288.3	56.7	36,650.5

3-YEAR TREND — ESTIMATED NUMBER OF EMPLOYEES

Year	Employee Size of Establishment									Total
	1-4 Emps.	5-9 Emps.	10-19 Emps.	20-49 Emps.	50-99 Emps.	100-249 Emps.	250-499 Emps.	>500 Emps.	Non-Employer	Employ-ment
2016	2,498	2,087	3,617	6,166	4,168	5,423	2,305	14,482	392	41,139
2017	2,658	2,221	3,848	6,560	4,435	5,770	2,452	15,408	418	43,770
2018	2,826	2,361	4,091	6,974	4,714	6,134	2,607	16,380	444	46,532

BREWERIES & BEER-MAKING INDUSTRY
NAICS 31212

SUB-INDUSTRIES – 2017 ESTIMATED INDUSTRY SALES, ESTABLISHMENTS & EMPLOYMENT

Sub-Industries	Category*	Establish-ments	Sales ($Mill)	Employ-ment
Malt beverages	Major1	1,304	2,800.4	14,327
Malt beverage products	Minor1	35	2,060.2	978
Brewers' grain	Minor2	72	165.5	490
Extract, malt	Minor2	7	15.4	69
Syrups, malt	Minor2	7	12.2	49
Ale (alcoholic beverage)	Minor2	81	1,382.9	1,064
Beer (alcoholic beverage)	Minor2	934	27,291.7	26,457
Liquors, malt	Minor2	69	80.8	298
Near beer	Minor2	9	14.1	38

*Category-Major categories (Major1) are more general descriptions for companies that self-selected to capture the many functions they perform in the industry. Minor categories (Minor1, Minor2) are more specific for companies that have more detailed functions (Minor1 is a larger category than Minor2). Minor categories figures (sales, etc.) can be aggregated to larger minor categories (Minor2 sums to Minor1) and major categories overall figures.

WINERIES & WINE-MAKING INDUSTRY
NAICS 31213

NAICS 31213: Wineries. This industry comprises establishments primarily engaged in one or more of the following: (1) growing grapes and manufacturing wine and brandies; (2) manufacturing wine and brandies from grapes and other fruits grown elsewhere; and (3) blending wines and brandies.

INDUSTRY ESTABLISHMENTS, SALES & EMPLOYMENT TRENDS

	Year					Percent Chg. Year-to-Year			
	2014	2015	2016	2017	2018	14-15	15-16	16-17	17-18
Establishments	3,826	4,015	4,184	4,306	4,419	4.9%	4.2%	2.9%	2.6%
Sales ($Millions)	12,310	12,434	12,430	12,248	11,982	1.0%	0.0%	-1.5%	-2.2%
Employment	42,397	44,491	46,358	47,716	48,962	4.9%	4.2%	2.9%	2.6%
Sales ($M)/Estab.	3.22	3.10	2.97	2.84	2.71	-3.8%	-4.1%	-4.3%	-4.7%
Sales ($)/Emp.	290,351	279,460	268,131	256,685	244,722	-3.8%	-4.1%	-4.3%	-4.7%

3-YEAR TREND – ESTIMATED NUMBER OF ESTABLISHMENTS

Year	Employee Size of Establishment									Total
	1-4 Emps.	5-9 Emps.	10-19 Emps.	20-49 Emps.	50-99 Emps.	100-249 Emps.	250-499 Emps.	>500 Emps.	Non-Employer	Employ-ment
2016	1,695	698	536	400	103	44	11	4	694	4,184
2017	1,744	718	551	412	106	45	11	5	714	4,306
2018	1,790	737	566	423	109	46	12	5	733	4,419

3-YEAR TREND – ESTIMATED INDUSTRY SALES ($MILLIONS)

Year	Employee Size of Establishment									Total
	1-4 Emps.	5-9 Emps.	10-19 Emps.	20-49 Emps.	50-99 Emps.	100-249 Emps.	250-499 Emps.	>500 Emps.	Non-Employer	Employ-ment
2016	706.9	764.7	1,477.0	2,920.1	1,648.6	1,890.8	1,593.2	1,354.3	74.6	12,430.2
2017	697.3	754.4	1,457.0	2,880.5	1,626.3	1,865.1	1,571.6	1,322.3	73.5	12,248.0
2018	682.8	738.7	1,426.7	2,820.7	1,592.5	1,826.4	1,539.0	1,283.3	72.0	11,982.2

3-YEAR TREND – ESTIMATED NUMBER OF EMPLOYEES

Year	Employee Size of Establishment									Total
	1-4 Emps.	5-9 Emps.	10-19 Emps.	20-49 Emps.	50-99 Emps.	100-249 Emps.	250-499 Emps.	>500 Emps.	Non-Employer	Employ-ment
2016	4,237	4,046	7,287	12,046	6,105	5,515	3,181	3,248	694	46,358
2017	4,361	4,165	7,500	12,399	6,284	5,677	3,274	3,343	714	47,716
2018	4,475	4,273	7,696	12,723	6,448	5,825	3,359	3,430	733	48,962

WINERIES & WINE-MAKING INDUSTRY
NAICS 31213

SUB-INDUSTRIES – 2017 ESTIMATED INDUSTRY SALES, ESTABLISHMENTS & EMPLOYMENT

Sub-Industries	Cate-gory*	Establish-ments	Sales ($Mill)	Employ-ment
Wines, brandy, and brandy spirits	Major1	877	8,355.8	12,447
Wines	Minor1	3,104	3,427.4	32,615
Wine coolers (beverages)	Minor2	18	11.2	82
Brandy	Minor2	15	132.0	198
Brandy spirits	Minor2	4	4.3	28
Neutral spirits, fruit	Minor2	4	1.4	11
Wine cellars, bonded: engaged in blending wines	Minor2	285	315.9	2,336

*Category-Major categories (Major1) are more general descriptions for companies that self-selected to capture the many functions they perform in the industry. Minor categories (Minor1, Minor2) are more specific for companies that have more detailed functions (Minor1 is a larger category than Minor2). Minor categories figures (sales, etc.) can be aggregated to larger minor categories (Minor2 sums to Minor1) and major categories overall figures.

DISTILLERIES & ALCOHOL-MAKING INDUSTRY
NAICS 31214

NAICS 31214: Distilleries. This industry comprises establishments primarily engaged in one or more of the following: (1) distilling potable liquors (except brandies); (2) distilling and blending liquors; and (3) blending and mixing liquors and other ingredients.

INDUSTRY ESTABLISHMENTS, SALES & EMPLOYMENT TRENDS

	Year					Percent Chg. Year-to-Year			
	2014	2015	2016	2017	2018	14-15	15-16	16-17	17-18
Establishments	578	623	660	714	772	7.9%	5.9%	8.2%	8.1%
Sales ($Millions)	6,861	7,967	9,020	10,376	11,866	16.1%	13.2%	15.0%	14.4%
Employment	8,338	8,997	9,529	10,306	11,138	7.9%	5.9%	8.2%	8.1%
Sales ($M)/Estab.	11.87	12.78	13.66	14.53	15.37	7.6%	6.9%	6.4%	5.8%
Sales ($)/Emp.	822,854	885,535	946,588	1,006,784	1,065,332	7.6%	6.9%	6.4%	5.8%

3-YEAR TREND — ESTIMATED NUMBER OF ESTABLISHMENTS

Year	Employee Size of Establishment									Total
	1-4 Emps.	5-9 Emps.	10-19 Emps.	20-49 Emps.	50-99 Emps.	100-249 Emps.	250-499 Emps.	>500 Emps.	Non-Employer	Employ-ment
2016	334	79	61	39	15	13	10	1	109	660
2017	361	85	66	42	16	14	11	1	118	714
2018	390	92	71	45	17	15	12	1	128	772

3-YEAR TREND — ESTIMATED INDUSTRY SALES ($MILLIONS)

Year	Employee Size of Establishment									Total
	1-4 Emps.	5-9 Emps.	10-19 Emps.	20-49 Emps.	50-99 Emps.	100-249 Emps.	250-499 Emps.	>500 Emps.	Non-Employer	Employ-ment
2016	384.0	238.5	460.7	782.2	657.4	1,499.3	4,134.5	849.1	14.6	9,020.2
2017	441.8	274.4	530.0	899.9	756.4	1,724.9	4,756.6	975.7	16.8	10,376.3
2018	505.2	313.8	606.1	1,029.2	865.0	1,972.7	5,440.0	1,114.6	19.2	11,865.8

3-YEAR TREND — ESTIMATED NUMBER OF EMPLOYEES

Year	Employee Size of Establishment									Total
	1-4 Emps.	5-9 Emps.	10-19 Emps.	20-49 Emps.	50-99 Emps.	100-249 Emps.	250-499 Emps.	>500 Emps.	Non-Employer	Employ-ment
2016	834	457	824	1,170	883	1,585	2,992	675	109	9,529
2017	902	495	891	1,265	955	1,715	3,236	730	118	10,306
2018	975	535	963	1,367	1,032	1,853	3,497	789	128	11,138

DISTILLERIES & ALCOHOL-MAKING INDUSTRY
NAICS 31214

SUB-INDUSTRIES – 2017 ESTIMATED INDUSTRY
SALES, ESTABLISHMENTS & EMPLOYMENT

Sub-Industries	Category*	Establish-ments	Sales ($Mill)	Employ-ment
Distilled and blended liquors	Major1	438	335.9	5,222
Distiller's dried grains and solubles, and alcohol	Minor1	32	45.1	222
Ethyl alcohol for beverage purposes	Minor2	6	0.9	12
Grain alcohol for beverage purposes	Minor2	17	266.3	196
Grain alcohol for medicinal purposes	Minor2	3	94.8	268
Neutral spirits, except fruit	Minor2	14	53.6	37
Cordials and premixed alcoholic cocktails	Minor1	6	4.4	31
Cocktails, alcoholic	Minor2	60	15.2	116
Cordials, alcoholic	Minor2	3	5.0	45
Applejack (alcoholic beverage)	Minor2	9	5.9	42
Bourbon whiskey	Minor2	32	9,446.1	2,769
Corn whiskey	Minor2	9	2.3	19
Gin (alcoholic beverage)	Minor2	3	0.6	4
Rum (alcoholic beverage)	Minor2	40	71.1	1,235
Scotch whiskey	Minor2	3	0.3	3
Vodka (alcoholic beverage)	Minor2	40	29.0	85

*Category-Major categories (Major1) are more general descriptions for companies that self-selected to capture the many functions they perform in the industry. Minor categories (Minor1, Minor2) are more specific for companies that have more detailed functions (Minor1 is a larger category than Minor2). Minor categories figures (sales, etc.) can be aggregated to larger minor categories (Minor2 sums to Minor1) and major categories overall figures.

Men's & Boys' Apparel Mfg. Industry
NAICS 31522

NAICS 31522: Men's & Boys' Apparel Manufacturing. This industry comprises establishments primarily engaged in manufacturing men's and boys' cut and sew apparel from purchased fabric. Men's and boys' clothing jobbers, who perform entrepreneurial functions involved in apparel manufacture, including buying raw materials, designing and preparing samples, arranging for apparel to be made from their materials, and marketing finished apparel, are included.

Industry Establishments, Sales & Employment Trends

	Year					Percent Chg. Year-to-Year			
	2014	2015	2016	2017	2018	14-15	15-16	16-17	17-18
Establishments	1,411	1,376	1,343	1,293	1,243	-2.5%	-2.4%	-3.7%	-3.9%
Sales ($Millions)	4,516	4,178	3,847	3,479	3,120	-7.5%	-7.9%	-9.6%	-10.3%
Employment	12,238	11,937	11,648	11,217	10,781	-2.5%	-2.4%	-3.7%	-3.9%
Sales ($M)/Estab.	3.20	3.04	2.86	2.69	2.51	-5.1%	-5.6%	-6.1%	-6.7%
Sales ($)/Emp.	368,982	349,994	330,267	310,175	289,345	-5.1%	-5.6%	-6.1%	-6.7%

3-Year Trend – Estimated Number of Establishments

Year	Employee Size of Establishment									Total
	1-4 Emps.	5-9 Emps.	10-19 Emps.	20-49 Emps.	50-99 Emps.	100-249 Emps.	250-499 Emps.	>500 Emps.	Non-Employer	Employ-ment
2016	239	65	51	52	30	24	6	2	875	1,343
2017	230	62	49	50	28	23	5	2	842	1,293
2018	221	60	48	48	27	22	5	2	809	1,243

3-Year Trend – Estimated Number of Establishments

Year	Employee Size of Establishment									Total
	1-4 Emps.	5-9 Emps.	10-19 Emps.	20-49 Emps.	50-99 Emps.	100-249 Emps.	250-499 Emps.	>500 Emps.	Non-Employer	Employ-ment
2016	106.9	76.1	152.0	409.8	507.8	1,103.7	892.8	546.6	51.3	3,847.0
2017	96.7	68.8	137.5	370.6	459.2	998.1	807.4	494.5	46.4	3,479.3
2018	86.7	61.7	123.3	332.3	411.7	894.9	723.9	443.5	41.6	3,119.5

3-Year Trend – Estimated Number of Establishments

Year	Employee Size of Establishment									Total
	1-4 Emps.	5-9 Emps.	10-19 Emps.	20-49 Emps.	50-99 Emps.	100-249 Emps.	250-499 Emps.	>500 Emps.	Non-Employer	Employ-ment
2016	597	375	699	1,576	1,753	3,000	1,661	1,112	875	11,648
2017	575	361	673	1,517	1,688	2,889	1,600	1,071	842	11,217
2018	553	347	647	1,458	1,622	2,777	1,538	1,029	809	10,781

MEN'S & BOYS' APPAREL MFG. INDUSTRY
NAICS 31522

SUB-INDUSTRIES — 2017 ESTIMATED INDUSTRY
SALES, ESTABLISHMENTS & EMPLOYMENT

Sub-Industries	Cate-gory*	Establish-ments	Sales ($Mill)	Employ-ment
Men's and boy's trousers and slacks	Major1	497	21.0	4,658
Men's and boys' jeans and dungarees	Minor1	83	423.5	565
Dungarees: men's, youths', and boys'	Minor2	30	0.1	698
Jeans: men's, youths', and boys'	Minor2	272	2,029.3	2,230
Men's and boys' dress slacks and shorts	Minor1	6	0.0	1
Shorts (outerwear): men's, youths', and boys'	Minor2	35	306.4	220
Slacks, dress: men's, youths', and boys'	Minor2	112	3.1	602
Men's and boy's suits and coats	Major1	72	77.8	390
Tailored suits and formal jackets	Minor1	18	15.1	19
Formal jackets, men's and youths': from purchased mater	Minor2	3	12.9	5
Jackets, tailored suit-type: men's and boys'	Minor2	5	16.6	9
Suits, men's and boys': made from purchased materials	Minor2	24	245.7	412
Tailored dress and sport coats: men's and boys'	Minor2	5	2.4	6
Tuxedos: made from purchased materials	Minor2	17	4.2	12
Coats, overcoats and vests	Minor1	10	5.8	18
Coats, tailored: men's and boys': from purchased material	Minor2	4	80.0	110
Overcoats and topcoats: men's, youths' and boys'	Minor2	1	0.2	1
Vests: made from purchased materials	Minor2	5	5.2	19
Men's and boys' uniforms	Minor1	29	103.2	277
Firemen's uniforms: made from purchased materials	Minor2	6	10.3	76
Military uniforms, men's and youths': purchased materials	Minor2	46	104.9	841
Policemen's uniforms: made from purchased materials	Minor2	13	11.5	48

*Category-Major categories (Major1) are more general descriptions for companies that self-selected to capture the many functions they perform in the industry. Minor categories (Minor1, Minor2) are more specific for companies that have more detailed functions (Minor1 is a larger category than Minor2). Minor categories figures (sales, etc.) can be aggregated to larger minor categories (Minor2 sums to Minor1) and major categories overall figures.

WOMEN'S & GIRLS' APPAREL MFG. INDUSTRY
NAICS 31524

NAICS 31524: Women's & Girls' Apparel Manufacturing Industry. This industry comprises establishments primarily engaged in manufacturing women's and girls' apparel from purchased fabric. Women's and girls' clothing jobbers, who perform entrepreneurial functions involved in apparel manufacture, including buying raw materials, designing and preparing samples, arranging for apparel to be made from their materials, and marketing finished apparel, are included.

INDUSTRY ESTABLISHMENTS, SALES & EMPLOYMENT TRENDS

	Year					Percent Chg. Year-to-Year			
	2014	2015	2016	2017	2018	14-15	15-16	16-17	17-18
Establishments	3,203	3,326	3,458	3,547	3,626	3.8%	3.9%	2.6%	2.2%
Sales ($Millions)	3,422	3,515	3,606	3,653	3,679	2.7%	2.6%	1.3%	0.7%
Employment	18,431	19,141	19,897	20,414	20,864	3.8%	3.9%	2.6%	2.2%
Sales ($M)/Estab.	1.07	1.06	1.04	1.03	1.01	-1.1%	-1.3%	-1.3%	-1.5%
Sales ($)/Emp.	185,660	183,628	181,245	178,934	176,338	-1.1%	-1.3%	-1.3%	-1.5%

3-YEAR TREND — ESTIMATED NUMBER OF ESTABLISHMENTS

Year	Employee Size of Establishment									Total
	1-4 Emps.	5-9 Emps.	10-19 Emps.	20-49 Emps.	50-99 Emps.	100-249 Emps.	250-499 Emps.	>500 Emps.	Non-Employer	Employ-ment
2016	607	230	152	140	51	21	3	2	2,252	3,458
2017	622	236	156	144	52	21	3	2	2,310	3,547
2018	636	241	160	147	53	22	3	2	2,361	3,626

3-YEAR TREND — ESTIMATED NUMBER OF ESTABLISHMENTS

Year	Employee Size of Establishment									Total
	1-4 Emps.	5-9 Emps.	10-19 Emps.	20-49 Emps.	50-99 Emps.	100-249 Emps.	250-499 Emps.	>500 Emps.	Non-Employer	Employ-ment
2016	179.0	178.3	296.9	724.5	575.8	627.3	333.8	545.4	145.2	3,606.2
2017	181.8	181.1	301.4	735.6	584.6	636.9	339.0	545.0	147.4	3,652.7
2018	183.4	182.7	304.2	742.4	590.0	642.8	342.1	542.6	148.7	3,679.0

3-YEAR TREND — ESTIMATED NUMBER OF ESTABLISHMENTS

Year	Employee Size of Establishment									Total
	1-4 Emps.	5-9 Emps.	10-19 Emps.	20-49 Emps.	50-99 Emps.	100-249 Emps.	250-499 Emps.	>500 Emps.	Non-Employer	Employ-ment
2016	1,517	1,334	2,070	4,224	3,014	2,586	942	1,958	2,252	19,897
2017	1,556	1,368	2,124	4,334	3,092	2,654	967	2,009	2,310	20,414
2018	1,590	1,398	2,171	4,429	3,160	2,712	988	2,053	2,361	20,864

WOMEN'S & GIRLS' APPAREL MFG. INDUSTRY
NAICS 31524

SUB-INDUSTRIES — 2017 ESTIMATED INDUSTRY SALES, ESTABLISHMENTS & EMPLOYMENT

Sub-Industries	Cate-gory*	Establish-ments	Sales ($Mill)	Employ-ment
Women's, junior's, and misses' dresses	Major1	1,166	2,712.1	11,083
Bridal and formal gowns	Minor1	423	39.1	1,294
Gowns, formal	Minor2	138	18.0	558
Wedding gowns and dresses	Minor2	875	50.8	2,062
Dresses,paper, cut and sewn	Minor2	170	85.9	1,040
Ensemble dresses: women's, misses', and juniors'	Minor2	46	11.7	227
Housedresses	Minor2	20	4.6	66
Women's and misses' blouses and shirts	Major1	476	486.9	1,746
Blouses, women's and juniors': made from purchased mat	Minor2	129	192.6	1,891
Shirts, women's and juniors': made from purchased mater	Minor2	17	5.1	65
T-shirts and tops, women's: made from purchased materi:	Minor2	88	46.0	381

*Category-Major categories (Major1) are more general descriptions for companies that self-selected to capture the many functions they perform in the industry. Minor categories (Minor1, Minor2) are more specific for companies that have more detailed functions (Minor1 is a larger category than Minor2). Minor categories figures (sales, etc.) can be aggregated to larger minor categories (Minor2 sums to Minor1) and major categories overall figures.

PAPER MILLS INDUSTRY
NAICS 32212

NAICS 32212: Paper Mills Industry. This industry comprises establishments primarily engaged in manufacturing paper from pulp. These establishments may manufacture or purchase pulp. In addition, the establishments may convert the paper they make. The activity of making paper classifies an establishment into this industry regardless of the output.

INDUSTRY ESTABLISHMENTS, SALES & EMPLOYMENT TRENDS

	Year					Percent Chg. Year-to-Year			
	2014	2015	2016	2017	2018	14-15	15-16	16-17	17-18
Establishments	263	245	225	215	203	-6.8%	-8.2%	-4.7%	-5.1%
Sales ($Millions)	38,137	38,842	38,868	39,869	40,544	1.8%	0.1%	2.6%	1.7%
Employment	49,216	45,885	42,133	40,173	38,105	-6.8%	-8.2%	-4.7%	-5.1%
Sales ($M)/Estab.	145.11	158.52	172.75	185.85	199.25	9.2%	9.0%	7.6%	7.2%
Sales ($)/Emp.	774,889	846,512	922,510	992,438	1,064,022	9.2%	9.0%	7.6%	7.2%

3-YEAR TREND — ESTIMATED NUMBER OF ESTABLISHMENTS

	Employee Size of Establishment									Total
Year	1-4 Emps.	5-9 Emps.	10-19 Emps.	20-49 Emps.	50-99 Emps.	100-249 Emps.	250-499 Emps.	>500 Emps.	Non-Employer	Employ-ment
2016	30	13	8	18	24	34	35	35	28	225
2017	29	12	7	17	23	33	33	33	27	215
2018	27	12	7	16	22	31	32	32	25	203

3-YEAR TREND — ESTIMATED NUMBER OF ESTABLISHMENTS

	Employee Size of Establishment									Total
Year	1-4 Emps.	5-9 Emps.	10-19 Emps.	20-49 Emps.	50-99 Emps.	100-249 Emps.	250-499 Emps.	>500 Emps.	Non-Employer	Employ-ment
2016	25.9	29.1	43.9	271.4	795.6	3,063.1	10,582.2	24,053.5	3.0	38,867.9
2017	26.2	29.5	44.6	275.3	806.9	3,106.8	10,733.1	24,843.3	3.1	39,868.9
2018	26.3	29.7	44.7	276.4	810.0	3,118.7	10,774.0	25,461.2	3.1	40,544.0

3-YEAR TREND — ESTIMATED NUMBER OF ESTABLISHMENTS

	Employee Size of Establishment									Total
Year	1-4 Emps.	5-9 Emps.	10-19 Emps.	20-49 Emps.	50-99 Emps.	100-249 Emps.	250-499 Emps.	>500 Emps.	Non-Employer	Employ-ment
2016	75	74	105	541	1,424	4,318	10,210	25,357	28	42,133
2017	71	71	100	516	1,358	4,117	9,735	24,177	27	40,173
2018	68	67	95	489	1,288	3,905	9,234	22,933	25	38,105

PAPER MILLS INDUSTRY
NAICS 32212

SUB-INDUSTRIES — 2017 ESTIMATED INDUSTRY SALES, ESTABLISHMENTS & EMPLOYMENT

Sub-Industries	Category*	Establish-ments	Sales ($Mill)	Employ-ment
Paper mills	Major1	46	29,523.2	21,441
Towels, tissues and napkins; paper and stock	Minor1	3	829.8	2,278
Cleansing paper	Minor2	0	3.5	21
Facial tissue stock	Minor2	0	2.3	33
Napkin stock, paper	Minor2	1	7.6	385
Pattern tissue	Minor2	1	0.5	4
Sanitary tissue paper	Minor2	1	0.4	242
Tissue paper	Minor2	3	117.5	1,050
Toilet tissue stock	Minor2	0	0.8	198
Toweling tissue (paper)	Minor2	0	2.4	20
Parchment, securites, and bank note papers	Minor1	2	573.2	1,067
Specialty or chemically treated papers	Minor1	9	126.9	1,421
Book, bond and printing papers	Minor1	12	935.7	2,079
Poster and art papers	Minor1	25	1,010.9	334
Stationary, envelope and tablet papers	Minor1	39	84.4	1,958
Catalog, magazine, and newsprint papers	Minor1	10	326.0	2,676
Wrapping and packaging papers	Minor1	20	97.3	2,440
Building and roofing paper, felts and insulation siding	Minor1	2	1,813.6	475
Pressed and molded pulp and fiber products	Minor2	1	0.2	69
Lath, fiber	Minor2	0	0.1	1
Molded pulp products	Minor2	2	12.8	168
Pressed pulp products	Minor2	0	0.1	240
Tube stock	Minor2	0	1.6	11
Fine paper	Minor2	2	4,328.0	948
Kraft paper	Minor2	1	0.4	52
Rope or jute paper	Minor2	0	1.2	9
Uncoated paper	Minor2	0		30
Wallpaper (hanging paper)	Minor2	17	33.6	239
Rope or jute paper	Minor2	0	1.2	9
Uncoated paper	Minor2	0		30
Wallpaper (hanging paper)	Minor2	17	33.6	239

*Category-Major categories (Major1) are more general descriptions for companies that self-selected to capture the many functions they perform in the industry. Minor categories (Minor1, Minor2) are more specific for companies that have more detailed functions (Minor1 is a larger category than Minor2). Minor categories figures (sales, etc.) can be aggregated to larger minor categories (Minor2 sums to Minor1) and major categories overall figures.

PRINTING INDUSTRY
NAICS 32311

NAICS 32311: Printing Industry. This industry comprises establishments primarily engaged in printing on apparel and textile products, paper, metal, glass, plastics, and other materials, except fabric (grey goods). The printing processes employed include, but are not limited to, lithographic, gravure, screen, flexographic, digital, and letterpress. Establishments in this industry do not manufacture the stock that they print but may perform postprinting activities, such as bending, cutting, or laminating the materials they print, and mailing.

INDUSTRY ESTABLISHMENTS, SALES & EMPLOYMENT TRENDS

	Year					Percent Chg. Year-to-Year			
	2014	2015	2016	2017	2018	14-15	15-16	16-17	17-18
Establishments	33,944	33,481	32,886	32,129	31,223	-1.4%	-1.8%	-2.3%	-2.8%
Sales ($Millions)	76,991	78,869	80,209	80,980	81,114	2.4%	1.7%	1.0%	0.2%
Employment	401,622	396,135	389,104	380,144	369,422	-1.4%	-1.8%	-2.3%	-2.8%
Sales ($M)/Estab.	2.27	2.36	2.44	2.52	2.60	3.9%	3.5%	3.3%	3.1%
Sales ($)/Emp.	191,700	199,097	206,139	213,025	219,570	3.9%	3.5%	3.3%	3.1%

3-YEAR TREND – ESTIMATED NUMBER OF ESTABLISHMENTS

Year	Employee Size of Establishment									Total
	1-4 Emps.	5-9 Emps.	10-19 Emps.	20-49 Emps.	50-99 Emps.	100-249 Emps.	250-499 Emps.	>500 Emps.	Non-Employer	Employ-ment
2016	11,940	4,682	3,034	2,387	923	615	138	58	9,108	32,886
2017	11,665	4,575	2,965	2,332	902	601	134	57	8,899	32,129
2018	11,336	4,446	2,881	2,266	877	584	131	55	8,648	31,223

3-YEAR TREND – ESTIMATED NUMBER OF ESTABLISHMENTS

Year	Employee Size of Establishment									Total
	1-4 Emps.	5-9 Emps.	10-19 Emps.	20-49 Emps.	50-99 Emps.	100-249 Emps.	250-499 Emps.	>500 Emps.	Non-Employer	Employ-ment
2016	3,463.9	3,570.3	5,818.4	12,116.0	10,301.0	18,499.0	13,942.8	11,668.7	829.2	80,209.3
2017	3,495.1	3,602.5	5,870.9	12,225.2	10,393.8	18,665.7	14,068.4	11,822.0	836.7	80,980.3
2018	3,498.2	3,605.7	5,876.1	12,236.2	10,403.2	18,682.5	14,081.1	11,893.4	837.4	81,114.0

3-YEAR TREND – ESTIMATED NUMBER OF ESTABLISHMENTS

Year	Employee Size of Establishment									Total
	1-4 Emps.	5-9 Emps.	10-19 Emps.	20-49 Emps.	50-99 Emps.	100-249 Emps.	250-499 Emps.	>500 Emps.	Non-Employer	Employ-ment
2016	29,850	27,158	41,268	71,855	54,844	77,578	40,020	37,424	9,108	389,104
2017	29,162	26,532	40,317	70,200	53,581	75,791	39,099	36,562	8,899	380,144
2018	28,340	25,784	39,180	68,220	52,070	73,654	37,996	35,531	8,648	369,422

SUB-INDUSTRIES – 2017 ESTIMATED INDUSTRY SALES, ESTABLISHMENTS & EMPLOYMENT

Sub-Industries	Cate-gory*	Establish-ments	Sales ($Mill)	Employ-ment
Commercial printing, lithographic	Major1	18,207	39,071.5	173,290
Offset and photolithographic printing	Minor1	462	780.5	5,665
Offset printing	Minor2	11,368	30,923.1	165,601
Photo-offset printing	Minor2	153	203.6	1,279
Photolithographic printing	Minor2	46	86.7	407
Promotional printing, lithographic	Minor1	134	419.2	2,510
Advertising posters, lithographed	Minor2	67	100.2	628
Catalogs, lithographed	Minor2	21	4,570.6	592
Circulars, lithographed	Minor2	4	66.5	564
Coupons, lithographed	Minor2	6	7.5	43
Business form and card printing, lithographic	Minor1	340	417.7	2,887
Billheads, lithographed	Minor2	2	1.0	5
Forms, business: lithographed	Minor2	116	569.1	3,141
Visiting cards, lithographed	Minor2	3	10.0	47
Calendar and card printing, lithographic	Minor1	26	11.5	586
Calendars, lithographed	Minor2	43	187.4	583
Cards, lithographed	Minor2	25	32.7	724
Playing cards, lithographed	Minor2	13	10.7	499
Post cards, picture: lithographed	Minor2	24	28.7	357
Souvenir cards, lithographed	Minor2	11	9.5	554
Atlas and map printing, lithographic	Minor1	3	0.7	6
Maps, lithographed	Minor2	28	57.7	242
Poster and decal printing, lithographic	Minor1	146	413.7	3,048
Tag, ticket, and schedule printing: lithographic	Minor1	44	107.2	1,091
Wrapper and seal printing, lithographic	Minor1	21	34.2	184
Publication printing, lithographic	Minor1	72	94.9	1,198
Newspapers, lithographed only	Minor2	27	76.4	583
Periodicals, lithographed	Minor2	9	15.2	2,207
Color lithography	Minor2	196	1,089.8	4,215
Fashion plates, lithographed	Minor2	16	35.5	157
Letters, circular or form: lithographed	Minor2	46	102.9	585
Lithographing on metal	Minor2	420	1,339.8	6,213
Menus, lithographed	Minor2	25	72.5	318
Trading stamps, lithographed	Minor2	6	32.0	134

*Category-Major categories (Major1) are more general descriptions for companies that self-selected to capture the many functions they perform in the industry. Minor categories (Minor1, Minor2) are more specific for companies that have more detailed functions (Minor1 is a larger category than Minor2). Minor categories figures (sales, etc.) can be aggregated to larger minor categories (Minor2 sums to Minor1) and major categories overall figures.

PETROLEUM REFINERIES INDUSTRY
NAICS 32411

NAICS 32411: Petroleum Refineries. Establishments primarily engaged in producing gasoline, kerosene, distillate fuel oils, residual fuel oils, and lubricants, through fractionation or straight distillation of crude oil, redistillation of unfinished petroleum derivatives, cracking or other processes. Establishments of this business also produce aliphatic and aromatic chemicals as byproducts. Natural gasoline from natural gas is classified in mining.

INDUSTRY ESTABLISHMENTS, SALES & EMPLOYMENT TRENDS

	Year					Percent Chg. Year-to-Year			
	2014	2015	2016	2017	2018	14-15	15-16	16-17	17-18
Establishments	242	234	225	216	207	-3.4%	-3.7%	-4.4%	-4.1%
Sales ($Millions)	632,541	665,029	693,039	715,807	737,285	5.1%	4.2%	3.3%	3.0%
Employment	55,540	53,664	51,667	49,417	47,406	-3.4%	-3.7%	-4.4%	-4.1%
Sales ($M)/Estab.	2,611.06	2,841.12	3,075.23	3,320.85	3,565.62	8.8%	8.2%	8.0%	7.4%
Sales ($)/Emp.	11,388,939	12,392,422	13,413,574	14,484,919	15,552,559	8.8%	8.2%	8.0%	7.4%

3-YEAR TREND — ESTIMATED NUMBER OF ESTABLISHMENTS

Year	Employee Size of Establishment									Total
	1-4 Emps.	5-9 Emps.	10-19 Emps.	20-49 Emps.	50-99 Emps.	100-249 Emps.	250-499 Emps.	>500 Emps.	Non-Employer	Employ-ment
2016	14	9	12	16	7	23	37	47	60	225
2017	13	9	12	15	7	22	36	44	57	216
2018	13	9	11	15	7	21	34	43	55	207

3-YEAR TREND — ESTIMATED NUMBER OF ESTABLISHMENTS

Year	Employee Size of Establishment									Total
	1-4 Emps.	5-9 Emps.	10-19 Emps.	20-49 Emps.	50-99 Emps.	100-249 Emps.	250-499 Emps.	>500 Emps.	Non-Employer	Employ-ment
2016	176.5	309.3	1,011.1	3,499.6	3,620.1	30,490.5	164,426.4	489,497.0	8.2	693,038.7
2017	179.5	314.6	1,028.4	3,559.6	3,682.2	31,013.0	167,244.0	508,777.5	8.4	715,807.1
2018	182.2	319.3	1,043.8	3,612.8	3,737.2	31,476.8	169,745.1	527,159.4	8.5	737,285.1

3-YEAR TREND — ESTIMATED NUMBER OF ESTABLISHMENTS

Year	Employee Size of Establishment									Total
	1-4 Emps.	5-9 Emps.	10-19 Emps.	20-49 Emps.	50-99 Emps.	100-249 Emps.	250-499 Emps.	>500 Emps.	Non-Employer	Employ-ment
2016	35	54	164	476	442	2,933	10,825	36,679	60	51,667
2017	33	52	157	455	423	2,805	10,353	35,082	57	49,417
2018	32	50	151	437	406	2,691	9,932	33,654	55	47,406

PETROLEUM REFINERIES INDUSTRY
NAICS 32411

SUB-INDUSTRIES — 2017 ESTIMATED INDUSTRY SALES, ESTABLISHMENTS & EMPLOYMENT

Sub-Industries	Category*	Establish-ments	Sales ($Mill)	Employ-ment
Petroleum refining	Major1	95	700,922.8	38,795
Gases and liquefied petroleum gases	Minor1	9	1,091.7	792
Gas, refinery	Minor2	9	11,783.0	2,457
Liquefied petroleum gases, LPG	Minor2	3	2.8	49
Light distillates	Minor1	1	3.7	272
Alkylates	Minor2	0	0.8	3
Gasoline blending plants	Minor2	3	10.9	442
Jet fuels	Minor2	3	11.6	218
Kerosene	Minor2	0	0.1	1
Solvents	Minor2	4	1,540.8	144
Intermediate distillates	Minor1	0	0.2	2
Acid oil	Minor2	0	0.1	1
Diesel fuels	Minor2	20	107.3	729
Oils, fuel	Minor2	25	84.4	2,086
Oils, illuminating	Minor2	0	1.5	14
Oils, partly refined: sold for rerunning	Minor2	1	3.7	87
Still oil	Minor2	0	0.3	3
Heavy distillates	Minor1	0	0.6	6
Mineral jelly	Minor2	0	0.1	1
Mineral oils, natural	Minor2	2	1.7	579
Mineral waxes, natural	Minor2	1	17.3	102
Oils, lubricating	Minor2	11	26.1	733
Paraffin wax	Minor2	1	49.9	21
Residues	Minor1	3	3.6	38
Asphalt or asphaltic materials, made in refineries	Minor2	5	37.7	301
Coke, petroleum	Minor2	2	1.3	371
Greases, lubricating	Minor2	1	1.7	48
Petrolatums, nonmedicinal	Minor2	1	0.4	141
Road materials, bituminous	Minor2	1	37.1	17
Road oils	Minor2	0	0.8	21
Aromatic chemical products	Minor1	6	3.5	124
Nonaromatic chemical products	Minor1	8	51.5	727
Fractionation products of crude petroleum, hydrocarbons,	Minor1	2	8.0	89

*Category-Major categories (Major1) are more general descriptions for companies that self-selected to capture the many functions they perform in the industry. Minor categories (Minor1, Minor2) are more specific for companies that have more detailed functions (Minor1 is a larger category than Minor2). Minor categories figures (sales, etc.) can be aggregated to larger minor categories (Minor2 sums to Minor1) and major categories overall figures.

PETROCHEMICAL MANUFACTURING INDUSTRY
NAICS 32511

NAICS 32511: Petrochemical Manufacturing Industry. This industry comprises establishments primarily engaged in (1) manufacturing acyclic (i.e., aliphatic) hydrocarbons such as ethylene, propylene, and butylene made from refined petroleum or liquid hydrocarbon and/or (2) manufacturing cyclic aromatic hydrocarbons such as benzene, toluene, styrene, xylene, ethyl benzene, and cumene made from refined petroleum or liquid hydrocarbons.

INDUSTRY ESTABLISHMENTS, SALES & EMPLOYMENT TRENDS

	Year					Percent Chg. Year-to-Year			
	2014	2015	2016	2017	2018	14-15	15-16	16-17	17-18
Establishments	66	68	71	73	75	2.7%	4.4%	3.0%	3.7%
Sales ($Millions)	40,160	45,564	51,978	58,034	64,767	13.5%	14.1%	11.7%	11.6%
Employment	7,623	7,830	8,175	8,419	8,732	2.7%	4.4%	3.0%	3.7%
Sales ($M)/Estab.	609.58	673.26	735.70	797.53	858.14	10.4%	9.3%	8.4%	7.6%
Sales ($)/Emp.	5,268,562	5,818,910	6,358,547	6,892,990	7,416,798	10.4%	9.3%	8.4%	7.6%

3-YEAR TREND — ESTIMATED NUMBER OF ESTABLISHMENTS

Year	Employee Size of Establishment									Total
	1-4 Emps.	5-9 Emps.	10-19 Emps.	20-49 Emps.	50-99 Emps.	100-249 Emps.	250-499 Emps.	>500 Emps.	Non-Employer	Employ-ment
2016	13	5	8	5	4	11	11	5	8	71
2017	13	6	8	6	4	11	11	6	9	73
2018	14	6	8	6	5	11	11	6	9	75

3-YEAR TREND — ESTIMATED NUMBER OF ESTABLISHMENTS

Year	Employee Size of Establishment									Total
	1-4 Emps.	5-9 Emps.	10-19 Emps.	20-49 Emps.	50-99 Emps.	100-249 Emps.	250-499 Emps.	>500 Emps.	Non-Employer	Employ-ment
2016	77.7	85.1	299.4	566.1	995.6	6,708.2	22,609.7	20,635.2	1.1	51,978.1
2017	86.7	95.0	334.3	632.1	1,111.6	7,490.1	25,244.8	23,037.9	1.2	58,033.8
2018	96.8	106.0	373.1	705.5	1,240.6	8,359.4	28,174.9	25,708.8	1.4	64,766.5

3-YEAR TREND — ESTIMATED NUMBER OF ESTABLISHMENTS

Year	Employee Size of Establishment									Total
	1-4 Emps.	5-9 Emps.	10-19 Emps.	20-49 Emps.	50-99 Emps.	100-249 Emps.	250-499 Emps.	>500 Emps.	Non-Employer	Employ-ment
2016	32	31	102	161	255	1,352	3,120	3,113	8	8,175
2017	33	32	105	166	262	1,393	3,213	3,206	9	8,419
2018	34	33	109	172	272	1,445	3,333	3,325	9	8,732

PETROCHEMICAL MANUFACTURING INDUSTRY
NAICS 32511

SUB-INDUSTRIES — 2017 ESTIMATED INDUSTRY SALES, ESTABLISHMENTS & EMPLOYMENT

Sub-Industries	Cate-gory*	Establish-ments	Sales ($Mill)	Employ-ment
Alcohols, non beverage	Minor1	1	447.9	210
Alcohols, industrial: denatured (non-beverage)	Minor2	1	133.4	250
Amyl alcohol	Minor2	0	0.3	55
Ethyl alcohol, ethanol	Minor2	16	15,261.4	2,973
Ethylene glycols	Minor2	1	3.7	62
Grain alcohol, industrial	Minor2	0	0.3	9
Methyl alcohol, synthetic, methanol	Minor2	0	553.9	211
Olefins	Minor1	1	28,799.9	663
Ethylene	Minor2	0	69.2	95
Propylene, butylene	Minor2	0	38.7	75
Coke, calcined petroleum: made from purchased material	Minor2	7	19.3	534
Fuel briquettes and waxes	Minor1	6	80.3	80
Fuel briquettes or boulets: made with petroleum binder	Minor2	13	19.3	1,836
Waxes, petroleum: not produced in petroleum refineries	Minor2	24	7,065.2	1,129
Phenol, alkylated and cumene	Minor2	0	46.6	30
Styrene	Minor2	0	114.8	25
Toluene	Minor2	0	0.5	0
Cyclic organic intermediates	Minor1	0	987.2	105
Tar, coal tar, and related chemicals	Minor1	0	1,903.1	20
Coal tar: crudes, intermediates, and distillates	Minor2	0	2,446.4	39
Tar	Minor2	1	23.7	9
Chemical indicators	Minor2	0	18.6	7

*Category-Major categories (Major1) are more general descriptions for companies that self-selected to capture the many functions they perform in the industry. Minor categories (Minor1, Minor2) are more specific for companies that have more detailed functions (Minor1 is a larger category than Minor2). Minor categories figures (sales, etc.) can be aggregated to larger minor categories (Minor2 sums to Minor1) and major categories overall figures.

PHARMACEUTICAL PREPARATION MFG. INDUSTRY (NAICS 325412)

NAICS 325412: Pharmaceutical Preparation Manufacturing . This U.S. industry comprises establishments primarily engaged in manufacturing in-vivo diagnostic substances and pharmaceutical preparations (except biological) intended for internal and external consumption in dose forms, such as ampoules, tablets, capsules, vials, ointments, powders, solutions, and suspensions.

INDUSTRY ESTABLISHMENTS, SALES & EMPLOYMENT TRENDS

	Year					Percent Chg. Year-to-Year			
	2014	2015	2016	2017	2018	14-15	15-16	16-17	17-18
Establishments	1,570	1,578	1,615	1,671	1,742	0.5%	2.3%	3.5%	4.2%
Sales ($Millions)	145,637	150,625	157,461	165,883	175,312	3.4%	4.5%	5.3%	5.7%
Employment	101,314	101,866	104,210	107,876	112,436	0.5%	2.3%	3.5%	4.2%
Sales ($M)/Estab.	92.77	95.43	97.52	99.24	100.63	2.9%	2.2%	1.8%	1.4%
Sales ($)/Emp.	1,437,483	1,478,656	1,510,994	1,537,719	1,559,217	2.9%	2.2%	1.8%	1.4%

3-YEAR TREND — ESTIMATED NUMBER OF ESTABLISHMENTS

Year	Employee Size of Establishment									Total
	1-4 Emps.	5-9 Emps.	10-19 Emps.	20-49 Emps.	50-99 Emps.	100-249 Emps.	250-499 Emps.	>500 Emps.	Non-Employer	Employ-ment
2016	358	171	140	193	120	118	79	63	372	1,615
2017	371	177	145	200	125	122	82	65	385	1,671
2018	386	184	151	209	130	128	85	68	402	1,742

3-YEAR TREND — ESTIMATED NUMBER OF ESTABLISHMENTS

Year	Employee Size of Establishment									Total
	1-4 Emps.	5-9 Emps.	10-19 Emps.	20-49 Emps.	50-99 Emps.	100-249 Emps.	250-499 Emps.	>500 Emps.	Non-Employer	Employ-ment
2016	568.0	712.1	1,467.1	5,368.1	7,343.7	19,454.2	43,903.0	78,607.4	37.7	157,461.3
2017	602.9	755.9	1,557.4	5,698.3	7,795.4	20,651.0	46,603.7	82,178.8	40.0	165,883.3
2018	642.8	805.9	1,660.5	6,075.5	8,311.5	22,018.2	49,689.2	86,065.8	42.6	175,312.1

3-YEAR TREND — ESTIMATED NUMBER OF ESTABLISHMENTS

Year	Employee Size of Establishment									Total
	1-4 Emps.	5-9 Emps.	10-19 Emps.	20-49 Emps.	50-99 Emps.	100-249 Emps.	250-499 Emps.	>500 Emps.	Non-Employer	Employ-ment
2016	895	990	1,902	5,821	7,149	14,916	23,040	49,126	372	104,210
2017	926	1,025	1,969	6,025	7,400	15,441	23,850	50,854	385	107,876
2018	966	1,068	2,053	6,280	7,713	16,094	24,858	53,003	402	112,436

PHARMACEUTICAL PREPARATION MFG. INDUSTRY (NAICS 325412)

SUB-INDUSTRIES – 2017 ESTIMATED INDUSTRY SALES, ESTABLISHMENTS & EMPLOYMENT

Sub-Industries	Cate-gory*	Establish-ments	Sales ($Mill)	Employ-ment
Pharmaceutical preparations	Major1	1,050	152,427.6	78,546
Drugs affecting neoplasms and endrocrine systems	Minor1	3	263.0	201
Adrenal pharmaceutical preparations	Minor2	9	30.3	93
Hormone preparations	Minor2	2	1.5	34
Insulin preparations	Minor2	1	0.2	1
Pituitary gland pharmaceutical preparations	Minor2	0	0.1	0
Thyroid preparations	Minor2	1	0.4	49
Drugs acting on the central nervous system & sense orgal	Minor1	5	72.7	873
Analgesics	Minor2	3	7.7	38
Barbituric acid pharmaceutical preparations	Minor2	1	5.0	34
Procaine pharmaceutical preparations	Minor2	1	0.4	0
Sodium salicylate tablets	Minor2	0	0.4	2
Tranquilizers or mental drug preparations	Minor2	1	0.1	4
Drugs acting on the cardiovascular system, except diagnc	Minor1	5	6.6	1,094
Digitalis pharmaceutical preparations	Minor2	2	4.1	33
Drugs acting on the respiratory system	Minor1	3	71.2	535
Antihistamine preparations	Minor2	0	0.3	128
Cold remedies	Minor2	1	0.8	6
Cough medicines	Minor2	5	1.8	190
Lozenges, pharmaceutical	Minor2	1	6.6	13
Syrups, pharmaceutical	Minor2	1	74.4	32
Drugs acting on the gastrointestinal or genitourinary syste	Minor1	4	180.3	64
Antacids	Minor2	1	0.5	5
Diuretics	Minor2	0	9.2	2
Effervescent salts	Minor2	1	20.7	74
Laxatives	Minor2	1	0.3	49
Dermatologicals	Minor1	52	396.2	1,022
Vitamin, nutrient, and hematinic preparations for human u	Minor1	174	1,857.0	8,214
Drugs affecting parasitic and infective diseases	Minor1	13	305.5	745
Chlorination tablets and kits (water purification)	Minor2	13	38.5	127
Druggists' preparations (pharmaceuticals)	Minor2	71	3,213.6	2,803
Emulsions, pharmaceutical	Minor2	0	0.4	3
Extracts of botanicals: powdered, pilular, solid, or fluid	Minor2	6	18.5	214
Misc. pharmaceutical preparations	Minor2	243	6,867.5	12,645

*Category-Major categories (Major1) are more general descriptions for companies that self-selected to capture the many functions they perform in the industry. Minor categories (Minor1, Minor2) are more specific for companies that have more detailed functions (Minor1 is a larger category than Minor2). Minor categories figures (sales, etc.) can be aggregated to larger minor categories (Minor2 sums to Minor1) and major categories overall figures.

ELECTRONIC COMPUTER MANUFACTURING INDUSTRY
(NAICS 334111)

NAICS 334111: Electronic Computer Manufacturing . This U.S. industry comprises establishments primarily engaged in manufacturing and/or assembling electronic computers, such as mainframes, personal computers, workstations, laptops, and computer servers. Computers can be analog, digital, or hybrid. Digital computers, the most common type, are devices that do all of the following: (1) store the processing program or programs and the data immediately necessary for the execution of the program; (2) can be freely programmed in accordance with the requirements of the user; (3) perform arithmetical computations specified by the user.

INDUSTRY ESTABLISHMENTS, SALES & EMPLOYMENT TRENDS

	Year					Percent Chg. Year-to-Year			
	2014	2015	2016	2017	2018	14-15	15-16	16-17	17-18
Establishments	522	498	479	475	479	-4.7%	-3.7%	-0.9%	0.7%
Sales ($Millions)	25,148	24,705	24,385	24,491	24,802	-1.8%	-1.3%	0.4%	1.3%
Employment	12,424	11,845	11,407	11,306	11,391	-4.7%	-3.7%	-0.9%	0.7%
Sales ($M)/Estab.	48.17	49.64	50.88	51.55	51.82	3.0%	2.5%	1.3%	0.5%
Sales ($)/Emp.	2,024,154	2,085,674	2,137,700	2,166,108	2,177,347	3.0%	2.5%	1.3%	0.5%

3-YEAR TREND – ESTIMATED NUMBER OF ESTABLISHMENTS

Year	Employee Size of Establishment									Total
	1-4 Emps.	5-9 Emps.	10-19 Emps.	20-49 Emps.	50-99 Emps.	100-249 Emps.	250-499 Emps.	>500 Emps.	Non-Employer	Employ-ment
2016	174	52	52	35	27	17	6	3	114	479
2017	172	52	52	35	26	17	5	3	113	475
2018	173	52	52	35	27	17	6	3	114	479

3-YEAR TREND – ESTIMATED NUMBER OF ESTABLISHMENTS

Year	Employee Size of Establishment									Total
	1-4 Emps.	5-9 Emps.	10-19 Emps.	20-49 Emps.	50-99 Emps.	100-249 Emps.	250-499 Emps.	>500 Emps.	Non-Employer	Employ-ment
2016	444.5	352.3	886.0	1,563.3	2,622.6	4,631.1	4,929.1	8,946.2	10.4	24,385.5
2017	444.9	352.7	886.9	1,565.0	2,625.3	4,635.8	4,934.2	9,035.4	10.4	24,490.5
2018	451.8	358.1	900.6	1,589.2	2,666.0	4,707.7	5,010.6	9,107.3	10.6	24,802.0

3-YEAR TREND – ESTIMATED NUMBER OF ESTABLISHMENTS

Year	Employee Size of Establishment									Total
	1-4 Emps.	5-9 Emps.	10-19 Emps.	20-49 Emps.	50-99 Emps.	100-249 Emps.	250-499 Emps.	>500 Emps.	Non-Employer	Employ-ment
2016	434	304	712	1,050	1,582	2,200	1,603	3,410	114	11,407
2017	430	301	705	1,041	1,568	2,180	1,588	3,380	113	11,306
2018	433	303	711	1,049	1,579	2,197	1,600	3,405	114	11,391

ELECTRONIC COMPUTER MANUFACTURING INDUSTRY (NAICS 334111)

SUB-INDUSTRIES — 2017 ESTIMATED INDUSTRY SALES, ESTABLISHMENTS & EMPLOYMENT

Sub-Industries	Cate-gory*	Establish-ments	Sales ($Mill)	Employ-ment
Electronic computers	Major1	327	6,290.0	6,166
Computers, digital, analog or hybrid	Minor2	40	11.2	810
Mainframe computers	Minor2	14	2.9	527
Minicomputers	Minor2	22	15.0	2,312
Personal computers (microcomputers)	Minor2	72	18,171.5	1,491

*Category-Major categories (Major1) are more general descriptions for companies that self-selected to capture the many functions they perform in the industry. Minor categories (Minor1, Minor2) are more specific for companies that have more detailed functions (Minor1 is a larger category than Minor2). Minor categories figures (sales, etc.) can be aggregated to larger minor categories (Minor2 sums to Minor1) and major categories overall figures.

TELEPHONE EQUIPMENT MFG. INDUSTRY
NAICS 33421

NAICS 33421: Telephone Apparatus Manufacturing This industry comprises establishments primarily engaged in manufacturing wire telephone and data communications equipment. These products may be standalone or board-level components of a larger system. Examples of products made by these establishments are central office switching equipment, cordless telephones (except cellular), PBX equipment, telephones, telephone answering machines, and data communications equipment, such as bridges, routers, and gateways.

INDUSTRY ESTABLISHMENTS, SALES & EMPLOYMENT TRENDS

	Year					Percent Chg. Year-to-Year			
	2014	2015	2016	2017	2018	14-15	15-16	16-17	17-18
Establishments	353	331	310	294	279	-6.1%	-6.4%	-5.1%	-5.3%
Sales ($Millions)	10,390	9,831	9,275	8,822	8,366	-5.4%	-5.7%	-4.9%	-5.2%
Employment	13,732	12,893	12,074	11,453	10,844	-6.1%	-6.4%	-5.1%	-5.3%
Sales ($M)/Estab.	29.45	29.68	29.90	29.98	30.03	0.8%	0.7%	0.3%	0.2%
Sales ($)/Emp.	756,572	762,548	768,193	770,252	771,508	0.8%	0.7%	0.3%	0.2%

3-YEAR TREND – ESTIMATED NUMBER OF ESTABLISHMENTS

Year	Employee Size of Establishment									Total
	1-4 Emps.	5-9 Emps.	10-19 Emps.	20-49 Emps.	50-99 Emps.	100-249 Emps.	250-499 Emps.	>500 Emps.	Non-Employer	Employ-ment
2016	67	31	41	43	23	23	4	4	74	310
2017	63	29	39	41	22	22	4	4	70	294
2018	60	28	37	39	21	21	4	4	66	279

3-YEAR TREND – ESTIMATED NUMBER OF ESTABLISHMENTS

Year	Employee Size of Establishment									Total
	1-4 Emps.	5-9 Emps.	10-19 Emps.	20-49 Emps.	50-99 Emps.	100-249 Emps.	250-499 Emps.	>500 Emps.	Non-Employer	Employ-ment
2016	58.6	71.0	239.7	661.3	771.4	2,079.0	1,347.5	4,040.3	6.4	9,275.1
2017	54.8	66.3	223.9	618.0	720.8	1,942.7	1,259.2	3,930.4	6.0	8,822.1
2018	51.0	61.7	208.4	575.0	670.7	1,807.7	1,171.7	3,814.7	5.6	8,366.5

3-YEAR TREND – ESTIMATED NUMBER OF ESTABLISHMENTS

Year	Employee Size of Establishment									Total
	1-4 Emps.	5-9 Emps.	10-19 Emps.	20-49 Emps.	50-99 Emps.	100-249 Emps.	250-499 Emps.	>500 Emps.	Non-Employer	Employ-ment
2016	167	178	562	1,297	1,358	2,883	1,279	4,277	74	12,074
2017	158	169	533	1,230	1,288	2,735	1,213	4,057	70	11,453
2018	150	160	505	1,165	1,220	2,589	1,149	3,841	66	10,844

TELEPHONE EQUIPMENT MFG. INDUSTRY
NAICS 33421

SUB-INDUSTRIES – 2017 ESTIMATED INDUSTRY SALES, ESTABLISHMENTS & EMPLOYMENT

Sub-Industries	Cate-gory*	Establish-ments	Sales ($Mill)	Employ-ment
Telephone and telegraph apparatus	Major1	113	5,031.3	6,213
Telephones and telephone apparatus	Minor1	48	1,483.0	1,479
Autotransformers for telephone switchboards	Minor2	1	1.1	4
Communication headgear, telephone	Minor2	7	23.7	140
Facsimile equipment	Minor2	2	2.3	13
Headsets, telephone	Minor2	10	14.8	190
Modems	Minor2	11	703.4	144
Switching equipment, telephone	Minor2	5	12.4	603
Telephone answering machines	Minor2	2	1.0	10
Telephone central office equipment, dial or manual	Minor2	3	4.0	73
Telephone dialing devices, automatic	Minor2	3	2.7	48
Telephone sets, all types except cellular radio	Minor2	10	39.3	193
Telephone station equipment and parts, wire	Minor2	5	3.4	56
Telephones, sound powered (no battery)	Minor2	1	0.4	3
Toll switching equipment, telephone	Minor2	1	0.4	10
Telegraph and related apparatus	Minor1	1	0.4	6
PBX equipment, manual or automatic	Minor2	3	4.4	38
Telegraph or telephone carrier and repeater equipment	Minor2	2	1.3	17
Telegraph station equipment and parts, wire	Minor2	0	0.1	1
Carrier equipment, telephone or telegraph	Minor2	5	102.0	51
Data sets, telephone or telegraph	Minor2	2	0.8	70
Electronic secretary	Minor2	2	2.1	14
Message concentrators	Minor2	9	151.3	67
Multiplex equipment, telephone and telegraph	Minor2	1	3.0	61
Switchboards, telephone or telegraph	Minor2	0	0.1	0
Telephone cords, jacks, adapters, etc.	Minor2	5	9.5	45
Fiber optics communications equipment	Minor2	44	1,223.6	1,904

*Category-Major categories (Major1) are more general descriptions for companies that self-selected to capture the many functions they perform in the industry. Minor categories (Minor1, Minor2) are more specific for companies that have more detailed functions (Minor1 is a larger category than Minor2). Minor categories figures (sales, etc.) can be aggregated to larger minor categories (Minor2 sums to Minor1) and major categories overall figures.

RADIO/TV BROADCAST EQUIPMENT INDUSTRY
NAICS 33422

NAICS 33422: Radio/TV Broadcast Equipment. Establishments primarily engaged in manufacturing radio and television broadcasting and communications equipment. Includes closed-circuit and cable television equipment; studio equipment; light communications equipment; transmitters, transceivers and receivers (except household and automotive); cellular radio telephones; communication antennas; receivers; RF power amplifiers; and fixed and mobile radio systems.

INDUSTRY ESTABLISHMENTS, SALES & EMPLOYMENT TRENDS

	Year					Percent Chg. Year-to-Year			
	2014	2015	2016	2017	2018	14-15	15-16	16-17	17-18
Establishments	1,006	960	924	907	904	-4.6%	-3.6%	-1.9%	-0.3%
Sales ($Millions)	33,438	32,077	30,913	30,086	29,511	-4.1%	-3.6%	-2.7%	-1.9%
Employment	47,040	44,868	43,230	42,392	42,260	-4.6%	-3.6%	-1.9%	-0.3%
Sales ($M)/Estab.	33.24	33.43	33.44	33.19	32.65	0.6%	0.0%	-0.7%	-1.6%
Sales ($)/Emp.	710,831	714,925	715,076	709,714	698,328	0.6%	0.0%	-0.7%	-1.6%

3-YEAR TREND — ESTIMATED NUMBER OF ESTABLISHMENTS

Year	Employee Size of Establishment									Total
	1-4 Emps.	5-9 Emps.	10-19 Emps.	20-49 Emps.	50-99 Emps.	100-249 Emps.	250-499 Emps.	>500 Emps.	Non-Employer	Employ-ment
2016	196	113	106	130	68	50	23	20	220	924
2017	192	111	104	127	67	49	23	20	215	907
2018	191	111	103	127	66	49	22	20	215	904

3-YEAR TREND — ESTIMATED NUMBER OF ESTABLISHMENTS

Year	Employee Size of Establishment									Total
	1-4 Emps.	5-9 Emps.	10-19 Emps.	20-49 Emps.	50-99 Emps.	100-249 Emps.	250-499 Emps.	>500 Emps.	Non-Employer	Employ-ment
2016	152.7	231.7	544.8	1,768.1	2,039.8	4,011.7	6,259.8	15,885.2	19.1	30,912.9
2017	147.5	223.8	526.3	1,707.9	1,970.4	3,875.2	6,046.9	15,569.9	18.5	30,086.4
2018	144.5	219.3	515.6	1,673.3	1,930.4	3,796.6	5,924.2	15,289.5	18.1	29,511.3

3-YEAR TREND — ESTIMATED NUMBER OF ESTABLISHMENTS

Year	Employee Size of Establishment									Total
	1-4 Emps.	5-9 Emps.	10-19 Emps.	20-49 Emps.	50-99 Emps.	100-249 Emps.	250-499 Emps.	>500 Emps.	Non-Employer	Employ-ment
2016	489	656	1,437	3,900	4,040	6,258	6,683	19,547	220	43,230
2017	480	643	1,409	3,825	3,961	6,137	6,554	19,168	215	42,392
2018	478	641	1,405	3,813	3,949	6,117	6,533	19,108	215	42,260

RADIO/TV BROADCAST EQUIPMENT INDUSTRY
NAICS 33422

SUB-INDUSTRIES – 2017 ESTIMATED INDUSTRY SALES, ESTABLISHMENTS & EMPLOYMENT

Sub-Industries	Category*	Establish-ments	Sales ($Mill)	Employ-ment
Radio and t.v. communications equipment	Major1	271	19,775.2	15,139
Radio broadcasting and communications equipment	Minor1	74	1,444.1	3,035
Airborne radio communications equipment	Minor2	9	25.8	616
Amplifiers, RF power and IF	Minor2	16	625.3	859
Carrier equipment, radio communications	Minor2	7	36.5	50
Cellular radio telephone	Minor2	26	112.0	1,077
Citizens' band (CB) radio	Minor2	1	5.6	20
Marine radio communications equipment	Minor2	5	19.0	58
Multiplex equipment	Minor2	1	6.4	12
Pagers (one-way)	Minor2	8	7.4	426
Radio receiver networks	Minor2	11	14.1	765
Receivers, radio communications	Minor2	8	26.9	130
Transmitter-receivers, radio	Minor2	9	142.7	292
Television broadcasting and communications equipment	Minor1	34	1,338.9	1,514
Cable television equipment	Minor2	19	65.4	1,159
Cameras, television	Minor2	9	10.2	477
Television antennas (transmitting) and ground equipment	Minor2	4	0.3	122
Television closed circuit equipment	Minor2	16	364.8	260
Television monitors	Minor2	7	38.8	114
Radio and t.v. communications equipment, nec	Minor2	14	44.7	113
Antennas, transmitting and communications	Minor2	36	189.8	2,221
Digital encoders	Minor2	17	85.2	164
Encryption devices	Minor2	3	51.9	111
Light communications equipment	Minor2	4	17.9	86
Microwave communication equipment	Minor2	25	1,102.0	2,153
Mobile communication equipment	Minor2	46	1,076.3	1,102
Radio and television switching equipment	Minor2	1	20.7	164
Receiver-transmitter units (transceiver)	Minor2	6	149.0	261
Satellites, communications	Minor2	145	468.6	3,319
Space satellite communications equipment	Minor2	29	2,709.9	3,718
Studio equipment, radio and television broadcasting	Minor2	24	52.4	543
Telemetering equipment, electronic	Minor2	15	41.5	2,160
Transmitting apparatus, radio or television	Minor2	8	17.2	153

*Category-Major categories (Major1) are more general descriptions for companies that self-selected to capture the many functions they perform in the industry. Minor categories (Minor1, Minor2) are more specific for companies that have more detailed functions (Minor1 is a larger category than Minor2). Minor categories figures (sales, etc.) can be aggregated to larger minor categories (Minor2 sums to Minor1) and major categories overall figures.

Audio & Visual Equipment Mfg. Industry
NAICS 33431

NAICS 33431: Audio & Video Equipment Manufacturing Industry.
This industry comprises establishments primarily engaged in manufacturing electronic audio and video equipment for home entertainment, motor vehicle, public address and musical instrument amplifications. Examples of products made by these establishments are video cassette recorders, televisions, stereo equipment, speaker systems, household-type video cameras, jukeboxes, and amplifiers for musical instruments and public address systems.

Industry Establishments, Sales & Employment Trends

	Year					Percent Chg. Year-to-Year			
	2014	2015	2016	2017	2018	14-15	15-16	16-17	17-18
Establishments	636	603	578	574	579	-5.2%	-4.3%	-0.7%	1.0%
Sales ($Millions)	2,647	2,512	2,402	2,380	2,392	-5.1%	-4.4%	-0.9%	0.5%
Employment	8,388	7,954	7,615	7,562	7,634	-5.2%	-4.3%	-0.7%	1.0%
Sales ($M)/Estab.	4.16	4.16	4.16	4.15	4.13	0.1%	-0.1%	-0.2%	-0.4%
Sales ($)/Emp.	315,562	315,797	315,396	314,655	313,272	0.1%	-0.1%	-0.2%	-0.4%

3-Year Trend — Estimated Number of Establishments

Year	Employee Size of Establishment									Total
	1-4 Emps.	5-9 Emps.	10-19 Emps.	20-49 Emps.	50-99 Emps.	100-249 Emps.	250-499 Emps.	>500 Emps.	Non-Employer	Employ-ment
2016	218	75	63	41	25	15	4	0	137	578
2017	216	75	62	41	25	14	4	0	136	574
2018	218	76	63	41	25	15	4	0	138	579

3-Year Trend — Estimated Number of Establishments

Year	Employee Size of Establishment									Total
	1-4 Emps.	5-9 Emps.	10-19 Emps.	20-49 Emps.	50-99 Emps.	100-249 Emps.	250-499 Emps.	>500 Emps.	Non-Employer	Employ-ment
2016	98.0	89.1	186.2	321.4	439.6	677.0	570.5	7.8	12.3	2,401.8
2017	97.1	88.2	184.5	318.4	435.5	670.7	565.2	7.8	12.1	2,379.5
2018	97.6	88.7	185.4	320.0	437.7	674.2	568.1	7.8	12.2	2,391.6

3-Year Trend — Estimated Number of Establishments

Year	Employee Size of Establishment									Total
	1-4 Emps.	5-9 Emps.	10-19 Emps.	20-49 Emps.	50-99 Emps.	100-249 Emps.	250-499 Emps.	>500 Emps.	Non-Employer	Employ-ment
2016	545	437	852	1,230	1,510	1,832	1,056	16	137	7,615
2017	541	434	846	1,221	1,499	1,819	1,049	16	136	7,562
2018	546	438	854	1,233	1,514	1,836	1,059	17	138	7,634

AUDIO & VISUAL EQUIPMENT MFG. INDUSTRY
NAICS 33431

SUB-INDUSTRIES — 2017 ESTIMATED INDUSTRY SALES, ESTABLISHMENTS & EMPLOYMENT

Sub-Industries	Cate-gory*	Establish-ments	Sales ($Mill)	Employ-ment
Household audio and video equipment	Major1	153	1,506.6	2,090
Household audio equipment	Minor1	33	66.6	698
Amplifiers: radio, public address, or musical instrument	Minor2	30	59.4	584
Audio electronic systems	Minor2	135	271.3	932
Coin-operated phonographs, juke boxes	Minor2	1	5.0	51
Compact disk players	Minor2	6	2.7	20
FM and AM radio tuners	Minor2	3	0.9	9
Loudspeakers, electrodynamic or magnetic	Minor2	12	27.1	275
Microphones	Minor2	9	23.5	186
Music distribution apparatus	Minor2	19	26.3	123
Phonograph and radio combinations	Minor2	0	0.0	0
Phonographs	Minor2	0	0.1	0
Pillows, stereo	Minor2	1	0.5	4
Public address systems	Minor2	2	5.5	28
Radio receiving sets	Minor2	2	1.4	48
Recording machines, except dictation and telephone ansv	Minor2	4	4.6	29
Sound reproducing equipment	Minor2	12	11.7	64
Speaker monitors	Minor2	5	8.6	39
Speaker systems	Minor2	35	88.5	736
Tape players, household use	Minor2	0	0.2	1
Tape recorders: cassette, cartridge or reel: household use	Minor2	3	2.7	19
Household video equipment	Minor2	8	6.7	493
Television receiving sets	Minor2	6	6.1	629
Video camera-audio recorders, household use	Minor2	10	11.1	48
Video cassette recorders/players and accessories	Minor2	9	8.5	55
Video triggers (remote control TV devices)	Minor2	4	131.8	40
Electronic kits for home assembly: radio, TV, phonograph	Minor2	16	12.3	97
Home entertainment equipment, electronic, nec	Minor2	54	89.8	265
Pickup heads, phonograph	Minor2	0	0.0	0

*Category-Major categories (Major1) are more general descriptions for companies that self-selected to capture the many functions they perform in the industry. Minor categories (Minor1, Minor2) are more specific for companies that have more detailed functions (Minor1 is a larger category than Minor2). Minor categories figures (sales, etc.) can be aggregated to larger minor categories (Minor2 sums to Minor1) and major categories overall figures.

NAICS 33441: Semiconductor and Other Electronic Component Manufacturing This industry comprises establishments primarily engaged in manufacturing semiconductors and other components for electronic applications. Examples of products made by these establishments are capacitors, resistors, microprocessors, bare and loaded printed circuit boards, electron tubes, electronic connectors, and computer modems.

INDUSTRY ESTABLISHMENTS, SALES & EMPLOYMENT TRENDS

	Year					Percent Chg. Year-to-Year			
	2014	2015	2016	2017	2018	14-15	15-16	16-17	17-18
Establishments	5,303	5,178	5,115	5,048	5,064	-2.3%	-1.2%	-1.3%	0.3%
Sales ($Millions)	148,075	151,949	156,844	161,357	167,782	2.6%	3.2%	2.9%	4.0%
Employment	213,818	208,803	206,254	203,546	204,206	-2.3%	-1.2%	-1.3%	0.3%
Sales ($M)/Estab.	27.92	29.34	30.66	31.96	33.13	5.1%	4.5%	4.2%	3.6%
Sales ($)/Emp.	692,528	727,713	760,443	792,729	821,630	5.1%	4.5%	4.2%	3.6%

3-YEAR TREND – ESTIMATED NUMBER OF ESTABLISHMENTS

Year	Employee Size of Establishment									Total
	1-4 Emps.	5-9 Emps.	10-19 Emps.	20-49 Emps.	50-99 Emps.	100-249 Emps.	250-499 Emps.	>500 Emps.	Non-Employer	Employ-ment
2016	960	546	570	794	458	373	127	71	1,215	5,115
2017	947	539	563	783	452	368	126	70	1,199	5,048
2018	950	541	564	786	454	370	126	71	1,203	5,064

3-YEAR TREND – ESTIMATED NUMBER OF ESTABLISHMENTS

Year	Employee Size of Establishment									Total
	1-4 Emps.	5-9 Emps.	10-19 Emps.	20-49 Emps.	50-99 Emps.	100-249 Emps.	250-499 Emps.	>500 Emps.	Non-Employer	Employ-ment
2016	838.5	1,253.7	3,291.9	12,133.7	15,394.1	33,803.3	38,860.6	51,149.8	118.6	156,844.1
2017	860.8	1,287.1	3,379.6	12,457.0	15,804.3	34,704.2	39,896.2	52,845.8	121.8	161,356.9
2018	895.6	1,339.0	3,516.0	12,959.6	16,442.0	36,104.3	41,505.9	54,892.7	126.7	167,781.7

3-YEAR TREND – ESTIMATED NUMBER OF ESTABLISHMENTS

Year	Employee Size of Establishment									Total
	1-4 Emps.	5-9 Emps.	10-19 Emps.	20-49 Emps.	50-99 Emps.	100-249 Emps.	250-499 Emps.	>500 Emps.	Non-Employer	Employ-ment
2016	2,399	3,167	7,753	23,896	27,217	47,074	37,040	56,492	1,215	206,254
2017	2,368	3,125	7,651	23,582	26,859	46,456	36,554	55,750	1,199	203,546
2018	2,376	3,135	7,676	23,659	26,947	46,607	36,673	55,931	1,203	204,206

SEMI-CONDUCTOR & ELECTRONIC COMPONENTS MFG.
NAICS 33441

SUB-INDUSTRIES — 2017 ESTIMATED INDUSTRY SALES, ESTABLISHMENTS & EMPLOYMENT

Sub-Industries	Cate-gory*	Establish-ments	Sales ($Mill)	Employ-ment
Semiconductors and related devices	Major1	1,974	35,993.1	65,079
Semiconductor diodes and rectifiers	Minor1	14	17.9	290
Controlled rectifiers, solid state	Minor2	1	1.7	0
Diodes, solid state (germanium, silicon, etc.)	Minor2	8	9.1	239
Light emitting diodes	Minor2	59	108.9	769
Thrystors	Minor2	1	1.4	17
Zener diodes	Minor2	1	0.3	5
Integrated circuits, semiconductor networks, etc.	Minor1	315	18,281.4	13,372
Computer logic modules	Minor2	59	197.5	488
Hybrid integrated circuits	Minor2	49	120.1	906
Magnetic bubble memory device	Minor2	5	11.7	72
Memories, solid state	Minor2	19	269.3	1,616
Metal oxide silicon (MOS) devices	Minor2	6	0.4	530
Microcircuits, integrated (semiconductor)	Minor2	110	8,118.3	8,978
Microprocessors	Minor2	45	39,334.9	15,661
Monolithic integrated circuits (solid state)	Minor2	6	0.5	4,545
Random access memory (RAM)	Minor2	22	41.8	726
Read-only memory (ROM)	Minor2	10	0.5	7
Semiconductor circuit networks	Minor2	59	473.0	4,085
Thin film circuits	Minor2	12	14.3	339
Wafers (semiconductor devices)	Minor2	42	160.1	3,934
Light sensitive devices	Minor1	247	4,886.8	4,986
Radiation sensors	Minor1	93	43.5	5,775
Misc. semiconductor devices	Minor1	266	2,659.0	7,524
Electronic components, nec	Major1	530	1,912.0	4,733
Electronic circuits	Minor1	864	42,962.7	44,868
Attenuators	Minor2	7	181.0	2,276
Commutators, electronic	Minor2	18	171.7	425
Delay lines	Minor2	5	22.2	75
Impedance conversion units, high frequency	Minor2	2	2.1	6
Microwave components	Minor2	142	4,497.8	7,490
Passive repeaters	Minor2	1	20.7	27
Pulse forming networks	Minor2	3	5.0	9
Misc. electronic components	Minor2	53	836.2	3,692

*Category-Major categories (Major1) are more general descriptions for companies that self-selected to capture the many functions they perform in the industry. Minor categories (Minor1, Minor2) are more specific for companies that have more detailed functions (Minor1 is a larger category than Minor2). Minor categories figures (sales, etc.) can be aggregated to larger minor categories (Minor2 sums to Minor1) and major categories overall figures.

SOFTWARE REPRODUCING INDUSTRY
(NAICS 334611)

NAICS 334611 Software Reproducing This U.S. industry comprises establishments primarily engaged in mass reproducing computer software. These establishments do not generally develop any software, they mass reproduce data and programs on magnetic media, such as diskettes, tapes, or cartridges. Establishments in this industry mass reproduce products, such as CD-ROMs and game cartridges.

INDUSTRY ESTABLISHMENTS, SALES & EMPLOYMENT TRENDS

	Year					Percent Chg. Year-to-Year			
	2014	2015	2016	2017	2018	14-15	15-16	16-17	17-18
Establishments	598	562	532	508	493	-6.1%	-5.3%	-4.5%	-2.9%
Sales ($Millions)	2,023	1,931	1,851	1,783	1,734	-4.6%	-4.1%	-3.7%	-2.8%
Employment	9,546	8,964	8,489	8,108	7,871	-6.1%	-5.3%	-4.5%	-2.9%
Sales ($M)/Estab.	3.38	3.44	3.48	3.51	3.52	1.6%	1.2%	0.9%	0.1%
Sales ($)/Emp.	211,966	215,414	218,036	219,962	220,266	1.6%	1.2%	0.9%	0.1%

3-YEAR TREND — ESTIMATED NUMBER OF ESTABLISHMENTS

Year	Employee Size of Establishment									Total
	1-4 Emps.	5-9 Emps.	10-19 Emps.	20-49 Emps.	50-99 Emps.	100-249 Emps.	250-499 Emps.	>500 Emps.	Non-Employer	Employment
2016	245	50	40	44	12	9	2	4	126	532
2017	234	48	38	42	12	8	2	3	121	508
2018	228	46	37	40	12	8	2	3	117	493

3-YEAR TREND — ESTIMATED NUMBER OF ESTABLISHMENTS

Year	Employee Size of Establishment									Total
	1-4 Emps.	5-9 Emps.	10-19 Emps.	20-49 Emps.	50-99 Emps.	100-249 Emps.	250-499 Emps.	>500 Emps.	Non-Employer	Employment
2016	65.6	35.0	70.7	203.9	128.0	246.5	166.1	923.9	11.2	1,851.0
2017	62.3	33.2	67.1	193.4	121.4	233.8	157.6	904.1	10.6	1,783.4
2018	59.9	31.9	64.5	186.0	116.8	224.9	151.6	887.7	10.2	1,733.6

3-YEAR TREND — ESTIMATED NUMBER OF ESTABLISHMENTS

Year	Employee Size of Establishment									Total
	1-4 Emps.	5-9 Emps.	10-19 Emps.	20-49 Emps.	50-99 Emps.	100-249 Emps.	250-499 Emps.	>500 Emps.	Non-Employer	Employment
2016	614	289	544	1,312	740	1,121	517	3,226	126	8,489
2017	586	276	520	1,253	706	1,071	494	3,081	121	8,108
2018	569	268	505	1,216	686	1,040	480	2,991	117	7,871

SOFTWARE REPRODUCING INDUSTRY (NAICS 334611)

SUB-INDUSTRIES — 2017 ESTIMATED INDUSTRY SALES, ESTABLISHMENTS & EMPLOYMENT

Sub-Industries	Cate-gory*	Establish-ments	Sales ($Mill)	Employ-ment
Computer related services, nec	Major1	111	96.8	720
Computer related maintenance services	Minor1	25	92.6	700
Disk and diskette conversion service	Minor2	1	2.4	13
Disk and diskette recertification service	Minor2	0	0.2	1
Tape recertification service	Minor2	0	0.1	1
Word processing equipment maintenance	Minor2	0	0.1	2
Computer data escrow service	Minor2	1	3.9	19
Computer related consulting services	Minor1	313	1,318.9	5,488
Computer hardware requirements analysis	Minor2	2	7.8	29
Data processing consultant	Minor2	11	44.6	225
Online services technology consultants	Minor2	44	216.0	910

*Category-Major categories (Major1) are more general descriptions for companies that self-selected to capture the many functions they perform in the industry. Minor categories (Minor1, Minor2) are more specific for companies that have more detailed functions (Minor1 is a larger category than Minor2). Minor categories figures (sales, etc.) can be aggregated to larger minor categories (Minor2 sums to Minor1) and major categories overall figures.

MAJOR APPLIANCE MANUFACTURING INDUSTRY
NAICS 33522

NAICS 33522: Appliance Manufacturing Industry. This industry comprises establishments primarily engaged in manufacturing household-type cooking appliances, household-type laundry equipment, household-type refrigerators, upright and chest freezers, and other electrical and nonelectrical major household-type appliances, such as dishwashers, water heaters, and garbage disposal units.

INDUSTRY ESTABLISHMENTS, SALES & EMPLOYMENT TRENDS

	Year					Percent Chg. Year-to-Year			
	2014	2015	2016	2017	2018	14-15	15-16	16-17	17-18
Establishments	215	204	194	185	176	-5.0%	-5.2%	-4.6%	-4.7%
Sales ($Millions)	14,003	13,674	13,327	13,003	12,666	-2.3%	-2.5%	-2.4%	-2.6%
Employment	29,544	28,059	26,610	25,374	24,190	-5.0%	-5.2%	-4.6%	-4.7%
Sales ($M)/Estab.	65.04	66.87	68.72	70.32	71.84	2.8%	2.8%	2.3%	2.2%
Sales ($)/Emp.	473,958	487,322	500,813	512,463	523,580	2.8%	2.8%	2.3%	2.2%

3-YEAR TREND – ESTIMATED NUMBER OF ESTABLISHMENTS

Year	Employee Size of Establishment									Total
	1-4 Emps.	5-9 Emps.	10-19 Emps.	20-49 Emps.	50-99 Emps.	100-249 Emps.	250-499 Emps.	>500 Emps.	Non-Employer	Employ-ment
2016	36	17	12	17	12	14	5	22	61	194
2017	34	16	11	16	11	13	4	21	58	185
2018	33	16	11	16	11	12	4	20	55	176

3-YEAR TREND – ESTIMATED NUMBER OF ESTABLISHMENTS

Year	Employee Size of Establishment									Total
	1-4 Emps.	5-9 Emps.	10-19 Emps.	20-49 Emps.	50-99 Emps.	100-249 Emps.	250-499 Emps.	>500 Emps.	Non-Employer	Employ-ment
2016	17.7	22.1	38.1	147.4	221.7	689.4	774.5	11,410.0	5.9	13,326.8
2017	16.7	20.9	36.0	139.2	209.3	650.9	731.2	11,193.7	5.6	13,003.5
2018	15.8	19.7	33.9	131.1	197.1	613.0	688.7	10,961.1	5.3	12,665.6

3-YEAR TREND – ESTIMATED NUMBER OF ESTABLISHMENTS

Year	Employee Size of Establishment									Total
	1-4 Emps.	5-9 Emps.	10-19 Emps.	20-49 Emps.	50-99 Emps.	100-249 Emps.	250-499 Emps.	>500 Emps.	Non-Employer	Employ-ment
2016	90	99	159	515	696	1,704	1,310	21,977	61	26,610
2017	86	95	152	491	663	1,625	1,249	20,956	58	25,374
2018	82	90	145	468	632	1,549	1,191	19,978	55	24,190

MAJOR APPLIANCE MANUFACTURING INDUSTRY
NAICS 33522

SUB-INDUSTRIES – 2017 ESTIMATED INDUSTRY
SALES, ESTABLISHMENTS & EMPLOYMENT

Sub-Industries	Cate-gory*	Establish-ments	Sales ($Mill)	Employ-ment
Household cooking equipment	Major1	38	139.3	9,597
Indoor cooking equipment	Minor1	2	1.1	2,182
Convection ovens, including portable: household	Minor2	3	12.3	426
Electric ranges, domestic	Minor2	1	8,333.4	67
Gas ranges, domestic	Minor2	4	0.3	1,705
Microwave ovens, including portable: household	Minor2	3	2.9	21
Stoves, disk	Minor2	3	16.4	18
Barbecues, grills, and braziers (outdoor cooking)	Minor2	68	163.3	2,900
Household refrigerators and freezers	Major1	32	1,311.2	1,481
Freezers, home and farm	Minor2	11	1,507.3	196
Ice boxes, household: metal or wood	Minor2	1	17.4	9
Refrigerator cabinets, household: metal and wood	Minor2	4	187.3	250
Refrigerators, mechanical and absorption: household	Minor2	14	1,311.2	6,522

*Category-Major categories (Major1) are more general descriptions for companies that self-selected to capture the many functions they perform in the industry. Minor categories (Minor1, Minor2) are more specific for companies that have more detailed functions (Minor1 is a larger category than Minor2). Minor categories figures (sales, etc.) can be aggregated to larger minor categories (Minor2 sums to Minor1) and major categories overall figures.

AUTOMOBILE & MOTOR VEHICLE MFG. INDUSTRY
NAICS 33611

NAICS 33611: Automobile & Light Motor Vehicle Manufacturing .
This industry comprises establishments primarily engaged in (1)
manufacturing complete automobile and light duty motor vehicles (i.e.,
body and chassis or unibody) or (2) manufacturing chassis only.

INDUSTRY ESTABLISHMENTS, SALES & EMPLOYMENT TRENDS

	Year					Percent Chg. Year-to-Year			
	2014	2015	2016	2017	2018	14-15	15-16	16-17	17-18
Establishments	309	307	302	297	292	-0.7%	-1.4%	-1.8%	-1.8%
Sales ($Millions)	195,693	197,097	197,981	198,593	198,812	0.7%	0.4%	0.3%	0.1%
Employment	58,497	58,065	57,265	56,255	55,240	-0.7%	-1.4%	-1.8%	-1.8%
Sales ($M)/Estab.	633.60	642.89	654.80	668.62	681.65	1.5%	1.9%	2.1%	1.9%
Sales ($)/Emp.	3,345,364	3,394,396	3,457,276	3,530,249	3,599,038	1.5%	1.9%	2.1%	1.9%

3-YEAR TREND – ESTIMATED NUMBER OF ESTABLISHMENTS

Year	Employee Size of Establishment									Total
	1-4 Emps.	5-9 Emps.	10-19 Emps.	20-49 Emps.	50-99 Emps.	100-249 Emps.	250-499 Emps.	>500 Emps.	Non-Employer	Employ-ment
2016	93	33	32	25	12	10	0	46	51	302
2017	91	33	32	25	12	10	0	45	50	297
2018	90	32	31	25	11	9	0	44	49	292

3-YEAR TREND – ESTIMATED NUMBER OF ESTABLISHMENTS

Year	Employee Size of Establishment									Total
	1-4 Emps.	5-9 Emps.	10-19 Emps.	20-49 Emps.	50-99 Emps.	100-249 Emps.	250-499 Emps.	>500 Emps.	Non-Employer	Employ-ment
2016	339.4	319.3	779.3	1,625.3	1,648.9	3,703.5	12.5	189,547.6	4.9	197,980.7
2017	335.1	315.2	769.3	1,604.4	1,627.7	3,655.8	12.3	190,268.7	4.8	198,593.4
2018	330.0	310.4	757.6	1,580.0	1,603.0	3,600.2	12.1	190,613.9	4.8	198,812.0

3-YEAR TREND – ESTIMATED NUMBER OF ESTABLISHMENTS

Year	Employee Size of Establishment									Total
	1-4 Emps.	5-9 Emps.	10-19 Emps.	20-49 Emps.	50-99 Emps.	100-249 Emps.	250-499 Emps.	>500 Emps.	Non-Employer	Employ-ment
2016	232	193	439	766	698	1,234	3	53,648	51	57,265
2017	228	190	432	753	685	1,213	3	52,702	50	56,255
2018	224	186	424	739	673	1,191	3	51,751	49	55,240

SUB-INDUSTRIES – 2017 ESTIMATED INDUSTRY SALES, ESTABLISHMENTS & EMPLOYMENT

Sub-Industries	Category*	Establish-ments	Sales ($Mill)	Employ-ment
Motor vehicles and car bodies	Major1	113	104,717.3	27,392
Automobile assembly, including specialty automobiles	Minor1	105	92,044.8	24,926
Ambulances (motor vehicles), assembly of	Minor2	7	306.8	615
Automobile bodies, passenger car, not including engine, e	Minor2	32	118.3	938
Cars, armored, assembly of	Minor2	9	138.9	341
Cars, electric, assembly of	Minor2	7	15.3	82
Chassis, motor vehicle	Minor2	21	1,244.5	1,643
Hearses (motor vehicles), assembly of	Minor2	1	6.2	149
Patrol wagons (motor vehicles), assembly of	Minor2	1	0.6	163
Station wagons (motor vehicles), assembly of	Minor2	0	0.1	0
Taxicabs, assembly of	Minor2	1	0.7	6

*Category-Major categories (Major1) are more general descriptions for companies that self-selected to capture the many functions they perform in the industry. Minor categories (Minor1, Minor2) are more specific for companies that have more detailed functions (Minor1 is a larger category than Minor2). Minor categories figures (sales, etc.) can be aggregated to larger minor categories (Minor2 sums to Minor1) and major categories overall figures.

HEAVY DUTY TRUCK MANUFACTURING INDUSTRY
NAICS 33612

NAICS 33612: Heavy Duty Truck Manufacturing Industry
This industry comprises establishments primarily engaged in (1) manufacturing heavy duty truck chassis and assembling complete heavy duty trucks, buses, heavy duty motor homes, and other special purpose heavy duty motor vehicles for highway use or (2) manufacturing heavy duty truck chassis only.

INDUSTRY ESTABLISHMENTS, SALES & EMPLOYMENT TRENDS

	Year					Percent Chg. Year-to-Year			
	2014	2015	2016	2017	2018	14-15	15-16	16-17	17-18
Establishments	95	96	95	92	90	1.3%	-1.3%	-2.8%	-2.8%
Sales ($Millions)	18,810	19,084	19,133	19,055	18,941	1.5%	0.3%	-0.4%	-0.6%
Employment	19,535	19,781	19,525	18,984	18,450	1.3%	-1.3%	-2.8%	-2.8%
Sales ($M)/Estab.	198.12	198.50	201.63	206.53	211.23	0.2%	1.6%	2.4%	2.3%
Sales ($)/Emp.	962,900	964,753	979,934	1,003,770	1,026,597	0.2%	1.6%	2.4%	2.3%

3-YEAR TREND — ESTIMATED NUMBER OF ESTABLISHMENTS

Year	Employee Size of Establishment									Total
	1-4 Emps.	5-9 Emps.	10-19 Emps.	20-49 Emps.	50-99 Emps.	100-249 Emps.	250-499 Emps.	>500 Emps.	Non-Employer	Employ-ment
2016	12	7	11	13	4	11	5	16	16	95
2017	12	7	11	13	4	11	5	16	15	92
2018	11	7	10	12	4	10	5	15	15	90

3-YEAR TREND — ESTIMATED NUMBER OF ESTABLISHMENTS

Year	Employee Size of Establishment									Total
	1-4 Emps.	5-9 Emps.	10-19 Emps.	20-49 Emps.	50-99 Emps.	100-249 Emps.	250-499 Emps.	>500 Emps.	Non-Employer	Employ-ment
2016	12.2	18.7	73.9	231.3	156.4	1,159.4	1,776.2	15,703.7	1.5	19,133.5
2017	11.9	18.3	72.4	226.3	153.1	1,134.7	1,738.4	15,698.8	1.5	19,055.4
2018	11.7	17.9	70.6	221.0	149.5	1,107.8	1,697.2	15,663.6	1.5	18,940.8

3-YEAR TREND — ESTIMATED NUMBER OF ESTABLISHMENTS

Year	Employee Size of Establishment									Total
	1-4 Emps.	5-9 Emps.	10-19 Emps.	20-49 Emps.	50-99 Emps.	100-249 Emps.	250-499 Emps.	>500 Emps.	Non-Employer	Employ-ment
2016	30	41	150	391	237	1,386	1,454	15,820	16	19,525
2017	29	39	145	380	231	1,348	1,413	15,382	15	18,984
2018	28	38	141	370	224	1,310	1,374	14,949	15	18,450

SUB-INDUSTRIES – 2017 ESTIMATED INDUSTRY SALES, ESTABLISHMENTS & EMPLOYMENT

Sub-Industries	Category*	Establish-ments	Sales ($Mill)	Employ-ment
Truck and tractor truck assembly	Minor1	12	13,675.8	4,886
Motor trucks, except off-highway, assembly of	Minor2	1	0.4	2,908
Truck tractors for highway use, assembly of	Minor2	3	1.0	2,495
Trucks, pickup, assembly of	Minor2	5	4.3	1,274
Military motor vehicle assembly	Minor1	5	495.6	2,117
Amphibian motor vehicles, assembly of	Minor2	0	0.1	3
Personnel carriers (motor vehicles), assembly of	Minor2	3	5.8	48
Reconnaissance cars, assembly of	Minor2	1	2.0	16
Scout cars (motor vehicles), assembly of	Minor2	1	0.4	25
Universal carriers, military, assembly of	Minor2	0	0.3	3
Bus and other large specialty vehicle assembly	Minor1	5	24.8	445
Brooms, powered (motor vehicles), assembly of	Minor2	0	0.1	2
Buses, all types, assembly of	Minor2	8	46.1	795
Fire department vehicles (motor vehicles), assembly of	Minor2	20	4,710.2	2,525
Mobile lounges (motor vehicle), assembly of	Minor2	1	0.7	7
Motor buses, except trackless trollies, assembly of	Minor2	1	11.7	214
Motor homes, self contained, assembly of	Minor2	2	7.3	288
Road oilers (motor vehicles), assembly of	Minor2	1	1.1	13
Snow plows (motor vehicles), assembly of	Minor2	6	21.7	218
Street sprinklers and sweepers (motor vehicles), assembly	Minor2	2	12.4	468
Wreckers (tow truck), assembly of	Minor2	14	33.5	232

*Category-Major categories (Major1) are more general descriptions for companies that self-selected to capture the many functions they perform in the industry. Minor categories (Minor1, Minor2) are more specific for companies that have more detailed functions (Minor1 is a larger category than Minor2). Minor categories figures (sales, etc.) can be aggregated to larger minor categories (Minor2 sums to Minor1) and major categories overall figures.

AUTOMOBILE GAS ENGINE & ENGINE PARTS MFG. NAICS 33631

NAICS 33631: Motor Vehicle Gas Engine & Engine Parts Manufacturing Industry. This industry comprises establishments primarily engaged in manufacturing and/or rebuilding motor vehicle gasoline engines, and engine parts, whether or not for vehicular use.

INDUSTRY ESTABLISHMENTS, SALES & EMPLOYMENT TRENDS

	Year					Percent Chg. Year-to-Year			
	2014	2015	2016	2017	2018	14-15	15-16	16-17	17-18
Establishments	1,031	1,007	957	932	907	-2.3%	-5.0%	-2.6%	-2.7%
Sales ($Millions)	23,017	21,908	20,334	19,214	18,088	-4.8%	-7.2%	-5.5%	-5.9%
Employment	46,285	45,201	42,943	41,820	40,710	-2.3%	-5.0%	-2.6%	-2.7%
Sales ($M)/Estab.	22.32	21.76	21.25	20.62	19.94	-2.5%	-2.3%	-3.0%	-3.3%
Sales ($)/Emp.	497,287	484,684	473,510	459,454	444,304	-2.5%	-2.3%	-3.0%	-3.3%

3-YEAR TREND – ESTIMATED NUMBER OF ESTABLISHMENTS

Year	Employee Size of Establishment									Total
	1-4 Emps.	5-9 Emps.	10-19 Emps.	20-49 Emps.	50-99 Emps.	100-249 Emps.	250-499 Emps.	>500 Emps.	Non-Employer	Employ-ment
2016	366	138	78	71	36	49	30	29	161	957
2017	356	135	76	69	35	48	29	28	156	932
2018	347	131	74	67	34	47	28	27	152	907

3-YEAR TREND – ESTIMATED NUMBER OF ESTABLISHMENTS

Year	Employee Size of Establishment									Total
	1-4 Emps.	5-9 Emps.	10-19 Emps.	20-49 Emps.	50-99 Emps.	100-249 Emps.	250-499 Emps.	>500 Emps.	Non-Employer	Employ-ment
2016	178.4	177.4	251.5	602.2	679.3	2,488.0	5,063.1	10,879.9	14.3	20,334.1
2017	167.7	166.7	236.4	566.1	638.5	2,338.8	4,759.4	10,327.5	13.5	19,214.5
2018	157.1	156.1	221.3	530.0	597.8	2,189.7	4,456.0	9,767.1	12.6	18,087.7

3-YEAR TREND – ESTIMATED NUMBER OF ESTABLISHMENTS

Year	Employee Size of Establishment									Total
	1-4 Emps.	5-9 Emps.	10-19 Emps.	20-49 Emps.	50-99 Emps.	100-249 Emps.	250-499 Emps.	>500 Emps.	Non-Employer	Employ-ment
2016	914	802	1,060	2,122	2,149	6,201	8,637	20,898	161	42,943
2017	890	781	1,032	2,067	2,093	6,039	8,411	20,351	156	41,820
2018	866	760	1,005	2,012	2,038	5,878	8,188	19,811	152	40,710

Automobile Gas Engine & Engine Parts Mfg. NAICS 33631

Sub-Industries — 2017 Estimated Industry Sales, Establishments & Employment

Sub-Industries	Category*	Establish-ments	Sales ($Mill)	Employ-ment
Motor vehicle parts and accessories	Major1	601	16,494.2	32,630
Motor vehicle engines and parts	Minor1	76	1,266.6	2,381
Acceleration equipment, motor vehicle	Minor2	5	3.3	121
Camshafts, motor vehicle	Minor2	6	10.5	237
Choker rods, motor vehicle	Minor2	0	0.0	0
Cleaners, air, motor vehicle	Minor2	6	1.1	147
Connecting rods, motor vehicle engine	Minor2	3	2.8	176
Crankshaft assemblies, motor vehicle	Minor2	3	17.6	91
Cylinder heads, motor vehicle	Minor2	15	18.6	188
Differentials and parts, motor vehicle	Minor2	3	5.9	44
Exhaust systems and parts, motor vehicle	Minor2	35	101.3	1,400
Filters: oil, fuel, and air, motor vehicle	Minor2	21	608.2	915
Fuel pipes, motor vehicle	Minor2	0	0.0	0
Fuel pumps, motor vehicle	Minor2	5	58.2	257
Fuel systems and parts, motor vehicle	Minor2	22	330.5	618
Gas tanks, motor vehicle	Minor2	4	0.8	73
Governors, motor vehicle	Minor2	1	0.6	5
Lubrication systems and parts, motor vehicle	Minor2	4	2.1	239
Manifolds, motor vehicle	Minor2	4	6.6	195
Mufflers (exhaust), motor vehicle	Minor2	18	25.5	628
Oil pump, motor vehicle	Minor2	3	0.5	13
Oil strainers, motor vehicle	Minor2	1	0.2	3
Propane conversion equipment, motor vehicle	Minor2	39	5.0	74
Radiators and radiator shells and cores, motor vehicle	Minor2	23	145.3	757
Rebuilding engines and transmissions, factory basis	Minor2	25	103.6	485
Tie rods, motor vehicle	Minor2	1	0.1	65
Water pump, motor vehicle	Minor2	6	5.4	78

*Category-Major categories (Major1) are more general descriptions for companies that self-selected to capture the many functions they perform in the industry. Minor categories (Minor1, Minor2) are more specific for companies that have more detailed functions (Minor1 is a larger category than Minor2). Minor categories figures (sales, etc.) can be aggregated to larger minor categories (Minor2 sums to Minor1) and major categories overall figures.

AIRCRAFT MANUFACTURING INDUSTRY
(NAICS 336411)

NAICS 336411: Aircraft Manufacturing . This U.S. industry comprises establishments primarily engaged in one or more of the following: (1) manufacturing or assembling complete aircraft; (2) developing and making aircraft prototypes; (3) aircraft conversion (i.e., major modifications to systems); and (4) complete aircraft overhaul and rebuilding (i.e., periodic restoration of aircraft to original design specifications).

INDUSTRY ESTABLISHMENTS, SALES & EMPLOYMENT TRENDS

	Year					Percent Chg. Year-to-Year			
	2014	2015	2016	2017	2018	14-15	15-16	16-17	17-18
Establishments	377	384	389	398	407	1.8%	1.2%	2.4%	2.3%
Sales ($Millions)	102,369	106,497	110,245	114,416	118,418	4.0%	3.5%	3.8%	3.5%
Employment	51,187	52,086	52,700	53,953	55,188	1.8%	1.2%	2.4%	2.3%
Sales ($M)/Estab.	271.28	277.35	283.76	287.66	291.05	2.2%	2.3%	1.4%	1.2%
Sales ($)/Emp.	1,999,909	2,044,653	2,091,930	2,120,670	2,145,700	2.2%	2.3%	1.4%	1.2%

3-YEAR TREND — ESTIMATED NUMBER OF ESTABLISHMENTS

Year	Employee Size of Establishment									Total
	1-4 Emps.	5-9 Emps.	10-19 Emps.	20-49 Emps.	50-99 Emps.	100-249 Emps.	250-499 Emps.	>500 Emps.	Non-Employer	Employ-ment
2016	98	42	35	48	19	25	18	39	65	389
2017	100	43	36	50	19	25	18	40	67	398
2018	102	44	37	51	19	26	18	41	68	407

3-YEAR TREND — ESTIMATED NUMBER OF ESTABLISHMENTS

Year	Employee Size of Establishment									Total
	1-4 Emps.	5-9 Emps.	10-19 Emps.	20-49 Emps.	50-99 Emps.	100-249 Emps.	250-499 Emps.	>500 Emps.	Non-Employer	Employ-ment
2016	218.9	248.3	517.8	1,894.6	1,595.0	5,731.9	13,684.3	86,348.0	6.6	110,245.4
2017	230.6	261.6	545.5	1,995.8	1,680.2	6,038.0	14,415.2	89,242.2	7.0	114,416.1
2018	242.1	274.6	572.6	2,095.3	1,763.9	6,338.9	15,133.4	91,989.8	7.3	118,417.9

3-YEAR TREND — ESTIMATED NUMBER OF ESTABLISHMENTS

Year	Employee Size of Establishment									Total
	1-4 Emps.	5-9 Emps.	10-19 Emps.	20-49 Emps.	50-99 Emps.	100-249 Emps.	250-499 Emps.	>500 Emps.	Non-Employer	Employ-ment
2016	245	245	476	1,457	1,101	3,116	5,092	40,905	65	52,700
2017	250	251	487	1,491	1,127	3,190	5,213	41,877	67	53,953
2018	256	256	499	1,525	1,153	3,263	5,332	42,836	68	55,188

AIRCRAFT MANUFACTURING INDUSTRY (NAICS 336411)

SUB-INDUSTRIES — 2017 ESTIMATED INDUSTRY SALES, ESTABLISHMENTS & EMPLOYMENT

Sub-Industries	Cate-gory*	Establish-ments	Sales ($Mill)	Employ-ment
Aircraft	Major1	303	50,399.0	34,577
Motorized aircraft	Minor1	4	5.6	124
Airplanes, fixed or rotary wing	Minor2	34	63,832.8	12,380
Helicopters	Minor2	34	141.0	6,665
Nonmotorized and lighter-than-air aircraft	Minor1	1	0.6	5
Airships	Minor2	4	17.9	74
Balloons, hot air (aircraft)	Minor2	8	6.8	38
Blimps	Minor2	2	6.1	48
Dirigibles	Minor2	1	0.3	2
Gliders (aircraft)	Minor2	2	1.0	7
Hang gliders	Minor2	6	4.7	29
Autogiros	Minor2	1	0.3	4

*Category-Major categories (Major1) are more general descriptions for companies that self-selected to capture the many functions they perform in the industry. Minor categories (Minor1, Minor2) are more specific for companies that have more detailed functions (Minor1 is a larger category than Minor2). Minor categories figures (sales, etc.) can be aggregated to larger minor categories (Minor2 sums to Minor1) and major categories overall figures.

KITCHEN CABINET & COUNTERTOP MFG. INDUSTRY
NAICS 33711

NAICS 33711: Kitchen Cabinet & Countertop Mfg Industry. This industry comprises establishments primarily engaged in manufacturing wood or plastics laminated on wood kitchen cabinets, bathroom vanities, and countertops (except freestanding). The cabinets and counters may be made on a stock or custom basis.

INDUSTRY ESTABLISHMENTS, SALES & EMPLOYMENT TRENDS

	Year					Percent Chg. Year-to-Year			
	2014	2015	2016	2017	2018	14-15	15-16	16-17	17-18
Establishments	9,088	8,618	8,210	7,853	7,551	-5.2%	-4.7%	-4.3%	-3.8%
Sales ($Millions)	12,554	12,691	12,820	12,952	13,097	1.1%	1.0%	1.0%	1.1%
Employment	83,694	79,360	75,604	72,318	69,538	-5.2%	-4.7%	-4.3%	-3.8%
Sales ($M)/Estab.	1.38	1.47	1.56	1.65	1.73	6.6%	6.0%	5.6%	5.2%
Sales ($)/Emp.	149,997	159,913	169,565	179,099	188,339	6.6%	6.0%	5.6%	5.2%

3-YEAR TREND — ESTIMATED NUMBER OF ESTABLISHMENTS

Year	Employee Size of Establishment									Total
	1-4 Emps.	5-9 Emps.	10-19 Emps.	20-49 Emps.	50-99 Emps.	100-249 Emps.	250-499 Emps.	>500 Emps.	Non-Employer	Employ-ment
2016	3,351	1,203	706	421	102	67	34	16	2,308	8,210
2017	3,206	1,151	676	403	98	64	33	16	2,208	7,853
2018	3,083	1,107	650	387	94	61	32	15	2,123	7,551

3-YEAR TREND — ESTIMATED NUMBER OF ESTABLISHMENTS

Year	Employee Size of Establishment									Total
	1-4 Emps.	5-9 Emps.	10-19 Emps.	20-49 Emps.	50-99 Emps.	100-249 Emps.	250-499 Emps.	>500 Emps.	Non-Employer	Employ-ment
2016	790.7	746.1	1,101.5	1,737.5	926.1	1,634.6	2,829.2	2,854.3	199.7	12,819.7
2017	796.5	751.6	1,109.7	1,750.3	933.0	1,646.7	2,850.1	2,913.0	201.2	12,952.1
2018	803.3	758.0	1,119.1	1,765.1	940.9	1,660.6	2,874.2	2,972.6	202.9	13,096.7

3-YEAR TREND — ESTIMATED NUMBER OF ESTABLISHMENTS

Year	Employee Size of Establishment									Total
	1-4 Emps.	5-9 Emps.	10-19 Emps.	20-49 Emps.	50-99 Emps.	100-249 Emps.	250-499 Emps.	>500 Emps.	Non-Employer	Employ-ment
2016	8,378	6,979	9,607	12,671	6,063	8,429	9,986	11,182	2,308	75,604
2017	8,014	6,676	9,190	12,120	5,800	8,063	9,552	10,696	2,208	72,318
2018	7,706	6,419	8,836	11,654	5,577	7,753	9,185	10,284	2,123	69,538

KITCHEN CABINET & COUNTERTOP MFG. INDUSTRY
NAICS 33711

SUB-INDUSTRIES — 2017 ESTIMATED INDUSTRY SALES, ESTABLISHMENTS & EMPLOYMENT

Sub-Industries	Cate-gory*	Establish-ments	Sales ($Mill)	Employ-ment
Wood kitchen cabinets	Major1	6,508	8,874.5	51,605
Vanities, bathroom: wood	Minor2	54	134.1	779
Counter and sink tops	Minor1	614	1,673.8	10,262
Counters or counter display cases, wood	Minor2	336	1,117.5	5,298
Drainboards, plastic laminated	Minor2	18	204.1	118
Sink tops, plastic laminated	Minor2	314	909.5	4,146
Table or counter tops, plastic laminated	Minor2	10	38.6	110

*Category-Major categories (Major1) are more general descriptions for companies that self-selected to capture the many functions they perform in the industry. Minor categories (Minor1, Minor2) are more specific for companies that have more detailed functions (Minor1 is a larger category than Minor2). Minor categories figures (sales, etc.) can be aggregated to larger minor categories (Minor2 sums to Minor1) and major categories overall figures.

HOUSEHOLD & INSTITUTIONAL FURNITURE MFG. NAICS 33712

NAICS 33712: Household and Institutional Furniture Manufacturing
This industry comprises establishments primarily engaged in manufacturing household-type and public building furniture (i.e., library, school, theater, and church furniture). The furniture may be made on a stock or custom basis and may be assembled or unassembled (i.e., knockdown).

INDUSTRY ESTABLISHMENTS, SALES & EMPLOYMENT TRENDS

	Year					Percent Chg. Year-to-Year			
	2014	2015	2016	2017	2018	14-15	15-16	16-17	17-18
Establishments	6,377	5,971	5,607	5,355	5,140	-6.4%	-6.1%	-4.5%	-4.0%
Sales ($Millions)	20,788	19,998	19,251	18,779	18,364	-3.8%	-3.7%	-2.5%	-2.2%
Employment	112,392	105,245	98,823	94,374	90,598	-6.4%	-6.1%	-4.5%	-4.0%
Sales ($M)/Estab.	3.26	3.35	3.43	3.51	3.57	2.7%	2.5%	2.1%	1.9%
Sales ($)/Emp.	184,960	190,015	194,800	198,982	202,702	2.7%	2.5%	2.1%	1.9%

3-YEAR TREND — ESTIMATED NUMBER OF ESTABLISHMENTS

Year	Employee Size of Establishment									Total
	1-4 Emps.	5-9 Emps.	10-19 Emps.	20-49 Emps.	50-99 Emps.	100-249 Emps.	250-499 Emps.	>500 Emps.	Non-Employer	Employ-ment
2016	1,971	737	517	391	183	157	39	35	1,577	5,607
2017	1,883	704	494	374	175	150	37	34	1,506	5,355
2018	1,807	675	474	359	168	144	35	32	1,445	5,140

3-YEAR TREND — ESTIMATED NUMBER OF ESTABLISHMENTS

Year	Employee Size of Establishment									Total
	1-4 Emps.	5-9 Emps.	10-19 Emps.	20-49 Emps.	50-99 Emps.	100-249 Emps.	250-499 Emps.	>500 Emps.	Non-Employer	Employ-ment
2016	467.6	459.4	810.6	1,623.8	1,668.4	3,869.7	3,206.0	7,020.1	125.2	19,250.7
2017	452.5	444.5	784.4	1,571.2	1,614.4	3,744.4	3,102.2	6,943.9	121.2	18,778.7
2018	439.2	431.5	761.4	1,525.2	1,567.1	3,634.8	3,011.4	6,876.2	117.6	18,364.3

3-YEAR TREND — ESTIMATED NUMBER OF ESTABLISHMENTS

Year	Employee Size of Establishment									Total
	1-4 Emps.	5-9 Emps.	10-19 Emps.	20-49 Emps.	50-99 Emps.	100-249 Emps.	250-499 Emps.	>500 Emps.	Non-Employer	Employ-ment
2016	4,928	4,274	7,031	11,777	10,864	19,847	11,254	27,271	1,577	98,823
2017	4,706	4,081	6,715	11,247	10,374	18,953	10,748	26,044	1,506	94,374
2018	4,518	3,918	6,446	10,797	9,959	18,195	10,318	25,001	1,445	90,598

HOUSEHOLD & INSTITUTIONAL FURNITURE MFG. NAICS 33712

SUB-INDUSTRIES — 2017 ESTIMATED INDUSTRY SALES, ESTABLISHMENTS & EMPLOYMENT

Sub-Industries	Cate-gory*	Establish-ments	Sales ($Mill)	Employ-ment
Wood household furniture	Major1	1,065	4,022.9	18,167
Wood bedroom furniture	Minor1	35	1,411.7	2,416
Bed frames, except water bed frames: wood	Minor2	21	126.5	1,131
Chiffoniers and chifforobes	Minor2	0	0.1	1
Commodes	Minor2	1	3.9	24
Dressers, household: wood	Minor2	3	1.8	97
Dressing tables: wood	Minor2	0	0.1	1
Headboards: wood	Minor2	3	20.6	92
Vanity dressers: wood	Minor2	1	0.4	7
Wardrobes, household: wood	Minor2	1	1.0	10
Waterbed frames: wood	Minor2	3	14.0	77
Kitchen and dining room furniture	Minor1	35	57.3	434
Buffets (furniture)	Minor2	1	1.1	5
Chairs, household, except upholstered: wood	Minor2	31	42.8	400
Chairs, Bentwood	Minor2	3	2.2	18
China closets	Minor2	8	7.1	58
Dining room furniture: wood	Minor2	12	55.3	1,013
Silverware chests: wood	Minor2	1	0.1	15
Stools, household: wood	Minor2	3	3.9	28
Tables, household: wood	Minor2	30	80.3	755
Children's wood furniture	Minor1	45	75.2	604
Wood game room furniture	Minor1	8	8.4	61
Wood desks, bookcases, and magazine racks	Minor1	18	37.6	213
Wood stands and chests, except bedside stands	Minor1	71	62.3	990
Wood lawn and garden furniture	Minor1	79	79.5	640
Misc. wood household furniture	Minor2	64	79.8	789
Upholstered household furniture	Major1	1,542	6,195.7	28,048
Public building and related furniture	Major1	728	191.8	10,231
Furniture and fixtures, nec	Major1	1,542	6,195.7	28,048

*Category-Major categories (Major1) are more general descriptions for companies that self-selected to capture the many functions they perform in the industry. Minor categories (Minor1, Minor2) are more specific for companies that have more detailed functions (Minor1 is a larger category than Minor2). Minor categories figures (sales, etc.) can be aggregated to larger minor categories (Minor2 sums to Minor1) and major categories overall figures.

OFFICE FURNITURE MANUFACTURING INDUSTRY
NAICS 33721

NAICS 33721: Office Furniture Manufacturing Industry. This industry comprises establishments primarily engaged in manufacturing office furniture and/or office and store fixtures. The furniture may be made on a stock or custom basis and may be assembled or unassembled (i.e., knockdown).

INDUSTRY ESTABLISHMENTS, SALES & EMPLOYMENT TRENDS

	Year					Percent Chg. Year-to-Year			
	2014	2015	2016	2017	2018	14-15	15-16	16-17	17-18
Establishments	5,048	4,997	4,988	4,935	4,909	-1.0%	-0.2%	-1.0%	-0.5%
Sales ($Millions)	21,578	22,050	22,648	23,033	23,482	2.2%	2.7%	1.7%	1.9%
Employment	97,214	96,218	96,046	95,038	94,534	-1.0%	-0.2%	-1.0%	-0.5%
Sales ($M)/Estab.	4.27	4.41	4.54	4.67	4.78	3.2%	2.9%	2.8%	2.5%
Sales ($)/Emp.	221,963	229,165	235,802	242,358	248,394	3.2%	2.9%	2.8%	2.5%

3-YEAR TREND – ESTIMATED NUMBER OF ESTABLISHMENTS

Year	Employee Size of Establishment									Total
	1-4 Emps.	5-9 Emps.	10-19 Emps.	20-49 Emps.	50-99 Emps.	100-249 Emps.	250-499 Emps.	>500 Emps.	Non-Employer	Employ-ment
2016	1,100	683	653	656	276	170	32	17	1,402	4,988
2017	1,088	676	646	649	273	168	31	17	1,388	4,935
2018	1,082	672	643	646	271	167	31	17	1,380	4,909

3-YEAR TREND – ESTIMATED NUMBER OF ESTABLISHMENTS

Year	Employee Size of Establishment									Total
	1-4 Emps.	5-9 Emps.	10-19 Emps.	20-49 Emps.	50-99 Emps.	100-249 Emps.	250-499 Emps.	>500 Emps.	Non-Employer	Employ-ment
2016	350.2	571.4	1,374.6	3,654.9	3,375.8	5,609.1	3,517.2	4,080.0	114.7	22,647.9
2017	355.9	580.7	1,397.0	3,714.5	3,430.9	5,700.6	3,574.6	4,162.5	116.5	23,033.4
2018	362.7	591.8	1,423.7	3,785.5	3,496.4	5,809.5	3,642.9	4,250.3	118.8	23,481.7

3-YEAR TREND – ESTIMATED NUMBER OF ESTABLISHMENTS

Year	Employee Size of Establishment									Total
	1-4 Emps.	5-9 Emps.	10-19 Emps.	20-49 Emps.	50-99 Emps.	100-249 Emps.	250-499 Emps.	>500 Emps.	Non-Employer	Employ-ment
2016	2,749	3,960	8,882	19,746	16,373	21,429	9,197	12,308	1,402	96,046
2017	2,720	3,918	8,788	19,539	16,202	21,204	9,100	12,179	1,388	95,038
2018	2,706	3,897	8,742	19,435	16,116	21,091	9,052	12,115	1,380	94,534

SUB-INDUSTRIES – 2017 ESTIMATED INDUSTRY SALES, ESTABLISHMENTS & EMPLOYMENT

Sub-Industries	Cate-gory*	Establish-ments	Sales ($Mill)	Employ-ment
Wood office furniture	Major1	543	2,766.2	13,788
Wood office chairs, benches and stools	Minor1	17	17.0	380
Benches, office: wood	Minor2	8	14.7	27
Chairs, office: padded, upholstered, or plain: wood	Minor2	32	165.4	1,250
Stools, office: wood	Minor2	2	6.2	38
Wood office filing cabinets and bookcases	Minor1	34	73.6	464
Bookcases, office: wood	Minor2	7	15.4	22
Cabinets, office: wood	Minor2	295	363.1	2,259
Filing cabinets (boxes), office: wood	Minor2	9	20.4	101
Wood office desks and tables	Minor1	11	38.4	263
Desks, office: wood	Minor2	21	56.1	384
Tables, office: wood	Minor2	17	92.0	99
Panel systems and partitions (free-standing), office: wood	Minor2	16	1,003.5	212
Office furniture, except wood	Major1	2,558	14,035.0	54,094
Office chairs, benches, and stools, except wood	Minor1	118	74.7	1,097
Benches, office: except wood	Minor2	31	13.9	110
Chairs, office: padded or plain: except wood	Minor2	205	493.7	7,205
Stools, office: except wood	Minor2	6	2.9	36
Office bookcases, wallcases and partitions, except wood	Minor1	31	7.3	62
Panel systems and partitions, office: except wood	Minor2	161	117.4	3,847
Wallcases, office: except wood	Minor2	19	1.5	15
Office cabinets and filing drawers, except wood	Minor1	155	129.3	1,192
Cabinets, office: except wood	Minor2	379	205.1	3,574
File drawer frames: except wood	Minor2	6	0.6	6
Filing boxes, cabinets, and cases: except wood	Minor2	106	21.2	2,079
Office desks and tables, except wood	Minor1	149	3,298.6	2,432

*Category-Major categories (Major1) are more general descriptions for companies that self-selected to capture the many functions they perform in the industry. Minor categories (Minor1, Minor2) are more specific for companies that have more detailed functions (Minor1 is a larger category than Minor2). Minor categories figures (sales, etc.) can be aggregated to larger minor categories (Minor2 sums to Minor1) and major categories overall figures.

MEDICAL EQUIPMENT & SUPPLIES MFG. INDUSTRY
NAICS 33911

NAICS 33911: Medical Equipment and Supplies Manufacturing This industry comprises establishments primarily engaged in manufacturing medical equipment and supplies. Examples of products made by these establishments are laboratory apparatus and furniture, surgical and medical instruments, surgical appliances and supplies, dental equipment and supplies, orthodontic goods, dentures, and orthodontic appliances.

INDUSTRY ESTABLISHMENTS, SALES & EMPLOYMENT TRENDS

	Year					Percent Chg. Year-to-Year			
	2014	2015	2016	2017	2018	14-15	15-16	16-17	17-18
Establishments	13,132	13,055	12,983	12,833	12,685	-0.6%	-0.6%	-1.2%	-1.2%
Sales ($Millions)	75,125	79,939	84,572	88,630	92,454	6.4%	5.8%	4.8%	4.3%
Employment	239,821	238,424	237,092	234,362	231,659	-0.6%	-0.6%	-1.2%	-1.2%
Sales ($M)/Estab.	5.72	6.12	6.51	6.91	7.29	7.0%	6.4%	6.0%	5.5%
Sales ($)/Emp.	313,253	335,280	356,705	378,175	399,094	7.0%	6.4%	6.0%	5.5%

3-YEAR TREND – ESTIMATED NUMBER OF ESTABLISHMENTS

Year	Employee Size of Establishment									Total
	1-4 Emps.	5-9 Emps.	10-19 Emps.	20-49 Emps.	50-99 Emps.	100-249 Emps.	250-499 Emps.	>500 Emps.	Non-Employer	Employ-ment
2016	6,212	1,773	1,107	873	417	329	144	76	2,050	12,983
2017	6,141	1,752	1,095	863	412	325	143	75	2,027	12,833
2018	6,070	1,732	1,082	853	408	322	141	74	2,003	12,685

3-YEAR TREND – ESTIMATED NUMBER OF ESTABLISHMENTS

Year	Employee Size of Establishment									Total
	1-4 Emps.	5-9 Emps.	10-19 Emps.	20-49 Emps.	50-99 Emps.	100-249 Emps.	250-499 Emps.	>500 Emps.	Non-Employer	Employ-ment
2016	2,683.8	2,012.7	3,161.7	6,597.7	6,931.3	14,741.2	21,783.5	26,437.3	222.7	84,571.8
2017	2,808.0	2,105.8	3,307.9	6,902.8	7,251.8	15,422.9	22,790.9	27,806.8	233.0	88,629.8
2018	2,924.2	2,193.0	3,444.8	7,188.5	7,552.0	16,061.3	23,734.3	29,112.9	242.6	92,453.7

3-YEAR TREND – ESTIMATED NUMBER OF ESTABLISHMENTS

Year	Employee Size of Establishment									Total
	1-4 Emps.	5-9 Emps.	10-19 Emps.	20-49 Emps.	50-99 Emps.	100-249 Emps.	250-499 Emps.	>500 Emps.	Non-Employer	Employ-ment
2016	15,531	10,281	15,059	26,276	24,782	41,513	41,988	59,612	2,050	237,092
2017	15,352	10,163	14,885	25,973	24,496	41,035	41,505	58,925	2,027	234,362
2018	15,175	10,045	14,714	25,674	24,214	40,562	41,026	58,246	2,003	231,659

SUB-INDUSTRIES – 2017 ESTIMATED INDUSTRY SALES, ESTABLISHMENTS & EMPLOYMENT

Sub-Industries	Category*	Establish-ments	Sales ($Mill)	Employ-ment
Surgical and medical instruments	Major1	2,786	11,635.8	43,042
Ophthalmic instruments and apparatus	Minor1	42	69.8	2,540
Muscle exercise apparatus, ophthalmic	Minor2	20	3.3	146
Ophthalmic lasers	Minor2	23	4.8	77
Diagnostic apparatus, medical	Minor1	388	944.5	8,928
Biopsy instruments and equipment	Minor2	12	1.9	42
Blood pressure apparatus	Minor2	20	13.2	263
Corneal microscopes	Minor2	2	0.3	3
Eye examining instruments and apparatus	Minor2	61	13.9	360
Gastroscopes, except electromedical	Minor2	3	1.9	24
Optometers	Minor2	32	7.0	104
Otoscopes, except electromedical	Minor2	2	0.3	6
Retinoscopes	Minor2	1	0.2	2
Tonometers, medical	Minor2	3	0.3	61
Veterinarians' instruments and apparatus	Minor1	68	27.6	314
Rifles, for propelling hypodermics into animals	Minor2	1	0.1	2
Surgical instruments and apparatus	Minor1	582	17,715.8	20,508
Medical instruments and equipment, blood and bone work	Minor1	320	635.8	5,763
Inhalation therapy equipment	Minor1	29	15.2	191
Operating tables	Minor1	5	2.8	29
Oxygen tents	Minor1	1	0.0	1
Physiotherapy equipment, electrical	Minor1	27	10.7	2,363
Skin grafting equipment	Minor1	34	5.5	68
Stethoscopes and stethographs	Minor1	2	1.1	13
Ultrasonic medical cleaning equipment	Minor1	14	15.5	70
Surgical appliances and supplies	Major1	1,671	29,981.6	58,786
Personal safety equipment	Minor1	923	5,141.3	24,547
Cotton and cotton applicators	Minor1	41	732.8	1,564
Prosthetic appliances	Minor1	2,008	10,010.8	20,952
Orthopedic appliances	Minor1	3,618	11,457.7	40,536
Bandages and dressings	Minor1	56	123.6	1,441
Bandages: plastic, muslin, plaster of paris, etc.	Minor2	17	10.3	524
Dressings, surgical	Minor2	19	35.1	1,048
Gauze, surgical	Minor2	3	9.1	43

*Category-Major categories (Major1) are more general descriptions for companies that self-selected to capture the many functions they perform in the industry. Minor categories (Minor1, Minor2) are more specific for companies that have more detailed functions (Minor1 is a larger category than Minor2). Minor categories figures (sales, etc.) can be aggregated to larger minor categories (Minor2 sums to Minor1) and major categories overall figures.

SIGN MANUFACTURING
NAICS 33995

NAICS 33995: Sign Manufacturing Industry. This industry comprises establishments primarily engaged in manufacturing signs and related displays of all materials (except printing paper and paperboard signs, notices, displays).

INDUSTRY ESTABLISHMENTS, SALES & EMPLOYMENT TRENDS

	Year					Percent Chg. Year-to-Year			
	2014	2015	2016	2017	2018	14-15	15-16	16-17	17-18
Establishments	16,430	15,951	15,476	15,138	14,807	-2.9%	-3.0%	-2.2%	-2.2%
Sales ($Millions)	12,206	12,587	12,907	13,291	13,632	3.1%	2.5%	3.0%	2.6%
Employment	79,586	77,266	74,964	73,328	71,725	-2.9%	-3.0%	-2.2%	-2.2%
Sales ($M)/Estab.	0.74	0.79	0.83	0.88	0.92	6.2%	5.7%	5.3%	4.9%
Sales ($)/Emp.	153,365	162,906	172,180	181,259	190,054	6.2%	5.7%	5.3%	4.9%

3-YEAR TREND – ESTIMATED NUMBER OF ESTABLISHMENTS

Year	Employee Size of Establishment									Total
	1-4 Emps.	5-9 Emps.	10-19 Emps.	20-49 Emps.	50-99 Emps.	100-249 Emps.	250-499 Emps.	>500 Emps.	Non-Employer	Employ-ment
2016	2,820	972	617	504	176	70	20	4	10,294	15,476
2017	2,759	951	603	493	172	68	19	4	10,069	15,138
2018	2,698	930	590	482	169	67	19	4	9,849	14,807

3-YEAR TREND – ESTIMATED NUMBER OF ESTABLISHMENTS

Year	Employee Size of Establishment									Total
	1-4 Emps.	5-9 Emps.	10-19 Emps.	20-49 Emps.	50-99 Emps.	100-249 Emps.	250-499 Emps.	>500 Emps.	Non-Employer	Employ-ment
2016	789.2	715.0	1,141.2	2,467.2	1,895.7	2,021.8	1,933.8	985.6	957.9	12,907.4
2017	811.8	735.4	1,173.8	2,537.7	1,949.9	2,079.6	1,989.1	1,028.7	985.3	13,291.3
2018	831.6	753.4	1,202.5	2,599.7	1,997.5	2,130.4	2,037.7	1,069.5	1,009.3	13,631.7

3-YEAR TREND – ESTIMATED NUMBER OF ESTABLISHMENTS

Year	Employee Size of Establishment									Total
	1-4 Emps.	5-9 Emps.	10-19 Emps.	20-49 Emps.	50-99 Emps.	100-249 Emps.	250-499 Emps.	>500 Emps.	Non-Employer	Employ-ment
2016	7,050	5,638	8,391	15,168	10,463	8,789	5,754	3,417	10,294	74,964
2017	6,896	5,515	8,207	14,837	10,234	8,598	5,628	3,343	10,069	73,328
2018	6,746	5,394	8,028	14,513	10,011	8,410	5,506	3,270	9,849	71,725

SIGN MANUFACTURING
NAICS 33995

SUB-INDUSTRIES — 2017 ESTIMATED INDUSTRY
SALES, ESTABLISHMENTS & EMPLOYMENT

Sub-Industries	Category*	Establish-ments	Sales ($Mill)	Employ-ment
Signs and advertising specialties	Major1	13,071	8,855.5	49,344
Electric signs	Minor1	434	1,238.5	6,954
Neon signs	Minor2	427	567.0	2,684
Scoreboards, electric	Minor2	29	581.4	420
Advertising artwork	Minor2	168	107.1	606
Advertising novelties	Minor2	175	426.9	3,173
Displays and cutouts, window and lobby	Minor2	166	684.9	4,480
Displays, paint process	Minor2	27	43.8	248
Letters for signs, metal	Minor2	25	25.9	141
Name plates: except engraved, etched, etc.: metal	Minor2	43	63.3	689
Signs, not made in custom sign painting shops	Minor2	573	696.8	4,589

*Category-Major categories (Major1) are more general descriptions for companies that self-selected to capture the many functions they perform in the industry. Minor categories (Minor1, Minor2) are more specific for companies that have more detailed functions (Minor1 is a larger category than Minor2). Minor categories figures (sales, etc.) can be aggregated to larger minor categories (Minor2 sums to Minor1) and major categories overall figures.

Automobile & Other Vehicles Wholesale (NAICS 42311)

NAICS 42311: Automobile & Other Vehicle Wholesale. This industry comprises establishments primarily engaged in wholesaling new and used passenger automobiles, trucks, trailers, and other motor vehicles, such as motorcycles, motor homes, and snowmobiles.

Industry Establishments, Sales & Employment Trends

	Year					Percent Chg. Year-to-Year			
	2014	2015	2016	2017	2018	14-15	15-16	16-17	17-18
Establishments	7,500	7,483	7,558	7,645	7,805	-0.2%	1.0%	1.1%	2.1%
Sales ($Millions)	397,238	389,970	386,482	383,010	382,052	-1.8%	-0.9%	-0.9%	-0.3%
Employment	110,260	110,013	111,117	112,390	114,748	-0.2%	1.0%	1.1%	2.1%
Sales ($M)/Estab.	52.97	52.11	51.13	50.10	48.95	-1.6%	-1.9%	-2.0%	-2.3%
Sales ($)/Emp.	3,602,751	3,544,747	3,478,163	3,407,878	3,329,488	-1.6%	-1.9%	-2.0%	-2.3%

3-Year Trend — Estimated Number of Establishments

Year	Employee Size of Establishment									Total
	1-4 Emps.	5-9 Emps.	10-19 Emps.	20-49 Emps.	50-99 Emps.	100-249 Emps.	250-499 Emps.	>500 Emps.	Non-Employer	Employ-ment
2016	3,203	858	836	987	436	156	17	7	1,058	7,558
2017	3,239	867	846	998	441	158	17	7	1,070	7,645
2018	3,307	886	864	1,019	451	161	18	7	1,093	7,805

3-Year Trend — Estimated Industry Sales ($Millions)

Year	Employee Size of Establishment									Total
	1-4 Emps.	5-9 Emps.	10-19 Emps.	20-49 Emps.	50-99 Emps.	100-249 Emps.	250-499 Emps.	>500 Emps.	Non-Employer	Employ-ment
2016	17,010.0	11,971.9	29,363.2	91,673.2	89,128.5	85,990.1	31,787.2	29,354.8	203.3	386,482.1
2017	16,863.3	11,868.6	29,110.0	90,882.6	88,359.8	85,248.5	31,513.1	28,963.0	201.5	383,010.2
2018	16,832.0	11,846.6	29,056.0	90,714.0	88,195.9	85,090.4	31,454.6	28,661.0	201.1	382,051.6

3-Year Trend — Estimated Number of Employees

Year	Employee Size of Establishment									Total
	1-4 Emps.	5-9 Emps.	10-19 Emps.	20-49 Emps.	50-99 Emps.	100-249 Emps.	250-499 Emps.	>500 Emps.	Non-Employer	Employ-ment
2016	8,007	4,974	11,376	29,697	25,920	19,697	4,984	5,404	1,058	111,117
2017	8,098	5,031	11,506	30,037	26,217	19,923	5,041	5,466	1,070	112,390
2018	8,268	5,137	11,748	30,667	26,767	20,341	5,147	5,580	1,093	114,748

AUTOMOBILE & OTHER VEHICLES WHOLESALE (NAICS 42311)

SUB-INDUSTRIES — 2017 ESTIMATED INDUSTRY SALES, ESTABLISHMENTS & EMPLOYMENT

Sub-Industries	Cate-gory*	Establish-ments	Sales ($Mill)	Employ-ment
Automobiles and other motor vehicles	Major1	1,688	92,445.6	26,603
Automotive brokers	Minor1	678	13,000.2	4,266
Automobile auction	Minor2	539	93,803.2	27,913
Automobiles	Minor2	1,560	40,283.1	13,565
Trucks, noncommercial	Minor2	124	3,337.2	699
Vans, noncommercial	Minor2	9	701.6	89
Commercial vehicles	Minor1	109	5,207.4	4,288
Ambulances	Minor2	284	4,767.7	1,853
Busses	Minor2	155	12,758.7	2,230
Fire trucks	Minor2	99	4,879.3	892
Taxicabs	Minor2	85	972.7	400
Trailers for trucks, new and used	Minor2	234	14,503.6	3,956
Truck bodies	Minor2	99	6,189.2	1,891
Truck tractors	Minor2	120	8,476.2	2,728
Trucks, commercial	Minor2	613	61,896.1	14,491
Vans, commercial	Minor2	30	369.0	486
Recreational vehicles, motor homes, and trailers	Minor1	112	4,772.3	1,320
Campers (pickup coaches) for mounting on trucks	Minor2	14	435.1	105
Motor homes	Minor2	15	635.5	150
Motor vehicles, kit form	Minor2	7	88.8	22
Pop-up campers	Minor2	2	22.8	9
Recreation vehicles, all-terrain	Minor2	39	631.0	222
Snowmobiles	Minor2	68	334.9	261
Trailers for passenger vehicles	Minor2	37	954.5	474
Motorized cycles	Minor1	35	592.3	158
Mopeds	Minor2	20	182.2	73
Motor scooters	Minor2	74	1,282.5	330
Motorcycles	Minor2	795	9,487.6	2,916

*Category-Major categories (Major1) are more general descriptions for companies that self-selected to capture the many functions they perform in the industry. Minor categories (Minor1, Minor2) are more specific for companies that have more detailed functions (Minor1 is a larger category than Minor2). Minor categories figures (sales, etc.) can be aggregated to larger minor categories (Minor2 sums to Minor1) and major categories overall figures.

MOTOR VEHICLE PARTS & SUPPLIES WHOLESALES (NAICS 42312)

NAICS 42312: Motor Vehicle Parts & Supplies Wholesale. Establishments primarily engaged in the wholesale distribution of new and used passenger automobiles, trucks, trailers, and other motor vehicles, including motorcycles, motor homes, and snowmobiles. Automotive distributors primarily engaged in selling at retail to individual consumers for personal use, and also selling a limited amount of new and used passenger automobiles and trucks at wholesale, are classified in SIC 5511.

INDUSTRY ESTABLISHMENTS, SALES & EMPLOYMENT TRENDS

	Year					Percent Chg. Year-to-Year			
	2014	2015	2016	2017	2018	14-15	15-16	16-17	17-18
Establishments	15,923	15,988	16,167	16,357	16,705	0.4%	1.1%	1.2%	2.1%
Sales ($Millions)	173,074	185,298	198,596	212,097	227,545	7.1%	7.2%	6.8%	7.3%
Employment	195,697	196,496	198,692	201,030	205,310	0.4%	1.1%	1.2%	2.1%
Sales ($M)/Estab.	10.87	11.59	12.28	12.97	13.62	6.6%	6.0%	5.6%	5.0%
Sales ($)/Emp.	884,395	943,014	999,515	1,055,052	1,108,301	6.6%	6.0%	5.6%	5.0%

3-YEAR TREND – ESTIMATED NUMBER OF ESTABLISHMENTS

Year	Employee Size of Establishment									Total
	1-4 Emps.	5-9 Emps.	10-19 Emps.	20-49 Emps.	50-99 Emps.	100-249 Emps.	250-499 Emps.	>500 Emps.	Non-Employer	Employ-ment
2016	5,661	3,214	2,599	1,642	530	209	35	13	2,263	16,167
2017	5,728	3,252	2,630	1,661	536	212	35	13	2,290	16,357
2018	5,850	3,322	2,686	1,696	548	216	36	14	2,338	16,705

3-YEAR TREND – ESTIMATED INDUSTRY SALES ($MILLIONS)

Year	Employee Size of Establishment									Total
	1-4 Emps.	5-9 Emps.	10-19 Emps.	20-49 Emps.	50-99 Emps.	100-249 Emps.	250-499 Emps.	>500 Emps.	Non-Employer	Employ-ment
2016	8,963.9	13,377.3	27,201.4	45,477.3	32,271.9	34,324.9	19,094.5	17,375.6	509.2	198,596.0
2017	9,578.4	14,294.4	29,066.2	48,595.1	34,484.3	36,678.1	20,403.5	18,452.5	544.1	212,096.6
2018	10,285.9	15,350.2	31,213.1	52,184.5	37,031.5	39,387.3	21,910.6	19,597.9	584.3	227,545.4

3-YEAR TREND – ESTIMATED NUMBER OF EMPLOYEES

Year	Employee Size of Establishment									Total
	1-4 Emps.	5-9 Emps.	10-19 Emps.	20-49 Emps.	50-99 Emps.	100-249 Emps.	250-499 Emps.	>500 Emps.	Non-Employer	Employ-ment
2016	14,153	18,644	35,349	49,417	31,481	26,374	10,042	10,969	2,263	198,692
2017	14,320	18,863	35,765	49,998	31,852	26,684	10,160	11,098	2,290	201,030
2018	14,625	19,265	36,526	51,062	32,530	27,253	10,376	11,335	2,338	205,310

MOTOR VEHICLE PARTS & SUPPLIES WHOLESALES (NAICS 42312)

SUB-INDUSTRIES – 2017 ESTIMATED INDUSTRY SALES, ESTABLISHMENTS & EMPLOYMENT

Sub-Industries	Category*	Establishments	Sales ($Mill)	Employment
Automobiles and other motor vehicles	Major1	3,611	51,192.9	47,585
Automotive brokers	Minor1	1,451	7,199.0	7,631
Automobile auction	Minor2	1,153	51,944.7	49,927
Automobiles	Minor2	3,338	22,307.2	24,264
Trucks, noncommercial	Minor2	265	1,848.0	1,251
Vans, noncommercial	Minor2	20	388.5	159
Commercial vehicles	Minor1	234	2,883.6	7,670
Ambulances	Minor2	608	2,640.2	3,315
Busses	Minor2	333	7,065.3	3,988
Fire trucks	Minor2	212	2,702.0	1,596
Taxicabs	Minor2	183	538.6	715
Trailers for trucks, new and used	Minor2	501	8,031.6	7,077
Truck bodies	Minor2	211	3,427.3	3,382
Truck tractors	Minor2	257	4,693.8	4,879
Trucks, commercial	Minor2	1,311	34,275.7	25,920
Vans, commercial	Minor2	64	204.4	869
Recreational vehicles, motor homes, and trailers	Minor1	240	2,642.7	2,361
Campers (pickup coaches) for mounting on trucks	Minor2	30	240.9	188
Motor homes	Minor2	33	351.9	268
Motor vehicles, kit form	Minor2	15	49.2	40
Pop-up campers	Minor2	3	12.6	17
Recreation vehicles, all-terrain	Minor2	84	349.4	397
Snowmobiles	Minor2	147	185.4	467
Trailers for passenger vehicles	Minor2	79	528.5	847
Motorized cycles	Minor1	76	328.0	283
Mopeds	Minor2	43	100.9	131
Motor scooters	Minor2	158	710.2	591
Motorcycles	Minor2	1,701	5,253.9	5,215

*Category-Major categories (Major1) are more general descriptions for companies that self-selected to capture the many functions they perform in the industry. Minor categories (Minor1, Minor2) are more specific for companies that have more detailed functions (Minor1 is a larger category than Minor2). Minor categories figures (sales, etc.) can be aggregated to larger minor categories (Minor2 sums to Minor1) and major categories overall figures.

FURNITURE WHOLESALE INDUSTRY
(NAICS 42321)

NAICS 42321: Furniture Wholesale. Establishments primarily engaged in the wholesale distribution of furniture, including bedsprings, mattresses, and other household furniture; office furniture; and furniture for public parks and buildings. Establishments primarily engaged in the wholesale distribution of partitions, shelving, lockers, and store fixtures are classified in SIC 5046.

INDUSTRY ESTABLISHMENTS, SALES & EMPLOYMENT TRENDS

	Year					Percent Chg. Year-to-Year			
	2014	2015	2016	2017	2018	14-15	15-16	16-17	17-18
Establishments	7,331	7,356	7,420	7,517	7,686	0.3%	0.9%	1.3%	2.3%
Sales ($Millions)	41,313	43,588	46,043	48,696	51,808	5.5%	5.6%	5.8%	6.4%
Employment	64,011	64,228	64,795	65,637	67,116	0.3%	0.9%	1.3%	2.3%
Sales ($M)/Estab.	5.64	5.93	6.20	6.48	6.74	5.2%	4.7%	4.4%	4.0%
Sales ($)/Emp.	645,399	678,644	710,598	741,905	771,918	5.2%	4.7%	4.4%	4.0%

3-YEAR TREND — ESTIMATED NUMBER OF ESTABLISHMENTS

Year	Employee Size of Establishment									Total
	1-4 Emps.	5-9 Emps.	10-19 Emps.	20-49 Emps.	50-99 Emps.	100-249 Emps.	250-499 Emps.	>500 Emps.	Non-Employer	Employ-ment
2016	3,043	1,021	806	575	165	70	7	1	1,733	7,420
2017	3,082	1,035	816	582	167	71	7	1	1,755	7,517
2018	3,152	1,058	835	596	171	72	7	1	1,795	7,686

3-YEAR TREND — ESTIMATED INDUSTRY SALES ($MILLIONS)

Year	Employee Size of Establishment									Total
	1-4 Emps.	5-9 Emps.	10-19 Emps.	20-49 Emps.	50-99 Emps.	100-249 Emps.	250-499 Emps.	>500 Emps.	Non-Employer	Employ-ment
2016	3,685.3	3,251.3	6,450.1	12,182.5	7,685.0	8,767.9	2,998.0	793.2	230.1	46,043.4
2017	3,897.6	3,438.6	6,821.8	12,884.5	8,127.9	9,273.1	3,170.8	838.7	243.4	48,696.5
2018	4,146.7	3,658.4	7,257.8	13,708.0	8,647.3	9,865.8	3,373.4	892.0	259.0	51,808.2

3-YEAR TREND — ESTIMATED NUMBER OF EMPLOYEES

Year	Employee Size of Establishment									Total
	1-4 Emps.	5-9 Emps.	10-19 Emps.	20-49 Emps.	50-99 Emps.	100-249 Emps.	250-499 Emps.	>500 Emps.	Non-Employer	Employ-ment
2016	7,607	5,924	10,958	17,306	9,801	8,808	2,061	598	1,733	64,795
2017	7,706	6,001	11,101	17,531	9,928	8,922	2,088	605	1,755	65,637
2018	7,880	6,136	11,351	17,926	10,152	9,123	2,135	619	1,795	67,116

FURNITURE WHOLESALE INDUSTRY (NAICS 42321)

SUB-INDUSTRIES – 2017 ESTIMATED INDUSTRY SALES, ESTABLISHMENTS & EMPLOYMENT

Sub-Industries	Cate-gory*	Establish-ments	Sales ($Mill)	Employ-ment
Furniture	Major1	3,482	19,840.5	26,353
Office and public building furniture	Minor1	382	4,001.0	4,191
Bar furniture	Minor2	16	152.4	149
Cafeteria furniture	Minor2	4	30.1	9
Church pews	Minor2	36	85.9	132
Filing units	Minor2	74	583.6	633
Lockers	Minor2	146	356.9	725
Office furniture, nec	Minor2	823	12,689.2	14,363
Public building furniture, nec	Minor2	37	378.8	459
Restaurant furniture, nec	Minor2	17	254.2	239
School desks	Minor2	38	430.3	383
Theater seats	Minor2	5	29.2	55
Household furniture	Minor1	462	4,644.7	6,284
Dining room furniture	Minor2	12	105.6	196
Dressers	Minor2	263	231.5	988
Juvenile furniture	Minor2	28	254.7	323
Sofas and couches	Minor2	15	69.1	105
Tables, occasional	Minor2	21	148.2	162
Beds and bedding	Minor1	65	582.3	629
Beds	Minor2	636	668.2	2,650
Bedsprings	Minor2	2	2.1	24
Mattresses	Minor2	177	602.1	1,563
Waterbeds	Minor2	16	25.8	210
Bookcases	Minor2	23	42.1	129
Chairs	Minor2	302	757.9	1,512
Desks, nec	Minor2	9	21.0	65
Outdoor and lawn furniture, nec	Minor2	117	940.9	1,042
Racks	Minor2	221	343.1	1,449
Shelving	Minor2	78	376.2	534
Unfinished furniture	Minor2	10	49.0	83

*Category-Major categories (Major1) are more general descriptions for companies that self-selected to capture the many functions they perform in the industry. Minor categories (Minor1, Minor2) are more specific for companies that have more detailed functions (Minor1 is a larger category than Minor2). Minor categories figures (sales, etc.) can be aggregated to larger minor categories (Minor2 sums to Minor1) and major categories overall figures.

HOME FURNISHINGS WHOLESALE INDUSTRY (NAICS 42322)

NAICS 42322: Home Furnishings Wholesales. Establishments primarily engaged in the wholesale distribution of homefurnishings and housewares, including antiques; china; glassware and earthenware; lamps (including electric); curtains and draperies; linens and towels; and carpets, linoleum, and all other types of hard and soft surface floor coverings. Wholesale distribution of other electrical household goods is classified in SIC 5064; precious metal flatware in SIC 5094.

INDUSTRY ESTABLISHMENTS, SALES & EMPLOYMENT TRENDS

	Year					Percent Chg. Year-to-Year			
	2014	2015	2016	2017	2018	14-15	15-16	16-17	17-18
Establishments	8,704	8,573	8,497	8,517	8,617	-1.5%	-0.9%	0.2%	1.2%
Sales ($Millions)	44,922	46,888	49,006	51,615	54,657	4.4%	4.5%	5.3%	5.9%
Employment	81,571	80,338	79,627	79,811	80,749	-1.5%	-0.9%	0.2%	1.2%
Sales ($M)/Estab.	5.16	5.47	5.77	6.06	6.34	6.0%	5.5%	5.1%	4.7%
Sales ($)/Emp.	550,707	583,629	615,448	646,715	676,879	6.0%	5.5%	5.1%	4.7%

3-YEAR TREND – ESTIMATED NUMBER OF ESTABLISHMENTS

Year	Employee Size of Establishment									Total
	1-4 Emps.	5-9 Emps.	10-19 Emps.	20-49 Emps.	50-99 Emps.	100-249 Emps.	250-499 Emps.	>500 Emps.	Non-Employer	Employ-ment
2016	3,246	1,311	1,017	635	191	95	18	1	1,984	8,497
2017	3,253	1,314	1,020	636	192	95	18	1	1,989	8,517
2018	3,291	1,329	1,031	643	194	96	18	1	2,012	8,617

3-YEAR TREND – ESTIMATED INDUSTRY SALES ($MILLIONS)

Year	Employee Size of Establishment									Total
	1-4 Emps.	5-9 Emps.	10-19 Emps.	20-49 Emps.	50-99 Emps.	100-249 Emps.	250-499 Emps.	>500 Emps.	Non-Employer	Employ-ment
2016	3,264.6	3,465.7	6,762.0	11,165.0	7,400.6	9,871.3	6,173.9	635.6	267.5	49,006.2
2017	3,438.4	3,650.2	7,122.0	11,759.3	7,794.6	10,396.8	6,502.6	669.5	281.7	51,615.0
2018	3,641.0	3,865.4	7,541.8	12,452.5	8,254.1	11,009.6	6,885.9	708.8	298.3	54,657.4

3-YEAR TREND – ESTIMATED NUMBER OF EMPLOYEES

Year	Employee Size of Establishment									Total
	1-4 Emps.	5-9 Emps.	10-19 Emps.	20-49 Emps.	50-99 Emps.	100-249 Emps.	250-499 Emps.	>500 Emps.	Non-Employer	Employ-ment
2016	8,114	7,604	13,833	19,099	11,365	11,940	5,111	576	1,984	79,627
2017	8,133	7,621	13,865	19,143	11,391	11,968	5,123	578	1,989	79,811
2018	8,229	7,711	14,028	19,368	11,525	12,108	5,183	584	2,012	80,749

HOME FURNISHINGS WHOLESALE INDUSTRY
(NAICS 42322)

SUB-INDUSTRIES – 2017 ESTIMATED INDUSTRY SALES, ESTABLISHMENTS & EMPLOYMENT

Sub-Industries	Category*	Establishments	Sales ($Mill)	Employment
Homefurnishings	Major1	1,002	7,596.1	13,626
Kitchenware	Minor1	223	3,019.2	3,814
Aluminumware	Minor2	11	147.4	253
China	Minor2	41	710.1	766
Crockery	Minor2	4	51.0	45
Glassware	Minor2	98	667.5	935
Kitchen tools and utensils, nec	Minor2	80	531.6	977
Stainless steel flatware	Minor2	21	212.9	363
Tupperware	Minor2	353	304.6	779
Grills, barbecue	Minor2	58	316.0	640
Linens and towels	Minor1	119	2,507.8	2,094
Bedspreads	Minor2	26	559.7	475
Blankets	Minor2	137	328.2	528
Linens, table	Minor2	32	164.9	221
Pillowcases	Minor2	9	67.0	90
Sheets, textile	Minor2	65	1,453.8	1,184
Slip covers (furniture)	Minor2	7	248.3	31
Towels	Minor2	71	558.6	388
Window furnishings	Minor1	112	885.7	1,683
Curtains	Minor2	27	148.9	353
Draperies	Minor2	163	752.8	1,488
Venetian blinds	Minor2	25	150.4	331
Vertical blinds	Minor2	58	250.9	388
Window covering parts and accessories	Minor2	195	736.8	1,376
Window shades	Minor2	34	195.0	301
Floor coverings	Minor1	1,312	11,027.3	15,927
Carpets	Minor2	1,738	5,488.1	9,240
Floor cushion and padding	Minor2	22	180.9	225
Resilient floor coverings: tile or sheet	Minor2	41	771.5	848
Rugs	Minor2	337	1,621.0	2,644
Wood flooring	Minor2	124	1,504.1	1,650
Decorative home furnishings and supplies	Minor1	1,829	7,444.9	14,072
Fireplace equipment and accessories	Minor2	60	528.1	785
Misc. home furnishings wholesales	Minor2	85	484.0	1,291

*Category-Major categories (Major1) are more general descriptions for companies that self-selected to capture the many functions they perform in the industry. Minor categories (Minor1, Minor2) are more specific for companies that have more detailed functions (Minor1 is a larger category than Minor2). Minor categories figures (sales, etc.) can be aggregated to larger minor categories (Minor2 sums to Minor1) and major categories overall figures.

OFFICE EQUIPMENT WHOLESALES INDUSTRY
(NAICS 42342)

NAICS 42342: Office Equipment Wholesales. Establishments primarily engaged in the wholesale distribution of office machines and related equipment, including photocopy and microfilm equipment and safes and vaults. These establishments frequently also sell office supplies, but wholesaling most office supplies is classified in SIC 5111-5113. Wholesaling office furniture is classified in SIC 5021, and wholesaling computers and peripheral equipment is classified in SIC 5045.

INDUSTRY ESTABLISHMENTS, SALES & EMPLOYMENT TRENDS

	Year					Percent Chg. Year-to-Year			
	2014	2015	2016	2017	2018	14-15	15-16	16-17	17-18
Establishments	9,562	9,513	9,529	9,878	10,336	-0.5%	0.2%	3.7%	4.6%
Sales ($Millions)	37,822	37,480	37,314	38,389	39,780	-0.9%	-0.4%	2.9%	3.6%
Employment	122,476	121,847	122,042	126,514	132,385	-0.5%	0.2%	3.7%	4.6%
Sales ($M)/Estab.	3.96	3.94	3.92	3.89	3.85	-0.4%	-0.6%	-0.8%	-1.0%
Sales ($)/Emp.	308,807	307,598	305,743	303,437	300,484	-0.4%	-0.6%	-0.8%	-1.0%

3-YEAR TREND — ESTIMATED NUMBER OF ESTABLISHMENTS

Year	Employee Size of Establishment									Total
	1-4 Emps.	5-9 Emps.	10-19 Emps.	20-49 Emps.	50-99 Emps.	100-249 Emps.	250-499 Emps.	>500 Emps.	Non-Employer	Employ-ment
2016	4,954	1,347	1,090	836	324	182	43	10	742	9,529
2017	5,136	1,397	1,130	867	336	189	44	10	769	9,878
2018	5,374	1,461	1,183	907	351	198	46	11	805	10,336

3-YEAR TREND — ESTIMATED INDUSTRY SALES ($MILLIONS)

Year	Employee Size of Establishment									Total
	1-4 Emps.	5-9 Emps.	10-19 Emps.	20-49 Emps.	50-99 Emps.	100-249 Emps.	250-499 Emps.	>500 Emps.	Non-Employer	Employ-ment
2016	2,207.2	1,577.5	3,210.0	6,516.1	5,548.5	8,420.5	6,668.7	3,057.0	107.9	37,313.5
2017	2,272.0	1,623.8	3,304.2	6,707.2	5,711.3	8,667.4	6,864.3	3,127.8	111.1	38,389.0
2018	2,355.7	1,683.6	3,425.9	6,954.3	5,921.7	8,986.7	7,117.2	3,219.4	115.2	39,779.7

3-YEAR TREND — ESTIMATED NUMBER OF EMPLOYEES

Year	Employee Size of Establishment									Total
	1-4 Emps.	5-9 Emps.	10-19 Emps.	20-49 Emps.	50-99 Emps.	100-249 Emps.	250-499 Emps.	>500 Emps.	Non-Employer	Employ-ment
2016	12,386	7,814	14,826	25,164	19,237	22,994	12,464	6,415	742	122,042
2017	12,840	8,100	15,369	26,086	19,941	23,837	12,921	6,650	769	126,514
2018	13,436	8,476	16,082	27,297	20,867	24,943	13,521	6,959	805	132,385

OFFICE EQUIPMENT WHOLESALES INDUSTRY (NAICS 42342)

SUB-INDUSTRIES – 2017 ESTIMATED INDUSTRY SALES, ESTABLISHMENTS & EMPLOYMENT

Sub-Industries	Cate-gory*	Establish-ments	Sales ($Mill)	Employ-ment
Office equipment	Major1	5,696	10,660.2	75,938
Calculating machines	Minor1	86	89.5	499
Accounting machines, excluding machine program readal	Minor2	78	63.4	668
Adding machines	Minor2	13	24.9	305
Cash registers	Minor2	808	732.8	4,589
Calculators, electronic	Minor2	19	33.5	114
Copying equipment	Minor1	966	1,423.3	10,845
Blueprinting equipment	Minor2	50	37.3	246
Duplicating machines	Minor2	200	339.2	3,544
Microfilm equipment	Minor2	100	122.5	1,044
Micrographic equipment	Minor2	39	68.5	610
Mimeograph machines	Minor2	4	2.1	77
Photocopy machines	Minor2	811	23,770.4	21,386
Whiteprinting equipment	Minor2	6	7.0	9
Typewriter and dictation equipment	Minor1	19	10.2	68
Dictating machines	Minor2	109	107.9	973
Typewriters	Minor2	85	66.9	457
Addressing and mailing machines	Minor1	47	45.2	297
Addressing machines	Minor2	10	4.4	46
Mailing machines	Minor2	202	219.4	1,899
Bank automatic teller machines	Minor2	155	251.1	1,209
Check writing, signing, and endorsing machines	Minor2	85	76.9	388
Vaults and safes	Minor2	290	232.5	1,302

*Category-Major categories (Major1) are more general descriptions for companies that self-selected to capture the many functions they perform in the industry. Minor categories (Minor1, Minor2) are more specific for companies that have more detailed functions (Minor1 is a larger category than Minor2). Minor categories figures (sales, etc.) can be aggregated to larger minor categories (Minor2 sums to Minor1) and major categories overall figures.

COMPUTER & EQUIPMENT WHOLESALE INDUSTRY
(NAICS 42343)

NAICS 42343: Computer & Peripheral Equipment and Software Wholesalers. This U.S. industry comprises establishments primarily engaged in wholesaling computers, computer peripheral equipment, loaded computer boards, and/or computer software.

INDUSTRY ESTABLISHMENTS, SALES & EMPLOYMENT TRENDS

	Year					Percent Chg. Year-to-Year			
	2014	2015	2016	2017	2018	14-15	15-16	16-17	17-18
Establishments	9,979	9,381	9,089	8,894	8,785	-6.0%	-3.1%	-2.1%	-1.2%
Sales ($Millions)	190,788	189,270	191,845	195,601	200,355	-0.8%	1.4%	2.0%	2.4%
Employment	178,070	167,395	162,183	158,709	156,772	-6.0%	-3.1%	-2.1%	-1.2%
Sales ($M)/Estab.	19.12	20.18	21.11	21.99	22.81	5.5%	4.6%	4.2%	3.7%
Sales ($)/Emp.	1,071,423	1,130,678	1,182,896	1,232,451	1,278,002	5.5%	4.6%	4.2%	3.7%

3-YEAR TREND — ESTIMATED NUMBER OF ESTABLISHMENTS

Year	Employee Size of Establishment									Total
	1-4 Emps.	5-9 Emps.	10-19 Emps.	20-49 Emps.	50-99 Emps.	100-249 Emps.	250-499 Emps.	>500 Emps.	Non-Employer	Employ-ment
2016	4,449	1,353	1,055	888	332	201	53	50	708	9,089
2017	4,354	1,324	1,032	869	325	197	52	49	692	8,894
2018	4,301	1,307	1,019	858	321	195	51	48	684	8,785

3-YEAR TREND — ESTIMATED INDUSTRY SALES ($MILLIONS)

Year	Employee Size of Establishment									Total
	1-4 Emps.	5-9 Emps.	10-19 Emps.	20-49 Emps.	50-99 Emps.	100-249 Emps.	250-499 Emps.	>500 Emps.	Non-Employer	Employ-ment
2016	6,763.9	5,404.3	10,597.8	23,618.1	19,435.8	31,716.8	28,055.1	66,140.8	112.9	191,845.4
2017	6,868.6	5,488.0	10,761.8	23,983.7	19,736.6	32,207.8	28,489.4	67,950.3	114.7	195,600.8
2018	7,019.2	5,608.4	10,997.9	24,509.9	20,169.6	32,914.4	29,114.4	69,904.0	117.2	200,355.0

3-YEAR TREND — ESTIMATED NUMBER OF EMPLOYEES

Year	Employee Size of Establishment									Total
	1-4 Emps.	5-9 Emps.	10-19 Emps.	20-49 Emps.	50-99 Emps.	100-249 Emps.	250-499 Emps.	>500 Emps.	Non-Employer	Employ-ment
2016	11,123	7,845	14,344	26,729	19,747	25,382	15,367	40,940	708	162,183
2017	10,885	7,677	14,036	26,157	19,324	24,838	15,038	40,063	692	158,709
2018	10,752	7,583	13,865	25,837	19,088	24,535	14,854	39,574	684	156,772

SUB-INDUSTRIES – 2017 ESTIMATED INDUSTRY SALES, ESTABLISHMENTS & EMPLOYMENT

Sub-Industries	Category*	Establishments	Sales ($Mill)	Employment
Computers, peripherals, and software	Major1	4,352	148,201.3	75,574
Computer peripheral equipment	Minor1	794	9,093.0	17,606
Disk drives	Minor2	18	40.0	518
Keying equipment	Minor2	9	11.4	94
Printers, computer	Minor2	130	773.9	5,958
Terminals, computer	Minor2	22	128.8	360
Accounting machines using machine readable programs	Minor2	12	16.8	97
Anti-static equipment and devices	Minor2	7	16.0	97
Computer software	Minor2	2,091	9,981.2	30,677
Computers and accessories, personal and home entertain	Minor2	327	5,633.7	4,280
Computers, nec	Minor2	1,093	21,151.6	21,852
Mainframe computers	Minor2	34	539.7	1,485
Word processing equipment	Minor2	4	13.2	112

*Category-Major categories (Major1) are more general descriptions for companies that self-selected to capture the many functions they perform in the industry. Minor categories (Minor1, Minor2) are more specific for companies that have more detailed functions (Minor1 is a larger category than Minor2). Minor categories figures (sales, etc.) can be aggregated to larger minor categories (Minor2 sums to Minor1) and major categories overall figures.

HARDWARE WHOLESALE INDUSTRY
(NAICS 42371)

NAICS 42371: Hardware Wholesales. Establishments primarily engaged in the wholesale distribution of cutlery and general hardware, including handsaws; saw blades; brads, staples, and tacks; and bolts, nuts, rivets, and screws. Establishments primarily engaged in the wholesale distribution of nails, noninsulated wire, and screening are classified in SIC 5051.

INDUSTRY ESTABLISHMENTS, SALES & EMPLOYMENT TRENDS

	Year					Percent Chg. Year-to-Year			
	2014	2015	2016	2017	2018	14-15	15-16	16-17	17-18
Establishments	6,709	6,556	6,466	6,463	6,521	-2.3%	-1.4%	0.0%	0.9%
Sales ($Millions)	49,061	50,321	51,857	53,975	56,490	2.6%	3.1%	4.1%	4.7%
Employment	83,357	81,451	80,327	80,296	81,021	-2.3%	-1.4%	0.0%	0.9%
Sales ($M)/Estab.	7.31	7.68	8.02	8.35	8.66	5.0%	4.5%	4.1%	3.7%
Sales ($)/Emp.	588,569	617,806	645,574	672,203	697,222	5.0%	4.5%	4.1%	3.7%

3-YEAR TREND – ESTIMATED NUMBER OF ESTABLISHMENTS

Year	Employee Size of Establishment									Total
	1-4 Emps.	5-9 Emps.	10-19 Emps.	20-49 Emps.	50-99 Emps.	100-249 Emps.	250-499 Emps.	>500 Emps.	Non-Employer	Employ-ment
2016	2,952	1,247	973	649	169	82	20	8	367	6,466
2017	2,951	1,246	973	648	169	82	20	8	366	6,463
2018	2,977	1,258	982	654	170	83	20	8	370	6,521

3-YEAR TREND – ESTIMATED INDUSTRY SALES ($MILLIONS)

Year	Employee Size of Establishment									Total
	1-4 Emps.	5-9 Emps.	10-19 Emps.	20-49 Emps.	50-99 Emps.	100-249 Emps.	250-499 Emps.	>500 Emps.	Non-Employer	Employ-ment
2016	2,906.8	3,227.6	6,335.2	11,173.5	6,386.8	8,360.9	6,962.1	6,449.7	54.5	51,857.1
2017	3,025.4	3,359.4	6,593.9	11,629.7	6,647.5	8,702.2	7,246.3	6,714.3	56.7	53,975.4
2018	3,168.3	3,518.0	6,905.1	12,178.7	6,961.3	9,113.0	7,588.4	6,997.8	59.4	56,489.9

3-YEAR TREND – ESTIMATED NUMBER OF EMPLOYEES

Year	Employee Size of Establishment									Total
	1-4 Emps.	5-9 Emps.	10-19 Emps.	20-49 Emps.	50-99 Emps.	100-249 Emps.	250-499 Emps.	>500 Emps.	Non-Employer	Employ-ment
2016	7,379	7,232	13,237	19,521	10,017	10,329	5,887	6,358	367	80,327
2017	7,376	7,230	13,232	19,514	10,013	10,325	5,885	6,356	366	80,296
2018	7,443	7,295	13,351	19,690	10,104	10,418	5,938	6,413	370	81,021

HARDWARE WHOLESALE INDUSTRY
(NAICS 42371)

SUB-INDUSTRIES – 2017 ESTIMATED INDUSTRY SALES, ESTABLISHMENTS & EMPLOYMENT

Sub-Industries	Cate-gory*	Establish-ments	Sales ($Mill)	Employ-ment
Hardware	Major1	1,992	30,915.0	36,037
Bolts, nuts, and screws	Minor1	143	1,328.5	2,496
Bolts	Minor2	188	973.1	2,467
Nuts (hardware)	Minor2	76	1,121.2	2,182
Rivets	Minor2	15	114.2	159
Screws	Minor2	47	2,143.9	1,588
Hand tools	Minor1	250	1,943.1	4,411
Cutlery	Minor2	56	2,131.2	864
Garden tools, hand	Minor2	17	218.9	185
Power tools and accessories	Minor1	126	1,455.4	1,876
Power handtools	Minor2	45	656.2	882
Saw blades	Minor2	29	212.7	388
Miscellaneous fasteners	Minor1	381	2,049.3	5,076
Brads	Minor2	2,236	2,160.8	8,378
Staples	Minor2	103	165.4	1,822
Tacks	Minor2	116	114.2	471
Builders' hardware, nec	Minor2	288	3,852.1	6,805
Casters and glides	Minor2	54	314.6	535
Chains	Minor2	142	515.8	718
Furniture hardware, nec	Minor2	46	538.5	1,320
Nozzles	Minor2	11	28.1	81
Padlocks	Minor2	5	44.2	87
Security devices, locks	Minor2	78	541.2	984
Shelf or light hardware	Minor2	19	437.7	485

*Category-Major categories (Major1) are more general descriptions for companies that self-selected to capture the many functions they perform in the industry. Minor categories (Minor1, Minor2) are more specific for companies that have more detailed functions (Minor1 is a larger category than Minor2). Minor categories figures (sales, etc.) can be aggregated to larger minor categories (Minor2 sums to Minor1) and major categories overall figures.

PRINTING & WRITING PAPER WHOLESALES (NAICS 42411)

NAICS 42411: Printing & Writing Paper Wholesales. Establishments primarily engaged in the wholesale distribution of printing and writing paper, including envelope paper; fine paper; and groundwood paper.

INDUSTRY ESTABLISHMENTS, SALES & EMPLOYMENT TRENDS

	Year					Percent Chg. Year-to-Year			
	2014	2015	2016	2017	2018	14-15	15-16	16-17	17-18
Establishments	1,141	1,095	1,004	959	925	-4.0%	-8.3%	-4.5%	-3.6%
Sales ($Millions)	18,692	19,029	18,417	18,505	18,693	1.8%	-3.2%	0.5%	1.0%
Employment	12,094	11,606	10,642	10,167	9,805	-4.0%	-8.3%	-4.5%	-3.6%
Sales ($M)/Estab.	16.39	17.38	18.35	19.30	20.21	6.1%	5.6%	5.2%	4.7%
Sales ($)/Emp.	1,545,519	1,639,560	1,730,656	1,820,120	1,906,479	6.1%	5.6%	5.2%	4.7%

3-YEAR TREND – ESTIMATED NUMBER OF ESTABLISHMENTS

Year	Employee Size of Establishment									Total
	1-4 Emps.	5-9 Emps.	10-19 Emps.	20-49 Emps.	50-99 Emps.	100-249 Emps.	250-499 Emps.	>500 Emps.	Non-Employer	Employ-ment
2016	467	143	103	99	21	12	3	1	154	1,004
2017	446	137	98	95	20	12	3	1	147	959
2018	430	132	95	92	19	11	2	1	142	925

3-YEAR TREND – ESTIMATED INDUSTRY SALES ($MILLIONS)

Year	Employee Size of Establishment									Total
	1-4 Emps.	5-9 Emps.	10-19 Emps.	20-49 Emps.	50-99 Emps.	100-249 Emps.	250-499 Emps.	>500 Emps.	Non-Employer	Employ-ment
2016	1,255.4	1,012.9	1,828.3	4,673.9	2,182.1	3,430.7	2,477.8	1,533.7	22.0	18,416.9
2017	1,261.3	1,017.7	1,836.9	4,695.9	2,192.4	3,446.9	2,489.5	1,542.4	22.1	18,505.2
2018	1,274.1	1,027.9	1,855.5	4,743.3	2,214.5	3,481.7	2,514.6	1,559.2	22.4	18,693.2

3-YEAR TREND – ESTIMATED NUMBER OF EMPLOYEES

Year	Employee Size of Establishment									Total
	1-4 Emps.	5-9 Emps.	10-19 Emps.	20-49 Emps.	50-99 Emps.	100-249 Emps.	250-499 Emps.	>500 Emps.	Non-Employer	Employ-ment
2016	1,168	832	1,400	2,993	1,254	1,553	768	519	154	10,642
2017	1,116	795	1,338	2,859	1,198	1,484	734	496	147	10,167
2018	1,076	766	1,290	2,758	1,156	1,431	708	479	142	9,805

PRINTING & WRITING PAPER WHOLESALES
(NAICS 42411)

SUB-INDUSTRIES — 2017 ESTIMATED INDUSTRY
SALES, ESTABLISHMENTS & EMPLOYMENT

Sub-Industries	Cate-gory*	Establish-ments	Sales ($Mill)	Employ-ment
Printing and writing paper	Major1	596	7,440.5	6,048
Fine paper	Minor2	112	2,906.0	1,678
Printing paper	Minor2	226	7,389.0	2,210
Writing paper	Minor2	24	769.7	231

*Category-Major categories (Major1) are more general descriptions for companies that self-selected to capture the many functions they perform in the industry. Minor categories (Minor1, Minor2) are more specific for companies that have more detailed functions (Minor1 is a larger category than Minor2). Minor categories figures (sales, etc.) can be aggregated to larger minor categories (Minor2 sums to Minor1) and major categories overall figures.

MEN'S & BOYS' CLOTHING WHOLESALES INDUSTRY (NAICS 42432)

NAICS 42432: Men's & Boys' Clothing Wholesales. Establishments primarily engaged in the wholesale distribution of men's and boys' apparel and furnishings, sportswear, hosiery, underwear, nightwear, and work clothing.

INDUSTRY ESTABLISHMENTS, SALES & EMPLOYMENT TRENDS

	Year					Percent Chg. Year-to-Year			
	2014	2015	2016	2017	2018	14-15	15-16	16-17	17-18
Establishments	5,834	5,864	5,872	5,929	6,043	0.5%	0.1%	1.0%	1.9%
Sales ($Millions)	45,096	47,924	50,513	53,488	56,938	6.3%	5.4%	5.9%	6.4%
Employment	54,585	54,857	54,935	55,468	56,533	0.5%	0.1%	1.0%	1.9%
Sales ($M)/Estab.	7.73	8.17	8.60	9.02	9.42	5.7%	5.3%	4.9%	4.4%
Sales ($)/Emp.	826,173	873,618	919,498	964,305	1,007,153	5.7%	5.3%	4.9%	4.4%

3-YEAR TREND – ESTIMATED NUMBER OF ESTABLISHMENTS

Year	Employee Size of Establishment									Total
	1-4 Emps.	5-9 Emps.	10-19 Emps.	20-49 Emps.	50-99 Emps.	100-249 Emps.	250-499 Emps.	>500 Emps.	Non-Employer	Employ-ment
2016	2,037	658	460	320	116	86	25	4	2,166	5,872
2017	2,057	665	464	323	117	86	25	4	2,187	5,929
2018	2,096	677	473	329	119	88	26	4	2,229	6,043

3-YEAR TREND – ESTIMATED INDUSTRY SALES ($MILLIONS)

Year	Employee Size of Establishment									Total
	1-4 Emps.	5-9 Emps.	10-19 Emps.	20-49 Emps.	50-99 Emps.	100-249 Emps.	250-499 Emps.	>500 Emps.	Non-Employer	Employ-ment
2016	2,721.0	2,310.9	4,060.8	7,479.3	5,945.7	11,844.3	11,741.4	4,115.9	293.2	50,512.5
2017	2,882.2	2,447.8	4,301.3	7,922.2	6,297.7	12,545.7	12,436.6	4,343.8	310.5	53,487.7
2018	3,069.8	2,607.1	4,581.4	8,438.0	6,707.8	13,362.5	13,246.3	4,593.9	330.7	56,937.5

3-YEAR TREND – ESTIMATED NUMBER OF EMPLOYEES

Year	Employee Size of Establishment									Total
	1-4 Emps.	5-9 Emps.	10-19 Emps.	20-49 Emps.	50-99 Emps.	100-249 Emps.	250-499 Emps.	>500 Emps.	Non-Employer	Employ-ment
2016	5,092	3,818	6,255	9,633	6,875	10,787	7,319	2,989	2,166	54,935
2017	5,142	3,855	6,316	9,727	6,942	10,892	7,390	3,018	2,187	55,468
2018	5,241	3,929	6,437	9,913	7,075	11,101	7,532	3,076	2,229	56,533

Men's & Boys' Clothing Wholesales Industry (NAICS 42432)

Sub-Industries – 2017 Estimated Industry Sales, Establishments & Employment

Sub-Industries	Cate-gory*	Establish-ments	Sales ($Mill)	Employ-ment
Men's and boy's clothing	Major1	2,956	23,990.4	26,448
Men's and boys' hats, scarves, and gloves	Minor1	30	164.4	163
Caps, men's and boys'	Minor2	93	597.0	1,278
Gloves, men's and boys'	Minor2	134	1,010.7	1,183
Hats, men's and boys'	Minor2	122	633.1	657
Mittens, men's and boys'	Minor2	2	14.7	80
Mufflers, men's and boys'	Minor2	1	2.0	2
Scarves, men's and boys'	Minor2	6	16.7	112
Men's and boys' robes, nightwear, and undergarments	Minor1	18	55.5	114
Nightwear, men's and boys'	Minor2	5	56.2	162
Robes, men's and boys'	Minor2	3	20.1	19
Underwear, men's and boys'	Minor2	53	342.9	333
Men's and boys' outerwear	Minor1	83	828.9	1,039
Coats, men's and boys'	Minor2	29	131.0	230
Leather and sheep lined clothing, men's and boys'	Minor2	39	161.8	379
Fur clothing, men's and boys'	Minor2	8	22.7	30
Men's and boys' furnishings	Minor1	29	251.3	207
Apparel belts, men's and boys'	Minor2	173	1,150.5	1,148
Handkerchiefs, men's and boys'	Minor2	1	6.7	7
Hosiery, men's and boys'	Minor2	60	308.8	333
Neckwear, men's and boys'	Minor2	55	488.0	265
Umbrellas, men's and boys'	Minor2	32	338.9	182
Men's and boys' suits and trousers	Minor1	38	252.0	336
Suits, men's and boys'	Minor2	21	164.4	305
Trousers, men's and boys'	Minor2	19	263.4	273
Men's and boys' sportswear and work clothing	Minor1	199	1,142.4	1,457
Beachwear, men's and boys'	Minor2	33	181.8	190
Sportswear, men's and boys'	Minor2	865	13,449.1	10,387
Uniforms, men's and boys'	Minor2	303	2,632.5	3,405
Work clothing, men's and boys'	Minor2	117	619.0	1,039
Shirts, men's and boys'	Minor2	363	3,147.2	3,422
Sweaters, men's and boys'	Minor2	37	1,043.5	281

*Category-Major categories (Major1) are more general descriptions for companies that self-selected to capture the many functions they perform in the industry. Minor categories (Minor1, Minor2) are more specific for companies that have more detailed functions (Minor1 is a larger category than Minor2). Minor categories figures (sales, etc.) can be aggregated to larger minor categories (Minor2 sums to Minor1) and major categories overall figures.

WOMEN'S & CHILDREN'S CLOTHING WHOLESALE (NAICS 42433)

NAICS 42433: Women's & Children's Clothing Wholesales.
Establishments primarily engaged in the wholesale distribution of women's, children's, and infants' clothing and accessories, including hosiery, lingerie, millinery, and furs.

INDUSTRY ESTABLISHMENTS, SALES & EMPLOYMENT TRENDS

	Year					Percent Chg. Year-to-Year			
	2014	2015	2016	2017	2018	14-15	15-16	16-17	17-18
Establishments	12,612	12,444	12,940	13,337	13,876	-1.3%	4.0%	3.1%	4.0%
Sales ($Millions)	70,809	72,190	77,181	81,681	87,010	2.0%	6.9%	5.8%	6.5%
Employment	93,439	92,194	95,867	98,811	102,803	-1.3%	4.0%	3.1%	4.0%
Sales ($M)/Estab.	5.61	5.80	5.96	6.12	6.27	3.3%	2.8%	2.7%	2.4%
Sales ($)/Emp.	757,809	783,023	805,085	826,640	846,375	3.3%	2.8%	2.7%	2.4%

3-YEAR TREND — ESTIMATED NUMBER OF ESTABLISHMENTS

Year	Employee Size of Establishment									Total
	1-4 Emps.	5-9 Emps.	10-19 Emps.	20-49 Emps.	50-99 Emps.	100-249 Emps.	250-499 Emps.	>500 Emps.	Non-Employer	Employ-ment
2016	4,998	1,296	896	605	223	115	28	6	4,774	12,940
2017	5,151	1,336	923	624	229	118	29	6	4,920	13,337
2018	5,359	1,390	960	649	239	123	30	7	5,119	13,876

3-YEAR TREND — ESTIMATED INDUSTRY SALES ($MILLIONS)

Year	Employee Size of Establishment									Total
	1-4 Emps.	5-9 Emps.	10-19 Emps.	20-49 Emps.	50-99 Emps.	100-249 Emps.	250-499 Emps.	>500 Emps.	Non-Employer	Employ-ment
2016	6,377.6	4,346.4	7,554.9	13,514.6	10,926.5	15,199.4	12,349.8	6,295.1	617.2	77,181.4
2017	6,757.2	4,605.0	8,004.5	14,318.8	11,576.7	16,103.9	13,084.7	6,576.1	653.9	81,680.8
2018	7,208.5	4,912.6	8,539.2	15,275.3	12,350.0	17,179.5	13,958.7	6,888.9	697.6	87,010.3

3-YEAR TREND — ESTIMATED NUMBER OF EMPLOYEES

Year	Employee Size of Establishment									Total
	1-4 Emps.	5-9 Emps.	10-19 Emps.	20-49 Emps.	50-99 Emps.	100-249 Emps.	250-499 Emps.	>500 Emps.	Non-Employer	Employ-ment
2016	12,494	7,516	12,181	18,221	13,225	14,490	8,058	4,908	4,774	95,867
2017	12,878	7,747	12,555	18,780	13,631	14,935	8,306	5,059	4,920	98,811
2018	13,398	8,060	13,063	19,539	14,182	15,539	8,641	5,263	5,119	102,803

WOMEN'S & CHILDREN'S CLOTHING WHOLESALE (NAICS 42433)

SUB-INDUSTRIES — 2017 ESTIMATED INDUSTRY SALES, ESTABLISHMENTS & EMPLOYMENT

Sub-Industries	Category*	Establishments	Sales ($Mill)	Employment
Women's and children's clothing	Major1	5,982	41,481.2	47,891
Women's and children's outerwear	Minor1	123	2,026.4	1,530
Coats: women's, children's, and infants'	Minor2	29	54.2	208
Fur clothing, women's and children's	Minor2	98	261.5	501
Leather and sheep lined clothing, women's and children's	Minor2	23	49.4	101
Women's and children's lingerie and undergarments	Minor1	126	2,097.7	1,259
Corsets	Minor2	31	33.2	91
Lingerie	Minor2	926	1,708.2	5,037
Nightwear: women's, children's, and infants'	Minor2	25	161.1	447
Underwear: women's, children's, and infants'	Minor2	56	223.4	311
Women's and children's sportswear and swimsuits	Minor1	181	870.3	1,320
Sportswear, women's and children's	Minor2	653	6,553.7	10,409
Swimsuits: women's, children's, and infants'	Minor2	123	437.2	686
Women's and children's accessories	Minor1	557	3,907.9	5,854
Apparel belts, women's and children's	Minor2	369	2,971.2	2,485
Caps and gowns	Minor2	22	66.4	121
Gloves, women's and children's	Minor2	26	92.3	129
Handbags	Minor2	582	6,204.7	4,401
Handkerchiefs, women's and children's	Minor2	1	2.4	3
Hats: women's, children's, and infants'	Minor2	95	288.2	491
Hosiery: women's, children's, and infants'	Minor2	233	2,895.9	1,873
Millinery	Minor2	42	50.2	150
Mittens: women's, children's, and infants'	Minor2	3	1.6	5
Purses	Minor2	982	736.7	2,416
Scarves, women's and children's	Minor2	32	43.7	99
Children's goods	Minor1	433	1,642.7	2,026
Baby goods	Minor2	642	2,126.8	2,833
Diapers	Minor2	313	947.2	809
Infants' wear	Minor2	148	779.6	1,056
Women's and children's dresses, suits, skirts, and blouses	Minor1	129	1,360.1	1,141
Blouses	Minor2	38	201.6	482
Dresses	Minor2	215	1,126.1	1,669
Skirts	Minor2	61	91.5	153
Suits: women's, children's, and infants'	Minor2	6	2.4	24
Coordinate sets: women's, children's, and infants'	Minor2	31	183.8	802

*Category-Major categories (Major1) are more general descriptions for companies that self-selected to capture the many functions they perform in the industry. Minor categories (Minor1, Minor2) are more specific for companies that have more detailed functions (Minor1 is a larger category than Minor2). Minor categories figures (sales, etc.) can be aggregated to larger minor categories (Minor2 sums to Minor1) and major categories overall figures.

GENERAL-LINE GROCERY WHOLESALE INDUSTRY (NAICS 42441)

NAICS 42441: General-Line Grocery Wholesale. Establishments primarily engaged in the wholesale distribution of a general line of groceries. Establishments primarily engaged in roasting coffee, blending tea, or grinding and packaging spices are classified under food processing.

INDUSTRY ESTABLISHMENTS, SALES & EMPLOYMENT TRENDS

	Year					Percent Chg. Year-to-Year			
	2014	2015	2016	2017	2018	14-15	15-16	16-17	17-18
Establishments	3,298	3,235	3,148	3,108	3,040	-1.9%	-2.7%	-1.3%	-2.2%
Sales ($Millions)	127,660	130,907	132,776	136,146	137,975	2.5%	1.4%	2.5%	1.3%
Employment	115,289	113,100	110,066	108,666	106,269	-1.9%	-2.7%	-1.3%	-2.2%
Sales ($M)/Estab.	38.71	40.47	42.18	43.80	45.39	4.5%	4.2%	3.9%	3.6%
Sales ($)/Emp.	1,107,303	1,157,451	1,206,324	1,252,890	1,298,351	4.5%	4.2%	3.9%	3.6%

3-YEAR TREND — ESTIMATED NUMBER OF ESTABLISHMENTS

Year	Employee Size of Establishment									Total
	1-4 Emps.	5-9 Emps.	10-19 Emps.	20-49 Emps.	50-99 Emps.	100-249 Emps.	250-499 Emps.	>500 Emps.	Non-Employer	Employ-ment
2016	1,233	404	268	269	197	166	118	36	457	3,148
2017	1,217	399	265	266	194	164	117	36	451	3,108
2018	1,190	390	259	260	190	160	114	35	441	3,040

3-YEAR TREND — ESTIMATED INDUSTRY SALES ($MILLIONS)

Year	Employee Size of Establishment									Total
	1-4 Emps.	5-9 Emps.	10-19 Emps.	20-49 Emps.	50-99 Emps.	100-249 Emps.	250-499 Emps.	>500 Emps.	Non-Employer	Employ-ment
2016	1,605.5	1,382.6	2,309.7	6,135.3	9,851.9	22,428.0	53,870.3	35,098.3	94.3	132,775.7
2017	1,644.5	1,416.2	2,365.9	6,284.5	10,091.6	22,973.6	55,180.9	36,092.2	96.6	136,146.1
2018	1,663.6	1,432.6	2,393.3	6,357.3	10,208.5	23,239.8	55,820.3	36,761.2	97.7	137,974.6

3-YEAR TREND — ESTIMATED NUMBER OF EMPLOYEES

Year	Employee Size of Establishment									Total
	1-4 Emps.	5-9 Emps.	10-19 Emps.	20-49 Emps.	50-99 Emps.	100-249 Emps.	250-499 Emps.	>500 Emps.	Non-Employer	Employ-ment
2016	3,081	2,342	3,648	8,104	11,682	20,948	34,438	25,366	457	110,066
2017	3,042	2,312	3,602	8,001	11,533	20,681	33,999	25,044	451	108,666
2018	2,975	2,261	3,523	7,824	11,279	20,225	33,250	24,491	441	106,269

GENERAL-LINE GROCERY WHOLESALE INDUSTRY (NAICS 42441)

SUB-INDUSTRIES — 2017 ESTIMATED INDUSTRY SALES, ESTABLISHMENTS & EMPLOYMENT

Sub-Industries	Cate-gory*	Establish-ments	Sales ($Mill)	Employ-ment
Groceries, general line	Major1	1,738	127,598.3	76,387
Food brokers	Minor2	1,370	8,547.8	32,279

*Category-Major categories (Major1) are more general descriptions for companies that self-selected to capture the many functions they perform in the industry. Minor categories (Minor1, Minor2) are more specific for companies that have more detailed functions (Minor1 is a larger category than Minor2). Minor categories figures (sales, etc.) can be aggregated to larger minor categories (Minor2 sums to Minor1) and major categories overall figures.

BEER & ALE WHOLESALE INDUSTRY (NAICS 42481)

NAICS 42481: Beer & Ale Wholesale. Establishments primarily engaged in the wholesale distribution of beer, ale, porter, and other fermented malt beverages.

INDUSTRY ESTABLISHMENTS, SALES & EMPLOYMENT TRENDS

	Year					Percent Chg. Year-to-Year			
	2014	2015	2016	2017	2018	14-15	15-16	16-17	17-18
Establishments	2,654	2,568	2,478	2,458	2,461	-3.2%	-3.5%	-0.8%	0.1%
Sales ($Millions)	58,222	61,146	63,520	67,435	71,845	5.0%	3.9%	6.2%	6.5%
Employment	94,766	91,713	88,490	87,771	87,878	-3.2%	-3.5%	-0.8%	0.1%
Sales ($M)/Estab.	21.94	23.81	25.63	27.44	29.20	8.5%	7.7%	7.0%	6.4%
Sales ($)/Emp.	614,382	666,711	717,813	768,298	817,553	8.5%	7.7%	7.0%	6.4%

3-YEAR TREND — ESTIMATED NUMBER OF ESTABLISHMENTS

Year	Employee Size of Establishment									Total
	1-4 Emps.	5-9 Emps.	10-19 Emps.	20-49 Emps.	50-99 Emps.	100-249 Emps.	250-499 Emps.	>500 Emps.	Non-Employer	Employ-ment
2016	443	167	202	381	291	264	64	4	662	2,478
2017	439	166	200	378	289	262	64	4	656	2,458
2018	440	166	200	378	289	262	64	4	657	2,461

3-YEAR TREND — ESTIMATED INDUSTRY SALES ($MILLIONS)

Year	Employee Size of Establishment									Total
	1-4 Emps.	5-9 Emps.	10-19 Emps.	20-49 Emps.	50-99 Emps.	100-249 Emps.	250-499 Emps.	>500 Emps.	Non-Employer	Employ-ment
2016	387.8	385.0	1,168.2	5,840.4	9,817.6	24,000.9	19,723.2	2,090.1	106.3	63,519.5
2017	411.7	408.7	1,240.2	6,200.4	10,422.7	25,480.2	20,938.8	2,219.0	112.9	67,434.6
2018	438.7	435.4	1,321.3	6,605.9	11,104.5	27,146.7	22,308.3	2,364.2	120.3	71,845.2

3-YEAR TREND — ESTIMATED NUMBER OF EMPLOYEES

Year	Employee Size of Establishment									Total
	1-4 Emps.	5-9 Emps.	10-19 Emps.	20-49 Emps.	50-99 Emps.	100-249 Emps.	250-499 Emps.	>500 Emps.	Non-Employer	Employ-ment
2016	1,107	969	2,743	11,468	17,306	33,323	18,743	2,170	662	88,490
2017	1,098	962	2,721	11,374	17,165	33,052	18,591	2,153	656	87,771
2018	1,099	963	2,724	11,388	17,186	33,093	18,613	2,155	657	87,878

BEER & ALE WHOLESALE INDUSTRY
(NAICS 42481)

SUB-INDUSTRIES – 2017 ESTIMATED INDUSTRY
SALES, ESTABLISHMENTS & EMPLOYMENT

Sub-Industries	Category*	Establish-ments	Sales ($Mill)	Employ-ment
Beer and ale	Major1	562	8,806.4	19,624
Ale	Minor2	93	701.5	1,094
Beer and other fermented malt liquors	Minor2	1,131	57,798.1	66,548
Porter	Minor2	672	128.6	505

*Category-Major categories (Major1) are more general descriptions for companies that self-selected to capture the many functions they perform in the industry. Minor categories (Minor1, Minor2) are more specific for companies that have more detailed functions (Minor1 is a larger category than Minor2). Minor categories figures (sales, etc.) can be aggregated to larger minor categories (Minor2 sums to Minor1) and major categories overall figures.

WINE & ALCOHOLIC BEVERAGES WHOLESALES (NAICS 42482)

NAICS 42482: Wine & Alcoholic Beverages Wholesales. Establishments primarily engaged in the wholesale distribution of distilled spirits, including neutral spirits and ethyl alcohol used in blended wines and distilled liquors.

INDUSTRY ESTABLISHMENTS, SALES & EMPLOYMENT TRENDS

	Year					Percent Chg. Year-to-Year			
	2014	2015	2016	2017	2018	14-15	15-16	16-17	17-18
Establishments	3,468	3,559	3,794	3,985	4,225	2.6%	6.6%	5.0%	6.0%
Sales ($Millions)	78,684	85,713	96,104	105,942	117,309	8.9%	12.1%	10.2%	10.7%
Employment	75,840	77,830	82,968	87,147	92,397	2.6%	6.6%	5.0%	6.0%
Sales ($M)/Estab.	22.69	24.08	25.33	26.58	27.76	6.1%	5.2%	5.0%	4.4%
Sales ($)/Emp.	1,037,503	1,101,289	1,158,324	1,215,673	1,269,617	6.1%	5.2%	5.0%	4.4%

3-YEAR TREND – ESTIMATED NUMBER OF ESTABLISHMENTS

Year	Employee Size of Establishment									Total
	1-4 Emps.	5-9 Emps.	10-19 Emps.	20-49 Emps.	50-99 Emps.	100-249 Emps.	250-499 Emps.	>500 Emps.	Non-Employer	Employ-ment
2016	1,374	470	323	264	131	128	60	31	1,013	3,794
2017	1,443	494	339	277	138	134	63	32	1,064	3,985
2018	1,530	524	359	294	146	143	67	34	1,128	4,225

3-YEAR TREND – ESTIMATED INDUSTRY SALES ($MILLIONS)

Year	Employee Size of Establishment									Total
	1-4 Emps.	5-9 Emps.	10-19 Emps.	20-49 Emps.	50-99 Emps.	100-249 Emps.	250-499 Emps.	>500 Emps.	Non-Employer	Employ-ment
2016	1,857.9	1,671.8	2,884.2	6,236.7	6,826.3	17,938.2	28,421.2	30,111.0	157.0	96,104.3
2017	2,057.7	1,851.6	3,194.5	6,907.6	7,560.6	19,867.9	31,478.6	32,849.4	173.9	105,941.8
2018	2,290.7	2,061.3	3,556.2	7,689.8	8,416.8	22,117.7	35,043.1	35,940.1	193.6	117,309.3

3-YEAR TREND – ESTIMATED NUMBER OF EMPLOYEES

Year	Employee Size of Establishment									Total
	1-4 Emps.	5-9 Emps.	10-19 Emps.	20-49 Emps.	50-99 Emps.	100-249 Emps.	250-499 Emps.	>500 Emps.	Non-Employer	Employ-ment
2016	3,435	2,728	4,389	7,936	7,798	16,141	17,503	22,024	1,013	82,968
2017	3,608	2,866	4,610	8,336	8,191	16,953	18,385	23,134	1,064	87,147
2018	3,826	3,039	4,888	8,838	8,684	17,975	19,493	24,527	1,128	92,397

WINE & ALCOHOLIC BEVERAGES WHOLESALES (NAICS 42482)

SUB-INDUSTRIES – 2017 ESTIMATED INDUSTRY SALES, ESTABLISHMENTS & EMPLOYMENT

Sub-Industries	Category*	Establishments	Sales ($Mill)	Employment
Wine and distilled beverages	Major1	393	21,534.9	18,482
Wine	Minor1	2,384	50,509.7	37,692
Brandy and brandy spirits	Minor2	8	316.3	97
Wine coolers, alcoholic	Minor2	13	575.6	433
Liquor	Minor1	1,095	29,626.6	27,113
Cocktails, alcoholic: premixed	Minor2	9	96.7	172
Neutral spirits	Minor2	8	130.3	224
Bottling wines and liquors	Minor2	75	3,151.7	2,933

*Category-Major categories (Major1) are more general descriptions for companies that self-selected to capture the many functions they perform in the industry. Minor categories (Minor1, Minor2) are more specific for companies that have more detailed functions (Minor1 is a larger category than Minor2). Minor categories figures (sales, etc.) can be aggregated to larger minor categories (Minor2 sums to Minor1) and major categories overall figures.

BOOK/PERIODICAL/NEWSPAPER WHOLESALES (NAICS 42492)

NAICS 42492: Book & Periodical & Newspaper Wholesales. Establishments primarily engaged in the wholesale distribution of books, periodicals, and newspapers.

INDUSTRY ESTABLISHMENTS, SALES & EMPLOYMENT TRENDS

	Year					Percent Chg. Year-to-Year			
	2014	2015	2016	2017	2018	14-15	15-16	16-17	17-18
Establishments	7,134	6,931	6,495	6,285	6,138	-2.8%	-6.3%	-3.2%	-2.3%
Sales ($Millions)	19,675	19,875	19,365	19,394	19,538	1.0%	-2.6%	0.1%	0.7%
Employment	43,134	41,905	39,272	38,000	37,115	-2.8%	-6.3%	-3.2%	-2.3%
Sales ($M)/Estab.	2.76	2.87	2.98	3.09	3.18	4.0%	4.0%	3.5%	3.1%
Sales ($)/Emp.	456,131	474,289	493,099	510,368	526,414	4.0%	4.0%	3.5%	3.1%

3-YEAR TREND – ESTIMATED NUMBER OF ESTABLISHMENTS

Year	Employee Size of Establishment									Total
	1-4 Emps.	5-9 Emps.	10-19 Emps.	20-49 Emps.	50-99 Emps.	100-249 Emps.	250-499 Emps.	>500 Emps.	Non-Employer	Employ-ment
2016	1,043	295	225	163	81	42	13	13	4,621	6,495
2017	1,010	285	218	158	78	41	12	12	4,471	6,285
2018	986	279	213	154	77	40	12	12	4,367	6,138

3-YEAR TREND – ESTIMATED INDUSTRY SALES ($MILLIONS)

Year	Employee Size of Establishment									Total
	1-4 Emps.	5-9 Emps.	10-19 Emps.	20-49 Emps.	50-99 Emps.	100-249 Emps.	250-499 Emps.	>500 Emps.	Non-Employer	Employ-ment
2016	727.7	540.7	1,036.6	1,988.5	2,173.3	3,027.5	3,105.5	6,463.7	301.6	19,365.1
2017	726.7	540.0	1,035.3	1,985.9	2,170.5	3,023.5	3,101.5	6,509.4	301.2	19,393.9
2018	730.6	542.9	1,040.8	1,996.5	2,182.1	3,039.7	3,118.1	6,584.4	302.8	19,537.8

3-YEAR TREND – ESTIMATED NUMBER OF EMPLOYEES

Year	Employee Size of Establishment									Total
	1-4 Emps.	5-9 Emps.	10-19 Emps.	20-49 Emps.	50-99 Emps.	100-249 Emps.	250-499 Emps.	>500 Emps.	Non-Employer	Employ-ment
2016	2,608	1,711	3,058	4,906	4,813	5,281	3,708	8,566	4,621	39,272
2017	2,524	1,656	2,959	4,747	4,657	5,110	3,588	8,288	4,471	38,000
2018	2,465	1,617	2,890	4,636	4,549	4,991	3,504	8,095	4,367	37,115

SUB-INDUSTRIES — 2017 ESTIMATED INDUSTRY SALES, ESTABLISHMENTS & EMPLOYMENT

Sub-Industries	Cate-gory*	Establish-ments	Sales ($Mill)	Employ-ment
Books, periodicals, and newspapers	Major1	336	2,554.2	7,541
Books	Minor2	4,466	11,202.9	20,088
Magazines	Minor2	1,101	3,929.6	7,365
Newspapers	Minor2	284	1,397.1	2,309
Periodicals	Minor2	32	227.4	529
Comic books	Minor2	67	82.7	166

*Category-Major categories (Major1) are more general descriptions for companies that self-selected to capture the many functions they perform in the industry. Minor categories (Minor1, Minor2) are more specific for companies that have more detailed functions (Minor1 is a larger category than Minor2). Minor categories figures (sales, etc.) can be aggregated to larger minor categories (Minor2 sums to Minor1) and major categories overall figures.

NEW CAR DEALERS INDUSTRY
(NAICS 44111)

NAICS 44111: New Car Dealers. Establishments primarily engaged in the retail sale of new automobiles or new and used automobiles. These establishments frequently maintain repair departments and carry stocks of replacement parts, tires, batteries, and automotive accessories. These establishments also frequently sell pickups and vans at retail.

INDUSTRY ESTABLISHMENTS, SALES & EMPLOYMENT TRENDS

	Year					Percent Chg. Year-to-Year			
	2014	2015	2016	2017	2018	14-15	15-16	16-17	17-18
Establishments	36,461	35,650	34,960	34,449	34,432	-2.2%	-1.9%	-1.5%	0.0%
Sales ($Millions)	687,139	702,621	717,866	735,142	761,232	2.3%	2.2%	2.4%	3.5%
Employment	953,494	932,293	914,247	900,880	900,449	-2.2%	-1.9%	-1.5%	0.0%
Sales ($M)/Estab.	18.85	19.71	20.53	21.34	22.11	4.6%	4.2%	3.9%	3.6%
Sales ($)/Emp.	720,654	753,648	785,200	816,027	845,392	4.6%	4.2%	3.9%	3.6%

3-YEAR TREND — ESTIMATED NUMBER OF ESTABLISHMENTS

Year	Employee Size of Establishment									Total
	1-4 Emps.	5-9 Emps.	10-19 Emps.	20-49 Emps.	50-99 Emps.	100-249 Emps.	250-499 Emps.	>500 Emps.	Non-Employer	Employ-ment
2016	2,975	1,293	2,095	6,300	5,158	2,470	154	6	14,509	34,960
2017	2,932	1,275	2,064	6,207	5,082	2,434	152	6	14,297	34,449
2018	2,930	1,274	2,063	6,204	5,080	2,433	152	6	14,290	34,432

3-YEAR TREND — ESTIMATED INDUSTRY SALES ($MILLIONS)

Year	Employee Size of Establishment									Total
	1-4 Emps.	5-9 Emps.	10-19 Emps.	20-49 Emps.	50-99 Emps.	100-249 Emps.	250-499 Emps.	>500 Emps.	Non-Employer	Employ-ment
2016	3,306.4	3,778.0	15,388.4	122,473.6	220,418.2	284,498.5	59,930.4	4,677.5	3,395.4	717,866.5
2017	3,385.8	3,868.8	15,758.3	125,417.6	225,716.6	291,337.3	61,371.0	4,809.6	3,477.0	735,142.1
2018	3,506.0	4,006.1	16,317.6	129,868.6	233,727.1	301,676.6	63,549.0	4,980.9	3,600.4	761,232.2

3-YEAR TREND — ESTIMATED NUMBER OF EMPLOYEES

Year	Employee Size of Establishment									Total
	1-4 Emps.	5-9 Emps.	10-19 Emps.	20-49 Emps.	50-99 Emps.	100-249 Emps.	250-499 Emps.	>500 Emps.	Non-Employer	Employ-ment
2016	7,438	7,502	28,493	189,617	306,361	311,463	44,907	3,956	14,509	914,247
2017	7,329	7,392	28,076	186,845	301,882	306,909	44,251	3,898	14,297	900,880
2018	7,326	7,389	28,063	186,755	301,737	306,762	44,229	3,896	14,290	900,449

NEW CAR DEALERS INDUSTRY
(NAICS 44111)

SUB-INDUSTRIES – 2017 ESTIMATED INDUSTRY SALES, ESTABLISHMENTS & EMPLOYMENT

Sub-Industries	Cate-gory*	Establish-ments	Sales ($Mill)	Employ-ment
New and used car dealers	Major1	9,941	139,896.8	86,572
Automobiles, new and used	Minor2	21,996	571,726.2	783,097
Pickups, new and used	Minor2	526	2,259.9	4,831
Trucks, tractors, and trailers: new and used	Minor2	1,947	20,811.9	25,961
Vans, new and used	Minor2	39	447.3	419

*Category-Major categories (Major1) are more general descriptions for companies that self-selected to capture the many functions they perform in the industry. Minor categories (Minor1, Minor2) are more specific for companies that have more detailed functions (Minor1 is a larger category than Minor2). Minor categories figures (sales, etc.) can be aggregated to larger minor categories (Minor2 sums to Minor1) and major categories overall figures.

FURNITURE STORES INDUSTRY
(NAICS 44211)

NAICS 44211: Furniture Stores. Establishments primarily engaged in the retail sale of household furniture. These stores may also sell homefurnishings, major appliances, and floor coverings.

INDUSTRY ESTABLISHMENTS, SALES & EMPLOYMENT TRENDS

	Year					Percent Chg. Year-to-Year			
	2014	2015	2016	2017	2018	14-15	15-16	16-17	17-18
Establishments	29,014	27,474	26,609	26,371	26,255	-5.3%	-3.1%	-0.9%	-0.4%
Sales ($Millions)	46,259	45,098	44,840	45,535	46,342	-2.5%	-0.6%	1.6%	1.8%
Employment	204,335	193,488	187,401	185,721	184,902	-5.3%	-3.1%	-0.9%	-0.4%
Sales ($M)/Estab.	1.59	1.64	1.69	1.73	1.77	3.0%	2.7%	2.5%	2.2%
Sales ($)/Emp.	226,387	233,079	239,272	245,183	250,629	3.0%	2.7%	2.5%	2.2%

3-YEAR TREND – ESTIMATED NUMBER OF ESTABLISHMENTS

Year	Employee Size of Establishment									Total
	1-4 Emps.	5-9 Emps.	10-19 Emps.	20-49 Emps.	50-99 Emps.	100-249 Emps.	250-499 Emps.	>500 Emps.	Non-Employer	Employ-ment
2016	11,869	4,782	3,083	1,548	225	62	39	6	4,996	26,609
2017	11,762	4,739	3,056	1,534	223	62	39	5	4,951	26,371
2018	11,710	4,718	3,042	1,527	222	62	39	5	4,929	26,255

3-YEAR TREND – ESTIMATED INDUSTRY SALES ($MILLIONS)

Year	Employee Size of Establishment									Total
	1-4 Emps.	5-9 Emps.	10-19 Emps.	20-49 Emps.	50-99 Emps.	100-249 Emps.	250-499 Emps.	>500 Emps.	Non-Employer	Employ-ment
2016	5,013.1	5,308.7	8,608.1	11,439.8	3,649.9	2,730.3	5,819.1	1,721.9	549.0	44,839.8
2017	5,090.3	5,390.5	8,740.8	11,616.1	3,706.1	2,772.4	5,908.8	1,752.9	557.4	45,535.4
2018	5,180.2	5,485.7	8,895.1	11,821.2	3,771.6	2,821.3	6,013.1	1,786.2	567.3	46,341.6

3-YEAR TREND – ESTIMATED NUMBER OF EMPLOYEES

Year	Employee Size of Establishment									Total
	1-4 Emps.	5-9 Emps.	10-19 Emps.	20-49 Emps.	50-99 Emps.	100-249 Emps.	250-499 Emps.	>500 Emps.	Non-Employer	Employ-ment
2016	29,671	27,735	41,934	46,598	13,347	7,864	11,472	3,784	4,996	187,401
2017	29,405	27,486	41,558	46,180	13,227	7,794	11,369	3,750	4,951	185,721
2018	29,276	27,365	41,375	45,977	13,169	7,759	11,319	3,734	4,929	184,902

FURNITURE STORES INDUSTRY
(NAICS 44211)

SUB-INDUSTRIES — 2017 ESTIMATED INDUSTRY SALES, ESTABLISHMENTS & EMPLOYMENT

Sub-Industries	Category*	Establishments	Sales ($Mill)	Employment
Furniture stores	Major1	18,489	34,850.1	135,684
Beds and accessories	Minor1	981	794.9	5,041
Bedding and bedsprings	Minor2	357	136.3	1,429
Mattresses	Minor2	1,659	1,083.0	7,857
Waterbeds and accessories	Minor2	119	82.1	1,020
Customized furniture and cabinets	Minor1	537	631.8	3,147
Cabinet work, custom	Minor2	1,539	2,061.1	7,948
Custom made furniture, except cabinets	Minor2	405	389.8	1,748
Bar fixtures, equipment and supplies	Minor2	44	50.5	196
Cabinets, except custom made: kitchen	Minor2	372	420.4	1,698
Juvenile furniture	Minor2	208	283.0	4,278
Office furniture	Minor2	1,109	4,045.7	12,436
Outdoor and garden furniture	Minor2	418	531.9	2,272
Unfinished furniture	Minor2	136	174.7	967

*Category-Major categories (Major1) are more general descriptions for companies that self-selected to capture the many functions they perform in the industry. Minor categories (Minor1, Minor2) are more specific for companies that have more detailed functions (Minor1 is a larger category than Minor2). Minor categories figures (sales, etc.) can be aggregated to larger minor categories (Minor2 sums to Minor1) and major categories overall figures.

APPLIANCE/TV/ELECTRONICS STORES INDUSTRY (NAICS 44311)

NAICS 44311: Appliance/TV/Electronics Stores. Establishments primarily engaged in the retail sale of electric and gas refrigerators, stoves, and other household appliances, such as electric irons, percolators, hot plates, and vacuum cleaners. Many such stores also sell radio and television sets. Retail stores operated by public utility companies and primarily engaged in the sale of electric and gas appliances for household use are classified in this business.

INDUSTRY ESTABLISHMENTS, SALES & EMPLOYMENT TRENDS

	Year					Percent Chg. Year-to-Year			
	2014	2015	2016	2017	2018	14-15	15-16	16-17	17-18
Establishments	56,777	55,927	56,483	59,147	62,222	-1.5%	1.0%	4.7%	5.2%
Sales ($Millions)	95,042	97,403	101,965	110,382	119,698	2.5%	4.7%	8.3%	8.4%
Employment	415,311	409,095	413,159	432,649	455,142	-1.5%	1.0%	4.7%	5.2%
Sales ($M)/Estab.	1.67	1.74	1.81	1.87	1.92	4.0%	3.7%	3.4%	3.1%
Sales ($)/Emp.	228,846	238,092	246,793	255,131	262,992	4.0%	3.7%	3.4%	3.1%

3-YEAR TREND – ESTIMATED NUMBER OF ESTABLISHMENTS

Year	Employee Size of Establishment									Total
	1-4 Emps.	5-9 Emps.	10-19 Emps.	20-49 Emps.	50-99 Emps.	100-249 Emps.	250-499 Emps.	>500 Emps.	Non-Employer	Employ-ment
2016	22,083	17,214	3,942	1,642	1,051	553	26	6	9,965	56,483
2017	23,125	18,026	4,128	1,720	1,100	579	27	6	10,435	59,147
2018	24,327	18,964	4,343	1,809	1,157	609	28	7	10,978	62,222

3-YEAR TREND – ESTIMATED INDUSTRY SALES ($MILLIONS)

Year	Employee Size of Establishment									Total
	1-4 Emps.	5-9 Emps.	10-19 Emps.	20-49 Emps.	50-99 Emps.	100-249 Emps.	250-499 Emps.	>500 Emps.	Non-Employer	Employ-ment
2016	9,525.2	19,516.0	11,239.9	12,394.2	17,426.2	24,728.8	3,897.5	2,322.3	915.0	101,965.0
2017	10,318.4	21,141.1	12,175.8	13,426.2	18,877.3	26,787.9	4,222.1	2,442.2	991.2	110,382.1
2018	11,197.0	22,941.4	13,212.6	14,569.6	20,484.8	29,069.1	4,581.6	2,566.8	1,075.6	119,698.5

3-YEAR TREND – ESTIMATED NUMBER OF EMPLOYEES

Year	Employee Size of Establishment									Total
	1-4 Emps.	5-9 Emps.	10-19 Emps.	20-49 Emps.	50-99 Emps.	100-249 Emps.	250-499 Emps.	>500 Emps.	Non-Employer	Employ-ment
2016	55,208	99,843	53,618	49,438	62,401	69,748	7,524	5,414	9,965	413,159
2017	57,812	104,553	56,147	51,770	65,345	73,039	7,879	5,669	10,435	432,649
2018	60,817	109,989	59,066	54,461	68,742	76,836	8,289	5,964	10,978	455,142

APPLIANCE/TV/ELECTRONICS STORES INDUSTRY (NAICS 44311)

SUB-INDUSTRIES – 2017 ESTIMATED INDUSTRY SALES, ESTABLISHMENTS & EMPLOYMENT

Sub-Industries	Category*	Establishments	Sales ($Mill)	Employment
Household appliance stores	Major1	6,993	20,003.6	92,810
Gas household appliances	Minor1	298	510.9	1,483
Gas ranges	Minor2	26	16.7	59
Electric household appliances	Minor1	1,944	3,260.4	10,624
Air conditioning room units, self-contained	Minor2	574	781.0	3,591
Electric household appliances, major	Minor2	1,958	4,371.9	11,694
Electric household appliances, small	Minor2	151	514.3	555
Electric ranges	Minor2	38	81.6	228
Fans, electric	Minor2	141	229.3	548
Garbage disposals	Minor2	129	185.9	583
Microwave ovens	Minor2	29	42.1	102
Vacuum cleaners	Minor2	4,116	3,160.3	10,991
Appliance parts	Minor2	521	512.2	2,016
Kitchens, complete (sinks, cabinets, etc.)	Minor2	578	1,160.5	2,647
Sewing machines	Minor2	2,053	1,777.4	5,771
Stoves, household, nec	Minor2	130	133.1	358
Suntanning equipment and supplies	Minor2	21	36.1	106
Kerosene heaters	Minor2	14	16.7	50
Radio, television, and electronic stores	Major1	19,202	68,065.5	173,256
Antennas	Minor1	482	162.4	1,718
Antennas, satellite dish	Minor2	3,782	651.4	21,462
Video cameras, recorders, and accessories	Minor1	545	337.4	3,936
Video cameras and accessories	Minor2	176	88.0	1,122
Video recorders, players, disc players, and accessories	Minor2	924	218.0	6,749
Video tapes, blank	Minor2	59	11.4	291
Automotive sound equipment	Minor2	3,451	599.9	15,022
Consumer electronic equipment, nec	Minor2	2,516	1,428.0	20,774
High fidelity stereo equipment	Minor2	3,298	717.5	18,594
Marine radios and radar equipment	Minor2	202	44.9	738
Phonographs	Minor2	2	0.1	2
Radios, receiver type	Minor2	188	55.2	931
Radios, two-way, citizens band, weather, short-wave, etc.	Minor2	1,882	532.1	9,718
Tape recorders and players	Minor2	25	3.0	83
Misc. household appliance stores	Minor2	2,696	673.1	14,036

*Category-Major categories (Major1) are more general descriptions for companies that self-selected to capture the many functions they perform in the industry. Minor categories (Minor1, Minor2) are more specific for companies that have more detailed functions (Minor1 is a larger category than Minor2). Minor categories figures (sales, etc.) can be aggregated to larger minor categories (Minor2 sums to Minor1) and major categories overall figures.

HOME CENTERS INDUSTRY
(NAICS 44411)

NAICS 44411: Home Centers. This industry comprises establishments known as home centers primarily engaged in retailing a general line of new home repair and improvement materials and supplies, such as lumber, plumbing goods, electrical goods, tools, housewares, hardware, and lawn and garden supplies, with no one merchandise line predominating. The merchandise lines are normally arranged in separate departments.

INDUSTRY ESTABLISHMENTS, SALES & EMPLOYMENT TRENDS

	Year					Percent Chg. Year-to-Year			
	2014	2015	2016	2017	2018	14-15	15-16	16-17	17-18
Establishments	7,706	7,747	7,985	8,161	8,380	0.5%	3.1%	2.2%	2.7%
Sales ($Millions)	158,068	164,149	174,258	183,136	192,862	3.8%	6.2%	5.1%	5.3%
Employment	548,822	551,739	568,662	581,254	596,857	0.5%	3.1%	2.2%	2.7%
Sales ($M)/Estab.	20.51	21.19	21.82	22.44	23.01	3.3%	3.0%	2.8%	2.6%
Sales ($)/Emp.	288,013	297,513	306,436	315,071	323,130	3.3%	3.0%	2.8%	2.6%

3-YEAR TREND – ESTIMATED NUMBER OF ESTABLISHMENTS

Year	Employee Size of Establishment									Total
	1-4 Emps.	5-9 Emps.	10-19 Emps.	20-49 Emps.	50-99 Emps.	100-249 Emps.	250-499 Emps.	>500 Emps.	Non-Employer	Employ-ment
2016	826	624	646	487	163	3,949	104	1	1,186	7,985
2017	844	638	660	498	166	4,036	106	1	1,213	8,161
2018	867	655	678	511	171	4,145	109	1	1,245	8,380

3-YEAR TREND – ESTIMATED INDUSTRY SALES ($MILLIONS)

Year	Employee Size of Establishment									Total
	1-4 Emps.	5-9 Emps.	10-19 Emps.	20-49 Emps.	50-99 Emps.	100-249 Emps.	250-499 Emps.	>500 Emps.	Non-Employer	Employ-ment
2016	307.5	610.5	1,588.8	3,172.7	2,329.7	152,413.8	13,479.5	249.5	106.4	174,258.4
2017	323.2	641.6	1,669.8	3,334.3	2,448.4	160,178.9	14,166.2	262.2	111.8	183,136.3
2018	340.4	675.7	1,758.5	3,511.4	2,578.4	168,685.9	14,918.6	276.0	117.7	192,862.5

3-YEAR TREND – ESTIMATED NUMBER OF EMPLOYEES

Year	Employee Size of Establishment									Total
	1-4 Emps.	5-9 Emps.	10-19 Emps.	20-49 Emps.	50-99 Emps.	100-249 Emps.	250-499 Emps.	>500 Emps.	Non-Employer	Employ-ment
2016	2,065	3,618	8,779	14,658	9,663	497,940	30,142	612	1,186	568,662
2017	2,110	3,698	8,973	14,983	9,877	508,965	30,809	625	1,213	581,254
2018	2,167	3,797	9,214	15,385	10,142	522,628	31,636	642	1,245	596,857

HOME CENTERS INDUSTRY
(NAICS 44411)

SUB-INDUSTRIES – 2017 ESTIMATED INDUSTRY SALES, ESTABLISHMENTS & EMPLOYMENT

Sub-Industries	Cate-gory*	Establish-ments	Sales ($Mill)	Employ-ment
Lumber and other building materials	Major1	2,679	163,754.7	354,544
Lumber products	Minor1	300	1,378.7	9,460
Flooring, wood	Minor2	91	508.5	1,611
Millwork and lumber	Minor2	194	1,540.3	8,839
Paneling	Minor2	7	23.5	183
Planing mill products and lumber	Minor2	296	766.5	6,399
Siding	Minor2	287	379.2	2,973
Wallboard (composition) and paneling	Minor2	6	24.8	162
Door and window products	Minor1	576	1,930.0	10,876
Doors, storm: wood or metal	Minor2	76	321.3	2,063
Doors, wood or metal, except storm	Minor2	64	240.3	1,111
Garage doors, sale and installation	Minor2	441	1,481.7	8,578
Jalousies	Minor2	1	4.0	14
Sash, wood or metal	Minor2	4	21.4	140
Screens, door and window	Minor2	86	157.4	973
Windows, storm: wood or metal	Minor2	83	315.9	2,062
Insulation and energy conservation products	Minor1	24	95.3	494
Energy conservation products	Minor2	76	288.6	1,312
Insulation material, building	Minor2	36	200.8	1,007
Solar heating equipment	Minor2	77	235.0	1,162
Prefabricated buildings	Minor1	103	361.8	1,692
Greenhouse kits, prefabricated	Minor2	9	26.2	166
Modular homes	Minor2	92	478.0	1,802
Masonry materials and supplies	Minor1	951	3,103.1	20,203
Bathroom fixtures, equipment and supplies	Minor2	95	357.8	1,901
Cabinets, kitchen	Minor2	344	1,274.2	6,263
Closets, interiors and accessories	Minor2	67	183.0	1,123
Counter tops	Minor2	149	1,555.1	2,646
Eavestroughing parts and supplies	Minor2	1	2.2	11
Electrical construction materials	Minor2	62	236.6	1,256
Fencing	Minor2	394	821.9	5,458
Home centers	Minor2	425	821.8	123,053
Roofing material	Minor2	61	235.1	1,659
Structural clay products	Minor2	5	11.2	58

*Category-Major categories (Major1) are more general descriptions for companies that self-selected to capture the many functions they perform in the industry. Minor categories (Minor1, Minor2) are more specific for companies that have more detailed functions (Minor1 is a larger category than Minor2). Minor categories figures (sales, etc.) can be aggregated to larger minor categories (Minor2 sums to Minor1) and major categories overall figures.

HARDWARE STORES INDUSTRY
(NAICS 44413)

NAICS 44413: Hardware Stores. Establishments primarily engaged
in the retail sale of a number of basic hardware lines, such as tools,
builders' hardware, paint and glass, housewares and household appliances,
and cutlery.

INDUSTRY ESTABLISHMENTS, SALES & EMPLOYMENT TRENDS

	Year					Percent Chg. Year-to-Year			
	2014	2015	2016	2017	2018	14-15	15-16	16-17	17-18
Establishments	16,707	16,986	17,698	18,245	18,895	1.7%	4.2%	3.1%	3.6%
Sales ($Millions)	20,708	21,450	22,719	23,778	24,949	3.6%	5.9%	4.7%	4.9%
Employment	142,843	145,226	151,318	155,992	161,550	1.7%	4.2%	3.1%	3.6%
Sales ($M)/Estab.	1.24	1.26	1.28	1.30	1.32	1.9%	1.7%	1.5%	1.3%
Sales ($)/Emp.	144,974	147,702	150,140	152,433	154,437	1.9%	1.7%	1.5%	1.3%

3-YEAR TREND – ESTIMATED NUMBER OF ESTABLISHMENTS

Year	Employee Size of Establishment									Total
	1-4 Emps.	5-9 Emps.	10-19 Emps.	20-49 Emps.	50-99 Emps.	100-249 Emps.	250-499 Emps.	>500 Emps.	Non-Employer	Employ-ment
2016	6,835	4,173	3,318	1,755	146	13	1	0	1,458	17,698
2017	7,046	4,302	3,420	1,810	151	13	1	0	1,503	18,245
2018	7,297	4,455	3,542	1,874	156	14	1	0	1,556	18,895

3-YEAR TREND – ESTIMATED INDUSTRY SALES ($MILLIONS)

Year	Employee Size of Establishment									Total
	1-4 Emps.	5-9 Emps.	10-19 Emps.	20-49 Emps.	50-99 Emps.	100-249 Emps.	250-499 Emps.	>500 Emps.	Non-Employer	Employ-ment
2016	1,982.0	3,180.3	6,359.2	8,905.0	1,630.3	382.1	107.3	5.3	167.4	22,718.9
2017	2,074.4	3,328.7	6,655.8	9,320.4	1,706.3	399.9	112.3	5.5	175.3	23,778.4
2018	2,176.6	3,492.6	6,983.5	9,779.4	1,790.3	419.6	117.9	5.6	183.9	24,949.3

3-YEAR TREND – ESTIMATED NUMBER OF EMPLOYEES

Year	Employee Size of Establishment									Total
	1-4 Emps.	5-9 Emps.	10-19 Emps.	20-49 Emps.	50-99 Emps.	100-249 Emps.	250-499 Emps.	>500 Emps.	Non-Employer	Employ-ment
2016	17,087	24,202	45,122	52,835	8,684	1,603	308	19	1,458	151,318
2017	17,615	24,949	46,516	54,467	8,952	1,652	318	20	1,503	155,992
2018	18,243	25,838	48,174	56,408	9,271	1,711	329	21	1,556	161,550

HARDWARE STORES INDUSTRY
(NAICS 44413)

SUB-INDUSTRIES — 2017 ESTIMATED INDUSTRY SALES, ESTABLISHMENTS & EMPLOYMENT

Sub-Industries	Cate-gory*	Establish-ments	Sales ($Mill)	Employ-ment
Hardware stores	Major1	12,569	19,923.6	127,167
Tools	Minor1	3,330	1,433.9	13,037
Chainsaws	Minor2	333	205.2	1,153
Snowblowers	Minor2	59	70.7	326
Tools, hand	Minor2	322	238.4	1,727
Tools, power	Minor2	282	338.1	2,622
Builders' hardware	Minor2	772	902.8	6,379
Door locks and lock sets	Minor2	194	269.9	1,131
Pumps and pumping equipment	Minor2	384	395.9	2,450

*Category-Major categories (Major1) are more general descriptions for companies that self-selected to capture the many functions they perform in the industry. Minor categories (Minor1, Minor2) are more specific for companies that have more detailed functions (Minor1 is a larger category than Minor2). Minor categories figures (sales, etc.) can be aggregated to larger minor categories (Minor2 sums to Minor1) and major categories overall figures.

GROCERY STORES INDUSTRY
(NAICS 44511)

NAICS 44511: Grocery Stores Industry. This industry comprises establishments generally known as supermarkets and grocery stores primarily engaged in retailing a general line of food, such as canned and frozen foods; fresh fruits and vegetables; and fresh and prepared meats, fish, and poultry. Included in this industry are delicatessen-type establishments primarily engaged in retailing a general line of food.

INDUSTRY ESTABLISHMENTS, SALES & EMPLOYMENT TRENDS

	Year					Percent Chg. Year-to-Year			
	2014	2015	2016	2017	2018	14-15	15-16	16-17	17-18
Establishments	77,669	76,788	77,840	79,530	81,631	-1.1%	1.4%	2.2%	2.6%
Sales ($Millions)	573,954	557,604	554,110	554,180	555,333	-2.8%	-0.6%	0.0%	0.2%
Employment	2,305,989	2,279,826	2,311,053	2,361,248	2,423,628	-1.1%	1.4%	2.2%	2.6%
Sales ($M)/Estab.	7.39	7.26	7.12	6.97	6.80	-1.7%	-2.0%	-2.1%	-2.4%
Sales ($)/Emp.	248,897	244,582	239,765	234,698	229,133	-1.7%	-2.0%	-2.1%	-2.4%

3-YEAR TREND – ESTIMATED NUMBER OF ESTABLISHMENTS

Year	Employee Size of Establishment									Total
	1-4 Emps.	5-9 Emps.	10-19 Emps.	20-49 Emps.	50-99 Emps.	100-249 Emps.	250-499 Emps.	>500 Emps.	Non-Employer	Employ-ment
2016	24,686	7,029	7,088	8,747	9,652	8,167	699	52	11,720	77,840
2017	25,222	7,182	7,241	8,937	9,862	8,344	714	53	11,974	79,530
2018	25,889	7,372	7,433	9,173	10,122	8,565	733	55	12,291	81,631

3-YEAR TREND – ESTIMATED INDUSTRY SALES ($MILLIONS)

Year	Employee Size of Establishment									Total
	1-4 Emps.	5-9 Emps.	10-19 Emps.	20-49 Emps.	50-99 Emps.	100-249 Emps.	250-499 Emps.	>500 Emps.	Non-Employer	Employ-ment
2016	7,847.5	5,873.3	14,891.9	48,647.2	118,000.4	269,094.4	77,574.7	10,695.3	1,485.0	554,109.6
2017	7,848.6	5,874.1	14,894.0	48,654.1	118,017.1	269,132.5	77,585.7	10,688.9	1,485.2	554,180.4
2018	7,865.1	5,886.4	14,925.3	48,756.1	118,264.6	269,696.8	77,748.3	10,702.0	1,488.3	555,332.9

3-YEAR TREND – ESTIMATED NUMBER OF EMPLOYEES

Year	Employee Size of Establishment									Total
	1-4 Emps.	5-9 Emps.	10-19 Emps.	20-49 Emps.	50-99 Emps.	100-249 Emps.	250-499 Emps.	>500 Emps.	Non-Employer	Employ-ment
2016	61,715	40,771	96,390	263,290	573,338	1,029,845	203,203	30,781	11,720	2,311,053
2017	63,056	41,656	98,484	269,008	585,790	1,052,213	207,616	31,450	11,974	2,361,248
2018	64,721	42,757	101,086	276,115	601,266	1,080,011	213,101	32,281	12,291	2,423,628

SUB-INDUSTRIES — 2017 ESTIMATED INDUSTRY SALES, ESTABLISHMENTS & EMPLOYMENT

Sub-Industries	Category*	Establishments	Sales ($Mill)	Employment
Grocery stores	Major1	48,162	56,681.2	721,757
Supermarkets	Minor1	6,341	131,158.2	212,294
Supermarkets, chain	Minor2	6,838	296,008.8	943,221
Supermarkets, greater than 100,000 square feet (hyperm	Minor2	52	52.3	11,823
Supermarkets, independent	Minor2	1,721	15,363.9	83,044
Supermarkets, 55,000 - 65,000 square feet (superstore)	Minor2	17	8,002.1	2,439
Supermarkets, 66,000 - 99,000 square feet	Minor2	13	23.0	1,625
Cooperative food stores	Minor2	253	921.4	7,710
Delicatessen stores	Minor2	4,858	6,003.7	37,484
Frozen food and freezer plans, except meat	Minor2	123	128.9	2,104
Grocery stores, chain	Minor2	1,369	9,833.6	140,331
Grocery stores, independent	Minor2	9,782	30,003.2	197,416

*Category-Major categories (Major1) are more general descriptions for companies that self-selected to capture the many functions they perform in the industry. Minor categories (Minor1, Minor2) are more specific for companies that have more detailed functions (Minor1 is a larger category than Minor2). Minor categories figures (sales, etc.) can be aggregated to larger minor categories (Minor2 sums to Minor1) and major categories overall figures.

BEER & WINE & LIQUOR STORES INDUSTRY (NAICS 44531)

NAICS 44531: Beer & Wine & Liquor Stores. Establishments primarily engaged in the retail sale of packaged alcoholic beverages, such as ale, beer, wine, and liquor, for consumption off the premises. Stores selling prepared drinks for consumption on the premises are classified in SIC 5813.

INDUSTRY ESTABLISHMENTS, SALES & EMPLOYMENT TRENDS

	Year					Percent Chg. Year-to-Year			
	2014	2015	2016	2017	2018	14-15	15-16	16-17	17-18
Establishments	36,250	36,382	37,438	38,688	40,164	0.4%	2.9%	3.3%	3.8%
Sales ($Millions)	40,648	42,509	45,421	48,628	52,149	4.6%	6.8%	7.1%	7.2%
Employment	167,121	167,732	172,597	178,361	185,165	0.4%	2.9%	3.3%	3.8%
Sales ($M)/Estab.	1.12	1.17	1.21	1.26	1.30	4.2%	3.8%	3.6%	3.3%
Sales ($)/Emp.	243,222	253,435	263,159	272,641	281,636	4.2%	3.8%	3.6%	3.3%

3-YEAR TREND — ESTIMATED NUMBER OF ESTABLISHMENTS

Year	Employee Size of Establishment									Total
	1-4 Emps.	5-9 Emps.	10-19 Emps.	20-49 Emps.	50-99 Emps.	100-249 Emps.	250-499 Emps.	>500 Emps.	Non-Employer	Employ-ment
2016	22,426	8,286	2,761	761	45	12	0	1	3,146	37,438
2017	23,174	8,563	2,853	787	47	13	0	1	3,251	38,688
2018	24,058	8,889	2,962	817	49	13	0	1	3,375	40,164

3-YEAR TREND — ESTIMATED INDUSTRY SALES ($MILLIONS)

Year	Employee Size of Establishment									Total
	1-4 Emps.	5-9 Emps.	10-19 Emps.	20-49 Emps.	50-99 Emps.	100-249 Emps.	250-499 Emps.	>500 Emps.	Non-Employer	Employ-ment
2016	12,617.2	12,253.0	10,265.9	7,492.1	983.2	722.7	2.0	375.8	708.6	45,420.6
2017	13,508.4	13,118.5	10,991.0	8,021.2	1,052.7	773.8	2.2	402.1	758.6	48,628.4
2018	14,486.4	14,068.3	11,786.8	8,602.0	1,128.9	829.8	2.3	431.0	813.5	52,148.9

3-YEAR TREND — ESTIMATED NUMBER OF EMPLOYEES

Year	Employee Size of Establishment									Total
	1-4 Emps.	5-9 Emps.	10-19 Emps.	20-49 Emps.	50-99 Emps.	100-249 Emps.	250-499 Emps.	>500 Emps.	Non-Employer	Employ-ment
2016	56,064	48,058	37,544	22,911	2,699	1,563	3	610	3,146	172,597
2017	57,936	49,663	38,798	23,676	2,789	1,615	3	630	3,251	178,361
2018	60,146	51,558	40,278	24,579	2,896	1,677	3	654	3,375	185,165

SUB-INDUSTRIES – 2017 ESTIMATED INDUSTRY SALES, ESTABLISHMENTS & EMPLOYMENT

Sub-Industries	Category*	Establishments	Sales ($Mill)	Employment
Liquor stores	Major1	23,114	27,957.1	105,068
Wine and beer	Minor1	673	754.7	3,231
Beer (packaged)	Minor2	4,562	7,271.1	23,110
Wine	Minor2	4,396	5,303.8	20,518
Hard liquor	Minor2	5,944	7,341.7	26,434

*Category-Major categories (Major1) are more general descriptions for companies that self-selected to capture the many functions they perform in the industry. Minor categories (Minor1, Minor2) are more specific for companies that have more detailed functions (Minor1 is a larger category than Minor2). Minor categories figures (sales, etc.) can be aggregated to larger minor categories (Minor2 sums to Minor1) and major categories overall figures.

PHARMACIES & DRUG STORES INDUSTRY
(NAICS 44611)

NAICS 44611 Pharmacies and Drug Stores – This industry comprises establishments known as pharmacies and drug stores engaged in retailing prescription or nonprescription drugs and medicines.

INDUSTRY ESTABLISHMENTS, SALES & EMPLOYMENT TRENDS

	Year					Percent Chg. Year-to-Year			
	2014	2015	2016	2017	2018	14-15	15-16	16-17	17-18
Establishments	47,064	47,378	48,895	50,326	52,036	0.7%	3.2%	2.9%	3.4%
Sales ($Millions)	190,182	201,465	217,843	234,229	252,120	5.9%	8.1%	7.5%	7.6%
Employment	717,499	722,282	745,413	767,222	793,301	0.7%	3.2%	2.9%	3.4%
Sales ($M)/Estab.	4.04	4.25	4.46	4.65	4.85	5.2%	4.8%	4.5%	4.1%
Sales ($)/Emp.	265,062	278,929	292,244	305,295	317,811	5.2%	4.8%	4.5%	4.1%

3-YEAR TREND – ESTIMATED NUMBER OF ESTABLISHMENTS

Year	Employee Size of Establishment									Total
	1-4 Emps.	5-9 Emps.	10-19 Emps.	20-49 Emps.	50-99 Emps.	100-249 Emps.	250-499 Emps.	>500 Emps.	Non-Employer	Employ-ment
2016	8,521	8,094	13,594	14,515	620	90	8	1	3,451	48,895
2017	8,770	8,331	13,992	14,939	638	93	9	1	3,552	50,326
2018	9,069	8,614	14,467	15,447	660	96	9	1	3,673	52,036

3-YEAR TREND – ESTIMATED INDUSTRY SALES ($MILLIONS)

Year	Employee Size of Establishment									Total
	1-4 Emps.	5-9 Emps.	10-19 Emps.	20-49 Emps.	50-99 Emps.	100-249 Emps.	250-499 Emps.	>500 Emps.	Non-Employer	Employ-ment
2016	4,510.1	11,260.0	47,556.7	134,400.2	12,624.5	4,958.5	1,536.8	618.7	377.2	217,842.8
2017	4,849.7	12,108.0	51,138.1	144,521.7	13,575.3	5,331.9	1,652.5	646.5	405.6	234,229.3
2018	5,220.6	13,033.9	55,049.0	155,574.2	14,613.5	5,739.7	1,778.9	673.2	436.7	252,119.6

3-YEAR TREND – ESTIMATED NUMBER OF EMPLOYEES

Year	Employee Size of Establishment									Total
	1-4 Emps.	5-9 Emps.	10-19 Emps.	20-49 Emps.	50-99 Emps.	100-249 Emps.	250-499 Emps.	>500 Emps.	Non-Employer	Employ-ment
2016	21,303	46,946	184,879	436,887	36,841	11,398	2,418	1,290	3,451	745,413
2017	21,926	48,319	190,288	449,670	37,919	11,731	2,488	1,328	3,552	767,222
2018	22,671	49,962	196,756	464,954	39,208	12,130	2,573	1,373	3,673	793,301

PHARMACIES & DRUG STORES INDUSTRY (NAICS 44611)

SUB-INDUSTRIES — 2017 ESTIMATED INDUSTRY SALES, ESTABLISHMENTS & EMPLOYMENT

Sub-Industries	Category*	Establishments	Sales ($Mill)	Employ-ment
Drug stores and proprietary stores	Major1	22,821	141,104.2	318,794
Drug stores	Minor2	26,564	92,644.4	438,253
Proprietary (non-prescription medicine) stores	Minor2	941	480.6	10,175

*Category-Major categories (Major1) are more general descriptions for companies that self-selected to capture the many functions they perform in the industry. Minor categories (Minor1, Minor2) are more specific for companies that have more detailed functions (Minor1 is a larger category than Minor2). Minor categories figures (sales, etc.) can be aggregated to larger minor categories (Minor2 sums to Minor1) and major categories overall figures.

GAS STATIONS WITH CONVENIENCE STORES (NAICS 44711)

NAICS 44711: Gas Stations with Convenience Stores. This industry comprises establishments primarily engaged in selling gasoline and lubricating oils. These establishments frequently sell other merchandise, such as tires, batteries, and other automobile parts, or perform minor repair work. Gasoline stations combined with other activities, such as grocery stores, convenience stores, or carwashes, are classified according to the primary activity.

INDUSTRY ESTABLISHMENTS, SALES & EMPLOYMENT TRENDS

	Year					Percent Chg. Year-to-Year			
	2014	2015	2016	2017	2018	14-15	15-16	16-17	17-18
Establishments	98,456	98,459	100,955	103,554	106,708	0.0%	2.5%	2.6%	3.0%
Sales ($Millions)	381,729	410,703	450,027	490,867	535,138	7.6%	9.6%	9.1%	9.0%
Employment	767,701	767,724	787,186	807,450	832,045	0.0%	2.5%	2.6%	3.0%
Sales ($M)/Estab.	3.88	4.17	4.46	4.74	5.01	7.6%	6.9%	6.3%	5.8%
Sales ($)/Emp.	497,237	534,961	571,690	607,922	643,160	7.6%	6.9%	6.3%	5.8%

3-YEAR TREND – ESTIMATED NUMBER OF ESTABLISHMENTS

Year	Employee Size of Establishment									Total
	1-4 Emps.	5-9 Emps.	10-19 Emps.	20-49 Emps.	50-99 Emps.	100-249 Emps.	250-499 Emps.	>500 Emps.	Non-Employer	Employ-ment
2016	34,782	35,623	22,925	5,328	212	49	2	0	2,034	100,955
2017	35,677	36,540	23,516	5,465	218	50	2	0	2,086	103,554
2018	36,764	37,653	24,232	5,631	224	52	2	0	2,150	106,708

3-YEAR TREND – ESTIMATED INDUSTRY SALES ($MILLIONS)

Year	Employee Size of Establishment									Total
	1-4 Emps.	5-9 Emps.	10-19 Emps.	20-49 Emps.	50-99 Emps.	100-249 Emps.	250-499 Emps.	>500 Emps.	Non-Employer	Employ-ment
2016	40,389.9	108,725.0	175,959.6	108,239.0	9,478.8	5,924.0	831.9	21.1	457.4	450,026.6
2017	44,055.4	118,592.0	191,928.2	118,061.8	10,339.0	6,461.6	907.4	22.6	498.9	490,867.0
2018	48,028.7	129,287.8	209,238.2	128,709.8	11,271.5	7,044.3	989.3	24.2	543.9	535,137.6

3-YEAR TREND – ESTIMATED NUMBER OF EMPLOYEES

Year	Employee Size of Establishment									Total
	1-4 Emps.	5-9 Emps.	10-19 Emps.	20-49 Emps.	50-99 Emps.	100-249 Emps.	250-499 Emps.	>500 Emps.	Non-Employer	Employ-ment
2016	86,955	206,612	311,786	160,369	12,608	6,206	597	19	2,034	787,186
2017	89,193	211,931	319,813	164,498	12,932	6,366	612	19	2,086	807,450
2018	91,910	218,386	329,554	169,508	13,326	6,560	631	20	2,150	832,045

GAS STATIONS WITH CONVENIENCE STORES (NAICS 44711)

SUB-INDUSTRIES — 2017 ESTIMATED INDUSTRY SALES, ESTABLISHMENTS & EMPLOYMENT

Sub-Industries	Category*	Establishments	Sales ($Mill)	Employment
Gasoline service stations	Major1	47,339	140,804.7	308,748
Gasoline service stations, nec	Minor2	235	298.2	1,936
Filling stations, gasoline	Minor2	53,299	302,878.2	434,694
Marine service station	Minor2	532	877.7	3,565
Truck stops	Minor2	2,150	46,008.1	58,507

*Category-Major categories (Major1) are more general descriptions for companies that self-selected to capture the many functions they perform in the industry. Minor categories (Minor1, Minor2) are more specific for companies that have more detailed functions (Minor1 is a larger category than Minor2). Minor categories figures (sales, etc.) can be aggregated to larger minor categories (Minor2 sums to Minor1) and major categories overall figures.

Men's Clothing Stores Industry
(NAICS 44811)

NAICS 44811: Men's Clothing Stores. This industry comprises establishments primarily engaged in retailing a general line of new men's and boys' clothing. These establishments may provide basic alterations, such as hemming, taking in or letting out seams, or lengthening or shortening sleeves.

INDUSTRY ESTABLISHMENTS, SALES & EMPLOYMENT TRENDS

	Year					Percent Chg. Year-to-Year			
	2014	2015	2016	2017	2018	14-15	15-16	16-17	17-18
Establishments	8,765	8,460	8,364	8,330	8,335	-3.5%	-1.1%	-0.4%	0.1%
Sales ($Millions)	8,093	8,170	8,418	8,715	9,035	1.0%	3.0%	3.5%	3.7%
Employment	57,990	55,969	55,340	55,115	55,144	-3.5%	-1.1%	-0.4%	0.1%
Sales ($M)/Estab.	0.92	0.97	1.01	1.05	1.08	4.6%	4.2%	3.9%	3.6%
Sales ($)/Emp.	139,556	145,976	152,117	158,117	163,838	4.6%	4.2%	3.9%	3.6%

3-YEAR TREND – ESTIMATED NUMBER OF ESTABLISHMENTS

Year	Employee Size of Establishment									Total
	1-4 Emps.	5-9 Emps.	10-19 Emps.	20-49 Emps.	50-99 Emps.	100-249 Emps.	250-499 Emps.	>500 Emps.	Non-Employer	Employ-ment
2016	3,042	1,727	1,603	353	41	8	1	0	1,589	8,364
2017	3,030	1,720	1,597	352	41	8	1	0	1,582	8,330
2018	3,032	1,721	1,598	352	41	8	1	0	1,583	8,335

3-YEAR TREND – ESTIMATED INDUSTRY SALES ($MILLIONS)

Year	Employee Size of Establishment									Total
	1-4 Emps.	5-9 Emps.	10-19 Emps.	20-49 Emps.	50-99 Emps.	100-249 Emps.	250-499 Emps.	>500 Emps.	Non-Employer	Employ-ment
2016	928.5	1,385.6	3,234.1	1,885.3	481.6	241.5	101.7	5.4	154.4	8,418.1
2017	961.2	1,434.4	3,348.0	1,951.7	498.6	250.0	105.3	5.6	159.9	8,714.7
2018	996.5	1,487.0	3,470.9	2,023.4	516.9	259.2	109.2	5.8	165.8	9,034.7

3-YEAR TREND – ESTIMATED NUMBER OF EMPLOYEES

Year	Employee Size of Establishment									Total
	1-4 Emps.	5-9 Emps.	10-19 Emps.	20-49 Emps.	50-99 Emps.	100-249 Emps.	250-499 Emps.	>500 Emps.	Non-Employer	Employ-ment
2016	7,606	10,018	21,804	10,628	2,437	963	278	17	1,589	55,340
2017	7,575	9,978	21,715	10,585	2,428	959	276	17	1,582	55,115
2018	7,579	9,983	21,727	10,590	2,429	959	277	17	1,583	55,144

MEN'S CLOTHING STORES INDUSTRY
(NAICS 44811)

SUB-INDUSTRIES — 2017 ESTIMATED INDUSTRY
SALES, ESTABLISHMENTS & EMPLOYMENT

Sub-Industries	Cate-gory*	Establish-ments	Sales ($Mill)	Employ-ment
Men's and boys' clothing stores	Major1	5,730	6,050.8	41,360
Clothing accessories: men's and boys'	Minor2	555	337.3	2,019
Clothing, male: everyday, except suits and sportswear	Minor2	307	111.6	2,716
Clothing, sportswear, men's and boys'	Minor2	926	257.8	5,203
Haberdashery stores	Minor2	31	12.6	83
Hats, men's and boys'	Minor2	147	34.5	290
Suits, men's	Minor2	566	1,895.2	3,176
Tie shops	Minor2	70	14.9	269

*Category-Major categories (Major1) are more general descriptions for companies that self-selected to capture the many functions they perform in the industry. Minor categories (Minor1, Minor2) are more specific for companies that have more detailed functions (Minor1 is a larger category than Minor2). Minor categories figures (sales, etc.) can be aggregated to larger minor categories (Minor2 sums to Minor1) and major categories overall figures.

WOMEN'S CLOTHING STORES INDUSTRY (NAICS 44812)

NAICS 44812: Women's Clothing Stores . This industry comprises establishments primarily engaged in retailing a general line of new women's, misses' and juniors' clothing, including maternity wear. These establishments may provide basic alterations, such as hemming, taking in or letting out seams, or lengthening or shortening sleeves.

INDUSTRY ESTABLISHMENTS, SALES & EMPLOYMENT TRENDS

	Year					Percent Chg. Year-to-Year			
	2014	2015	2016	2017	2018	14-15	15-16	16-17	17-18
Establishments	44,307	44,890	46,616	47,974	49,598	1.3%	3.8%	2.9%	3.4%
Sales ($Millions)	44,681	47,008	50,514	53,689	57,165	5.2%	7.5%	6.3%	6.5%
Employment	365,466	370,271	384,513	395,712	409,109	1.3%	3.8%	2.9%	3.4%
Sales ($M)/Estab.	1.01	1.05	1.08	1.12	1.15	3.8%	3.5%	3.3%	3.0%
Sales ($)/Emp.	122,257	126,956	131,372	135,677	139,730	3.8%	3.5%	3.3%	3.0%

3-YEAR TREND — ESTIMATED NUMBER OF ESTABLISHMENTS

	Employee Size of Establishment									Total
Year	1-4 Emps.	5-9 Emps.	10-19 Emps.	20-49 Emps.	50-99 Emps.	100-249 Emps.	250-499 Emps.	>500 Emps.	Non-Employer	Employ-ment
2016	12,746	10,998	10,714	2,771	393	142	16	6	8,829	46,616
2017	13,118	11,318	11,026	2,852	405	146	16	6	9,087	47,974
2018	13,562	11,701	11,399	2,949	419	151	17	7	9,394	49,598

3-YEAR TREND — ESTIMATED INDUSTRY SALES ($MILLIONS)

	Employee Size of Establishment									Total
Year	1-4 Emps.	5-9 Emps.	10-19 Emps.	20-49 Emps.	50-99 Emps.	100-249 Emps.	250-499 Emps.	>500 Emps.	Non-Employer	Employ-ment
2016	3,152.1	7,148.3	17,511.7	11,989.6	3,742.2	3,640.6	1,363.4	1,236.3	729.9	50,514.2
2017	3,351.3	7,600.0	18,618.4	12,747.2	3,978.7	3,870.7	1,449.6	1,297.1	776.0	53,689.1
2018	3,569.6	8,095.0	19,830.9	13,577.4	4,237.8	4,122.8	1,544.0	1,360.9	826.6	57,164.8

3-YEAR TREND — ESTIMATED NUMBER OF EMPLOYEES

	Employee Size of Establishment									Total
Year	1-4 Emps.	5-9 Emps.	10-19 Emps.	20-49 Emps.	50-99 Emps.	100-249 Emps.	250-499 Emps.	>500 Emps.	Non-Employer	Employ-ment
2016	31,866	63,787	145,707	83,416	23,373	17,911	4,591	5,033	8,829	384,513
2017	32,794	65,645	149,950	85,845	24,054	18,432	4,725	5,180	9,087	395,712
2018	33,904	67,867	155,027	88,751	24,869	19,056	4,885	5,355	9,394	409,109

WOMEN'S CLOTHING STORES INDUSTRY (NAICS 44812)

SUB-INDUSTRIES – 2017 ESTIMATED INDUSTRY SALES, ESTABLISHMENTS & EMPLOYMENT

Sub-Industries	Cate-gory*	Establish-ments	Sales ($Mill)	Employ-ment
Women's clothing stores	Major1	20,595	16,632.1	181,172
Women's specialty clothing stores	Minor1	795	288.2	6,966
Boutiques	Minor2	7,317	2,138.5	26,414
Bridal shops	Minor2	3,506	1,555.9	22,307
Dress shops	Minor2	460	208.3	3,524
Women's sportswear	Minor2	274	181.2	2,393
Maternity wear	Minor2	575	121.0	3,134
Ready-to-wear apparel, women's	Minor2	14,366	32,518.8	148,585
Teenage apparel	Minor2	87	45.1	1,217

*Category-Major categories (Major1) are more general descriptions for companies that self-selected to capture the many functions they perform in the industry. Minor categories (Minor1, Minor2) are more specific for companies that have more detailed functions (Minor1 is a larger category than Minor2). Minor categories figures (sales, etc.) can be aggregated to larger minor categories (Minor2 sums to Minor1) and major categories overall figures.

FAMILY CLOTHING STORES INDUSTRY (NAICS 44814)

NAICS 44814: Family Clothing Stores . This industry comprises establishments primarily engaged in retailing a general line of new clothing for men, women, and children, without specializing in sales for an individual gender or age group. These establishments may provide basic alterations, such as hemming, taking in or letting out seams, or lengthening or shortening sleeves.

INDUSTRY ESTABLISHMENTS, SALES & EMPLOYMENT TRENDS

	Year					Percent Chg. Year-to-Year			
	2014	2015	2016	2017	2018	14-15	15-16	16-17	17-18
Establishments	34,069	34,058	34,909	35,931	37,153	0.0%	2.5%	2.9%	3.4%
Sales ($Millions)	101,391	104,987	111,115	117,867	125,272	3.5%	5.8%	6.1%	6.3%
Employment	669,584	669,361	686,083	706,171	730,190	0.0%	2.5%	2.9%	3.4%
Sales ($M)/Estab.	2.98	3.08	3.18	3.28	3.37	3.6%	3.3%	3.1%	2.8%
Sales ($)/Emp.	151,424	156,847	161,955	166,910	171,560	3.6%	3.3%	3.1%	2.8%

3-YEAR TREND – ESTIMATED NUMBER OF ESTABLISHMENTS

Year	Employee Size of Establishment									Total
	1-4 Emps.	5-9 Emps.	10-19 Emps.	20-49 Emps.	50-99 Emps.	100-249 Emps.	250-499 Emps.	>500 Emps.	Non-Employer	Employ-ment
2016	5,850	3,991	6,831	7,911	3,775	349	102	22	6,077	34,909
2017	6,021	4,108	7,031	8,143	3,885	360	105	22	6,255	35,931
2018	6,226	4,248	7,270	8,420	4,017	372	109	23	6,468	37,153

3-YEAR TREND – ESTIMATED INDUSTRY SALES ($MILLIONS)

Year	Employee Size of Establishment									Total
	1-4 Emps.	5-9 Emps.	10-19 Emps.	20-49 Emps.	50-99 Emps.	100-249 Emps.	250-499 Emps.	>500 Emps.	Non-Employer	Employ-ment
2016	1,501.7	2,692.8	11,590.9	35,530.1	37,265.9	9,296.8	9,189.0	3,641.6	406.2	111,114.9
2017	1,593.0	2,856.7	12,296.3	37,692.1	39,533.5	9,862.5	9,748.1	3,854.2	430.9	117,867.3
2018	1,693.3	3,036.4	13,069.8	40,063.3	42,020.6	10,483.0	10,361.4	4,085.9	458.0	125,271.6

3-YEAR TREND – ESTIMATED NUMBER OF EMPLOYEES

Year	Employee Size of Establishment									Total
	1-4 Emps.	5-9 Emps.	10-19 Emps.	20-49 Emps.	50-99 Emps.	100-249 Emps.	250-499 Emps.	>500 Emps.	Non-Employer	Employ-ment
2016	14,624	23,148	92,906	238,129	224,222	44,060	29,807	13,111	6,077	686,083
2017	15,052	23,825	95,626	245,101	230,787	45,350	30,680	13,495	6,255	706,171
2018	15,564	24,636	98,878	253,438	238,637	46,892	31,723	13,954	6,468	730,190

FAMILY CLOTHING STORES INDUSTRY (NAICS 44814)

SUB-INDUSTRIES – 2017 ESTIMATED INDUSTRY SALES, ESTABLISHMENTS & EMPLOYMENT

Sub-Industries	Cate-gory*	Establish-ments	Sales ($Mill)	Employ-ment
Family clothing stores	Major1	29,639	116,648.9	639,939
Jeans stores	Minor2	554	339.2	11,121
Unisex clothing stores	Minor2	5,737	879.2	55,111

*Category-Major categories (Major1) are more general descriptions for companies that self-selected to capture the many functions they perform in the industry. Minor categories (Minor1, Minor2) are more specific for companies that have more detailed functions (Minor1 is a larger category than Minor2). Minor categories figures (sales, etc.) can be aggregated to larger minor categories (Minor2 sums to Minor1) and major categories overall figures.

BOOK STORES RETAILING INDUSTRY (NAICS 451211)

NAICS 451211: Book Stores. This industry comprises establishments primarily engaged in the retail sale of new books and magazines. Establishments primarily engaged in the retail sale of used books are classified in 5932.

INDUSTRY ESTABLISHMENTS, SALES & EMPLOYMENT TRENDS

	Year					Percent Chg. Year-to-Year			
	2014	2015	2016	2017	2018	14-15	15-16	16-17	17-18
Establishments	10,773	10,055	9,583	9,223	8,917	-6.7%	-4.7%	-3.8%	-3.3%
Sales ($Millions)	11,423	11,260	11,278	11,369	11,471	-1.4%	0.2%	0.8%	0.9%
Employment	95,851	89,467	85,266	82,062	79,339	-6.7%	-4.7%	-3.8%	-3.3%
Sales ($M)/Estab.	1.06	1.12	1.18	1.23	1.29	5.6%	5.1%	4.7%	4.4%
Sales ($)/Emp.	119,172	125,855	132,266	138,546	144,585	5.6%	5.1%	4.7%	4.4%

3-YEAR TREND – ESTIMATED NUMBER OF ESTABLISHMENTS

Year	Employee Size of Establishment									Total Employ-ment
	1-4 Emps.	5-9 Emps.	10-19 Emps.	20-49 Emps.	50-99 Emps.	100-249 Emps.	250-499 Emps.	>500 Emps.	Non-Employer	
2016	2,316	1,346	1,108	1,096	225	33	2	3	3,456	9,583
2017	2,229	1,295	1,066	1,055	217	32	2	3	3,326	9,223
2018	2,155	1,252	1,031	1,020	209	31	2	2	3,216	8,917

3-YEAR TREND – ESTIMATED INDUSTRY SALES ($MILLIONS)

Year	Employee Size of Establishment									Total Employ-ment
	1-4 Emps.	5-9 Emps.	10-19 Emps.	20-49 Emps.	50-99 Emps.	100-249 Emps.	250-499 Emps.	>500 Emps.	Non-Employer	
2016	538.3	822.3	1,701.6	4,457.0	2,012.0	793.0	144.5	533.0	276.1	11,277.8
2017	542.1	828.2	1,713.8	4,489.0	2,026.4	798.7	145.5	547.5	278.0	11,369.3
2018	546.5	834.9	1,727.7	4,525.4	2,042.8	805.2	146.7	561.7	280.3	11,471.3

3-YEAR TREND – ESTIMATED NUMBER OF EMPLOYEES

Year	Employee Size of Establishment									Total Employ-ment
	1-4 Emps.	5-9 Emps.	10-19 Emps.	20-49 Emps.	50-99 Emps.	100-249 Emps.	250-499 Emps.	>500 Emps.	Non-Employer	
2016	5,789	7,806	15,062	32,988	13,369	4,150	518	2,128	3,456	85,266
2017	5,571	7,513	14,496	31,749	12,866	3,995	498	2,048	3,326	82,062
2018	5,386	7,264	14,015	30,695	12,439	3,862	482	1,980	3,216	79,339

BOOK STORES RETAILING INDUSTRY (NAICS 451211)

SUB-INDUSTRIES — 2017 ESTIMATED INDUSTRY SALES, ESTABLISHMENTS & EMPLOYMENT

Sub-Industries	Category*	Establishments	Sales ($Mill)	Employment
Book stores	Major1	6,980	9,445.4	64,443
Books, foreign	Minor2	38	11.2	158
Books, religious	Minor2	881	791.3	6,443
Children's books	Minor2	137	38.7	436
College book stores	Minor2	566	961.9	9,117
Comic books	Minor2	622	120.9	1,466

*Category-Major categories (Major1) are more general descriptions for companies that self-selected to capture the many functions they perform in the industry. Minor categories (Minor1, Minor2) are more specific for companies that have more detailed functions (Minor1 is a larger category than Minor2). Minor categories figures (sales, etc.) can be aggregated to larger minor categories (Minor2 sums to Minor1) and major categories overall figures.

DEPARTMENT STORES INDUSTRY (NAICS 45211)

NAICS 45211: Department Stores Industry . This industry comprises establishments known as department stores primarily engaged in retailing a wide range of the following new products with no one merchandise line predominating: apparel, furniture, appliances and home furnishings; and selected additional items, such as paint, hardware, toiletries, cosmetics, photographic equipment, jewelry, toys, and sporting goods. Merchandise lines are normally arranged in separate departments.

INDUSTRY ESTABLISHMENTS, SALES & EMPLOYMENT TRENDS

	Year					Percent Chg. Year-to-Year			
	2014	2015	2016	2017	2018	14-15	15-16	16-17	17-18
Establishments	10,195	9,844	9,737	9,689	9,684	-3.4%	-1.1%	-0.5%	0.0%
Sales ($Millions)	136,921	133,944	133,934	134,557	135,527	-2.2%	0.0%	0.5%	0.7%
Employment	847,176	818,004	809,170	805,112	804,757	-3.4%	-1.1%	-0.5%	0.0%
Sales ($M)/Estab.	13.43	13.61	13.75	13.89	13.99	1.3%	1.1%	1.0%	0.8%
Sales ($)/Emp.	161,621	163,745	165,520	167,128	168,407	1.3%	1.1%	1.0%	0.8%

3-YEAR TREND – ESTIMATED NUMBER OF ESTABLISHMENTS

Year	Employee Size of Establishment									Total
	1-4 Emps.	5-9 Emps.	10-19 Emps.	20-49 Emps.	50-99 Emps.	100-249 Emps.	250-499 Emps.	>500 Emps.	Non-Employer	Employ-ment
2016	51	7	11	344	2,970	3,654	476	32	2,194	9,737
2017	50	7	11	342	2,955	3,636	473	31	2,183	9,689
2018	50	7	11	342	2,953	3,634	473	31	2,182	9,684

3-YEAR TREND – ESTIMATED INDUSTRY SALES ($MILLIONS)

Year	Employee Size of Establishment									Total
	1-4 Emps.	5-9 Emps.	10-19 Emps.	20-49 Emps.	50-99 Emps.	100-249 Emps.	250-499 Emps.	>500 Emps.	Non-Employer	Employ-ment
2016	9.8	3.4	14.7	1,170.2	22,214.8	73,680.8	32,324.0	4,328.7	187.7	133,934.2
2017	9.9	3.4	14.8	1,175.6	22,317.3	74,020.8	32,473.2	4,353.2	188.5	134,556.7
2018	10.0	3.5	14.9	1,184.1	22,478.1	74,554.3	32,707.2	4,385.0	189.9	135,526.9

3-YEAR TREND – ESTIMATED NUMBER OF EMPLOYEES

Year	Employee Size of Establishment									Total
	1-4 Emps.	5-9 Emps.	10-19 Emps.	20-49 Emps.	50-99 Emps.	100-249 Emps.	250-499 Emps.	>500 Emps.	Non-Employer	Employ-ment
2016	127	39	156	10,350	176,390	460,814	138,369	20,732	2,194	809,170
2017	126	39	155	10,298	175,505	458,503	137,675	20,628	2,183	805,112
2018	126	39	155	10,293	175,428	458,301	137,614	20,619	2,182	804,757

DEPARTMENT STORES INDUSTRY
(NAICS 45211)

SUB-INDUSTRIES – 2017 ESTIMATED INDUSTRY
SALES, ESTABLISHMENTS & EMPLOYMENT

Sub-Industries	Cate-gory*	Establish-ments	Sales ($Mill)	Employ-ment
Department stores	Major1	2,892	13,533.8	127,742
Department stores, discount	Minor2	5,341	106,706.8	548,040
Department stores, non-discount	Minor2	1,456	14,316.2	129,330

*Category-Major categories (Major1) are more general descriptions for companies that self-selected to capture the many functions they perform in the industry. Minor categories (Minor1, Minor2) are more specific for companies that have more detailed functions (Minor1 is a larger category than Minor2). Minor categories figures (sales, etc.) can be aggregated to larger minor categories (Minor2 sums to Minor1) and major categories overall figures.

WAREHOUSE CLUBS & SUPERSTORES INDUSTRY (NAICS 45291)

NAICS 45291: Warehouse Clubs and Superstores This industry comprises establishments known as warehouse clubs, superstores or supercenters primarily engaged in retailing a general line of groceries in combination with general lines of new merchandise, such as apparel, furniture, and appliances.

INDUSTRY ESTABLISHMENTS, SALES & EMPLOYMENT TRENDS

	Year					Percent Chg. Year-to-Year			
	2014	2015	2016	2017	2018	14-15	15-16	16-17	17-18
Establishments	6,850	7,295	7,803	8,218	8,485	6.5%	7.0%	5.3%	3.3%
Sales ($Millions)	520,593	574,681	635,186	689,891	732,664	10.4%	10.5%	8.6%	6.2%
Employment	1,123,960	1,196,972	1,280,310	1,348,330	1,392,153	6.5%	7.0%	5.3%	3.3%
Sales ($M)/Estab.	76.00	78.77	81.40	83.95	86.35	3.7%	3.3%	3.1%	2.9%
Sales ($)/Emp.	463,178	480,112	496,119	511,663	526,281	3.7%	3.3%	3.1%	2.9%

3-YEAR TREND — ESTIMATED NUMBER OF ESTABLISHMENTS

Year	Employee Size of Establishment									Total
	1-4 Emps.	5-9 Emps.	10-19 Emps.	20-49 Emps.	50-99 Emps.	100-249 Emps.	250-499 Emps.	>500 Emps.	Non-Employer	Employ-ment
2016	175	2	5	93	54	2,452	3,217	47	1,758	7,803
2017	185	2	5	98	56	2,583	3,388	49	1,851	8,218
2018	191	2	5	102	58	2,667	3,498	51	1,911	8,485

3-YEAR TREND — ESTIMATED INDUSTRY SALES ($MILLIONS)

Year	Employee Size of Establishment									Total
	1-4 Emps.	5-9 Emps.	10-19 Emps.	20-49 Emps.	50-99 Emps.	100-249 Emps.	250-499 Emps.	>500 Emps.	Non-Employer	Employ-ment
2016	78.9	2.7	13.5	735.2	926.3	114,357.2	505,557.9	13,357.5	157.3	635,186.5
2017	85.7	2.9	14.7	798.5	1,006.0	124,206.1	549,099.0	14,507.6	170.9	689,891.4
2018	91.0	3.1	15.6	848.0	1,068.4	131,906.9	583,142.9	15,406.9	181.5	732,664.2

3-YEAR TREND — ESTIMATED NUMBER OF EMPLOYEES

Year	Employee Size of Establishment									Total
	1-4 Emps.	5-9 Emps.	10-19 Emps.	20-49 Emps.	50-99 Emps.	100-249 Emps.	250-499 Emps.	>500 Emps.	Non-Employer	Employ-ment
2016	439	13	62	2,812	3,180	309,260	935,778	27,009	1,758	1,280,310
2017	462	14	65	2,961	3,349	325,690	985,494	28,444	1,851	1,348,330
2018	477	14	67	3,057	3,458	336,276	1,017,524	29,368	1,911	1,392,153

SUB-INDUSTRIES – 2017 ESTIMATED INDUSTRY SALES, ESTABLISHMENTS & EMPLOYMENT

Sub-Industries	Cate-gory*	Establish-ments	Sales ($Mill)	Employ-ment
Department stores	Major1	1,635	46,259.7	142,621
Department stores, discount	Minor2	3,020	364,733.8	611,873
Department stores, non-discount	Minor2	823	48,934.1	144,393
Warehouse club stores	Minor2	2,739	229,963.8	449,443

*Category-Major categories (Major1) are more general descriptions for companies that self-selected to capture the many functions they perform in the industry. Minor categories (Minor1, Minor2) are more specific for companies that have more detailed functions (Minor1 is a larger category than Minor2). Minor categories figures (sales, etc.) can be aggregated to larger minor categories (Minor2 sums to Minor1) and major categories overall figures.

OFFICE SUPPLIES & STATIONERY STORES INDUSTRY (NAICS 45321)

NAICS 45321: Office Supplies and Stationery Stores . This industry comprises establishments primarily engaged in one or more of the following: (1) retailing new stationery, school supplies, and office supplies; (2) selling a combination of new office equipment, furniture, and supplies; and (3) selling new office equipment, furniture, and supplies in combination with selling new computers.

INDUSTRY ESTABLISHMENTS, SALES & EMPLOYMENT TRENDS

	Year					Percent Chg. Year-to-Year			
	2014	2015	2016	2017	2018	14-15	15-16	16-17	17-18
Establishments	8,689	8,376	8,271	8,102	7,973	-3.6%	-1.3%	-2.0%	-1.6%
Sales ($Millions)	15,206	14,669	14,467	14,138	13,853	-3.5%	-1.4%	-2.3%	-2.0%
Employment	88,820	85,621	84,549	82,820	81,499	-3.6%	-1.3%	-2.0%	-1.6%
Sales ($M)/Estab.	1.75	1.75	1.75	1.75	1.74	0.1%	-0.1%	-0.2%	-0.4%
Sales ($)/Emp.	171,197	171,321	171,102	170,712	169,979	0.1%	-0.1%	-0.2%	-0.4%

3-YEAR TREND – ESTIMATED NUMBER OF ESTABLISHMENTS

Year	Employee Size of Establishment									Total
	1-4 Emps.	5-9 Emps.	10-19 Emps.	20-49 Emps.	50-99 Emps.	100-249 Emps.	250-499 Emps.	>500 Emps.	Non-Employer	Employ-ment
2016	2,565	730	1,537	1,637	18	7	0	0	1,776	8,271
2017	2,513	715	1,506	1,604	18	7	0	0	1,740	8,102
2018	2,473	704	1,482	1,578	17	6	0	0	1,712	7,973

3-YEAR TREND – ESTIMATED INDUSTRY SALES ($MILLIONS)

Year	Employee Size of Establishment									Total
	1-4 Emps.	5-9 Emps.	10-19 Emps.	20-49 Emps.	50-99 Emps.	100-249 Emps.	250-499 Emps.	>500 Emps.	Non-Employer	Employ-ment
2016	820.5	613.7	3,249.7	9,160.9	222.5	220.9	1.1	5.7	171.6	14,466.6
2017	801.8	599.8	3,176.0	8,953.0	217.4	215.9	1.0	5.6	167.7	14,138.3
2018	785.7	587.7	3,111.9	8,772.4	213.0	211.5	1.0	5.5	164.3	13,853.1

3-YEAR TREND – ESTIMATED NUMBER OF EMPLOYEES

Year	Employee Size of Establishment									Total
	1-4 Emps.	5-9 Emps.	10-19 Emps.	20-49 Emps.	50-99 Emps.	100-249 Emps.	250-499 Emps.	>500 Emps.	Non-Employer	Employ-ment
2016	6,414	4,235	20,908	49,282	1,074	840	3	17	1,776	84,549
2017	6,282	4,148	20,480	48,274	1,052	823	3	17	1,740	82,820
2018	6,182	4,082	20,153	47,504	1,036	810	3	17	1,712	81,499

OFFICE SUPPLIES & STATIONERY STORES INDUSTRY (NAICS 45321)

SUB-INDUSTRIES — 2017 ESTIMATED INDUSTRY SALES, ESTABLISHMENTS & EMPLOYMENT

Sub-Industries	Category*	Establishments	Sales ($Mill)	Employment
Stationery stores	Major1	1,411	4,331.8	21,139
Notary and corporate seals	Minor2	24	2.9	76
Office forms and supplies	Minor2	1,019	298.0	5,543
School supplies	Minor2	150	70.6	529
Writing supplies	Minor2	97	9.5	319
Stationery and office supplies	Major1	1,422	7,124.3	20,129
Writing instruments and supplies	Minor1	23	17.5	411
Marking devices	Minor2	23	29.8	382
Pens and/or pencils	Minor2	58	40.7	649
Writing ink	Minor2	15	7.2	107
Social stationery and greeting cards	Minor1	58	20.6	821
Greeting cards	Minor2	220	112.1	1,892
Stationery	Minor2	193	98.7	1,233
Albums, scrapbooks and binders	Minor1	52	13.7	244
Albums (photo) and scrapbooks	Minor2	92	50.0	1,425
Looseleaf binders	Minor2	23	7.0	79
Computer and photocopying supplies	Minor1	205	186.1	3,441
Computer paper	Minor2	52	77.6	422
Data processing supplies	Minor2	69	38.5	621
Mimeograph paper	Minor2	2	10.8	82
Photocopying supplies	Minor2	40	26.2	641
Laser printer supplies	Minor2	94	66.1	856
Office filing supplies	Minor1	93	35.2	548
File cards	Minor2	6	10.4	96
File folders	Minor2	9	7.1	74
Blank books	Minor2	4	3.1	48
Business forms	Minor2	1,554	715.2	9,661
Carbon paper	Minor2	3	6.1	23
Envelopes	Minor2	117	61.4	1,301
Inked ribbons	Minor2	27	12.0	136
Manifold business forms	Minor2	16	4.1	226
Office supplies, nec	Minor2	855	606.7	9,024
Sales and receipt books	Minor2	45	13.7	201
Stationers, commercial	Minor2	25	23.4	436
Tabulation cards	Minor2	3	0.3	4

*Category-Major categories (Major1) are more general descriptions for companies that self-selected to capture the many functions they perform in the industry. Minor categories (Minor1, Minor2) are more specific for companies that have more detailed functions (Minor1 is a larger category than Minor2). Minor categories figures (sales, etc.) can be aggregated to larger minor categories (Minor2 sums to Minor1) and major categories overall figures.

ELECTRONIC SHOPPING & MAIL ORDER HOUSES (NAICS 45411)

NAICS 45411: Electronic Shopping and Mail-Order Houses This industry comprises establishments primarily engaged in retailing all types of merchandise by means of mail or by electronic media, such as interactive television or computer. Included in this industry are establishments primarily engaged in retailing from catalogue showrooms of mail-order houses.

INDUSTRY ESTABLISHMENTS, SALES & EMPLOYMENT TRENDS

	Year					Percent Chg. Year-to-Year			
	2014	2015	2016	2017	2018	14-15	15-16	16-17	17-18
Establishments	80,990	86,436	92,617	99,772	105,374	6.7%	7.2%	7.7%	5.6%
Sales ($Millions)	351,725	397,814	449,185	507,782	561,426	13.1%	12.9%	13.0%	10.6%
Employment	421,321	449,652	481,808	519,028	548,172	6.7%	7.2%	7.7%	5.6%
Sales ($M)/Estab.	4.34	4.60	4.85	5.09	5.33	6.0%	5.4%	4.9%	4.7%
Sales ($)/Emp.	834,813	884,716	932,291	978,332	1,024,177	6.0%	5.4%	4.9%	4.7%

3-YEAR TREND – ESTIMATED NUMBER OF ESTABLISHMENTS

Year	Employee Size of Establishment									Total
	1-4 Emps.	5-9 Emps.	10-19 Emps.	20-49 Emps.	50-99 Emps.	100-249 Emps.	250-499 Emps.	>500 Emps.	Non-Employer	Employ-ment
2016	25,646	5,180	3,059	1,870	612	443	192	117	55,499	92,617
2017	27,627	5,581	3,295	2,014	659	477	207	126	59,787	99,772
2018	29,178	5,894	3,480	2,127	696	504	219	133	63,144	105,374

3-YEAR TREND – ESTIMATED INDUSTRY SALES ($MILLIONS)

Year	Employee Size of Establishment									Total
	1-4 Emps.	5-9 Emps.	10-19 Emps.	20-49 Emps.	50-99 Emps.	100-249 Emps.	250-499 Emps.	>500 Emps.	Non-Employer	Employ-ment
2016	36,270.4	19,256.7	28,595.7	46,262.4	33,276.2	64,875.2	94,921.3	120,242.3	5,485.1	449,185.3
2017	41,272.7	21,912.5	32,539.5	52,642.8	37,865.5	73,822.6	108,012.6	133,472.1	6,241.6	507,782.0
2018	45,841.3	24,338.1	36,141.3	58,470.0	42,056.9	81,994.2	119,968.8	145,682.6	6,932.5	561,425.7

3-YEAR TREND – ESTIMATED NUMBER OF EMPLOYEES

Year	Employee Size of Establishment									Total
	1-4 Emps.	5-9 Emps.	10-19 Emps.	20-49 Emps.	50-99 Emps.	100-249 Emps.	250-499 Emps.	>500 Emps.	Non-Employer	Employ-ment
2016	64,114	30,046	41,603	56,279	36,341	55,807	55,887	86,232	55,499	481,808
2017	69,067	32,367	44,817	60,626	39,149	60,118	60,205	92,893	59,787	519,028
2018	72,945	34,185	47,333	64,031	41,347	63,494	63,585	98,109	63,144	548,172

ELECTRONIC SHOPPING & MAIL ORDER HOUSES (NAICS 45411)

SUB-INDUSTRIES – 2017 ESTIMATED INDUSTRY SALES, ESTABLISHMENTS & EMPLOYMENT

Sub-Industries	Cate-gory*	Establish-ments	Sales ($Mill)	Employ-ment
Catalog and mail-order houses	Major1	22,528	38,620.5	113,282
Food, mail order	Minor1	1,191	693.1	6,910
Cheese, mail order	Minor2	85	24.6	4,120
Fruit, mail order	Minor2	998	253.2	4,510
Computer equipment and electronics, mail order	Minor1	2,757	10,337.9	8,603
Computer software, mail order	Minor2	2,183	52,600.5	14,247
Computers and peripheral equipment, mail order	Minor2	992	18,862.9	5,013
Electronic kits and parts, mail order	Minor2	447	236.6	1,914
Book and record clubs	Minor1	453	140,538.6	6,682
Book club, mail order	Minor2	520	212.5	6,424
Magazines, mail order	Minor2	593	260.6	2,953
Record and/or tape (music or video) club, mail order	Minor2	2,122	2,345.8	18,374
Stamps, coins, and other collectibles, mail order	Minor1	1,886	329.4	2,238
Coins, mail order	Minor2	345	379.8	1,683
Collectibles and antiques, mail order	Minor2	7,467	985.8	11,209
Stamps, mail order	Minor2	514	296.2	2,354
Catalog and mail-order houses, nec	Minor2	1,179	50,454.7	3,435
Arts and crafts equipment and supplies, mail order	Minor2	2,116	255.5	3,997
Automotive supplies and equipment, mail order	Minor2	1,905	2,447.1	7,390
Books, mail order (except book clubs)	Minor2	3,065	924.0	7,767
Cards, mail order	Minor2	568	279.0	4,282
Catalog sales	Minor2	6,917	9,837.3	56,653
Clothing, mail order (except women's)	Minor2	1,512	802.0	8,332
Cosmetics and perfumes, mail order	Minor2	1,548	685.7	2,579
Educational supplies and equipment, mail order	Minor2	1,826	1,040.8	5,389
Fishing, hunting and camping equipment and supplies: by	Minor2	810	15,298.7	14,727
Fitness and sporting goods, mail order	Minor2	1,820	1,091.2	9,185
Flowers, plants and bulbs: mail order	Minor2	943	362.6	2,771
Furniture and furnishings, mail order	Minor2	992	589.4	3,789
General merchandise, mail order	Minor2	8,537	8,002.5	20,596
Gift items, mail order	Minor2	4,129	1,535.2	13,100
Jewelry, mail order	Minor2	2,013	1,150.8	3,201
Mail order house, nec	Minor2	7,775	7,171.9	62,376
Misc. mail order items	Minor2	7,038	138,875.6	78,941

*Category-Major categories (Major1) are more general descriptions for companies that self-selected to capture the many functions they perform in the industry. Minor categories (Minor1, Minor2) are more specific for companies that have more detailed functions (Minor1 is a larger category than Minor2). Minor categories figures (sales, etc.) can be aggregated to larger minor categories (Minor2 sums to Minor1) and major categories overall figures.

SCHEDULED AIR TRANSPORTATION INDUSTRY (NAICS 48111)

NAICS 48111: Scheduled Air Transportation Industry. This industry comprises establishments primarily engaged in providing air transportation of passengers and/or cargo over regular routes and on regular schedules. Establishments in this industry operate flights even if partially loaded. Establishments primarily engaged in providing scheduled air transportation of mail on a contract basis are included in this industry.

INDUSTRY ESTABLISHMENTS, SALES & EMPLOYMENT TRENDS

	Year					Percent Chg. Year-to-Year			
	2014	2015	2016	2017	2018	14-15	15-16	16-17	17-18
Establishments	5,962	5,790	5,663	5,603	5,564	-2.9%	-2.2%	-1.1%	-0.7%
Sales ($Millions)	129,084	138,869	148,656	159,058	169,425	7.6%	7.0%	7.0%	6.5%
Employment	196,888	191,201	187,001	185,020	183,739	-2.9%	-2.2%	-1.1%	-0.7%
Sales ($M)/Estab.	21.65	23.99	26.25	28.39	30.45	10.8%	9.5%	8.1%	7.3%
Sales ($)/Emp.	655,623	726,301	794,948	859,680	922,095	10.8%	9.5%	8.1%	7.3%

3-YEAR TREND — ESTIMATED NUMBER OF ESTABLISHMENTS

Year	Employee Size of Establishment									Total
	1-4 Emps.	5-9 Emps.	10-19 Emps.	20-49 Emps.	50-99 Emps.	100-249 Emps.	250-499 Emps.	>500 Emps.	Non-Employer	Employ-ment
2016	737	292	356	430	209	182	81	104	3,271	5,663
2017	729	288	352	426	207	180	80	103	3,236	5,603
2018	724	286	350	423	205	179	79	103	3,214	5,564

3-YEAR TREND — ESTIMATED INDUSTRY SALES ($MILLIONS)

Year	Employee Size of Establishment									Total
	1-4 Emps.	5-9 Emps.	10-19 Emps.	20-49 Emps.	50-99 Emps.	100-249 Emps.	250-499 Emps.	>500 Emps.	Non-Employer	Employ-ment
2016	637.1	662.5	2,034.9	6,506.5	6,946.1	16,338.4	24,378.9	90,722.3	429.3	148,656.2
2017	678.3	705.3	2,166.5	6,927.2	7,395.2	17,394.7	25,955.1	97,378.2	457.1	159,057.6
2018	720.1	748.8	2,300.2	7,354.7	7,851.6	18,468.2	27,556.8	103,939.5	485.3	169,425.2

3-YEAR TREND — ESTIMATED NUMBER OF EMPLOYEES

Year	Employee Size of Establishment									Total
	1-4 Emps.	5-9 Emps.	10-19 Emps.	20-49 Emps.	50-99 Emps.	100-249 Emps.	250-499 Emps.	>500 Emps.	Non-Employer	Employ-ment
2016	1,843	1,691	4,844	12,951	12,412	22,995	23,485	103,510	3,271	187,001
2017	1,823	1,673	4,793	12,813	12,280	22,752	23,236	102,413	3,236	185,020
2018	1,810	1,662	4,759	12,725	12,195	22,594	23,075	101,704	3,214	183,739

SCHEDULED AIR TRANSPORTATION INDUSTRY (NAICS 48111)

SUB-INDUSTRIES – 2017 ESTIMATED INDUSTRY SALES, ESTABLISHMENTS & EMPLOYMENT

Sub-Industries	Cate-gory*	Establish-ments	Sales ($Mill)	Employ-ment
Air transportation, scheduled	Major1	1,925	25,308.8	40,984
Air cargo carrier, scheduled	Minor2	984	1,731.3	17,524
Air passenger carrier, scheduled	Minor2	2,394	131,511.8	123,326
Helicopter carrier, scheduled	Minor2	299	505.9	3,185

*Category-Major categories (Major1) are more general descriptions for companies that self-selected to capture the many functions they perform in the industry. Minor categories (Minor1, Minor2) are more specific for companies that have more detailed functions (Minor1 is a larger category than Minor2). Minor categories figures (sales, etc.) can be aggregated to larger minor categories (Minor2 sums to Minor1) and major categories overall figures.

LOCAL FREIGHT TRUCKING INDUSTRY
(NAICS 48411)

NAICS 48411: Freight Trucking, Local. This industry comprises establishments primarily engaged in providing local general freight trucking. General freight establishments handle a wide variety of commodities, generally palletized and transported in a container or van trailer. Local general freight trucking establishments usually provide trucking within a metropolitan area which may cross state lines. Generally the trips are same-day return.

INDUSTRY ESTABLISHMENTS, SALES & EMPLOYMENT TRENDS

	Year					Percent Chg. Year-to-Year			
	2014	2015	2016	2017	2018	14-15	15-16	16-17	17-18
Establishments	57,317	58,262	59,639	61,404	63,484	1.6%	2.4%	3.0%	3.4%
Sales ($Millions)	21,610	21,864	22,230	22,708	23,243	1.2%	1.7%	2.2%	2.4%
Employment	226,466	230,201	235,639	242,615	250,833	1.6%	2.4%	3.0%	3.4%
Sales ($M)/Estab.	0.38	0.38	0.37	0.37	0.37	-0.5%	-0.7%	-0.8%	-1.0%
Sales ($)/Emp.	95,423	94,979	94,338	93,598	92,665	-0.5%	-0.7%	-0.8%	-1.0%

3-YEAR TREND — ESTIMATED NUMBER OF ESTABLISHMENTS

Year	Employee Size of Establishment									Total
	1-4 Emps.	5-9 Emps.	10-19 Emps.	20-49 Emps.	50-99 Emps.	100-249 Emps.	250-499 Emps.	>500 Emps.	Non-Employer	Employ-ment
2016	20,407	3,997	2,622	1,616	388	120	15	6	30,468	59,639
2017	21,012	4,115	2,700	1,664	400	123	15	6	31,370	61,404
2018	21,723	4,254	2,791	1,720	413	127	16	7	32,433	63,484

3-YEAR TREND — ESTIMATED INDUSTRY SALES ($MILLIONS)

Year	Employee Size of Establishment									Total
	1-4 Emps.	5-9 Emps.	10-19 Emps.	20-49 Emps.	50-99 Emps.	100-249 Emps.	250-499 Emps.	>500 Emps.	Non-Employer	Employ-ment
2016	3,431.0	1,766.1	2,913.8	4,752.9	2,509.4	2,085.2	855.6	751.3	3,164.4	22,229.7
2017	3,505.8	1,804.5	2,977.3	4,856.5	2,564.1	2,130.6	874.2	761.9	3,233.4	22,708.3
2018	3,589.4	1,847.6	3,048.3	4,972.3	2,625.2	2,181.4	895.1	773.6	3,310.5	23,243.5

3-YEAR TREND — ESTIMATED NUMBER OF EMPLOYEES

Year	Employee Size of Establishment									Total
	1-4 Emps.	5-9 Emps.	10-19 Emps.	20-49 Emps.	50-99 Emps.	100-249 Emps.	250-499 Emps.	>500 Emps.	Non-Employer	Employ-ment
2016	51,019	23,180	35,660	48,639	23,054	15,089	4,238	4,293	30,468	235,639
2017	52,529	23,866	36,716	50,079	23,736	15,536	4,363	4,420	31,370	242,615
2018	54,308	24,675	37,960	51,775	24,540	16,062	4,511	4,570	32,433	250,833

SUB-INDUSTRIES – 2017 ESTIMATED INDUSTRY SALES, ESTABLISHMENTS & EMPLOYMENT

Sub-Industries	Cate-gory*	Establish-ments	Sales ($Mill)	Employ-ment
Local trucking, without storage	Major1	44,705	14,290.2	150,969
Animal and farm product transportation services	Minor1	237	97.5	990
Animal transport	Minor2	278	90.4	943
Farm to market haulage, local	Minor2	264	133.6	1,254
Live poultry haulage	Minor2	19	16.1	167
Liquid transfer services	Minor1	89	99.5	945
Liquid haulage, local	Minor2	285	292.2	2,383
Petroleum haulage, local	Minor2	181	374.5	2,530
Lumber and timber trucking	Minor1	125	67.5	640
Lumber (log) trucking, local	Minor2	280	137.5	1,312
Timber trucking, local	Minor2	66	47.2	470
Moving services	Minor1	2,275	1,039.9	13,575
Furniture moving, local: without storage	Minor2	263	138.9	1,803
Safe moving, local	Minor2	19	11.4	100
Baggage transfer	Minor2	24	64.2	740
Coal haulage, local	Minor2	153	116.9	1,246
Delivery service, vehicular	Minor2	4,608	1,735.6	20,654
Draying, local: without storage	Minor2	42	37.3	418
Dump truck haulage	Minor2	2,320	1,222.0	11,653
Garbage collection and transport, no disposal	Minor2	935	655.4	11,402
Hazardous waste transport	Minor2	128	212.7	2,087
Heavy machinery transport, local	Minor2	200	141.4	1,291
Light haulage and cartage, local	Minor2	3,016	734.6	8,596
Mail carriers, contract	Minor2	489	419.9	4,143
Star routes, local	Minor2	6	10.9	81
Steel hauling, local	Minor2	87	42.8	408
Truck rental with drivers	Minor2	311	478.3	1,814

*Category-Major categories (Major1) are more general descriptions for companies that self-selected to capture the many functions they perform in the industry. Minor categories (Minor1, Minor2) are more specific for companies that have more detailed functions (Minor1 is a larger category than Minor2). Minor categories figures (sales, etc.) can be aggregated to larger minor categories (Minor2 sums to Minor1) and major categories overall figures.

FREIGHT TRUCKING LONG DISTANCE INDUSTRY (NAICS 48412)

NAICS 48412: Freight Trucking, Long-Distance. This industry comprises establishments primarily engaged in providing long-distance general freight trucking. General freight establishments handle a wide variety of commodities, generally palletized and transported in a container or van trailer. Long-distance general freight trucking establishments usually provide trucking between metropolitan areas which may cross North American country borders. Included in this industry are establishments operating as truckload (TL) or less than truckload (LTL) carriers.

INDUSTRY ESTABLISHMENTS, SALES & EMPLOYMENT TRENDS

	Year					Percent Chg. Year-to-Year			
	2014	2015	2016	2017	2018	14-15	15-16	16-17	17-18
Establishments	70,767	71,482	72,476	74,478	76,877	1.0%	1.4%	2.8%	3.2%
Sales ($Millions)	127,986	135,995	144,384	154,755	165,981	6.3%	6.2%	7.2%	7.3%
Employment	689,849	696,819	706,507	726,023	749,408	1.0%	1.4%	2.8%	3.2%
Sales ($M)/Estab.	1.81	1.90	1.99	2.08	2.16	5.2%	4.7%	4.3%	3.9%
Sales ($)/Emp.	185,528	195,165	204,363	213,154	221,482	5.2%	4.7%	4.3%	3.9%

3-YEAR TREND – ESTIMATED NUMBER OF ESTABLISHMENTS

Year	Employee Size of Establishment									Total
	1-4 Emps.	5-9 Emps.	10-19 Emps.	20-49 Emps.	50-99 Emps.	100-249 Emps.	250-499 Emps.	>500 Emps.	Non-Employer	Employ-ment
2016	27,053	4,461	3,634	3,702	1,700	1,121	286	128	30,391	72,476
2017	27,800	4,584	3,734	3,805	1,747	1,152	294	132	31,230	74,478
2018	28,696	4,732	3,854	3,927	1,803	1,190	303	136	32,236	76,877

3-YEAR TREND – ESTIMATED INDUSTRY SALES ($MILLIONS)

Year	Employee Size of Establishment									Total
	1-4 Emps.	5-9 Emps.	10-19 Emps.	20-49 Emps.	50-99 Emps.	100-249 Emps.	250-499 Emps.	>500 Emps.	Non-Employer	Employ-ment
2016	7,463.0	3,234.7	6,625.6	17,868.3	18,036.5	32,066.1	27,537.4	27,100.7	4,451.9	144,384.1
2017	8,014.9	3,473.9	7,115.5	19,189.5	19,370.1	34,437.1	29,573.5	28,799.1	4,781.0	154,754.5
2018	8,615.5	3,734.2	7,648.7	20,627.5	20,821.7	37,017.7	31,789.7	30,586.3	5,139.3	165,980.6

3-YEAR TREND – ESTIMATED NUMBER OF EMPLOYEES

Year	Employee Size of Establishment									Total
	1-4 Emps.	5-9 Emps.	10-19 Emps.	20-49 Emps.	50-99 Emps.	100-249 Emps.	250-499 Emps.	>500 Emps.	Non-Employer	Employ-ment
2016	67,632	25,875	49,418	111,439	100,985	141,414	83,121	96,233	30,391	706,507
2017	69,500	26,590	50,783	114,517	103,774	145,320	85,417	98,891	31,230	726,023
2018	71,739	27,446	52,419	118,206	107,117	150,001	88,168	102,076	32,236	749,408

FREIGHT TRUCKING LONG DISTANCE INDUSTRY (NAICS 48412)

SUB-INDUSTRIES — 2017 ESTIMATED INDUSTRY SALES, ESTABLISHMENTS & EMPLOYMENT

Sub-Industries	Category*	Establishments	Sales ($Mill)	Employment
Trucking, except local	Major1	51,040	107,341.3	471,162
Automobiles, transport and delivery	Minor2	2,743	2,323.7	15,431
Building materials transport	Minor2	466	508.4	7,197
Contract haulers	Minor2	8,492	16,150.8	118,111
Heavy hauling, nec	Minor2	4,800	3,762.7	27,255
Heavy machinery transport	Minor2	553	838.0	4,896
Household goods transport	Minor2	1,947	5,690.0	27,849
Less-than-truckload (LTL)	Minor2	407	10,047.0	16,578
Liquid petroleum transport, non-local	Minor2	587	2,366.2	12,913
Mobile homes transport	Minor2	1,669	586.5	4,844
Refrigerated products transport	Minor2	1,446	4,976.3	18,178
Trailer or container on flat car (TOFC/COFC)	Minor2	327	163.5	1,608

*Category-Major categories (Major1) are more general descriptions for companies that self-selected to capture the many functions they perform in the industry. Minor categories (Minor1, Minor2) are more specific for companies that have more detailed functions (Minor1 is a larger category than Minor2). Minor categories figures (sales, etc.) can be aggregated to larger minor categories (Minor2 sums to Minor1) and major categories overall figures.

GENERAL WAREHOUSING & STORAGE INDUSTRY (NAICS 49311)

NAICS 49311: General Warehousing and Storage . This industry comprises establishments primarily engaged in operating merchandise warehousing and storage facilities. These establishments generally handle goods in containers, such as boxes, barrels, and/or drums, using equipment, such as forklifts, pallets, and racks. They are not specialized in handling bulk products of any particular type, size, or quantity of goods or products.

INDUSTRY ESTABLISHMENTS, SALES & EMPLOYMENT TRENDS

	Year					Percent Chg. Year-to-Year			
	2014	2015	2016	2017	2018	14-15	15-16	16-17	17-18
Establishments	13,429	13,248	13,191	13,558	14,121	-1.4%	-0.4%	2.8%	4.2%
Sales ($Millions)	45,582	47,317	49,328	52,780	56,965	3.8%	4.3%	7.0%	7.9%
Employment	553,362	545,875	543,525	558,668	581,856	-1.4%	-0.4%	2.8%	4.2%
Sales ($M)/Estab.	3.39	3.57	3.74	3.89	4.03	5.2%	4.7%	4.1%	3.6%
Sales ($)/Emp.	82,373	86,681	90,757	94,475	97,903	5.2%	4.7%	4.1%	3.6%

3-YEAR TREND — ESTIMATED NUMBER OF ESTABLISHMENTS

Year	Employee Size of Establishment									Total
	1-4 Emps.	5-9 Emps.	10-19 Emps.	20-49 Emps.	50-99 Emps.	100-249 Emps.	250-499 Emps.	>500 Emps.	Non-Employer	Employ-ment
2016	2,926	1,630	1,610	1,685	909	783	361	290	2,998	13,191
2017	3,008	1,675	1,655	1,731	934	805	372	298	3,082	13,558
2018	3,132	1,744	1,723	1,803	973	838	387	310	3,209	14,121

3-YEAR TREND — ESTIMATED INDUSTRY SALES ($MILLIONS)

Year	Employee Size of Establishment									Total
	1-4 Emps.	5-9 Emps.	10-19 Emps.	20-49 Emps.	50-99 Emps.	100-249 Emps.	250-499 Emps.	>500 Emps.	Non-Employer	Employ-ment
2016	289.7	424.0	1,053.4	2,917.4	3,459.0	8,032.5	12,500.5	20,360.3	291.8	49,328.5
2017	310.7	454.8	1,129.9	3,129.5	3,710.4	8,616.4	13,409.1	21,706.5	313.0	52,780.4
2018	336.6	492.7	1,224.0	3,389.9	4,019.2	9,333.4	14,525.0	23,305.5	339.1	56,965.3

3-YEAR TREND — ESTIMATED NUMBER OF EMPLOYEES

Year	Employee Size of Establishment									Total
	1-4 Emps.	5-9 Emps.	10-19 Emps.	20-49 Emps.	50-99 Emps.	100-249 Emps.	250-499 Emps.	>500 Emps.	Non-Employer	Employ-ment
2016	7,315	9,451	21,894	50,704	53,968	98,715	105,148	193,331	2,998	543,525
2017	7,519	9,714	22,504	52,116	55,472	101,465	108,078	198,717	3,082	558,668
2018	7,831	10,118	23,438	54,280	57,774	105,677	112,564	206,965	3,209	581,856

GENERAL WAREHOUSING & STORAGE INDUSTRY (NAICS 49311)

SUB-INDUSTRIES – 2017 ESTIMATED INDUSTRY SALES, ESTABLISHMENTS & EMPLOYMENT

Sub-Industries	Cate-gory*	Establish-ments	Sales ($Mill)	Employ-ment
General warehousing and storage	Major1	6,048	24,104.5	358,061
General warehousing	Minor2	2,548	19,983.2	126,233
Miniwarehouse, warehousing	Minor2	1,638	2,303.0	20,789
Warehousing, self storage	Minor2	3,324	6,389.7	53,586

*Category-Major categories (Major1) are more general descriptions for companies that self-selected to capture the many functions they perform in the industry. Minor categories (Minor1, Minor2) are more specific for companies that have more detailed functions (Minor1 is a larger category than Minor2). Minor categories figures (sales, etc.) can be aggregated to larger minor categories (Minor2 sums to Minor1) and major categories overall figures.

NEWSPAPER PUBLISHING INDUSTRY
(NAICS 51111)

NAICS 51111: Newspaper Publishers . Establishments primarily engaged in publishing newspapers, or in publishing and printing newspapers. These establishments carry on the various operations necessary for issuing newspapers, including the gathering of news and the preparation of editorials and advertisements, but may or may not perform their own printing.

INDUSTRY ESTABLISHMENTS, SALES & EMPLOYMENT TRENDS

	Year					Percent Chg. Year-to-Year			
	2014	2015	2016	2017	2018	14-15	15-16	16-17	17-18
Establishments	18,185	18,020	18,007	18,029	18,289	-0.9%	-0.1%	0.1%	1.4%
Sales ($Millions)	33,037	33,194	33,537	33,907	34,624	0.5%	1.0%	1.1%	2.1%
Employment	196,420	194,640	194,504	194,740	197,548	-0.9%	-0.1%	0.1%	1.4%
Sales ($M)/Estab.	1.82	1.84	1.86	1.88	1.89	1.4%	1.1%	1.0%	0.7%
Sales ($)/Emp.	168,196	170,540	172,425	174,115	175,271	1.4%	1.1%	1.0%	0.7%

3-YEAR TREND – ESTIMATED NUMBER OF ESTABLISHMENTS

Year	Employee Size of Establishment									Total
	1-4 Emps.	5-9 Emps.	10-19 Emps.	20-49 Emps.	50-99 Emps.	100-249 Emps.	250-499 Emps.	>500 Emps.	Non-Employer	Employment
2016	2,625	1,586	1,287	988	413	269	97	47	10,694	18,007
2017	2,628	1,588	1,289	989	413	270	97	47	10,707	18,029
2018	2,666	1,611	1,307	1,004	419	274	99	47	10,862	18,289

3-YEAR TREND – ESTIMATED INDUSTRY SALES ($MILLIONS)

Year	Employee Size of Establishment									Total
	1-4 Emps.	5-9 Emps.	10-19 Emps.	20-49 Emps.	50-99 Emps.	100-249 Emps.	250-499 Emps.	>500 Emps.	Non-Employer	Employment
2016	591.6	939.6	1,917.4	3,896.1	3,578.5	6,291.0	7,639.5	7,986.5	697.3	33,537.4
2017	598.1	950.0	1,938.7	3,939.4	3,618.3	6,361.0	7,724.5	8,071.8	705.1	33,907.0
2018	611.5	971.3	1,982.1	4,027.7	3,699.4	6,503.5	7,897.6	8,210.4	720.9	34,624.4

3-YEAR TREND – ESTIMATED NUMBER OF EMPLOYEES

Year	Employee Size of Establishment									Total
	1-4 Emps.	5-9 Emps.	10-19 Emps.	20-49 Emps.	50-99 Emps.	100-249 Emps.	250-499 Emps.	>500 Emps.	Non-Employer	Employment
2016	6,563	9,201	17,508	29,747	24,528	33,965	28,230	34,068	10,694	194,504
2017	6,571	9,212	17,529	29,783	24,558	34,006	28,264	34,110	10,707	194,740
2018	6,666	9,345	17,782	30,212	24,912	34,496	28,672	34,602	10,862	197,548

SUB-INDUSTRIES — 2017 ESTIMATED INDUSTRY SALES, ESTABLISHMENTS & EMPLOYMENT

Sub-Industries	Cate-gory*	Establish-ments	Sales ($Mill)	Employ-ment
Newspapers	Major1	7,480	3,344.7	54,941
Newspapers, publishing and printing	Minor1	5,864	26,705.9	89,566
Commercial printing and newspaper publishing combined	Minor2	817	480.6	13,334
Job printing and newspaper publishing combined	Minor2	527	173.5	3,709
Newspapers: publishing only, not printed on site	Minor2	3,341	3,202.4	33,190

*Category-Major categories (Major1) are more general descriptions for companies that self-selected to capture the many functions they perform in the industry. Minor categories (Minor1, Minor2) are more specific for companies that have more detailed functions (Minor1 is a larger category than Minor2). Minor categories figures (sales, etc.) can be aggregated to larger minor categories (Minor2 sums to Minor1) and major categories overall figures.

PERIODICAL PUBLISHING INDUSTRY
(NAICS 51112)

NAICS 51112: Periodical Publishing . Establishments primarily engaged in publishing periodicals, or in publishing and printing periodicals. These establishments carry on the various operations necessary for issuing periodicals, but may or may not perform their own printing. Establishments not engaged in publishing periodicals, but which print periodicals for publishers, are classified in SIC 2752-2759.

INDUSTRY ESTABLISHMENTS, SALES & EMPLOYMENT TRENDS

	Year					Percent Chg. Year-to-Year			
	2014	2015	2016	2017	2018	14-15	15-16	16-17	17-18
Establishments	14,942	14,709	14,597	14,390	14,372	-1.6%	-0.8%	-1.4%	-0.1%
Sales ($Millions)	27,527	27,450	27,506	27,376	27,498	-0.3%	0.2%	-0.5%	0.4%
Employment	106,190	104,536	103,743	102,266	102,139	-1.6%	-0.8%	-1.4%	-0.1%
Sales ($M)/Estab.	1.84	1.87	1.88	1.90	1.91	1.3%	1.0%	1.0%	0.6%
Sales ($)/Emp.	259,223	262,585	265,131	267,692	269,217	1.3%	1.0%	1.0%	0.6%

3-YEAR TREND — ESTIMATED NUMBER OF ESTABLISHMENTS

Year	Employee Size of Establishment									Total
	1-4 Emps.	5-9 Emps.	10-19 Emps.	20-49 Emps.	50-99 Emps.	100-249 Emps.	250-499 Emps.	>500 Emps.	Non-Employer	Employ-ment
2016	3,209	1,018	789	527	201	135	29	20	8,669	14,597
2017	3,164	1,003	778	519	198	133	29	19	8,546	14,390
2018	3,160	1,002	777	518	198	133	29	19	8,535	14,372

3-YEAR TREND — ESTIMATED INDUSTRY SALES ($MILLIONS)

Year	Employee Size of Establishment									Total
	1-4 Emps.	5-9 Emps.	10-19 Emps.	20-49 Emps.	50-99 Emps.	100-249 Emps.	250-499 Emps.	>500 Emps.	Non-Employer	Employ-ment
2016	1,243.1	1,036.4	2,021.0	3,568.4	2,997.9	5,412.7	3,965.9	6,697.6	562.5	27,505.5
2017	1,234.6	1,029.3	2,007.2	3,544.0	2,977.4	5,375.8	3,938.8	6,710.0	558.7	27,375.7
2018	1,239.9	1,033.7	2,015.7	3,559.1	2,990.1	5,398.7	3,955.6	6,743.7	561.1	27,497.6

3-YEAR TREND — ESTIMATED NUMBER OF EMPLOYEES

Year	Employee Size of Establishment									Total
	1-4 Emps.	5-9 Emps.	10-19 Emps.	20-49 Emps.	50-99 Emps.	100-249 Emps.	250-499 Emps.	>500 Emps.	Non-Employer	Employ-ment
2016	8,023	5,904	10,736	15,850	11,954	17,001	8,526	17,079	8,669	103,743
2017	7,909	5,820	10,583	15,624	11,784	16,759	8,405	16,836	8,546	102,266
2018	7,899	5,813	10,570	15,605	11,770	16,738	8,394	16,815	8,535	102,139

SUB-INDUSTRIES – 2017 ESTIMATED INDUSTRY SALES, ESTABLISHMENTS & EMPLOYMENT

Sub-Industries	Category*	Establishments	Sales ($Mill)	Employment
Periodicals	Major1	6,005	2,802.6	25,912
Periodicals, publishing only	Minor1	1,099	1,360.4	8,721
Comic books: publishing only, not printed on site	Minor2	74	46.6	281
Magazines: publishing only, not printed on site	Minor2	3,145	5,227.0	32,029
Statistical reports (periodicals): publishing only	Minor2	100	1,102.5	2,742
Television schedules: publishing only, not printed on site	Minor2	10	4.6	123
Trade journals: publishing only, not printed on site	Minor2	611	11,176.8	7,251
Periodicals, publishing and printing	Minor1	327	471.0	4,612
Comic books: publishing and printing	Minor2	105	21.0	179
Magazines: publishing and printing	Minor2	2,507	4,523.5	16,568
Statistical reports (periodicals): publishing and printing	Minor2	81	28.6	1,096
Television schedules: publishing and printing	Minor2	16	58.6	410
Trade journals: publishing and printing	Minor2	310	552.6	2,343

*Category-Major categories (Major1) are more general descriptions for companies that self-selected to capture the many functions they perform in the industry. Minor categories (Minor1, Minor2) are more specific for companies that have more detailed functions (Minor1 is a larger category than Minor2). Minor categories figures (sales, etc.) can be aggregated to larger minor categories (Minor2 sums to Minor1) and major categories overall figures.

BOOK PUBLISHING INDUSTRY
(NAICS 51113)

NAICS 51113: Book Publishers . This U.S. industry comprises establishments known as book publishers. Establishments in this industry carry out design, editing, and marketing activities necessary for producing and distributing books. These establishments may publish books in print, electronic, or audio form.

INDUSTRY ESTABLISHMENTS, SALES & EMPLOYMENT TRENDS

	Year					Percent Chg. Year-to-Year			
	2014	2015	2016	2017	2018	14-15	15-16	16-17	17-18
Establishments	6,476	6,278	6,129	6,052	6,054	-3.1%	-2.4%	-1.3%	0.0%
Sales ($Millions)	20,811	20,967	21,186	21,570	22,139	0.8%	1.0%	1.8%	2.6%
Employment	60,698	58,845	57,446	56,723	56,747	-3.1%	-2.4%	-1.3%	0.0%
Sales ($M)/Estab.	3.21	3.34	3.46	3.56	3.66	3.9%	3.5%	3.1%	2.6%
Sales ($)/Emp.	342,854	356,315	368,799	380,263	390,135	3.9%	3.5%	3.1%	2.6%

3-YEAR TREND – ESTIMATED NUMBER OF ESTABLISHMENTS

Year	Employee Size of Establishment									Total
	1-4 Emps.	5-9 Emps.	10-19 Emps.	20-49 Emps.	50-99 Emps.	100-249 Emps.	250-499 Emps.	>500 Emps.	Non-Employer	Employ-ment
2016	1,449	327	256	233	98	86	20	19	3,640	6,129
2017	1,431	323	253	230	97	85	20	19	3,594	6,052
2018	1,431	323	253	230	97	85	20	19	3,596	6,054

3-YEAR TREND – ESTIMATED INDUSTRY SALES ($MILLIONS)

Year	Employee Size of Establishment									Total
	1-4 Emps.	5-9 Emps.	10-19 Emps.	20-49 Emps.	50-99 Emps.	100-249 Emps.	250-499 Emps.	>500 Emps.	Non-Employer	Employ-ment
2016	694.5	412.5	812.5	1,952.2	1,814.2	4,278.4	3,327.7	7,647.3	246.8	21,186.2
2017	705.4	419.0	825.3	1,982.9	1,842.7	4,345.6	3,380.0	7,818.0	250.7	21,569.5
2018	724.1	430.1	847.1	2,035.4	1,891.5	4,460.7	3,469.5	8,023.3	257.3	22,139.0

3-YEAR TREND – ESTIMATED NUMBER OF EMPLOYEES

Year	Employee Size of Establishment									Total
	1-4 Emps.	5-9 Emps.	10-19 Emps.	20-49 Emps.	50-99 Emps.	100-249 Emps.	250-499 Emps.	>500 Emps.	Non-Employer	Employ-ment
2016	3,622	1,899	3,488	7,008	5,847	10,860	5,782	15,300	3,640	57,446
2017	3,577	1,875	3,444	6,920	5,773	10,724	5,709	15,107	3,594	56,723
2018	3,578	1,876	3,446	6,923	5,775	10,728	5,711	15,114	3,596	56,747

BOOK PUBLISHING INDUSTRY
(NAICS 51113)

SUB-INDUSTRIES – 2017 ESTIMATED INDUSTRY SALES, ESTABLISHMENTS & EMPLOYMENT

Sub-Industries	Cate-gory*	Establish-ments	Sales ($Mill)	Employ-ment
Book publishing	Major1	3,750	2,629.5	20,778
Books, publishing only	Minor1	1,263	15,376.5	19,049
Book clubs: publishing only, not printed on site	Minor2	34	29.0	149
Book music: publishing only, not printed on site	Minor2	49	25.6	153
Pamphlets: publishing only, not printed on site	Minor2	75	84.4	506
Textbooks: publishing only, not printed on site	Minor2	156	2,557.6	2,401
Books, publishing and printing	Minor1	404	486.5	8,869
Book clubs: publishing and printing	Minor2	62	99.6	392
Book music: publishing and printing	Minor2	86	25.3	254
Pamphlets: publishing and printing	Minor2	90	172.1	1,159
Textbooks: publishing and printing	Minor2	84	83.6	3,012

*Category-Major categories (Major1) are more general descriptions for companies that self-selected to capture the many functions they perform in the industry. Minor categories (Minor1, Minor2) are more specific for companies that have more detailed functions (Minor1 is a larger category than Minor2). Minor categories figures (sales, etc.) can be aggregated to larger minor categories (Minor2 sums to Minor1) and major categories overall figures.

DATABASE & DIRECTORY PUBLISHING INDUSTRY (NAICS 51114)

NAICS 51114: Database and Directory Publishers . This U.S. industry comprises establishments primarily engaged in publishing compilations and collections of information or facts that are logically organized to facilitate their use. These collections may be published in print or electronic form. Electronic versions may be provided directly to customers by the establishment or offered through on-line services or third-party vendors.

INDUSTRY ESTABLISHMENTS, SALES & EMPLOYMENT TRENDS

	Year					Percent Chg. Year-to-Year			
	2014	2015	2016	2017	2018	14-15	15-16	16-17	17-18
Establishments	2,487	2,427	2,386	2,264	2,177	-2.4%	-1.7%	-5.1%	-3.9%
Sales ($Millions)	6,323	6,309	6,318	6,158	6,050	-0.2%	0.1%	-2.5%	-1.8%
Employment	24,443	23,852	23,450	22,251	21,392	-2.4%	-1.7%	-5.1%	-3.9%
Sales ($M)/Estab.	2.54	2.60	2.65	2.72	2.78	2.3%	1.8%	2.7%	2.2%
Sales ($)/Emp.	258,666	264,521	269,408	276,746	282,798	2.3%	1.8%	2.7%	2.2%

3-YEAR TREND – ESTIMATED NUMBER OF ESTABLISHMENTS

Year	Employee Size of Establishment									Total
	1-4 Emps.	5-9 Emps.	10-19 Emps.	20-49 Emps.	50-99 Emps.	100-249 Emps.	250-499 Emps.	>500 Emps.	Non-Employer	Employ-ment
2016	429	171	174	113	41	27	9	6	1,417	2,386
2017	407	162	165	107	39	25	8	5	1,345	2,264
2018	391	156	158	103	38	25	8	5	1,293	2,177

3-YEAR TREND – ESTIMATED INDUSTRY SALES ($MILLIONS)

Year	Employee Size of Establishment									Total
	1-4 Emps.	5-9 Emps.	10-19 Emps.	20-49 Emps.	50-99 Emps.	100-249 Emps.	250-499 Emps.	>500 Emps.	Non-Employer	Employ-ment
2016	154.6	161.8	413.9	714.2	572.1	1,004.0	1,087.7	2,116.4	92.9	6,317.5
2017	148.6	155.5	397.7	686.3	549.8	964.8	1,045.2	2,120.6	89.3	6,157.9
2018	144.4	151.1	386.5	666.9	534.2	937.5	1,015.6	2,126.8	86.8	6,049.7

3-YEAR TREND – ESTIMATED NUMBER OF EMPLOYEES

Year	Employee Size of Establishment									Total
	1-4 Emps.	5-9 Emps.	10-19 Emps.	20-49 Emps.	50-99 Emps.	100-249 Emps.	250-499 Emps.	>500 Emps.	Non-Employer	Employ-ment
2016	1,072	990	2,362	3,407	2,450	3,387	2,512	5,852	1,417	23,450
2017	1,017	940	2,241	3,233	2,325	3,214	2,383	5,553	1,345	22,251
2018	978	904	2,154	3,108	2,235	3,090	2,291	5,339	1,293	21,392

SUB-INDUSTRIES — 2017 ESTIMATED INDUSTRY SALES, ESTABLISHMENTS & EMPLOYMENT

Sub-Industries	Cate-gory*	Establish-ments	Sales ($Mill)	Employ-ment
Telephone and other directory publishing	Minor1	767	1,711.6	3,404
Directories, nec: publishing and printing	Minor2	193	2,089.8	1,999
Directories, nec: publishing only, not printed on site	Minor2	319	130.3	4,468
Directories, telephone: publishing and printing	Minor2	75	63.5	1,097
Directories, telephone: publishing only, not printed on site	Minor2	155	110.1	3,866
Mailing list compilers	Minor2	68	133.9	457
Mailing service	Minor2	632	1,657.5	6,506
Mailing list management	Minor2	12	87.8	128
Mailing list brokers	Minor2	42	173.4	326

*Category-Major categories (Major1) are more general descriptions for companies that self-selected to capture the many functions they perform in the industry. Minor categories (Minor1, Minor2) are more specific for companies that have more detailed functions (Minor1 is a larger category than Minor2). Minor categories figures (sales, etc.) can be aggregated to larger minor categories (Minor2 sums to Minor1) and major categories overall figures.

SOFTWARE PUBLISHING INDUSTRY
(NAICS 51121)

NAICS 51121: Software Publishers . This industry comprises establishments primarily engaged in computer software publishing or publishing and reproduction. Establishments in this industry carry out operations necessary for producing and distributing computer software, such as designing, providing documentation, assisting in installation, and providing support services to software purchasers. These establishments may design, develop, and publish, or publish only.

INDUSTRY ESTABLISHMENTS, SALES & EMPLOYMENT TRENDS

	Year					Percent Chg. Year-to-Year			
	2014	2015	2016	2017	2018	14-15	15-16	16-17	17-18
Establishments	22,617	21,815	21,177	21,618	22,358	-3.5%	-2.9%	2.1%	3.4%
Sales ($Millions)	175,162	189,463	203,561	225,497	250,361	8.2%	7.4%	10.8%	11.0%
Employment	351,337	338,873	328,973	335,814	347,318	-3.5%	-2.9%	2.1%	3.4%
Sales ($M)/Estab.	7.74	8.69	9.61	10.43	11.20	12.1%	10.7%	8.5%	7.3%
Sales ($)/Emp.	498,558	559,098	618,776	671,493	720,840	12.1%	10.7%	8.5%	7.3%

3-YEAR TREND – ESTIMATED NUMBER OF ESTABLISHMENTS

Year	Employee Size of Establishment									Total
	1-4 Emps.	5-9 Emps.	10-19 Emps.	20-49 Emps.	50-99 Emps.	100-249 Emps.	250-499 Emps.	>500 Emps.	Non-Employer	Employment
2016	3,646	1,216	1,178	1,245	561	458	163	133	12,577	21,177
2017	3,722	1,242	1,202	1,271	573	467	166	136	12,838	21,618
2018	3,849	1,284	1,244	1,315	592	483	172	140	13,278	22,358

3-YEAR TREND – ESTIMATED INDUSTRY SALES ($MILLIONS)

Year	Employee Size of Establishment									Total
	1-4 Emps.	5-9 Emps.	10-19 Emps.	20-49 Emps.	50-99 Emps.	100-249 Emps.	250-499 Emps.	>500 Emps.	Non-Employer	Employment
2016	2,678.2	2,348.2	5,718.8	16,003.4	15,843.7	34,859.9	41,807.5	83,320.7	980.2	203,560.6
2017	2,979.8	2,612.7	6,362.8	17,805.5	17,627.8	38,785.5	46,515.4	91,716.5	1,090.5	225,496.6
2018	3,331.6	2,921.1	7,114.0	19,907.7	19,709.0	43,364.5	52,007.0	100,786.7	1,219.3	250,360.9

3-YEAR TREND – ESTIMATED NUMBER OF EMPLOYEES

Year	Employee Size of Establishment									Total
	1-4 Emps.	5-9 Emps.	10-19 Emps.	20-49 Emps.	50-99 Emps.	100-249 Emps.	250-499 Emps.	>500 Emps.	Non-Employer	Employment
2016	9,115	7,055	16,020	37,485	33,316	57,738	47,395	108,274	12,577	328,973
2017	9,305	7,201	16,353	38,264	34,009	58,938	48,380	110,525	12,838	335,814
2018	9,624	7,448	16,913	39,575	35,174	60,958	50,038	114,311	13,278	347,318

SOFTWARE PUBLISHING INDUSTRY (NAICS 51121)

SUB-INDUSTRIES — 2017 ESTIMATED INDUSTRY SALES, ESTABLISHMENTS & EMPLOYMENT

Sub-Industries	Category*	Establishments	Sales ($Mill)	Employment
Prepackaged software	Major1	17,990	175,101.6	234,198
Application computer software	Minor2	972	20,493.4	37,372
Business oriented computer software	Minor2	1,183	17,147.6	43,895
Educational computer software	Minor2	551	2,282.6	9,221
Home entertainment computer software	Minor2	125	8,565.3	1,931
Operating systems computer software	Minor2	235	1,477.1	3,326
Publisher's computer software	Minor2	409	289.7	3,868
Utility computer software	Minor2	100	124.0	1,831
Word processing computer software	Minor2	51	15.4	171

*Category-Major categories (Major1) are more general descriptions for companies that self-selected to capture the many functions they perform in the industry. Minor categories (Minor1, Minor2) are more specific for companies that have more detailed functions (Minor1 is a larger category than Minor2). Minor categories figures (sales, etc.) can be aggregated to larger minor categories (Minor2 sums to Minor1) and major categories overall figures.

MOTION PICTURES & VIDEO PRODUCTION INDUSTRY (NAICS 51211)

NAICS 51211: Motion Picture and Video Production Industry . This industry comprises establishments primarily engaged in producing, or producing and distributing motion pictures, videos, television programs, or television and video commercials.

INDUSTRY ESTABLISHMENTS, SALES & EMPLOYMENT TRENDS

	Year					Percent Chg. Year-to-Year			
	2014	2015	2016	2017	2018	14-15	15-16	16-17	17-18
Establishments	34,740	35,054	35,683	36,838	38,533	0.9%	1.8%	3.2%	4.6%
Sales ($Millions)	54,513	58,342	62,493	67,351	72,978	7.0%	7.1%	7.8%	8.4%
Employment	136,498	137,730	140,203	144,743	151,400	0.9%	1.8%	3.2%	4.6%
Sales ($M)/Estab.	1.57	1.66	1.75	1.83	1.89	6.1%	5.2%	4.4%	3.6%
Sales ($)/Emp.	399,367	423,599	445,728	465,316	482,020	6.1%	5.2%	4.4%	3.6%

3-YEAR TREND – ESTIMATED NUMBER OF ESTABLISHMENTS

Year	Employee Size of Establishment									Total
	1-4 Emps.	5-9 Emps.	10-19 Emps.	20-49 Emps.	50-99 Emps.	100-249 Emps.	250-499 Emps.	>500 Emps.	Non-Employer	Employ-ment
2016	12,076	1,153	620	377	141	93	29	33	21,160	35,683
2017	12,467	1,191	640	389	145	96	30	34	21,845	36,838
2018	13,041	1,246	670	407	152	101	31	35	22,850	38,533

3-YEAR TREND – ESTIMATED INDUSTRY SALES ($MILLIONS)

Year	Employee Size of Establishment									Total
	1-4 Emps.	5-9 Emps.	10-19 Emps.	20-49 Emps.	50-99 Emps.	100-249 Emps.	250-499 Emps.	>500 Emps.	Non-Employer	Employ-ment
2016	8,831.9	2,217.3	2,998.9	4,823.2	3,957.8	7,085.4	7,348.0	23,476.8	1,753.3	62,492.5
2017	9,608.7	2,412.3	3,262.7	5,247.4	4,305.9	7,708.6	7,994.3	24,903.6	1,907.5	67,351.1
2018	10,547.2	2,647.9	3,581.4	5,759.9	4,726.5	8,461.5	8,775.1	26,384.6	2,093.8	72,977.8

3-YEAR TREND – ESTIMATED NUMBER OF EMPLOYEES

Year	Employee Size of Establishment									Total
	1-4 Emps.	5-9 Emps.	10-19 Emps.	20-49 Emps.	50-99 Emps.	100-249 Emps.	250-499 Emps.	>500 Emps.	Non-Employer	Employ-ment
2016	30,190	6,690	8,437	11,347	8,359	11,787	8,366	33,867	21,160	140,203
2017	31,168	6,907	8,711	11,714	8,629	12,168	8,637	34,963	21,845	144,743
2018	32,601	7,224	9,111	12,253	9,026	12,728	9,034	36,572	22,850	151,400

MOTION PICTURES & VIDEO PRODUCTION INDUSTRY (NAICS 51211)

SUB-INDUSTRIES — 2017 ESTIMATED INDUSTRY SALES, ESTABLISHMENTS & EMPLOYMENT

Sub-Industries	Cate-gory*	Establish-ments	Sales ($Mill)	Employ-ment
Motion picture and video production	Major1	20,225	56,246.2	57,624
Motion picture production	Minor1	1,181	841.3	6,817
Cartoon motion picture production	Minor2	137	1,267.1	744
Educational motion picture production	Minor2	176	123.9	1,196
Educational motion picture production, television	Minor2	98	138.6	771
Industrial motion picture production	Minor2	63	46.0	448
Motion picture production and distribution	Minor2	424	302.1	16,790
Motion picture production and distribution, television	Minor2	194	163.3	3,150
Non-theatrical motion picture production	Minor2	42	16.4	114
Non-theatrical motion picture production, television	Minor2	55	25.6	237
Religious motion picture production	Minor2	19	5.0	97
Television film production	Minor2	2,384	2,808.9	16,939
Training motion picture production	Minor2	56	44.1	275
Video production	Minor1	6,883	1,984.9	16,894
Music video production	Minor2	727	250.6	2,217
Video tape production	Minor2	1,516	1,259.0	8,531
Audio-visual program production	Minor2	1,967	1,194.5	7,902
Cartoon production, television	Minor2	87	26.6	862
Commercials, television: tape or film	Minor2	603	606.9	3,135

*Category-Major categories (Major1) are more general descriptions for companies that self-selected to capture the many functions they perform in the industry. Minor categories (Minor1, Minor2) are more specific for companies that have more detailed functions (Minor1 is a larger category than Minor2). Minor categories figures (sales, etc.) can be aggregated to larger minor categories (Minor2 sums to Minor1) and major categories overall figures.

MUSIC PUBLISHING INDUSTRY
(NAICS 51223)

NAICS 51223: Music Publishers . This U.S. industry comprises establishments known as music publishers. Establishments in this industry carry out design, editing, and marketing activities necessary for producing and distributing music books. These establishments may publish books in print, electronic, or audio form.

INDUSTRY ESTABLISHMENTS, SALES & EMPLOYMENT TRENDS

	Year					Percent Chg. Year-to-Year			
	2014	2015	2016	2017	2018	14-15	15-16	16-17	17-18
Establishments	3,074	3,292	3,545	3,678	3,866	7.1%	7.7%	3.7%	5.1%
Sales ($Millions)	2,839	3,124	3,449	3,662	3,931	10.1%	10.4%	6.2%	7.3%
Employment	8,477	9,078	9,778	10,144	10,663	7.1%	7.7%	3.7%	5.1%
Sales ($M)/Estab.	0.92	0.95	0.97	1.00	1.02	2.8%	2.5%	2.4%	2.1%
Sales ($)/Emp.	334,861	344,136	352,737	361,035	368,652	2.8%	2.5%	2.4%	2.1%

3-YEAR TREND – ESTIMATED NUMBER OF ESTABLISHMENTS

Year	Employee Size of Establishment									Total
	1-4 Emps.	5-9 Emps.	10-19 Emps.	20-49 Emps.	50-99 Emps.	100-249 Emps.	250-499 Emps.	>500 Emps.	Non-Employer	Employ-ment
2016	654	84	52	32	10	10	2	1	2,699	3,545
2017	679	87	54	34	11	11	2	1	2,800	3,678
2018	713	92	57	35	11	11	3	1	2,943	3,866

3-YEAR TREND – ESTIMATED INDUSTRY SALES ($MILLIONS)

Year	Employee Size of Establishment									Total
	1-4 Emps.	5-9 Emps.	10-19 Emps.	20-49 Emps.	50-99 Emps.	100-249 Emps.	250-499 Emps.	>500 Emps.	Non-Employer	Employ-ment
2016	448.0	151.6	235.0	387.0	273.5	737.0	552.0	510.0	154.9	3,449.0
2017	475.7	161.0	249.6	411.0	290.4	782.7	586.2	541.3	164.5	3,662.4
2018	510.7	172.8	267.9	441.2	311.7	840.2	629.3	580.7	176.6	3,931.0

3-YEAR TREND – ESTIMATED NUMBER OF EMPLOYEES

Year	Employee Size of Establishment									Total
	1-4 Emps.	5-9 Emps.	10-19 Emps.	20-49 Emps.	50-99 Emps.	100-249 Emps.	250-499 Emps.	>500 Emps.	Non-Employer	Employ-ment
2016	1,635	488	706	972	617	1,309	671	681	2,699	9,778
2017	1,696	507	732	1,009	640	1,358	696	706	2,800	10,144
2018	1,783	533	770	1,060	672	1,428	732	743	2,943	10,663

SUB-INDUSTRIES – 2017 ESTIMATED INDUSTRY
SALES, ESTABLISHMENTS & EMPLOYMENT

Sub-Industries	Cate-gory*	Establish-ments	Sales ($Mill)	Employ-ment
Book music: publishing only, not printed on site	Minor2	39	11.7	26
Book music: publishing and printing	Minor2	70	11.6	44
Song writings	Minor1	649	739.4	1,708
Music arranging and composing	Minor2	2,920	2,899.7	8,366

*Category-Major categories (Major1) are more general descriptions for companies that self-selected to capture the many functions they perform in the industry. Minor categories (Minor1, Minor2) are more specific for companies that have more detailed functions (Minor1 is a larger category than Minor2). Minor categories figures (sales, etc.) can be aggregated to larger minor categories (Minor2 sums to Minor1) and major categories overall figures.

RADIO BROADCASTING INDUSTRY
(NAICS 51511)

NAICS 51511: Radio Broadcasting . This industry comprises establishments primarily engaged in broadcasting audio signals. These establishments operate radio broadcasting studios and facilities for the transmission of aural programming by radio to the public, to affiliates, or to subscribers. The radio programs may include entertainment, news, talk shows, business data, or religious services.

INDUSTRY ESTABLISHMENTS, SALES & EMPLOYMENT TRENDS

	Year					Percent Chg. Year-to-Year			
	2014	2015	2016	2017	2018	14-15	15-16	16-17	17-18
Establishments	12,528	12,339	12,252	12,288	12,487	-1.5%	-0.7%	0.3%	1.6%
Sales ($Millions)	14,227	14,444	14,740	15,166	15,767	1.5%	2.0%	2.9%	4.0%
Employment	96,196	94,746	94,077	94,358	95,888	-1.5%	-0.7%	0.3%	1.6%
Sales ($M)/Estab.	1.14	1.17	1.20	1.23	1.26	3.1%	2.8%	2.6%	2.3%
Sales ($)/Emp.	147,899	152,447	156,677	160,726	164,434	3.1%	2.8%	2.6%	2.3%

3-YEAR TREND – ESTIMATED NUMBER OF ESTABLISHMENTS

Year	Employee Size of Establishment									Total
	1-4 Emps.	5-9 Emps.	10-19 Emps.	20-49 Emps.	50-99 Emps.	100-249 Emps.	250-499 Emps.	>500 Emps.	Non-Employer	Employ-ment
2016	2,629	1,449	1,288	869	245	66	10	6	5,689	12,252
2017	2,637	1,454	1,292	872	246	66	10	6	5,706	12,288
2018	2,679	1,477	1,313	886	250	67	10	6	5,799	12,487

3-YEAR TREND – ESTIMATED INDUSTRY SALES ($MILLIONS)

Year	Employee Size of Establishment									Total
	1-4 Emps.	5-9 Emps.	10-19 Emps.	20-49 Emps.	50-99 Emps.	100-249 Emps.	250-499 Emps.	>500 Emps.	Non-Employer	Employ-ment
2016	695.9	1,008.4	2,253.5	4,026.4	2,498.9	1,797.8	904.4	1,130.3	423.9	14,739.6
2017	716.0	1,037.6	2,318.8	4,143.0	2,571.3	1,849.9	930.6	1,162.1	436.2	15,165.7
2018	744.7	1,079.1	2,411.6	4,308.8	2,674.2	1,923.9	967.8	1,203.4	453.7	15,767.2

3-YEAR TREND – ESTIMATED NUMBER OF EMPLOYEES

Year	Employee Size of Establishment									Total
	1-4 Emps.	5-9 Emps.	10-19 Emps.	20-49 Emps.	50-99 Emps.	100-249 Emps.	250-499 Emps.	>500 Emps.	Non-Employer	Employ-ment
2016	6,572	8,406	17,517	26,169	14,581	8,263	2,845	4,035	5,689	94,077
2017	6,592	8,431	17,569	26,247	14,624	8,287	2,853	4,047	5,706	94,358
2018	6,698	8,568	17,854	26,673	14,862	8,422	2,900	4,113	5,799	95,888

RADIO BROADCASTING INDUSTRY
(NAICS 51511)

SUB-INDUSTRIES – 2017 ESTIMATED INDUSTRY SALES, ESTABLISHMENTS & EMPLOYMENT

Sub-Industries	Cate-gory*	Establish-ments	Sales ($Mill)	Employ-ment
Radio broadcasting stations	Major1	10,215	14,681.6	86,081
Radio broadcasting stations, music format	Minor1	188	61.2	1,926
Big band	Minor2	56	7.1	110
Classical	Minor2	21	13.0	117
Contemporary	Minor2	30	13.0	507
Country	Minor2	45	56.0	434
Easy listening	Minor2	16	11.7	216
Gospel	Minor2	113	9.6	145
Jazz	Minor2	24	4.6	33
Rhythm and blues	Minor2	4	0.3	3
Rock	Minor2	143	14.4	260
Radio broadcasting stations, except music format	Minor1	54	12.5	191
Educational	Minor2	375	77.6	1,188
News	Minor2	109	20.7	615
Religious	Minor2	351	83.2	772
Sports	Minor2	438	82.1	1,360
Talk	Minor2	80	11.9	213
Ethnic programming	Minor2	26	5.2	186

*Category-Major categories (Major1) are more general descriptions for companies that self-selected to capture the many functions they perform in the industry. Minor categories (Minor1, Minor2) are more specific for companies that have more detailed functions (Minor1 is a larger category than Minor2). Minor categories figures (sales, etc.) can be aggregated to larger minor categories (Minor2 sums to Minor1) and major categories overall figures.

TELEVISION BROADCASTING SERVICES INDUSTRY (NAICS 51512)

NAICS 51512: Television Broadcasting . This industry comprises establishments primarily engaged in broadcasting images together with sound. These establishments operate television broadcasting studios and facilities for the programming and transmission of programs to the public. These establishments also produce or transmit visual programming to affiliated broadcast television stations, which in turn broadcast the programs to the public on a predetermined schedule. Programming may originate in their own studios, from an affiliated network, or from external sources.

INDUSTRY ESTABLISHMENTS, SALES & EMPLOYMENT TRENDS

	Year					Percent Chg. Year-to-Year			
	2014	2015	2016	2017	2018	14-15	15-16	16-17	17-18
Establishments	4,010	4,066	4,158	4,234	4,367	1.4%	2.3%	1.8%	3.2%
Sales ($Millions)	38,271	38,455	38,863	39,073	39,661	0.5%	1.1%	0.5%	1.5%
Employment	102,188	103,601	105,963	107,880	111,281	1.4%	2.3%	1.8%	3.2%
Sales ($M)/Estab.	9.54	9.46	9.35	9.23	9.08	-0.9%	-1.2%	-1.2%	-1.6%
Sales ($)/Emp.	374,514	371,183	366,762	362,189	356,402	-0.9%	-1.2%	-1.2%	-1.6%

3-YEAR TREND – ESTIMATED NUMBER OF ESTABLISHMENTS

Year	Employee Size of Establishment									Total
	1-4 Emps.	5-9 Emps.	10-19 Emps.	20-49 Emps.	50-99 Emps.	100-249 Emps.	250-499 Emps.	>500 Emps.	Non-Employer	Employ-ment
2016	738	220	231	311	344	329	35	19	1,931	4,158
2017	752	224	235	317	350	335	36	19	1,966	4,234
2018	775	231	243	327	362	345	37	20	2,028	4,367

3-YEAR TREND – ESTIMATED INDUSTRY SALES ($MILLIONS)

Year	Employee Size of Establishment									Total
	1-4 Emps.	5-9 Emps.	10-19 Emps.	20-49 Emps.	50-99 Emps.	100-249 Emps.	250-499 Emps.	>500 Emps.	Non-Employer	Employ-ment
2016	341.2	267.0	706.4	2,515.2	6,118.7	15,745.9	5,692.1	7,343.2	133.6	38,863.3
2017	343.7	269.0	711.6	2,533.8	6,163.8	15,862.0	5,734.1	7,320.4	134.6	39,073.0
2018	350.1	274.0	724.7	2,580.4	6,277.4	16,154.4	5,839.8	7,323.0	137.1	39,660.8

3-YEAR TREND – ESTIMATED NUMBER OF EMPLOYEES

Year	Employee Size of Establishment									Total
	1-4 Emps.	5-9 Emps.	10-19 Emps.	20-49 Emps.	50-99 Emps.	100-249 Emps.	250-499 Emps.	>500 Emps.	Non-Employer	Employ-ment
2016	1,846	1,275	3,145	9,364	20,449	41,451	10,256	16,247	1,931	105,963
2017	1,879	1,298	3,202	9,533	20,819	42,200	10,442	16,541	1,966	107,880
2018	1,938	1,339	3,303	9,834	21,476	43,531	10,771	17,062	2,028	111,281

TELEVISION BROADCASTING SERVICES INDUSTRY
(NAICS 51512)

SUB-INDUSTRIES – 2017 ESTIMATED INDUSTRY SALES, ESTABLISHMENTS & EMPLOYMENT

Sub-Industries	Cate-gory*	Establish-ments	Sales ($Mill)	Employ-ment
Television broadcasting stations	Major1	4,051	38,993.3	105,519
Television translator station	Minor2	183	79.7	2,362

*Category-Major categories (Major1) are more general descriptions for companies that self-selected to capture the many functions they perform in the industry. Minor categories (Minor1, Minor2) are more specific for companies that have more detailed functions (Minor1 is a larger category than Minor2). Minor categories figures (sales, etc.) can be aggregated to larger minor categories (Minor2 sums to Minor1) and major categories overall figures.

CABLE TELEVISION NETWORKS INDUSTRY (NAICS 51521)

NAICS 51521: Cable Networks . This industry comprises establishments primarily engaged in operating studios and facilities for the broadcasting of programs on a subscription or fee basis. The broadcast programming is typically narrowcast in nature (e.g., limited format, such as news, sports, education, or youth-oriented). These establishments produce programming in their own facilities or acquire programming from external sources. The programming material is usually delivered to a third party, such as cable systems or direct-to-home satellite systems, for transmission to viewers.

INDUSTRY ESTABLISHMENTS, SALES & EMPLOYMENT TRENDS

	Year					Percent Chg. Year-to-Year			
	2014	2015	2016	2017	2018	14-15	15-16	16-17	17-18
Establishments	1,402	1,462	1,536	1,597	1,683	4.2%	5.1%	4.0%	5.4%
Sales ($Millions)	61,261	67,365	74,064	80,531	87,996	10.0%	9.9%	8.7%	9.3%
Employment	43,090	44,920	47,200	49,081	51,711	4.2%	5.1%	4.0%	5.4%
Sales ($M)/Estab.	43.69	46.09	48.22	50.42	52.30	5.5%	4.6%	4.6%	3.7%
Sales ($)/Emp.	1,421,711	1,499,657	1,569,135	1,640,774	1,701,706	5.5%	4.6%	4.6%	3.7%

3-YEAR TREND – ESTIMATED NUMBER OF ESTABLISHMENTS

Year	Employee Size of Establishment									Total
	1-4 Emps.	5-9 Emps.	10-19 Emps.	20-49 Emps.	50-99 Emps.	100-249 Emps.	250-499 Emps.	>500 Emps.	Non-Employer	Employ-ment
2016	314	133	103	95	67	65	21	25	713	1,536
2017	327	138	107	99	69	67	22	26	742	1,597
2018	344	145	113	104	73	71	23	28	781	1,683

3-YEAR TREND – ESTIMATED INDUSTRY SALES ($MILLIONS)

Year	Employee Size of Establishment									Total
	1-4 Emps.	5-9 Emps.	10-19 Emps.	20-49 Emps.	50-99 Emps.	100-249 Emps.	250-499 Emps.	>500 Emps.	Non-Employer	Employ-ment
2016	571.8	633.6	1,237.8	3,032.4	4,673.7	12,183.6	13,224.0	38,449.7	57.1	74,063.7
2017	629.3	697.3	1,362.3	3,337.4	5,143.8	13,408.9	14,554.0	41,335.6	62.8	80,531.4
2018	698.5	774.0	1,512.1	3,704.3	5,709.3	14,883.1	16,154.1	44,491.1	69.7	87,996.1

3-YEAR TREND – ESTIMATED NUMBER OF EMPLOYEES

Year	Employee Size of Establishment									Total
	1-4 Emps.	5-9 Emps.	10-19 Emps.	20-49 Emps.	50-99 Emps.	100-249 Emps.	250-499 Emps.	>500 Emps.	Non-Employer	Employ-ment
2016	786	769	1,400	2,869	3,969	8,150	6,054	22,491	713	47,200
2017	817	799	1,456	2,983	4,127	8,474	6,296	23,387	742	49,081
2018	861	842	1,534	3,143	4,348	8,928	6,633	24,640	781	51,711

CABLE TELEVISION NETWORKS INDUSTRY (NAICS 51521)

SUB-INDUSTRIES – 2017 ESTIMATED INDUSTRY SALES, ESTABLISHMENTS & EMPLOYMENT

Sub-Industries	Cate-gory*	Establish-ments	Sales ($Mill)	Employ-ment
Cable and other pay television services	Major1	451	39,256.1	16,757
Cable television services	Minor2	963	28,030.7	27,796
Closed circuit television services	Minor2	10	25.2	255
Direct broadcast satellite services (DBS)	Minor2	77	12,663.5	2,704
Multipoint distribution systems services (MDS)	Minor2	9	11.6	65
Satellite master antenna systems services (SMATV)	Minor2	75	267.9	792
Subscription television services	Minor2	12	276.4	712

*Category-Major categories (Major1) are more general descriptions for companies that self-selected to capture the many functions they perform in the industry. Minor categories (Minor1, Minor2) are more specific for companies that have more detailed functions (Minor1 is a larger category than Minor2). Minor categories figures (sales, etc.) can be aggregated to larger minor categories (Minor2 sums to Minor1) and major categories overall figures.

WIRED TELECOMMUNICATIONS CARRIERS INDUSTRY (NAICS 51711)

NAICS 51711: Wired Telecommunications Carriers . This industry comprises establishments engaged in (1) operating and maintaining switching and transmission facilities to provide direct communications via landlines, microwave, or a combination of landlines and satellite linkups or (2) furnishing telegraph and other nonvocal communications using their own facilities.

INDUSTRY ESTABLISHMENTS, SALES & EMPLOYMENT TRENDS

	Year					Percent Chg. Year-to-Year			
	2014	2015	2016	2017	2018	14-15	15-16	16-17	17-18
Establishments	42,383	41,168	40,275	40,417	41,095	-2.9%	-2.2%	0.4%	1.7%
Sales ($Millions)	371,016	363,049	356,880	358,714	364,179	-2.1%	-1.7%	0.5%	1.5%
Employment	682,080	662,533	648,153	650,441	661,347	-2.9%	-2.2%	0.4%	1.7%
Sales ($M)/Estab.	8.75	8.82	8.86	8.88	8.86	0.7%	0.5%	0.2%	-0.2%
Sales ($)/Emp.	543,948	547,971	550,611	551,494	550,662	0.7%	0.5%	0.2%	-0.2%

3-YEAR TREND – ESTIMATED NUMBER OF ESTABLISHMENTS

Year	Employee Size of Establishment									Total
	1-4 Emps.	5-9 Emps.	10-19 Emps.	20-49 Emps.	50-99 Emps.	100-249 Emps.	250-499 Emps.	>500 Emps.	Non-Employer	Employ-ment
2016	17,843	5,084	3,768	3,080	1,530	915	284	190	7,581	40,275
2017	17,906	5,102	3,781	3,091	1,535	918	285	191	7,608	40,417
2018	18,206	5,187	3,844	3,142	1,561	934	290	194	7,735	41,095

3-YEAR TREND – ESTIMATED INDUSTRY SALES ($MILLIONS)

Year	Employee Size of Establishment									Total
	1-4 Emps.	5-9 Emps.	10-19 Emps.	20-49 Emps.	50-99 Emps.	100-249 Emps.	250-499 Emps.	>500 Emps.	Non-Employer	Employ-ment
2016	12,588.2	9,427.0	17,569.4	38,012.5	41,509.0	66,916.2	70,026.6	100,182.4	649.0	356,880.3
2017	12,656.8	9,478.4	17,665.1	38,219.6	41,735.1	67,280.7	70,408.0	100,617.9	652.5	358,714.0
2018	12,868.1	9,636.6	17,960.0	38,857.6	42,431.8	68,403.8	71,583.3	101,774.0	663.4	364,178.6

3-YEAR TREND – ESTIMATED NUMBER OF EMPLOYEES

Year	Employee Size of Establishment									Total
	1-4 Emps.	5-9 Emps.	10-19 Emps.	20-49 Emps.	50-99 Emps.	100-249 Emps.	250-499 Emps.	>500 Emps.	Non-Employer	Employ-ment
2016	44,608	29,487	51,242	92,702	90,877	115,394	82,653	133,610	7,581	648,153
2017	44,765	29,591	51,423	93,029	91,198	115,801	82,944	134,082	7,608	650,441
2018	45,516	30,087	52,285	94,589	92,727	117,743	84,335	136,330	7,735	661,347

WIRED TELECOMMUNICATIONS CARRIERS INDUSTRY (NAICS 51711)

SUB-INDUSTRIES – 2017 ESTIMATED INDUSTRY SALES, ESTABLISHMENTS & EMPLOYMENT

Sub-Industries	Category*	Establishments	Sales ($Mill)	Employment
Telephone communication, except radio	Major1	10,225	101,209.0	267,639
Local and long distance telephone communications	Minor1	3,033	188,046.9	98,622
Data telephone communications	Minor2	568	1,750.2	14,167
Local telephone communications	Minor2	1,790	36,989.7	91,839
Long distance telephone communications	Minor2	1,570	4,362.5	30,751
Voice telephone communications	Minor2	601	5,323.3	9,338
Online service providers	Minor1	6,159	7,023.2	40,360
Internet connectivity services	Minor2	6,136	6,220.6	32,187
Internet host services	Minor2	7,942	5,017.3	45,211
Proprietary online service networks	Minor2	1,055	425.2	6,687
Telephone cable service, land or submarine	Minor2	194	396.3	1,550
Wire telephone	Minor2	145	108.3	1,919
Telephone/video communications	Minor2	271	513.5	5,565
Telephone communications broker	Minor2	728	1,328.0	4,605

*Category-Major categories (Major1) are more general descriptions for companies that self-selected to capture the many functions they perform in the industry. Minor categories (Minor1, Minor2) are more specific for companies that have more detailed functions (Minor1 is a larger category than Minor2). Minor categories figures (sales, etc.) can be aggregated to larger minor categories (Minor2 sums to Minor1) and major categories overall figures.

WIRELESS TELECOMMUNICATIONS CARRIERS (NAICS 51721)

NAICS 51721: Wireless Telecommunications Carriers. This industry comprises establishments primarily engaged in providing two-way radiotelephone communications services, such as cellular telephone services. This business also includes establishments primarily engaged in providing telephone paging and beeper services and those engaged in leasing telephone lines or other methods of telephone transmission, such as optical fiber lines and microwave or satellite facilities, and reselling the use of such methods to others.

INDUSTRY ESTABLISHMENTS, SALES & EMPLOYMENT TRENDS

	Year					Percent Chg. Year-to-Year			
	2014	2015	2016	2017	2018	14-15	15-16	16-17	17-18
Establishments	12,830	13,389	14,083	14,454	15,031	4.4%	5.2%	2.6%	4.0%
Sales ($Millions)	134,522	149,939	167,236	181,696	198,755	11.5%	11.5%	8.6%	9.4%
Employment	223,500	233,238	245,318	251,786	261,833	4.4%	5.2%	2.6%	4.0%
Sales ($M)/Estab.	10.48	11.20	11.88	12.57	13.22	6.8%	6.0%	5.9%	5.2%
Sales ($)/Emp.	601,889	642,858	681,709	721,627	759,089	6.8%	6.0%	5.9%	5.2%

3-YEAR TREND — ESTIMATED NUMBER OF ESTABLISHMENTS

Year	Employee Size of Establishment									Total
	1-4 Emps.	5-9 Emps.	10-19 Emps.	20-49 Emps.	50-99 Emps.	100-249 Emps.	250-499 Emps.	>500 Emps.	Non-Employer	Employ-ment
2016	3,121	2,398	3,789	1,617	180	147	89	91	2,651	14,083
2017	3,203	2,462	3,889	1,659	185	151	91	94	2,721	14,454
2018	3,331	2,560	4,044	1,726	192	157	95	97	2,829	15,031

3-YEAR TREND — ESTIMATED INDUSTRY SALES ($MILLIONS)

Year	Employee Size of Establishment									Total
	1-4 Emps.	5-9 Emps.	10-19 Emps.	20-49 Emps.	50-99 Emps.	100-249 Emps.	250-499 Emps.	>500 Emps.	Non-Employer	Employ-ment
2016	2,859.1	5,775.5	22,945.9	25,916.2	6,342.8	13,967.9	28,457.5	60,712.9	257.9	167,235.6
2017	3,115.5	6,293.4	25,003.5	28,240.2	6,911.6	15,220.4	31,009.4	65,620.6	281.0	181,695.6
2018	3,422.7	6,914.0	27,469.1	31,024.9	7,593.1	16,721.3	34,067.3	71,233.5	308.7	198,754.8

3-YEAR TREND — ESTIMATED NUMBER OF EMPLOYEES

Year	Employee Size of Establishment									Total
	1-4 Emps.	5-9 Emps.	10-19 Emps.	20-49 Emps.	50-99 Emps.	100-249 Emps.	250-499 Emps.	>500 Emps.	Non-Employer	Employ-ment
2016	7,801	13,910	51,530	48,666	10,693	18,547	25,863	65,658	2,651	245,318
2017	8,007	14,277	52,889	49,949	10,974	19,036	26,545	67,389	2,721	251,786
2018	8,327	14,847	54,999	51,942	11,412	19,796	27,604	70,078	2,829	261,833

WIRELESS TELECOMMUNICATIONS CARRIERS (NAICS 51721)

SUB-INDUSTRIES – 2017 ESTIMATED INDUSTRY SALES, ESTABLISHMENTS & EMPLOYMENT

Sub-Industries	Category*	Establish-ments	Sales ($Mill)	Employ-ment
Radiotelephone communication	Major1	2,202	1,283.5	102,666
Cellular telephone services	Minor2	11,604	179,814.0	140,490
Paging services	Minor2	509	461.8	7,031
Radio pager (beeper) communication services	Minor2	139	136.3	1,599

*Category-Major categories (Major1) are more general descriptions for companies that self-selected to capture the many functions they perform in the industry. Minor categories (Minor1, Minor2) are more specific for companies that have more detailed functions (Minor1 is a larger category than Minor2). Minor categories figures (sales, etc.) can be aggregated to larger minor categories (Minor2 sums to Minor1) and major categories overall figures.

DATA PROCESSING SERVICES INDUSTRY
(NAICS 51821)

NAICS 51821: Data Processing Services. This industry comprises establishments primarily engaged in providing computer processing and data preparation services. The service may consist of complete processing and preparation of reports from data supplied by the customer or a specialized service, such as data entry or making data processing equipment available on an hourly or time-sharing basis.

INDUSTRY ESTABLISHMENTS, SALES & EMPLOYMENT TRENDS

	Year					Percent Chg. Year-to-Year			
	2014	2015	2016	2017	2018	14-15	15-16	16-17	17-18
Establishments	37,012	39,620	42,656	45,190	48,506	7.0%	7.7%	5.9%	7.3%
Sales ($Millions)	95,624	100,657	106,322	110,702	116,380	5.3%	5.6%	4.1%	5.1%
Employment	464,571	497,307	535,414	567,218	608,838	7.0%	7.7%	5.9%	7.3%
Sales ($M)/Estab.	2.58	2.54	2.49	2.45	2.40	-1.7%	-1.9%	-1.7%	-2.1%
Sales ($)/Emp.	205,833	202,404	198,578	195,166	191,152	-1.7%	-1.9%	-1.7%	-2.1%

3-YEAR TREND – ESTIMATED NUMBER OF ESTABLISHMENTS

Year	Employee Size of Establishment									Total
	1-4 Emps.	5-9 Emps.	10-19 Emps.	20-49 Emps.	50-99 Emps.	100-249 Emps.	250-499 Emps.	>500 Emps.	Non-Employer	Employ-ment
2016	7,650	2,154	1,933	2,049	984	768	302	183	26,633	42,656
2017	8,105	2,282	2,048	2,171	1,043	813	320	194	28,215	45,190
2018	8,699	2,449	2,198	2,330	1,119	873	343	208	30,285	48,506

3-YEAR TREND – ESTIMATED INDUSTRY SALES ($MILLIONS)

Year	Employee Size of Establishment									Total
	1-4 Emps.	5-9 Emps.	10-19 Emps.	20-49 Emps.	50-99 Emps.	100-249 Emps.	250-499 Emps.	>500 Emps.	Non-Employer	Employ-ment
2016	1,885.3	1,395.2	3,148.2	8,834.7	9,328.0	19,606.1	25,995.9	34,315.3	1,812.9	106,321.6
2017	1,978.8	1,464.4	3,304.3	9,272.9	9,790.6	20,578.6	27,285.3	35,123.8	1,902.8	110,701.6
2018	2,099.9	1,554.0	3,506.4	9,840.0	10,389.4	21,837.1	28,954.0	36,180.7	2,019.2	116,380.5

3-YEAR TREND – ESTIMATED NUMBER OF EMPLOYEES

Year	Employee Size of Establishment									Total
	1-4 Emps.	5-9 Emps.	10-19 Emps.	20-49 Emps.	50-99 Emps.	100-249 Emps.	250-499 Emps.	>500 Emps.	Non-Employer	Employ-ment
2016	19,126	12,493	26,285	61,679	58,463	96,789	87,838	146,108	26,633	535,414
2017	20,262	13,235	27,846	65,343	61,936	102,538	93,056	154,787	28,215	567,218
2018	21,748	14,206	29,890	70,137	66,480	110,062	99,884	166,145	30,285	608,838

DATA PROCESSING SERVICES INDUSTRY (NAICS 51821)

SUB-INDUSTRIES – 2017 ESTIMATED INDUSTRY SALES, ESTABLISHMENTS & EMPLOYMENT

Sub-Industries	Cate-gory*	Establish-ments	Sales ($Mill)	Employ-ment
Data processing and preparation	Major1	8,687	33,331.3	153,257
Computer processing services	Minor1	713	480.8	27,328
Calculating service (computer)	Minor2	103	63.2	1,335
Computer graphics service	Minor2	28,585	7,787.3	98,368
Computer time-sharing	Minor2	149	79.2	2,426
Service bureau, computer	Minor2	437	246.2	7,929
Data entry service	Minor2	1,105	3,932.9	19,102
Data processing service	Minor2	4,720	64,069.8	248,922
Data verification service	Minor2	220	379.7	2,951
Keypunch service	Minor2	43	38.2	614
Optical scanning data service	Minor2	405	245.5	4,167
Tabulating service	Minor2	23	47.5	819

*Category-Major categories (Major1) are more general descriptions for companies that self-selected to capture the many functions they perform in the industry. Minor categories (Minor1, Minor2) are more specific for companies that have more detailed functions (Minor1 is a larger category than Minor2). Minor categories figures (sales, etc.) can be aggregated to larger minor categories (Minor2 sums to Minor1) and major categories overall figures.

COMMERCIAL BANKING INDUSTRY
(NAICS 52211)

NAICS 52211: Commercial Banking. This industry comprises commercial banks and trust companies (accepting deposits) chartered under the National Bank Act. Trust companies engaged in fiduciary business, but not regularly engaged in deposit banking, are classified in 6091.

INDUSTRY ESTABLISHMENTS, SALES & EMPLOYMENT TRENDS

	Year					Percent Chg. Year-to-Year			
	2014	2015	2016	2017	2018	14-15	15-16	16-17	17-18
Establishments	95,471	96,784	98,847	100,873	104,052	1.4%	2.1%	2.0%	3.2%
Sales ($Millions)	479,659	497,431	517,845	537,991	562,850	3.7%	4.1%	3.9%	4.6%
Employment	1,433,624	1,453,344	1,484,322	1,514,735	1,562,479	1.4%	2.1%	2.0%	3.2%
Sales ($M)/Estab.	5.02	5.14	5.24	5.33	5.41	2.3%	1.9%	1.8%	1.4%
Sales ($)/Emp.	334,578	342,266	348,877	355,172	360,229	2.3%	1.9%	1.8%	1.4%

3-YEAR TREND — ESTIMATED NUMBER OF ESTABLISHMENTS

Year	Employee Size of Establishment									Total
	1-4 Emps.	5-9 Emps.	10-19 Emps.	20-49 Emps.	50-99 Emps.	100-249 Emps.	250-499 Emps.	>500 Emps.	Non-Employer	Employ-ment
2016	19,615	41,427	23,792	8,241	1,915	941	372	333	2,211	98,847
2017	20,017	42,276	24,279	8,410	1,955	960	379	340	2,256	100,873
2018	20,648	43,608	25,044	8,675	2,016	991	391	351	2,327	104,052

3-YEAR TREND — ESTIMATED INDUSTRY SALES ($MILLIONS)

Year	Employee Size of Establishment									Total
	1-4 Emps.	5-9 Emps.	10-19 Emps.	20-49 Emps.	50-99 Emps.	100-249 Emps.	250-499 Emps.	>500 Emps.	Non-Employer	Employ-ment
2016	10,074.8	55,926.1	80,769.7	74,056.8	37,834.9	50,104.0	66,694.5	142,244.7	139.5	517,845.0
2017	10,498.1	58,275.9	84,163.3	77,168.3	39,424.5	52,209.2	69,496.7	146,609.7	145.4	537,991.1
2018	11,032.5	61,242.2	88,447.3	81,096.2	41,431.3	54,866.7	73,034.2	151,546.9	152.8	562,849.9

3-YEAR TREND — ESTIMATED NUMBER OF EMPLOYEES

Year	Employee Size of Establishment									Total
	1-4 Emps.	5-9 Emps.	10-19 Emps.	20-49 Emps.	50-99 Emps.	100-249 Emps.	250-499 Emps.	>500 Emps.	Non-Employer	Employ-ment
2016	49,037	240,276	323,566	248,069	113,776	118,678	108,126	280,581	2,211	1,484,322
2017	50,042	245,200	330,196	253,152	116,107	121,110	110,342	286,331	2,256	1,514,735
2018	51,619	252,928	340,604	261,131	119,767	124,928	113,820	295,356	2,327	1,562,479

COMMERCIAL BANKING INDUSTRY
(NAICS 52211)

SUB-INDUSTRIES — 2017 ESTIMATED INDUSTRY SALES, ESTABLISHMENTS & EMPLOYMENT

Sub-Industries	Cate-gory*	Establish-ments	Sales ($Mill)	Employ-ment
National commercial banks	Major1	32,032	177,535.4	474,175
National trust companies with deposits, commercial	Minor2	1,592	1,794.9	30,737
State commercial banks	Major1	61,398	336,919.7	900,353
State trust companies accepting deposits, commercial	Minor2	5,850	21,741.1	109,470

*Category-Major categories (Major1) are more general descriptions for companies that self-selected to capture the many functions they perform in the industry. Minor categories (Minor1, Minor2) are more specific for companies that have more detailed functions (Minor1 is a larger category than Minor2). Minor categories figures (sales, etc.) can be aggregated to larger minor categories (Minor2 sums to Minor1) and major categories overall figures.

MORTGAGE & NON-MORTGAGE LOAN BROKERS (NAICS 52231)

NAICS 52231: Mortgage & Non-Mortgage Loan Brokers. This industry comprises establishments primarily engaged in arranging loans for others. These establishments operate mostly on a commission or fee basis and do not ordinarily have any continuing relationship with either borrower or lender.

INDUSTRY ESTABLISHMENTS, SALES & EMPLOYMENT TRENDS

	Year					Percent Chg. Year-to-Year			
	2014	2015	2016	2017	2018	14-15	15-16	16-17	17-18
Establishments	8,903	8,019	7,273	6,659	6,018	-9.9%	-9.3%	-8.4%	-9.6%
Sales ($Millions)	8,690	7,764	6,969	6,306	5,627	-10.7%	-10.2%	-9.5%	-10.8%
Employment	41,429	37,318	33,846	30,987	28,004	-9.9%	-9.3%	-8.4%	-9.6%
Sales ($M)/Estab.	0.98	0.97	0.96	0.95	0.94	-0.8%	-1.0%	-1.2%	-1.3%
Sales ($)/Emp.	209,758	208,044	205,911	203,517	200,948	-0.8%	-1.0%	-1.2%	-1.3%

3-YEAR TREND – ESTIMATED NUMBER OF ESTABLISHMENTS

Year	Employee Size of Establishment									Total Employ-ment
	1-4 Emps.	5-9 Emps.	10-19 Emps.	20-49 Emps.	50-99 Emps.	100-249 Emps.	250-499 Emps.	>500 Emps.	Non-Employer	
2016	4,733	697	287	128	36	30	5	2	1,355	7,273
2017	4,334	638	263	117	33	28	4	1	1,241	6,659
2018	3,916	577	237	106	30	25	4	1	1,121	6,018

3-YEAR TREND – ESTIMATED INDUSTRY SALES ($MILLIONS)

Year	Employee Size of Establishment									Total Employ-ment
	1-4 Emps.	5-9 Emps.	10-19 Emps.	20-49 Emps.	50-99 Emps.	100-249 Emps.	250-499 Emps.	>500 Emps.	Non-Employer	
2016	1,745.8	675.6	699.1	827.6	509.9	1,155.6	631.6	620.2	103.9	6,969.3
2017	1,570.9	607.9	629.0	744.7	458.8	1,039.8	568.3	593.7	93.5	6,306.5
2018	1,391.8	538.6	557.3	659.8	406.5	921.2	503.5	565.8	82.9	5,627.3

3-YEAR TREND – ESTIMATED NUMBER OF EMPLOYEES

Year	Employee Size of Establishment									Total Employ-ment
	1-4 Emps.	5-9 Emps.	10-19 Emps.	20-49 Emps.	50-99 Emps.	100-249 Emps.	250-499 Emps.	>500 Emps.	Non-Employer	
2016	11,834	4,042	3,900	3,861	2,135	3,812	1,426	1,482	1,355	33,846
2017	10,834	3,700	3,570	3,535	1,955	3,490	1,305	1,357	1,241	30,987
2018	9,791	3,344	3,227	3,194	1,767	3,154	1,180	1,226	1,121	28,004

MORTGAGE & NON-MORTGAGE LOAN BROKERS (NAICS 52231)

SUB-INDUSTRIES — 2017 ESTIMATED INDUSTRY SALES, ESTABLISHMENTS & EMPLOYMENT

Sub-Industries	Category*	Establish-ments	Sales ($Mill)	Employ-ment
Loan brokers	Major1	1,652	1,768.8	6,639
Agents, farm or business loan	Minor2	28	207.8	97
Brokers, farm or business loan	Minor2	55	18.6	268
Loan agents	Minor2	532	193.2	1,825
Mortgage brokers arranging for loans, using money of oth	Minor2	4,392	4,118.1	22,157

*Category-Major categories (Major1) are more general descriptions for companies that self-selected to capture the many functions they perform in the industry. Minor categories (Minor1, Minor2) are more specific for companies that have more detailed functions (Minor1 is a larger category than Minor2). Minor categories figures (sales, etc.) can be aggregated to larger minor categories (Minor2 sums to Minor1) and major categories overall figures.

INVESTMENT BANKING & SECURITIES DEALING (NAICS 52311)

NAICS 52311: Investment Banking & Securities Dealing. This industry compromises establishments primarily engaged in the purchase, sale, and brokerage of securities; and those, generally known as investment bankers, primarily engaged in originating, underwriting, and distributing issues of securities. Establishments primarily engaged in issuing shares of mutual and money market funds, unit investment trusts, and face amount certificates are classified in 6722 or 6726.

INDUSTRY ESTABLISHMENTS, SALES & EMPLOYMENT TRENDS

	Year					Percent Chg. Year-to-Year			
	2014	2015	2016	2017	2018	14-15	15-16	16-17	17-18
Establishments	6,041	5,598	5,210	4,964	4,782	-7.3%	-6.9%	-4.7%	-3.7%
Sales ($Millions)	101,472	109,701	117,188	125,649	134,275	8.1%	6.8%	7.2%	6.9%
Employment	74,091	68,662	63,894	60,885	58,645	-7.3%	-6.9%	-4.7%	-3.7%
Sales ($M)/Estab.	16.80	19.60	22.49	25.31	28.08	16.7%	14.8%	12.5%	10.9%
Sales ($)/Emp.	1,369,559	1,597,705	1,834,106	2,063,701	2,289,610	16.7%	14.8%	12.5%	10.9%

3-YEAR TREND — ESTIMATED NUMBER OF ESTABLISHMENTS

Year	Employee Size of Establishment									Total
	1-4 Emps.	5-9 Emps.	10-19 Emps.	20-49 Emps.	50-99 Emps.	100-249 Emps.	250-499 Emps.	>500 Emps.	Non-Employer	Employ-ment
2016	2,412	498	296	178	55	61	28	25	1,656	5,210
2017	2,298	475	282	169	53	58	27	24	1,578	4,964
2018	2,214	458	271	163	51	56	26	23	1,520	4,782

3-YEAR TREND — ESTIMATED INDUSTRY SALES ($MILLIONS)

Year	Employee Size of Establishment									Total
	1-4 Emps.	5-9 Emps.	10-19 Emps.	20-49 Emps.	50-99 Emps.	100-249 Emps.	250-499 Emps.	>500 Emps.	Non-Employer	Employ-ment
2016	5,200.4	2,824.6	4,215.2	6,700.8	4,576.2	13,682.7	21,434.6	58,108.7	444.7	117,187.9
2017	5,471.8	2,972.0	4,435.2	7,050.4	4,815.0	14,396.7	22,553.1	63,486.5	468.0	125,648.8
2018	5,760.3	3,128.7	4,668.9	7,422.1	5,068.8	15,155.7	23,742.0	68,835.9	492.6	134,275.0

3-YEAR TREND — ESTIMATED NUMBER OF EMPLOYEES

Year	Employee Size of Establishment									Total
	1-4 Emps.	5-9 Emps.	10-19 Emps.	20-49 Emps.	50-99 Emps.	100-249 Emps.	250-499 Emps.	>500 Emps.	Non-Employer	Employ-ment
2016	6,030	2,891	4,023	5,347	3,278	7,721	8,279	24,669	1,656	63,894
2017	5,746	2,755	3,833	5,095	3,124	7,357	7,889	23,507	1,578	60,885
2018	5,535	2,654	3,692	4,908	3,009	7,087	7,598	22,643	1,520	58,645

Investment Banking & Securities Dealing (NAICS 52311)

Sub-Industries – 2017 Estimated Industry Sales, Establishments & Employment

Sub-Industries	Category*	Establishments	Sales ($Mill)	Employment
Flotation companies	Minor1	19	231.8	212
Distributors, security	Minor2	75	445.3	507
Investment bankers	Minor2	961	54,225.5	17,856
Investment certificate sales	Minor2	24	203.7	151
Investment firm, general brokerage	Minor2	1,548	24,374.3	20,829
Securities flotation companies	Minor2	307	770.0	1,397
Syndicate shares (real estate, entertainment, equip.) sale	Minor2	33	115.9	343
Underwriters, security	Minor2	148	28,857.9	1,712
Mineral, oil, and gas leasing and royalty dealers	Minor1	44	378.7	397
Mineral leasing dealers	Minor2	16	72.3	70
Mineral royalties dealers	Minor2	8	1,350.1	41
Oil and gas lease brokers	Minor2	183	1,400.6	1,077
Oil royalties dealers	Minor2	47	185.3	162
Mortgages, buying and selling	Minor2	1,249	7,742.8	9,215
Mutual funds, selling by independent salesperson	Minor2	301	5,294.4	6,916

*Category-Major categories (Major1) are more general descriptions for companies that self-selected to capture the many functions they perform in the industry. Minor categories (Minor1, Minor2) are more specific for companies that have more detailed functions (Minor1 is a larger category than Minor2). Minor categories figures (sales, etc.) can be aggregated to larger minor categories (Minor2 sums to Minor1) and major categories overall figures.

SECURITIES BROKERAGE INDUSTRY (NAICS 52312)

NAICS 52312: Securities Brokerage Industry. This industry comprises establishments primarily engaged in the purchase, sale, and brokerage of securities; and those, generally known as investment bankers, primarily engaged in originating, underwriting, and distributing issues of securities. Establishments primarily engaged in issuing shares of mutual and money market funds, unit investment trusts, and face amount certificates are classified in 6722 or 6726.

INDUSTRY ESTABLISHMENTS, SALES & EMPLOYMENT TRENDS

	Year					Percent Chg. Year-to-Year			
	2014	2015	2016	2017	2018	14-15	15-16	16-17	17-18
Establishments	42,161	45,434	46,780	49,405	51,594	7.8%	3.0%	5.6%	4.4%
Sales ($Millions)	137,039	155,255	168,155	185,635	202,120	13.3%	8.3%	10.4%	8.9%
Employment	300,531	323,860	333,456	352,165	367,772	7.8%	3.0%	5.6%	4.4%
Sales ($M)/Estab.	3.25	3.42	3.59	3.76	3.92	5.1%	5.2%	4.5%	4.3%
Sales ($)/Emp.	455,991	479,389	504,279	527,123	549,581	5.1%	5.2%	4.5%	4.3%

3-YEAR TREND – ESTIMATED NUMBER OF ESTABLISHMENTS

Year	Employee Size of Establishment									Total
	1-4 Emps.	5-9 Emps.	10-19 Emps.	20-49 Emps.	50-99 Emps.	100-249 Emps.	250-499 Emps.	>500 Emps.	Non-Employer	Employ-ment
2016	34,522	3,488	2,371	1,687	584	249	77	63	3,740	46,780
2017	36,459	3,684	2,504	1,781	616	262	81	67	3,950	49,405
2018	38,074	3,847	2,615	1,860	644	274	84	70	4,125	51,594

3-YEAR TREND – ESTIMATED INDUSTRY SALES ($MILLIONS)

Year	Employee Size of Establishment									Total
	1-4 Emps.	5-9 Emps.	10-19 Emps.	20-49 Emps.	50-99 Emps.	100-249 Emps.	250-499 Emps.	>500 Emps.	Non-Employer	Employ-ment
2016	27,057.3	7,186.3	12,283.5	23,125.7	17,591.7	20,191.0	20,962.6	39,028.4	728.2	168,154.7
2017	30,051.5	7,981.6	13,642.9	25,684.9	19,538.4	22,425.4	23,282.4	42,218.5	808.8	185,634.5
2018	32,871.6	8,730.6	14,923.1	28,095.2	21,371.9	24,529.8	25,467.2	45,246.3	884.7	202,120.4

3-YEAR TREND – ESTIMATED NUMBER OF EMPLOYEES

Year	Employee Size of Establishment									Total
	1-4 Emps.	5-9 Emps.	10-19 Emps.	20-49 Emps.	50-99 Emps.	100-249 Emps.	250-499 Emps.	>500 Emps.	Non-Employer	Employ-ment
2016	86,304	20,233	32,247	50,764	34,667	31,341	22,271	51,887	3,740	333,456
2017	91,146	21,368	34,057	53,613	36,613	33,099	23,521	54,799	3,950	352,165
2018	95,186	22,315	35,566	55,989	38,235	34,566	24,563	57,227	4,125	367,772

SECURITIES BROKERAGE INDUSTRY (NAICS 52312)

SUB-INDUSTRIES – 2017 ESTIMATED INDUSTRY SALES, ESTABLISHMENTS & EMPLOYMENT

Sub-Industries	Cate-gory*	Establish-ments	Sales ($Mill)	Employ-ment
Security brokers and dealers	Major1	27,063	102,980.0	155,576
Security brokers and dealers	Minor1	7,832	19,814.9	65,870
Bond dealers and brokers	Minor2	687	4,891.2	6,383
Brokers, security	Minor2	7,488	40,673.6	66,739
Dealers, security	Minor2	639	5,661.3	17,044
Floor traders, security	Minor2	50	145.8	397
Note brokers	Minor2	477	109.2	584
Stock brokers and dealers	Minor2	4,572	10,979.8	34,682
Stock option dealers	Minor2	117	91.5	1,262
Tax certificate dealers	Minor2	60	65.9	425
Traders, security	Minor2	420	221.2	3,205

*Category-Major categories (Major1) are more general descriptions for companies that self-selected to capture the many functions they perform in the industry. Minor categories (Minor1, Minor2) are more specific for companies that have more detailed functions (Minor1 is a larger category than Minor2). Minor categories figures (sales, etc.) can be aggregated to larger minor categories (Minor2 sums to Minor1) and major categories overall figures.

LIFE INSURANCE CARRIERS INDUSTRY
(NAICS 524113)

NAICS 524113: Life Insurance Carriers. This industry comprises establishments primarily engaged in underwriting life insurance. These establishments are operated by enterprises that may be owned by stockholders, policyholders, or other carriers.

INDUSTRY ESTABLISHMENTS, SALES & EMPLOYMENT TRENDS

	Year					Percent Chg. Year-to-Year			
	2014	2015	2016	2017	2018	14-15	15-16	16-17	17-18
Establishments	9,682	9,801	9,996	10,265	10,654	1.2%	2.0%	2.7%	3.8%
Sales ($Millions)	543,106	562,521	584,310	609,083	638,556	3.6%	3.9%	4.2%	4.8%
Employment	284,489	287,982	293,714	301,592	313,026	1.2%	2.0%	2.7%	3.8%
Sales ($M)/Estab.	56.09	57.39	58.45	59.34	59.94	2.3%	1.8%	1.5%	1.0%
Sales ($)/Emp.	1,909,059	1,953,319	1,989,383	2,019,561	2,039,945	2.3%	1.8%	1.5%	1.0%

3-YEAR TREND — ESTIMATED NUMBER OF ESTABLISHMENTS

Year	Employee Size of Establishment									Total
	1-4 Emps.	5-9 Emps.	10-19 Emps.	20-49 Emps.	50-99 Emps.	100-249 Emps.	250-499 Emps.	>500 Emps.	Non-Employer	Employ-ment
2016	5,704	1,160	997	1,071	384	287	133	153	107	9,996
2017	5,857	1,192	1,024	1,099	394	295	137	157	110	10,265
2018	6,079	1,237	1,063	1,141	409	306	142	163	114	10,654

3-YEAR TREND — ESTIMATED INDUSTRY SALES ($MILLIONS)

Year	Employee Size of Establishment									Total
	1-4 Emps.	5-9 Emps.	10-19 Emps.	20-49 Emps.	50-99 Emps.	100-249 Emps.	250-499 Emps.	>500 Emps.	Non-Employer	Employ-ment
2016	13,194.2	7,055.1	15,247.7	43,325.2	34,164.4	68,811.9	107,620.6	294,878.8	12.0	584,309.8
2017	13,853.5	7,407.6	16,009.6	45,490.2	35,871.6	72,250.5	112,998.4	305,189.3	12.6	609,083.3
2018	14,669.0	7,843.7	16,952.0	48,167.9	37,983.1	76,503.4	119,650.0	316,773.7	13.3	638,556.2

3-YEAR TREND — ESTIMATED NUMBER OF EMPLOYEES

Year	Employee Size of Establishment									Total
	1-4 Emps.	5-9 Emps.	10-19 Emps.	20-49 Emps.	50-99 Emps.	100-249 Emps.	250-499 Emps.	>500 Emps.	Non-Employer	Employ-ment
2016	14,260	6,731	13,564	32,226	22,813	36,193	38,743	129,078	107	293,714
2017	14,643	6,911	13,927	33,090	23,425	37,163	39,782	132,540	110	301,592
2018	15,198	7,173	14,455	34,345	24,313	38,572	41,290	137,565	114	313,026

SUB-INDUSTRIES – 2017 ESTIMATED INDUSTRY SALES, ESTABLISHMENTS & EMPLOYMENT

Sub-Industries	Category*	Establish-ments	Sales ($Mill)	Employ-ment
Life insurance	Major1	7,700	130,969.8	142,223
Mutual association life insurance	Minor1	207	11,081.9	9,538
Cooperative life insurance organizations	Minor2	56	19,028.3	1,744
Fraternal life insurance organizations	Minor2	286	14,828.8	4,856
Fraternal protective associations	Minor2	21	10.9	87
Assessment life insurance agents	Minor2	137	131.3	1,085
Benevolent insurance associations	Minor2	23	186.4	289
Burial insurance societies	Minor2	19	12.9	103
Funeral insurance	Minor2	43	61.8	556
Legal reserve life insurance	Minor2	88	1,083.9	651
Life insurance carriers	Minor2	1,572	421,323.4	135,035
Life insurance funds, savings bank	Minor2	23	6,525.2	179
Life reinsurance carriers	Minor2	90	3,838.7	5,246

*Category-Major categories (Major1) are more general descriptions for companies that self-selected to capture the many functions they perform in the industry. Minor categories (Minor1, Minor2) are more specific for companies that have more detailed functions (Minor1 is a larger category than Minor2). Minor categories figures (sales, etc.) can be aggregated to larger minor categories (Minor2 sums to Minor1) and major categories overall figures.

HEALTH & MEDICAL INSURANCE CARRIERS (NAICS 524114)

NAICS 524114: Health & Medical Insurance Carrier. This industry comprises establishments primarily engaged in providing hospital, medical, and other health services to subscribers or members in accordance with prearranged agreements or service plans, generally in return for specified subscription charges. The plans may be through a contract with a participating hospital or physician. Other plans provide for partial indemnity and service benefits. Includes separate establishments of HMOs which provide insurance.

INDUSTRY ESTABLISHMENTS, SALES & EMPLOYMENT TRENDS

	Year					Percent Chg. Year-to-Year			
	2014	2015	2016	2017	2018	14-15	15-16	16-17	17-18
Establishments	5,193	5,200	5,247	5,418	5,655	0.1%	0.9%	3.3%	4.4%
Sales ($Millions)	522,604	561,951	603,640	655,751	714,392	7.5%	7.4%	8.6%	8.9%
Employment	364,270	364,696	368,038	380,026	396,642	0.1%	0.9%	3.3%	4.4%
Sales ($M)/Estab.	100.63	108.08	115.04	121.03	126.33	7.4%	6.4%	5.2%	4.4%
Sales ($)/Emp.	1,434,663	1,540,876	1,640,154	1,725,545	1,801,100	7.4%	6.4%	5.2%	4.4%

3-YEAR TREND — ESTIMATED NUMBER OF ESTABLISHMENTS

Year	Employee Size of Establishment									Total
	1-4 Emps.	5-9 Emps.	10-19 Emps.	20-49 Emps.	50-99 Emps.	100-249 Emps.	250-499 Emps.	>500 Emps.	Non-Employer	Employ-ment
2016	2,407	610	493	498	341	375	215	252	56	5,247
2017	2,485	630	509	514	353	387	222	260	58	5,418
2018	2,594	658	531	537	368	404	232	271	60	5,655

3-YEAR TREND — ESTIMATED INDUSTRY SALES ($MILLIONS)

Year	Employee Size of Establishment									Total
	1-4 Emps.	5-9 Emps.	10-19 Emps.	20-49 Emps.	50-99 Emps.	100-249 Emps.	250-499 Emps.	>500 Emps.	Non-Employer	Employ-ment
2016	4,140.0	2,759.2	5,606.1	14,990.6	22,592.2	66,835.0	129,329.2	357,380.4	6.8	603,639.7
2017	4,541.1	3,026.5	6,149.2	16,442.8	24,780.8	73,309.6	141,857.8	385,636.1	7.5	655,751.4
2018	5,009.7	3,338.8	6,783.7	18,139.7	27,338.1	80,874.9	156,497.2	416,401.2	8.3	714,391.7

3-YEAR TREND — ESTIMATED NUMBER OF EMPLOYEES

Year	Employee Size of Establishment									Total
	1-4 Emps.	5-9 Emps.	10-19 Emps.	20-49 Emps.	50-99 Emps.	100-249 Emps.	250-499 Emps.	>500 Emps.	Non-Employer	Employ-ment
2016	6,017	3,539	6,705	14,993	20,285	47,267	62,603	206,573	56	368,038
2017	6,213	3,655	6,924	15,481	20,946	48,807	64,642	213,301	58	380,026
2018	6,484	3,815	7,227	16,158	21,861	50,941	67,468	222,628	60	396,642

HEALTH & MEDICAL INSURANCE CARRIERS (NAICS 524114)

SUB-INDUSTRIES — 2017 ESTIMATED INDUSTRY SALES, ESTABLISHMENTS & EMPLOYMENT

Sub-Industries	Category*	Establishments	Sales ($Mill)	Employment
Hospital and medical service plans	Major1	2,930	365,981.3	221,724
Dental insurance	Minor2	425	7,504.3	17,840
Group hospitalization plans	Minor2	508	77,675.4	45,597
Health Maintenance Organization (HMO), insurance only	Minor2	1,554	204,590.4	94,865

*Category-Major categories (Major1) are more general descriptions for companies that self-selected to capture the many functions they perform in the industry. Minor categories (Minor1, Minor2) are more specific for companies that have more detailed functions (Minor1 is a larger category than Minor2). Minor categories figures (sales, etc.) can be aggregated to larger minor categories (Minor2 sums to Minor1) and major categories overall figures.

PROPERTY & CASUALTY INSURANCE CARRIERS (NAICS 524126)

NAICS 524126: Property & Casualty Insurance Carriers. This industry comprises establishments primarily engaged in underwriting fire, marine, and casualty insurance. These establishments are operated by enterprises that may be owned by stockholders, policyholders, or other carriers.

INDUSTRY ESTABLISHMENTS, SALES & EMPLOYMENT TRENDS

	Year					Percent Chg. Year-to-Year			
	2014	2015	2016	2017	2018	14-15	15-16	16-17	17-18
Establishments	13,508	12,926	12,516	12,571	12,740	-4.3%	-3.2%	0.4%	1.3%
Sales ($Millions)	448,469	463,952	481,437	510,884	543,205	3.5%	3.8%	6.1%	6.3%
Employment	410,818	393,120	380,656	382,318	387,453	-4.3%	-3.2%	0.4%	1.3%
Sales ($M)/Estab.	33.20	35.89	38.46	40.64	42.64	8.1%	7.2%	5.7%	4.9%
Sales ($)/Emp.	1,091,647	1,180,181	1,264,758	1,336,280	1,401,989	8.1%	7.2%	5.7%	4.9%

3-YEAR TREND – ESTIMATED NUMBER OF ESTABLISHMENTS

Year	Employee Size of Establishment									Total
	1-4 Emps.	5-9 Emps.	10-19 Emps.	20-49 Emps.	50-99 Emps.	100-249 Emps.	250-499 Emps.	>500 Emps.	Non-Employer	Employ-ment
2016	7,150	1,467	1,241	1,119	563	463	196	183	134	12,516
2017	7,182	1,473	1,246	1,124	566	465	196	184	134	12,571
2018	7,278	1,493	1,263	1,139	573	472	199	187	136	12,740

3-YEAR TREND – ESTIMATED INDUSTRY SALES ($MILLIONS)

Year	Employee Size of Establishment									Total
	1-4 Emps.	5-9 Emps.	10-19 Emps.	20-49 Emps.	50-99 Emps.	100-249 Emps.	250-499 Emps.	>500 Emps.	Non-Employer	Employ-ment
2016	10,147.0	5,470.8	11,637.1	27,788.5	30,744.7	68,143.6	96,922.5	230,566.9	16.2	481,437.4
2017	10,780.5	5,812.4	12,363.6	29,523.4	32,664.2	72,397.9	102,973.5	244,351.7	17.2	510,884.3
2018	11,504.1	6,202.5	13,193.5	31,505.2	34,856.8	77,257.8	109,885.9	258,780.4	18.3	543,204.7

3-YEAR TREND – ESTIMATED NUMBER OF EMPLOYEES

Year	Employee Size of Establishment									Total
	1-4 Emps.	5-9 Emps.	10-19 Emps.	20-49 Emps.	50-99 Emps.	100-249 Emps.	250-499 Emps.	>500 Emps.	Non-Employer	Employ-ment
2016	17,876	8,507	16,873	33,691	33,464	58,421	56,873	154,817	134	380,656
2017	17,954	8,544	16,947	33,838	33,610	58,676	57,122	155,493	134	382,318
2018	18,195	8,659	17,175	34,293	34,061	59,464	57,889	157,581	136	387,453

SUB-INDUSTRIES – 2017 ESTIMATED INDUSTRY SALES, ESTABLISHMENTS & EMPLOYMENT

Sub-Industries	Cate-gory*	Establish-ments	Sales ($Mill)	Employ-ment
Fire, marine, and casualty insurance	Major1	4,164	160,817.0	142,739
Agricultural insurance	Minor1	141	1,267.1	1,821
Federal Crop Insurance Corporation	Minor2	82	11.8	338
Fire, marine and casualty insurance and carriers	Minor1	941	50,493.9	52,532
Associated factory mutuals, fire and marine insurance	Minor2	18	5.2	73
Fire, marine, and casualty insurance: mutual	Minor2	562	11,304.8	21,572
Fire, marine, and casualty insurance: stock	Minor2	82	27,218.9	12,895
Assessment associations: fire, marine and casualty insura	Minor2	77	23.9	3,879
Automobile insurance	Minor2	2,150	50,954.5	39,278
Boiler insurance	Minor2	14	538.1	393
Burglary and theft insurance	Minor2	11	10.0	229
Contact lens insurance	Minor2	4	0.9	15
Plate glass insurance	Minor2	5	0.9	38
Property damage insurance	Minor2	3,561	194,219.7	70,441
Reciprocal interinsurance exchanges: fire, marine, casual	Minor2	36	4,475.6	4,516
Workers' compensation insurance	Minor2	724	9,541.8	31,559

*Category-Major categories (Major1) are more general descriptions for companies that self-selected to capture the many functions they perform in the industry. Minor categories (Minor1, Minor2) are more specific for companies that have more detailed functions (Minor1 is a larger category than Minor2). Minor categories figures (sales, etc.) can be aggregated to larger minor categories (Minor2 sums to Minor1) and major categories overall figures.

INSURANCE AGENCIES & BROKERAGES INDUSTRY (NAICS 52421)

NAICS 52421: Insurance Agencies & Brokerages. This industry comprises establishments primarily representing one or more insurance carriers, or brokers not representing any particular carriers primarily engaged as independent contractors in the sale or placement of insurance contracts with carriers, but not employees of the insurance carriers they represent. This business also includes independent organizations concerned with insurance services.

INDUSTRY ESTABLISHMENTS, SALES & EMPLOYMENT TRENDS

	Year					Percent Chg. Year-to-Year			
	2014	2015	2016	2017	2018	14-15	15-16	16-17	17-18
Establishments	234,363	230,295	228,157	230,310	234,997	-1.7%	-0.9%	0.9%	2.0%
Sales ($Millions)	125,180	127,774	131,054	136,640	143,584	2.1%	2.6%	4.3%	5.1%
Employment	806,888	792,883	785,521	792,934	809,069	-1.7%	-0.9%	0.9%	2.0%
Sales ($M)/Estab.	0.53	0.55	0.57	0.59	0.61	3.9%	3.5%	3.3%	3.0%
Sales ($)/Emp.	155,139	161,152	166,838	172,322	177,468	3.9%	3.5%	3.3%	3.0%

3-YEAR TREND — ESTIMATED NUMBER OF ESTABLISHMENTS

Year	Employee Size of Establishment									Total
	1-4 Emps.	5-9 Emps.	10-19 Emps.	20-49 Emps.	50-99 Emps.	100-249 Emps.	250-499 Emps.	>500 Emps.	Non-Employer	Employ-ment
2016	96,350	21,654	6,903	3,204	821	348	67	25	98,785	228,157
2017	97,260	21,858	6,968	3,234	828	351	68	26	99,717	230,310
2018	99,239	22,303	7,110	3,300	845	358	69	26	101,746	234,997

3-YEAR TREND — ESTIMATED INDUSTRY SALES ($MILLIONS)

Year	Employee Size of Establishment									Total
	1-4 Emps.	5-9 Emps.	10-19 Emps.	20-49 Emps.	50-99 Emps.	100-249 Emps.	250-499 Emps.	>500 Emps.	Non-Employer	Employ-ment
2016	32,108.3	18,966.4	15,205.2	18,678.7	10,517.6	12,004.5	7,820.1	6,266.4	9,487.2	131,054.4
2017	33,481.4	19,777.5	15,855.5	19,477.5	10,967.4	12,517.9	8,154.5	6,515.5	9,892.9	136,640.2
2018	35,193.1	20,788.6	16,666.0	20,473.3	11,528.0	13,157.8	8,571.4	6,806.7	10,398.7	143,583.6

3-YEAR TREND — ESTIMATED NUMBER OF EMPLOYEES

Year	Employee Size of Establishment									Total
	1-4 Emps.	5-9 Emps.	10-19 Emps.	20-49 Emps.	50-99 Emps.	100-249 Emps.	250-499 Emps.	>500 Emps.	Non-Employer	Employ-ment
2016	240,876	125,593	93,884	96,436	48,748	43,826	19,541	17,833	98,785	785,521
2017	243,149	126,778	94,770	97,346	49,208	44,239	19,725	18,001	99,717	792,934
2018	248,096	129,358	96,698	99,327	50,210	45,139	20,126	18,368	101,746	809,069

INSURANCE AGENCIES & BROKERAGES INDUSTRY (NAICS 52421)

SUB-INDUSTRIES – 2017 ESTIMATED INDUSTRY SALES, ESTABLISHMENTS & EMPLOYMENT

Sub-Industries	Category*	Establish-ments	Sales ($Mill)	Employ-ment
Insurance agents, brokers, and service	Major1	154,520	59,715.6	409,614
Insurance information and consulting services	Minor1	3,563	5,877.1	17,606
Advisory services, insurance	Minor2	679	410.3	3,616
Education services, insurance	Minor2	146	103.9	925
Information bureaus, insurance	Minor2	108	82.9	1,626
Pension and retirement plan consultants	Minor2	2,001	2,475.2	10,684
Policyholders' consulting service	Minor2	97	40.6	3,093
Insurance adjusters	Minor1	2,439	667.0	12,005
Insurance claim adjusters, not employed by insurance cor	Minor2	2,912	992.5	13,853
Insurance agents and brokers	Minor1	23,586	8,789.3	87,259
Insurance agents, nec	Minor2	26,486	18,305.6	124,857
Insurance brokers, nec	Minor2	4,935	18,410.9	44,586
Life insurance agents	Minor2	2,490	1,130.5	13,194
Real estate insurance agents	Minor2	1,065	241.7	2,498
Property and casualty insurance agent	Minor2	1,843	17,040.7	16,415
Title insurance agents	Minor2	365	164.2	1,987
Fire loss appraisal	Minor2	70	40.0	297
Fire Insurance Underwriters' Laboratories	Minor2	39	75.6	157
Inspection and investigation services, insurance	Minor2	924	345.7	4,109
Insurance claim processing, except medical	Minor2	709	507.2	6,841
Loss prevention services, insurance	Minor2	113	78.8	1,751
Medical insurance claim processing, contract or fee basis	Minor2	787	877.3	10,524
Patrol services, insurance	Minor2	18	31.9	2,449
Professional standards services, insurance	Minor2	118	69.3	715
Ratemaking organizations, insurance	Minor2	31	43.0	582
Reporting services, insurance	Minor2	71	51.2	548
Research services, insurance	Minor2	194	72.4	1,145

*Category-Major categories (Major1) are more general descriptions for companies that self-selected to capture the many functions they perform in the industry. Minor categories (Minor1, Minor2) are more specific for companies that have more detailed functions (Minor1 is a larger category than Minor2). Minor categories figures (sales, etc.) can be aggregated to larger minor categories (Minor2 sums to Minor1) and major categories overall figures.

OFFICES OF REAL ESTATE AGENTS & BROKERS (NAICS 53121)

NAICS 53121: Real Estate Agents & Brokers. This industry comprises establishments primarily engaged in renting, buying, selling, managing, and appraising real estate for others.

INDUSTRY ESTABLISHMENTS, SALES & EMPLOYMENT TRENDS

	Year					Percent Chg. Year-to-Year			
	2014	2015	2016	2017	2018	14-15	15-16	16-17	17-18
Establishments	273,191	279,574	290,338	304,596	320,003	2.3%	3.9%	4.9%	5.1%
Sales ($Millions)	85,876	87,735	90,755	94,727	98,811	2.2%	3.4%	4.4%	4.3%
Employment	547,821	560,620	582,205	610,797	641,693	2.3%	3.9%	4.9%	5.1%
Sales ($M)/Estab.	0.31	0.31	0.31	0.31	0.31	-0.2%	-0.4%	-0.5%	-0.7%
Sales ($)/Emp.	156,759	156,497	155,882	155,088	153,985	-0.2%	-0.4%	-0.5%	-0.7%

3-YEAR TREND – ESTIMATED NUMBER OF ESTABLISHMENTS

	Employee Size of Establishment									Total
Year	1-4 Emps.	5-9 Emps.	10-19 Emps.	20-49 Emps.	50-99 Emps.	100-249 Emps.	250-499 Emps.	>500 Emps.	Non-Employer	Employ-ment
2016	90,494	7,656	2,699	1,161	303	131	26	13	187,855	290,338
2017	94,938	8,032	2,832	1,218	318	137	27	13	197,081	304,596
2018	99,741	8,438	2,975	1,279	334	144	28	14	207,050	320,003

3-YEAR TREND – ESTIMATED INDUSTRY SALES ($MILLIONS)

	Employee Size of Establishment									Total
Year	1-4 Emps.	5-9 Emps.	10-19 Emps.	20-49 Emps.	50-99 Emps.	100-249 Emps.	250-499 Emps.	>500 Emps.	Non-Employer	Employ-ment
2016	31,531.1	7,011.5	6,216.8	7,074.4	4,058.6	4,720.9	3,104.7	3,502.7	23,534.6	90,755.2
2017	32,938.7	7,324.5	6,494.3	7,390.2	4,239.8	4,931.7	3,243.3	3,579.8	24,585.1	94,727.3
2018	34,386.9	7,646.5	6,779.8	7,715.1	4,426.2	5,148.5	3,385.9	3,656.2	25,666.1	98,811.3

3-YEAR TREND – ESTIMATED NUMBER OF EMPLOYEES

	Employee Size of Establishment									Total
Year	1-4 Emps.	5-9 Emps.	10-19 Emps.	20-49 Emps.	50-99 Emps.	100-249 Emps.	250-499 Emps.	>500 Emps.	Non-Employer	Employ-ment
2016	226,236	44,406	36,712	34,932	17,992	16,484	7,420	10,169	187,855	582,205
2017	237,346	46,586	38,515	36,648	18,875	17,293	7,784	10,668	197,081	610,797
2018	249,352	48,943	40,463	38,501	19,830	18,168	8,178	11,208	207,050	641,693

OFFICES OF REAL ESTATE AGENTS & BROKERS (NAICS 53121)

SUB-INDUSTRIES – 2017 ESTIMATED INDUSTRY SALES, ESTABLISHMENTS & EMPLOYMENT

Sub-Industries	Cate-gory*	Establish-ments	Sales ($Mill)	Employ-ment
Real estate agents and managers	Major1	117,200	36,717.5	248,933
Real estate brokers and agents	Minor1	145,095	32,236.1	232,340
Broker of manufactured homes, on site	Minor2	450	236.5	1,177
Buying agent, real estate	Minor2	2,248	708.3	3,446
Escrow agent, real estate	Minor2	921	296.9	2,771
Real estate agent, commercial	Minor2	12,025	11,622.9	32,082
Real estate agent, residential	Minor2	24,600	12,222.6	84,458
Selling agent, real estate	Minor2	2,057	686.4	5,589

*Category-Major categories (Major1) are more general descriptions for companies that self-selected to capture the many functions they perform in the industry. Minor categories (Minor1, Minor2) are more specific for companies that have more detailed functions (Minor1 is a larger category than Minor2). Minor categories figures (sales, etc.) can be aggregated to larger minor categories (Minor2 sums to Minor1) and major categories overall figures.

REAL ESTATE PROPERTY MANAGERS INDUSTRY (NAICS 53131)

NAICS 53131: Real Estate Property Managers. This industry comprises establishments primarily engaged in renting, buying, selling, managing, and appraising real estate for others.

INDUSTRY ESTABLISHMENTS, SALES & EMPLOYMENT TRENDS

	Year					Percent Chg. Year-to-Year			
	2014	2015	2016	2017	2018	14-15	15-16	16-17	17-18
Establishments	109,700	109,367	111,929	115,698	119,749	-0.3%	2.3%	3.4%	3.5%
Sales ($Millions)	46,454	45,905	46,406	47,305	48,176	-1.2%	1.1%	1.9%	1.8%
Employment	602,892	601,060	615,143	635,855	658,121	-0.3%	2.3%	3.4%	3.5%
Sales ($M)/Estab.	0.42	0.42	0.41	0.41	0.40	-0.9%	-1.2%	-1.4%	-1.6%
Sales ($)/Emp.	77,052	76,373	75,439	74,396	73,202	-0.9%	-1.2%	-1.4%	-1.6%

3-YEAR TREND – ESTIMATED NUMBER OF ESTABLISHMENTS

Year	Employee Size of Establishment									Total
	1-4 Emps.	5-9 Emps.	10-19 Emps.	20-49 Emps.	50-99 Emps.	100-249 Emps.	250-499 Emps.	>500 Emps.	Non-Employer	Employ-ment
2016	40,702	11,846	6,146	3,313	1,066	554	118	59	48,124	111,929
2017	42,072	12,245	6,353	3,425	1,102	573	122	61	49,745	115,698
2018	43,545	12,674	6,576	3,544	1,141	593	127	63	51,487	119,749

3-YEAR TREND – ESTIMATED INDUSTRY SALES ($MILLIONS)

Year	Employee Size of Establishment									Total
	1-4 Emps.	5-9 Emps.	10-19 Emps.	20-49 Emps.	50-99 Emps.	100-249 Emps.	250-499 Emps.	>500 Emps.	Non-Employer	Employ-ment
2016	4,786.8	3,661.7	4,777.8	6,816.5	4,822.4	6,753.6	4,862.7	5,450.6	4,473.6	46,405.8
2017	4,887.5	3,738.8	4,878.4	6,959.9	4,923.9	6,895.7	4,965.1	5,488.0	4,567.7	47,305.0
2018	4,985.7	3,813.8	4,976.3	7,099.7	5,022.8	7,034.2	5,064.8	5,519.0	4,659.5	48,175.7

3-YEAR TREND – ESTIMATED NUMBER OF EMPLOYEES

Year	Employee Size of Establishment									Total
	1-4 Emps.	5-9 Emps.	10-19 Emps.	20-49 Emps.	50-99 Emps.	100-249 Emps.	250-499 Emps.	>500 Emps.	Non-Employer	Employ-ment
2016	101,754	68,706	83,591	99,721	63,334	69,864	34,430	45,618	48,124	615,143
2017	105,180	71,020	86,406	103,078	65,467	72,216	35,589	47,154	49,745	635,855
2018	108,863	73,507	89,431	106,688	67,759	74,745	36,836	48,806	51,487	658,121

REAL ESTATE PROPERTY MANAGERS INDUSTRY
(NAICS 53131)

SUB-INDUSTRIES – 2017 ESTIMATED INDUSTRY SALES, ESTABLISHMENTS & EMPLOYMENT

Sub-Industries	Cate-gory*	Establish-ments	Sales ($Mill)	Employ-ment
Real estate managers	Minor1	96,861	40,604.0	537,334
Cemetery management service	Minor2	897	242.8	6,181
Condominium manager	Minor2	15,393	5,257.1	74,439
Cooperative apartment manager	Minor2	2,546	1,201.1	17,901

*Category-Major categories (Major1) are more general descriptions for companies that self-selected to capture the many functions they perform in the industry. Minor categories (Minor1, Minor2) are more specific for companies that have more detailed functions (Minor1 is a larger category than Minor2). Minor categories figures (sales, etc.) can be aggregated to larger minor categories (Minor2 sums to Minor1) and major categories overall figures.

OFFICES OF LAWYERS INDUSTRY
(NAICS 54111)

NAICS 54111: Offices of Lawyers. This industry comprises offices of legal practitioners known as lawyers or attorneys (i.e., counselors-at-law) primarily engaged in the practice of law. Establishments in this industry may provide expertise in a range or in specific areas of law, such as criminal law, corporate law, family and estate law, patent law, real estate law, or tax law.

INDUSTRY ESTABLISHMENTS, SALES & EMPLOYMENT TRENDS

	Year					Percent Chg. Year-to-Year			
	2014	2015	2016	2017	2018	14-15	15-16	16-17	17-18
Establishments	249,973	255,238	257,842	261,260	265,925	2.1%	1.0%	1.3%	1.8%
Sales ($Millions)	193,760	209,055	222,143	235,974	250,837	7.9%	6.3%	6.2%	6.3%
Employment	1,185,139	1,210,099	1,222,448	1,238,652	1,260,767	2.1%	1.0%	1.3%	1.8%
Sales ($M)/Estab.	0.78	0.82	0.86	0.90	0.94	5.7%	5.2%	4.8%	4.4%
Sales ($)/Emp.	163,492	172,758	181,720	190,508	198,956	5.7%	5.2%	4.8%	4.4%

3-YEAR TREND – ESTIMATED NUMBER OF ESTABLISHMENTS

Year	Employee Size of Establishment									Total
	1-4 Emps.	5-9 Emps.	10-19 Emps.	20-49 Emps.	50-99 Emps.	100-249 Emps.	250-499 Emps.	>500 Emps.	Non-Employer	Employ-ment
2016	131,992	25,830	11,809	6,173	1,768	853	209	66	79,140	257,842
2017	133,742	26,173	11,966	6,255	1,791	864	212	67	80,189	261,260
2018	136,130	26,640	12,180	6,367	1,823	880	216	68	81,621	265,925

3-YEAR TREND – ESTIMATED INDUSTRY SALES ($MILLIONS)

Year	Employee Size of Establishment									Total
	1-4 Emps.	5-9 Emps.	10-19 Emps.	20-49 Emps.	50-99 Emps.	100-249 Emps.	250-499 Emps.	>500 Emps.	Non-Employer	Employ-ment
2016	42,563.6	21,892.9	25,170.6	34,827.7	21,925.0	28,511.7	23,588.5	14,836.2	8,827.1	222,143.3
2017	45,221.5	23,260.0	26,742.4	37,002.5	23,294.2	30,292.1	25,061.5	15,720.9	9,378.4	235,973.5
2018	48,081.1	24,730.8	28,433.4	39,342.4	24,767.1	32,207.6	26,646.3	16,656.4	9,971.4	250,836.5

3-YEAR TREND – ESTIMATED NUMBER OF EMPLOYEES

Year	Employee Size of Establishment									Total
	1-4 Emps.	5-9 Emps.	10-19 Emps.	20-49 Emps.	50-99 Emps.	100-249 Emps.	250-499 Emps.	>500 Emps.	Non-Employer	Employ-ment
2016	329,981	149,816	160,608	185,820	105,017	107,568	60,912	43,586	79,140	1,222,448
2017	334,355	151,802	162,737	188,283	106,409	108,994	61,719	44,164	80,189	1,238,652
2018	340,325	154,512	165,643	191,644	108,309	110,940	62,821	44,953	81,621	1,260,767

OFFICES OF LAWYERS INDUSTRY (NAICS 54111)

SUB-INDUSTRIES – 2017 ESTIMATED INDUSTRY SALES, ESTABLISHMENTS & EMPLOYMENT

Sub-Industries	Cate-gory*	Establish-ments	Sales ($Mill)	Employ-ment
Legal services	Major1	88,113	61,362.4	324,624
Specialized legal services	Minor1	1,383	1,881.5	8,243
Bankruptcy referee	Minor2	195	408.7	1,459
Patent solicitor	Minor2	101	183.4	1,212
Specialized law offices, attorneys	Minor1	8,466	8,205.2	41,430
Administrative and government law	Minor2	446	1,509.3	4,086
Antitrust and trade regulation law	Minor2	32	42.1	914
Bankrupcy law	Minor2	1,372	1,049.6	5,161
Corporate, partnership and business law	Minor2	1,299	2,949.1	15,280
Criminal law	Minor2	2,814	1,681.5	8,333
Debt collection law	Minor2	194	356.5	1,567
Divorce and family law	Minor2	2,340	1,431.0	7,075
Environmental law	Minor2	159	215.1	865
Immigration and naturalization law	Minor2	1,176	820.9	3,967
Labor and employment law	Minor2	1,124	1,035.8	5,075
Malpractice and negligence law	Minor2	559	817.3	4,100
Patent, trademark and copyright law	Minor2	772	983.2	4,703
Product liability law	Minor2	49	45.9	327
Real estate law	Minor2	2,084	2,051.0	9,135
Securities law	Minor2	100	124.7	743
Taxation law	Minor2	410	512.9	1,568
Will, estate and trust law	Minor2	1,491	959.5	4,473
General practice attorney, lawyer	Minor2	108,640	85,320.7	444,837
General practice law office	Minor2	36,848	58,890.0	328,906
Legal aid service	Minor2	1,095	3,136.3	10,570

*Category-Major categories (Major1) are more general descriptions for companies that self-selected to capture the many functions they perform in the industry. Minor categories (Minor1, Minor2) are more specific for companies that have more detailed functions (Minor1 is a larger category than Minor2). Minor categories figures (sales, etc.) can be aggregated to larger minor categories (Minor2 sums to Minor1) and major categories overall figures.

OFFICES OF CERTIFIED PUBLIC ACCOUNTANTS (NAICS 541211)

NAICS 541211: Offices of Certified Public Accountants This U.S. industry comprises establishments of accountants that are certified to audit the accounting records of public and private organizations and to attest to compliance with generally accepted accounting practices. Offices of certified public accountants (CPAs) may provide one or more of the following accounting services: (1) auditing financial statements; (2) designing accounting systems; (3) preparing financial statements; (4) developing budgets; and (5) providing advice on matters related to accounting.

INDUSTRY ESTABLISHMENTS, SALES & EMPLOYMENT TRENDS

	Year					Percent Chg. Year-to-Year			
	2014	2015	2016	2017	2018	14-15	15-16	16-17	17-18
Establishments	68,348	68,646	70,313	71,453	72,936	0.4%	2.4%	1.6%	2.1%
Sales ($Millions)	61,201	65,741	71,445	76,757	82,413	7.4%	8.7%	7.4%	7.4%
Employment	452,280	454,254	465,286	472,829	482,642	0.4%	2.4%	1.6%	2.1%
Sales ($M)/Estab.	0.90	0.96	1.02	1.07	1.13	7.0%	6.1%	5.7%	5.2%
Sales ($)/Emp.	135,316	144,722	153,552	162,335	170,754	7.0%	6.1%	5.7%	5.2%

3-YEAR TREND — ESTIMATED NUMBER OF ESTABLISHMENTS

Year	Employee Size of Establishment									Total
	1-4 Emps.	5-9 Emps.	10-19 Emps.	20-49 Emps.	50-99 Emps.	100-249 Emps.	250-499 Emps.	>500 Emps.	Non-Employer	Employ-ment
2016	38,745	11,185	5,056	2,122	666	337	85	62	12,055	70,313
2017	39,373	11,366	5,138	2,157	676	343	87	63	12,250	71,453
2018	40,190	11,602	5,245	2,201	690	350	89	64	12,505	72,936

3-YEAR TREND — ESTIMATED INDUSTRY SALES ($MILLIONS)

Year	Employee Size of Establishment									Total
	1-4 Emps.	5-9 Emps.	10-19 Emps.	20-49 Emps.	50-99 Emps.	100-249 Emps.	250-499 Emps.	>500 Emps.	Non-Employer	Employ-ment
2016	9,699.8	7,359.5	8,366.8	9,295.4	6,408.3	8,755.9	7,467.8	12,876.4	1,215.7	71,445.5
2017	10,437.2	7,919.0	9,002.8	10,002.0	6,895.4	9,421.5	8,035.5	13,735.4	1,308.1	76,757.0
2018	11,228.3	8,519.2	9,685.2	10,760.1	7,418.1	10,135.6	8,644.5	14,614.8	1,407.2	82,413.1

3-YEAR TREND — ESTIMATED NUMBER OF EMPLOYEES

Year	Employee Size of Establishment									Total
	1-4 Emps.	5-9 Emps.	10-19 Emps.	20-49 Emps.	50-99 Emps.	100-249 Emps.	250-499 Emps.	>500 Emps.	Non-Employer	Employ-ment
2016	96,863	64,871	68,766	63,882	39,537	42,550	24,839	51,923	12,055	465,286
2017	98,433	65,923	69,881	64,918	40,178	43,240	25,242	52,765	12,250	472,829
2018	100,476	67,291	71,331	66,265	41,012	44,137	25,766	53,860	12,505	482,642

OFFICES OF CERTIFIED PUBLIC ACCOUNTANTS (NAICS 541211)

SUB-INDUSTRIES – 2017 ESTIMATED INDUSTRY SALES, ESTABLISHMENTS & EMPLOYMENT

Sub-Industries	Category*	Establish-ments	Sales ($Mill)	Employ-ment
Accounting, auditing, and bookkeeping	Major1	22,178	12,334.6	123,889
Auditing services	Minor1	784	872.8	10,123
Certified public accountant	Minor2	34,495	48,013.3	213,768
Accounting services, except auditing	Minor1	4,349	2,878.7	42,851
Calculating and statistical service	Minor2	79	49.6	394
Payroll accounting service	Minor2	1,106	7,650.7	27,879
Billing and bookkeeping service	Minor2	8,462	4,957.3	53,925

*Category-Major categories (Major1) are more general descriptions for companies that self-selected to capture the many functions they perform in the industry. Minor categories (Minor1, Minor2) are more specific for companies that have more detailed functions (Minor1 is a larger category than Minor2). Minor categories figures (sales, etc.) can be aggregated to larger minor categories (Minor2 sums to Minor1) and major categories overall figures.

ARCHITECTURAL SERVICES INDUSTRY
(NAICS 54131)

NAICS 54131: Architectural Services. This industry comprises establishments primarily engaged in planning and designing residential, institutional, leisure, commercial, and industrial buildings and structures by applying knowledge of design, construction procedures, zoning regulations, building codes, and building materials.

INDUSTRY ESTABLISHMENTS, SALES & EMPLOYMENT TRENDS

	Year					Percent Chg. Year-to-Year			
	2014	2015	2016	2017	2018	14-15	15-16	16-17	17-18
Establishments	37,142	36,530	35,989	35,526	35,185	-1.6%	-1.5%	-1.3%	-1.0%
Sales ($Millions)	25,880	27,273	28,610	29,937	31,278	5.4%	4.9%	4.6%	4.5%
Employment	176,667	173,757	171,181	168,983	167,359	-1.6%	-1.5%	-1.3%	-1.0%
Sales ($M)/Estab.	0.70	0.75	0.79	0.84	0.89	7.1%	6.5%	6.0%	5.5%
Sales ($)/Emp.	146,493	156,959	167,133	177,161	186,891	7.1%	6.5%	6.0%	5.5%

3-YEAR TREND — ESTIMATED NUMBER OF ESTABLISHMENTS

Year	Employee Size of Establishment									Total
	1-4 Emps.	5-9 Emps.	10-19 Emps.	20-49 Emps.	50-99 Emps.	100-249 Emps.	250-499 Emps.	>500 Emps.	Non-Employer	Employ-ment
2016	13,441	3,615	2,023	1,094	296	128	18	2	15,371	35,989
2017	13,269	3,569	1,997	1,080	292	126	18	2	15,174	35,526
2018	13,141	3,534	1,978	1,070	289	125	18	2	15,028	35,185

3-YEAR TREND — ESTIMATED INDUSTRY SALES ($MILLIONS)

Year	Employee Size of Establishment									Total
	1-4 Emps.	5-9 Emps.	10-19 Emps.	20-49 Emps.	50-99 Emps.	100-249 Emps.	250-499 Emps.	>500 Emps.	Non-Employer	Employ-ment
2016	4,138.9	2,925.8	4,117.6	5,893.1	3,499.6	4,082.1	1,980.4	547.5	1,425.0	28,610.0
2017	4,330.1	3,061.0	4,307.9	6,165.5	3,661.3	4,270.7	2,071.9	577.7	1,490.8	29,937.1
2018	4,523.5	3,197.7	4,500.3	6,440.8	3,824.9	4,461.5	2,164.4	607.4	1,557.4	31,277.9

3-YEAR TREND — ESTIMATED NUMBER OF EMPLOYEES

Year	Employee Size of Establishment									Total
	1-4 Emps.	5-9 Emps.	10-19 Emps.	20-49 Emps.	50-99 Emps.	100-249 Emps.	250-499 Emps.	>500 Emps.	Non-Employer	Employ-ment
2016	33,603	20,968	27,515	32,928	17,554	16,128	5,355	1,758	15,371	171,181
2017	33,172	20,699	27,162	32,505	17,329	15,921	5,287	1,735	15,174	168,983
2018	32,853	20,500	26,901	32,193	17,163	15,768	5,236	1,718	15,028	167,359

ARCHITECTURAL SERVICES INDUSTRY
(NAICS 54131)

SUB-INDUSTRIES – 2017 ESTIMATED INDUSTRY SALES, ESTABLISHMENTS & EMPLOYMENT

Sub-Industries	Category*	Establish-ments	Sales ($Mill)	Employ-ment
Architectural services	Major1	31,421	20,591.3	137,714
Architectural engineering	Minor1	511	499.6	3,945
Architectural engineering	Minor2	2,255	8,513.3	24,335
House designer	Minor2	1,340	333.0	2,989

*Category-Major categories (Major1) are more general descriptions for companies that self-selected to capture the many functions they perform in the industry. Minor categories (Minor1, Minor2) are more specific for companies that have more detailed functions (Minor1 is a larger category than Minor2). Minor categories figures (sales, etc.) can be aggregated to larger minor categories (Minor2 sums to Minor1) and major categories overall figures.

Engineering Services Industry (NAICS 54133)

NAICS 54133: Engineering Services. This industry comprises establishments primarily engaged in applying physical laws and principles of engineering in the design, development, and utilization of machines, materials, instruments, structures, processes, and systems. The assignments undertaken by these establishments may involve any of the following activities: provision of advice, preparation of feasibility studies, preparation of preliminary and final plans and designs, provision of technical services during the construction or installation phase, inspection and evaluation of engineering projects, and related services.

Industry Establishments, Sales & Employment Trends

	Year					Percent Chg. Year-to-Year			
	2014	2015	2016	2017	2018	14-15	15-16	16-17	17-18
Establishments	89,378	91,132	93,251	95,661	97,623	2.0%	2.3%	2.6%	2.1%
Sales ($Millions)	192,469	208,811	225,983	244,129	261,368	8.5%	8.2%	8.0%	7.1%
Employment	915,346	933,309	955,014	979,693	999,782	2.0%	2.3%	2.6%	2.1%
Sales ($M)/Estab.	2.15	2.29	2.42	2.55	2.68	6.4%	5.8%	5.3%	4.9%
Sales ($)/Emp.	210,269	223,732	236,628	249,189	261,425	6.4%	5.8%	5.3%	4.9%

3-Year Trend – Estimated Number of Establishments

	Employee Size of Establishment									Total
Year	1-4 Emps.	5-9 Emps.	10-19 Emps.	20-49 Emps.	50-99 Emps.	100-249 Emps.	250-499 Emps.	>500 Emps.	Non-Employer	Employment
2016	34,606	9,445	7,778	5,919	2,195	1,132	313	154	31,708	93,251
2017	35,501	9,689	7,979	6,072	2,252	1,161	321	158	32,527	95,661
2018	36,229	9,888	8,143	6,196	2,298	1,185	328	162	33,194	97,623

3-Year Trend – Estimated Industry Sales ($Millions)

	Employee Size of Establishment									Total
Year	1-4 Emps.	5-9 Emps.	10-19 Emps.	20-49 Emps.	50-99 Emps.	100-249 Emps.	250-499 Emps.	>500 Emps.	Non-Employer	Employment
2016	11,740.8	8,422.5	17,441.7	35,130.8	28,641.1	39,807.2	37,097.1	44,304.6	3,397.1	225,982.8
2017	12,719.9	9,124.9	18,896.2	38,060.4	31,029.5	43,126.8	40,190.7	47,299.7	3,680.4	244,128.5
2018	13,648.5	9,791.0	20,275.7	40,839.1	33,294.9	46,275.3	43,124.9	50,169.2	3,949.1	261,367.7

3-Year Trend – Estimated Number of Employees

	Employee Size of Establishment									Total
Year	1-4 Emps.	5-9 Emps.	10-19 Emps.	20-49 Emps.	50-99 Emps.	100-249 Emps.	250-499 Emps.	>500 Emps.	Non-Employer	Employment
2016	86,516	54,783	105,782	178,157	130,394	142,748	91,052	133,875	31,708	955,014
2017	88,752	56,199	108,515	182,761	133,763	146,437	93,405	137,334	32,527	979,693
2018	90,572	57,351	110,740	186,509	136,506	149,439	95,320	140,150	33,194	999,782

ENGINEERING SERVICES INDUSTRY
(NAICS 54133)

SUB-INDUSTRIES – 2017 ESTIMATED INDUSTRY
SALES, ESTABLISHMENTS & EMPLOYMENT

Sub-Industries	Cate-gory*	Establish-ments	Sales ($Mill)	Employ-ment
Engineering services	Major1	49,506	145,935.3	514,950
Sanitary engineers	Minor1	166	657.3	1,952
Pollution control engineering	Minor2	233	619.1	3,148
Industrial engineers	Minor1	603	10,867.3	8,213
Machine tool design	Minor2	455	414.7	2,415
Mechanical engineering	Minor2	2,122	2,469.2	17,677
Petroleum, mining, and chemical engineers	Minor1	136	719.7	1,428
Chemical engineering	Minor2	333	470.2	3,944
Mining engineer	Minor2	132	83.6	1,013
Petroleum engineering	Minor2	331	899.2	2,988
Construction and civil engineering	Minor1	1,467	2,225.0	17,780
Building construction consultant	Minor2	2,612	1,777.1	11,441
Civil engineering	Minor2	5,924	17,354.6	86,062
Heating and ventilation engineering	Minor2	355	499.5	2,537
Structural engineering	Minor2	2,401	1,841.0	14,989
Acoustical engineering	Minor2	315	243.9	2,421
Aviation and/or aeronautical engineering	Minor2	1,138	7,546.8	16,846
Consulting engineer	Minor2	19,448	36,719.0	203,045
Designing: ship, boat, machine, and product	Minor2	953	1,182.0	11,566
Electrical or electronic engineering	Minor2	2,860	5,257.0	29,303
Energy conservation engineering	Minor2	701	1,201.2	6,550
Fire protection engineering	Minor2	322	413.8	2,664
Marine engineering	Minor2	385	1,181.4	3,913
Professional engineer	Minor2	2,762	3,550.8	12,846

*Category-Major categories (Major1) are more general descriptions for companies that self-selected to capture the many functions they perform in the industry. Minor categories (Minor1, Minor2) are more specific for companies that have more detailed functions (Minor1 is a larger category than Minor2). Minor categories figures (sales, etc.) can be aggregated to larger minor categories (Minor2 sums to Minor1) and major categories overall figures.

INTERIOR DESIGN SERVICES INDUSTRY (NAICS 54141)

NAICS 54141: Interior Design Services . This industry comprises establishments primarily engaged in planning, designing, and administering projects in interior spaces to meet the physical and aesthetic needs of people using them, taking into consideration building codes, health and safety regulations, traffic patterns and floor planning, mechanical and electrical needs, and interior fittings and furniture. Interior designers and interior design consultants work in areas, such as hospitality design, health care design, institutional design, commercial and corporate design, and residential design.

INDUSTRY ESTABLISHMENTS, SALES & EMPLOYMENT TRENDS

	Year					Percent Chg. Year-to-Year			
	2014	2015	2016	2017	2018	14-15	15-16	16-17	17-18
Establishments	51,338	48,931	47,630	46,412	45,319	-4.7%	-2.7%	-2.6%	-2.4%
Sales ($Millions)	9,371	9,241	9,278	9,309	9,335	-1.4%	0.4%	0.3%	0.3%
Employment	87,228	83,139	80,928	78,858	77,002	-4.7%	-2.7%	-2.6%	-2.4%
Sales ($M)/Estab.	0.18	0.19	0.19	0.20	0.21	3.5%	3.2%	3.0%	2.7%
Sales ($)/Emp.	107,427	111,147	114,652	118,049	121,232	3.5%	3.2%	3.0%	2.7%

3-YEAR TREND – ESTIMATED NUMBER OF ESTABLISHMENTS

Year	Employee Size of Establishment									Total
	1-4 Emps.	5-9 Emps.	10-19 Emps.	20-49 Emps.	50-99 Emps.	100-249 Emps.	250-499 Emps.	>500 Emps.	Non-Employer	Employ-ment
2016	9,304	1,135	393	190	32	10	1	0	36,565	47,630
2017	9,066	1,106	383	185	31	10	1	0	35,630	46,412
2018	8,852	1,080	374	181	30	10	1	0	34,791	45,319

3-YEAR TREND – ESTIMATED INDUSTRY SALES ($MILLIONS)

Year	Employee Size of Establishment									Total
	1-4 Emps.	5-9 Emps.	10-19 Emps.	20-49 Emps.	50-99 Emps.	100-249 Emps.	250-499 Emps.	>500 Emps.	Non-Employer	Employ-ment
2016	2,978.8	954.8	832.5	1,065.3	388.4	338.7	103.8	5.6	2,610.7	9,278.5
2017	2,988.6	958.0	835.2	1,068.8	389.7	339.8	104.1	5.7	2,619.3	9,309.1
2018	2,996.9	960.6	837.5	1,071.8	390.8	340.7	104.4	5.8	2,626.5	9,335.1

3-YEAR TREND – ESTIMATED NUMBER OF EMPLOYEES

Year	Employee Size of Establishment									Total
	1-4 Emps.	5-9 Emps.	10-19 Emps.	20-49 Emps.	50-99 Emps.	100-249 Emps.	250-499 Emps.	>500 Emps.	Non-Employer	Employ-ment
2016	23,259	6,581	5,350	5,725	1,874	1,287	270	17	36,565	80,928
2017	22,665	6,413	5,213	5,578	1,826	1,254	263	16	35,630	78,858
2018	22,131	6,262	5,090	5,447	1,783	1,224	257	16	34,791	77,002

INTERIOR DESIGN SERVICES INDUSTRY (NAICS 54141)

SUB-INDUSTRIES – 2017 ESTIMATED INDUSTRY SALES, ESTABLISHMENTS & EMPLOYMENT

Sub-Industries	Cate-gory*	Establish-ments	Sales ($Mill)	Employ-ment
Interior design services	Minor1	29,028	5,000.0	45,926
Decoration service for special events	Minor2	1,306	411.6	4,077
Interior designer	Minor2	9,176	2,448.6	17,501
Interior decorating	Minor2	6,902	1,449.0	11,354

*Category-Major categories (Major1) are more general descriptions for companies that self-selected to capture the many functions they perform in the industry. Minor categories (Minor1, Minor2) are more specific for companies that have more detailed functions (Minor1 is a larger category than Minor2). Minor categories figures (sales, etc.) can be aggregated to larger minor categories (Minor2 sums to Minor1) and major categories overall figures.

GRAPHIC DESIGNS SERVICES INDUSTRY (NAICS 54143)

NAICS 54143: Graphic Design Services . This industry comprises establishments primarily engaged in planning, designing, and managing the production of visual communication in order to convey specific messages or concepts, clarify complex information, or project visual identities. These services can include the design of printed materials, packaging, advertising, signage systems, and corporate identification (logos). This industry also includes commercial artists engaged exclusively in generating drawings and illustrations requiring technical accuracy or interpretative skills.

INDUSTRY ESTABLISHMENTS, SALES & EMPLOYMENT TRENDS

	Year					Percent Chg. Year-to-Year			
	2014	2015	2016	2017	2018	14-15	15-16	16-17	17-18
Establishments	65,676	65,872	65,631	65,563	65,759	0.3%	-0.4%	-0.1%	0.3%
Sales ($Millions)	10,479	10,505	10,441	10,394	10,367	0.2%	-0.6%	-0.5%	-0.3%
Employment	114,949	115,291	114,869	114,751	115,094	0.3%	-0.4%	-0.1%	0.3%
Sales ($M)/Estab.	0.16	0.16	0.16	0.16	0.16	0.0%	-0.2%	-0.3%	-0.6%
Sales ($)/Emp.	91,163	91,119	90,893	90,576	90,076	0.0%	-0.2%	-0.3%	-0.6%

3-YEAR TREND – ESTIMATED NUMBER OF ESTABLISHMENTS

Year	Employee Size of Establishment									Total
	1-4 Emps.	5-9 Emps.	10-19 Emps.	20-49 Emps.	50-99 Emps.	100-249 Emps.	250-499 Emps.	>500 Emps.	Non-Employer	Employ-ment
2016	12,604	1,600	676	307	42	15	3	0	50,384	65,631
2017	12,591	1,598	675	306	42	15	3	0	50,332	65,563
2018	12,629	1,603	677	307	42	15	3	0	50,483	65,759

3-YEAR TREND – ESTIMATED INDUSTRY SALES ($MILLIONS)

Year	Employee Size of Establishment									Total
	1-4 Emps.	5-9 Emps.	10-19 Emps.	20-49 Emps.	50-99 Emps.	100-249 Emps.	250-499 Emps.	>500 Emps.	Non-Employer	Employ-ment
2016	2,890.4	964.3	1,023.9	1,230.8	370.1	356.3	240.2	4.1	3,360.7	10,440.8
2017	2,877.3	959.9	1,019.3	1,225.2	368.5	354.7	239.1	4.1	3,345.5	10,393.6
2018	2,870.0	957.5	1,016.7	1,222.1	367.5	353.8	238.5	4.1	3,337.1	10,367.2

3-YEAR TREND – ESTIMATED NUMBER OF EMPLOYEES

Year	Employee Size of Establishment									Total
	1-4 Emps.	5-9 Emps.	10-19 Emps.	20-49 Emps.	50-99 Emps.	100-249 Emps.	250-499 Emps.	>500 Emps.	Non-Employer	Employ-ment
2016	31,511	9,279	9,187	9,234	2,493	1,890	872	18	50,384	114,869
2017	31,478	9,270	9,178	9,225	2,490	1,888	871	18	50,332	114,751
2018	31,572	9,298	9,205	9,252	2,498	1,894	874	18	50,483	115,094

GRAPHIC DESIGNS SERVICES INDUSTRY (NAICS 54143)

SUB-INDUSTRIES – 2017 ESTIMATED INDUSTRY SALES, ESTABLISHMENTS & EMPLOYMENT

Sub-Industries	Cate-gory*	Establish-ments	Sales ($Mill)	Employ-ment
Commercial art and graphic design	Major1	36,452	4,924.2	53,629
Art design services	Minor1	3,022	475.3	5,272
Chart and graph design	Minor2	951	85.4	1,353
Creative services to advertisers, except writers	Minor2	1,036	247.1	2,519
Graphic arts and related design	Minor2	18,041	3,372.1	37,289
Package design	Minor2	506	279.6	2,306
Silk screen design	Minor2	1,834	610.4	7,086
Film strip, slide, and still film production	Minor1	652	109.3	1,351
Film strip and slide producer	Minor2	135	20.1	270
Still film producer	Minor2	76	18.0	154
Commercial art and illustration	Minor2	2,858	252.2	3,521

*Category-Major categories (Major1) are more general descriptions for companies that self-selected to capture the many functions they perform in the industry. Minor categories (Minor1, Minor2) are more specific for companies that have more detailed functions (Minor1 is a larger category than Minor2). Minor categories figures (sales, etc.) can be aggregated to larger minor categories (Minor2 sums to Minor1) and major categories overall figures.

COMPUTER SYSTEMS DESIGNS SERVICES INDUSTRY (NAICS 54151)

NAICS 54151: Computer Systems Design and Related Services .
This industry comprises establishments primarily engaged in providing expertise in the field of information technologies through one or more of the following activities: (1) writing, modifying, testing, and supporting software to meet the needs of a particular customer; (2) planning and designing computer systems that integrate computer hardware, software, and communication technologies; (3) on-site management and operation of clients' computer systems and/or data processing facilities; and (4) other professional and technical computer-related advice and services.

INDUSTRY ESTABLISHMENTS, SALES & EMPLOYMENT TRENDS

	Year					Percent Chg. Year-to-Year			
	2014	2015	2016	2017	2018	14-15	15-16	16-17	17-18
Establishments	265,346	271,516	281,191	292,008	304,587	2.3%	3.6%	3.8%	4.3%
Sales ($Millions)	307,499	330,055	356,552	385,038	416,055	7.3%	8.0%	8.0%	8.1%
Employment	1,643,947	1,682,175	1,742,113	1,809,129	1,887,061	2.3%	3.6%	3.8%	4.3%
Sales ($M)/Estab.	1.16	1.22	1.27	1.32	1.37	4.9%	4.3%	4.0%	3.6%
Sales ($)/Emp.	187,049	196,207	204,667	212,830	220,478	4.9%	4.3%	4.0%	3.6%

3-YEAR TREND — ESTIMATED NUMBER OF ESTABLISHMENTS

Year	Employee Size of Establishment									Total
	1-4 Emps.	5-9 Emps.	10-19 Emps.	20-49 Emps.	50-99 Emps.	100-249 Emps.	250-499 Emps.	>500 Emps.	Non-Employer	Employ-ment
2016	104,935	14,954	9,970	7,718	3,080	1,916	599	356	137,664	281,191
2017	108,972	15,529	10,353	8,015	3,198	1,990	622	370	142,960	292,008
2018	113,666	16,198	10,799	8,360	3,336	2,075	649	386	149,118	304,587

3-YEAR TREND — ESTIMATED INDUSTRY SALES ($MILLIONS)

Year	Employee Size of Establishment									Total
	1-4 Emps.	5-9 Emps.	10-19 Emps.	20-49 Emps.	50-99 Emps.	100-249 Emps.	250-499 Emps.	>500 Emps.	Non-Employer	Employ-ment
2016	31,214.6	11,691.4	19,602.0	40,164.9	35,229.0	59,073.4	62,219.8	84,619.2	12,738.2	356,552.5
2017	33,853.1	12,679.7	21,258.8	43,559.9	38,206.8	64,066.7	67,479.1	90,118.6	13,814.9	385,037.6
2018	36,749.6	13,764.5	23,077.8	47,287.0	41,475.9	69,548.3	73,252.7	95,902.8	14,996.9	416,055.4

3-YEAR TREND — ESTIMATED NUMBER OF EMPLOYEES

Year	Employee Size of Establishment									Total
	1-4 Emps.	5-9 Emps.	10-19 Emps.	20-49 Emps.	50-99 Emps.	100-249 Emps.	250-499 Emps.	>500 Emps.	Non-Employer	Employ-ment
2016	262,337	86,731	135,589	232,309	182,924	241,603	174,173	288,783	137,664	1,742,113
2017	272,429	90,067	140,805	241,245	189,961	250,897	180,873	299,892	142,960	1,809,129
2018	284,165	93,947	146,870	251,637	198,144	261,705	188,665	312,810	149,118	1,887,061

SUB-INDUSTRIES – 2017 ESTIMATED INDUSTRY SALES, ESTABLISHMENTS & EMPLOYMENT

Sub-Industries	Cate-gory*	Establish-ments	Sales ($Mill)	Employ-ment
Custom computer programming services	Major1	100,156	67,775.7	471,148
Custom computer programming services	Minor1	8,976	12,418.6	59,016
Computer software systems analysis and design, custom	Minor2	42,183	37,781.5	191,486
Computer software writing services	Minor1	3,431	2,233.8	14,522
Computer code authors	Minor2	421	129.5	1,627
Computer software writers, freelance	Minor2	2,125	490.9	5,420
Computer software development and applications	Minor1	28,630	112,215.6	233,417
Computer software development	Minor2	95,703	141,724.1	772,329
Software programming applications	Minor2	10,382	10,267.8	60,165

*Category-Major categories (Major1) are more general descriptions for companies that self-selected to capture the many functions they perform in the industry. Minor categories (Minor1, Minor2) are more specific for companies that have more detailed functions (Minor1 is a larger category than Minor2). Minor categories figures (sales, etc.) can be aggregated to larger minor categories (Minor2 sums to Minor1) and major categories overall figures.

MANAGEMENT CONSULTING SERVICES INDUSTRY (NAICS 54161)

NAICS 54161: Management Consulting Services . This industry comprises establishments primarily engaged in providing advice and assistance to businesses and other organizations on management issues, such as strategic and organizational planning; financial planning and budgeting; marketing objectives and policies; human resource policies, practices, and planning; production scheduling; and control planning.

INDUSTRY ESTABLISHMENTS, SALES & EMPLOYMENT TRENDS

	Year					Percent Chg. Year-to-Year			
	2014	2015	2016	2017	2018	14-15	15-16	16-17	17-18
Establishments	349,947	354,576	369,157	385,309	403,884	1.3%	4.1%	4.4%	4.8%
Sales ($Millions)	138,558	144,768	154,543	165,090	176,623	4.5%	6.8%	6.8%	7.0%
Employment	1,174,570	1,190,106	1,239,047	1,293,258	1,355,604	1.3%	4.1%	4.4%	4.8%
Sales ($M)/Estab.	0.40	0.41	0.42	0.43	0.44	3.1%	2.5%	2.3%	2.1%
Sales ($)/Emp.	117,965	121,643	124,727	127,655	130,291	3.1%	2.5%	2.3%	2.1%

3-YEAR TREND — ESTIMATED NUMBER OF ESTABLISHMENTS

Year	Employee Size of Establishment									Total
	1-4 Emps.	5-9 Emps.	10-19 Emps.	20-49 Emps.	50-99 Emps.	100-249 Emps.	250-499 Emps.	>500 Emps.	Non-Employer	Employ-ment
2016	113,284	10,735	6,325	4,342	1,653	986	254	177	231,401	369,157
2017	118,241	11,204	6,602	4,532	1,725	1,029	265	185	241,525	385,309
2018	123,941	11,744	6,920	4,750	1,809	1,079	278	194	253,168	403,884

3-YEAR TREND — ESTIMATED INDUSTRY SALES ($MILLIONS)

Year	Employee Size of Establishment									Total
	1-4 Emps.	5-9 Emps.	10-19 Emps.	20-49 Emps.	50-99 Emps.	100-249 Emps.	250-499 Emps.	>500 Emps.	Non-Employer	Employ-ment
2016	22,885.0	5,699.7	8,445.6	15,345.4	12,842.2	20,652.4	17,941.7	29,411.5	21,319.6	154,542.9
2017	24,551.7	6,114.8	9,060.6	16,462.9	13,777.5	22,156.4	19,248.3	30,845.9	22,872.2	165,090.3
2018	26,385.6	6,571.5	9,737.4	17,692.6	14,806.6	23,811.5	20,686.1	32,350.7	24,580.7	176,622.8

3-YEAR TREND — ESTIMATED NUMBER OF EMPLOYEES

Year	Employee Size of Establishment									Total
	1-4 Emps.	5-9 Emps.	10-19 Emps.	20-49 Emps.	50-99 Emps.	100-249 Emps.	250-499 Emps.	>500 Emps.	Non-Employer	Employ-ment
2016	283,210	62,261	86,022	130,693	98,189	124,376	73,955	148,941	231,401	1,239,047
2017	295,601	64,985	89,786	136,411	102,485	129,818	77,191	155,457	241,525	1,293,258
2018	309,852	68,118	94,114	142,987	107,426	136,076	80,912	162,951	253,168	1,355,604

MANAGEMENT CONSULTING SERVICES INDUSTRY (NAICS 54161)

SUB-INDUSTRIES — 2017 ESTIMATED INDUSTRY SALES, ESTABLISHMENTS & EMPLOYMENT

Sub-Industries	Category*	Establish-ments	Sales ($Mill)	Employ-ment
Management consulting services	Major1	117,406	65,481.9	398,627
Industrial and labor consulting services	Minor1	1,188	426.3	4,695
Automation and robotics consultant	Minor2	1,319	398.3	4,406
Industrial consultant	Minor2	1,916	500.6	5,042
Industrial hygiene consultant	Minor2	346	102.3	1,093
Maintenance management consultant	Minor2	1,172	482.9	7,273
Management engineering	Minor2	521	543.1	2,808
Manufacturing management consultant	Minor2	3,670	1,882.2	10,087
Quality assurance consultant	Minor2	1,282	641.6	8,080
Human resource consulting services	Minor1	7,739	3,285.3	63,421
Compensation and benefits planning consultant	Minor2	2,279	4,209.1	17,982
Incentive or award program consultant	Minor2	685	1,511.4	5,309
Labor and union relations consultant	Minor2	457	131.5	1,068
Personnel management consultant	Minor2	2,091	681.2	9,278
Programmed instruction service	Minor2	551	105.7	1,807
Training and development consultant	Minor2	9,656	3,731.3	28,715
Marketing consulting services	Minor1	81,863	19,077.0	197,654
Distribution channels consultant	Minor2	544	207.4	2,148
Franchising consultant	Minor2	386	85.0	901
Merchandising consultant	Minor2	745	364.4	5,212
New products and services consultants	Minor2	828	267.9	3,268
Sales (including sales management) consultant	Minor2	5,409	1,287.5	13,126
Industry specialist consultants	Minor1	50,826	30,922.4	238,337
Business planning and organizing services	Minor1	25,819	4,616.7	53,748
Administrative services consultant	Minor2	3,220	1,394.9	17,045
Business management consultant	Minor2	13,413	6,052.1	52,131
Foreign trade consultant	Minor2	1,756	586.9	3,872
General management consultant	Minor2	5,781	3,029.0	17,979
Management information systems consultant	Minor2	2,194	1,136.9	14,129
Productivity improvement consultant	Minor2	469	113.8	1,377
Site location consultant	Minor2	395	126.7	1,384
Financial consultant	Minor2	39,382	11,707.0	101,255

*Category-Major categories (Major1) are more general descriptions for companies that self-selected to capture the many functions they perform in the industry. Minor categories (Minor1, Minor2) are more specific for companies that have more detailed functions (Minor1 is a larger category than Minor2). Minor categories figures (sales, etc.) can be aggregated to larger minor categories (Minor2 sums to Minor1) and major categories overall figures.

ADVERTISING AGENCIES INDUSTRY (NAICS 54181)

NAICS 54181: Advertising Agencies . This industry comprises establishments primarily engaged in designing and implementing public relations campaigns. These campaigns are designed to promote the interests and image of their clients. Establishments providing lobbying, political consulting, or public relations consulting are included in this industry.

INDUSTRY ESTABLISHMENTS, SALES & EMPLOYMENT TRENDS

	Year					Percent Chg. Year-to-Year			
	2014	2015	2016	2017	2018	14-15	15-16	16-17	17-18
Establishments	33,697	32,667	31,705	30,795	29,963	-3.1%	-2.9%	-2.9%	-2.7%
Sales ($Millions)	65,647	66,578	67,353	68,026	68,610	1.4%	1.2%	1.0%	0.9%
Employment	193,972	188,044	182,505	177,266	172,476	-3.1%	-2.9%	-2.9%	-2.7%
Sales ($M)/Estab.	1.95	2.04	2.12	2.21	2.29	4.6%	4.2%	4.0%	3.7%
Sales ($)/Emp.	338,434	354,058	369,049	383,750	397,795	4.6%	4.2%	4.0%	3.7%

3-YEAR TREND – ESTIMATED NUMBER OF ESTABLISHMENTS

Year	Employee Size of Establishment									Total
	1-4 Emps.	5-9 Emps.	10-19 Emps.	20-49 Emps.	50-99 Emps.	100-249 Emps.	250-499 Emps.	>500 Emps.	Non-Employer	Employ-ment
2016	7,927	1,824	1,234	867	326	211	72	34	19,211	31,705
2017	7,699	1,772	1,198	843	316	205	69	33	18,660	30,795
2018	7,491	1,724	1,166	820	308	199	68	32	18,155	29,963

3-YEAR TREND – ESTIMATED INDUSTRY SALES ($MILLIONS)

Year	Employee Size of Establishment									Total
	1-4 Emps.	5-9 Emps.	10-19 Emps.	20-49 Emps.	50-99 Emps.	100-249 Emps.	250-499 Emps.	>500 Emps.	Non-Employer	Employ-ment
2016	4,307.7	2,605.7	4,430.5	8,247.3	6,803.4	11,871.0	13,574.9	13,537.9	1,975.1	67,353.4
2017	4,343.4	2,627.4	4,467.3	8,315.8	6,859.9	11,969.6	13,687.7	13,763.3	1,991.5	68,026.0
2018	4,373.7	2,645.7	4,498.4	8,373.8	6,907.7	12,053.0	13,783.1	13,969.3	2,005.4	68,610.0

3-YEAR TREND – ESTIMATED NUMBER OF EMPLOYEES

Year	Employee Size of Establishment									Total
	1-4 Emps.	5-9 Emps.	10-19 Emps.	20-49 Emps.	50-99 Emps.	100-249 Emps.	250-499 Emps.	>500 Emps.	Non-Employer	Employ-ment
2016	19,817	10,581	16,776	26,112	19,337	26,577	20,801	23,293	19,211	182,505
2017	19,249	10,278	16,294	25,362	18,782	25,814	20,204	22,624	18,660	177,266
2018	18,728	10,000	15,854	24,677	18,275	25,116	19,658	22,013	18,155	172,476

ADVERTISING AGENCIES INDUSTRY (NAICS 54181)

SUB-INDUSTRIES — 2017 ESTIMATED INDUSTRY SALES, ESTABLISHMENTS & EMPLOYMENT

Sub-Industries	Cate-gory*	Establish-ments	Sales ($Mill)	Employ-ment
Advertising agencies	Major1	25,008	63,451.1	157,038
Advertising consultant	Minor2	5,787	4,574.8	20,228

*Category-Major categories (Major1) are more general descriptions for companies that self-selected to capture the many functions they perform in the industry. Minor categories (Minor1, Minor2) are more specific for companies that have more detailed functions (Minor1 is a larger category than Minor2). Minor categories figures (sales, etc.) can be aggregated to larger minor categories (Minor2 sums to Minor1) and major categories overall figures.

PUBLIC RELATIONS AGENCIES INDUSTRY (NAICS 54182)

NAICS 54182: Public Relations Agencies . This industry comprises establishments primarily engaged in designing and implementing public relations campaigns. These campaigns are designed to promote the interests and image of their clients. Establishments providing lobbying, political consulting, or public relations consulting are included in this industry.

INDUSTRY ESTABLISHMENTS, SALES & EMPLOYMENT TRENDS

	Year					Percent Chg. Year-to-Year			
	2014	2015	2016	2017	2018	14-15	15-16	16-17	17-18
Establishments	21,090	22,509	23,722	25,046	26,543	6.7%	5.4%	5.6%	6.0%
Sales ($Millions)	10,921	12,399	13,829	15,390	17,116	13.5%	11.5%	11.3%	11.2%
Employment	69,689	74,378	78,386	82,762	87,706	6.7%	5.4%	5.6%	6.0%
Sales ($M)/Estab.	0.52	0.55	0.58	0.61	0.64	6.4%	5.8%	5.4%	4.9%
Sales ($)/Emp.	156,717	166,703	176,420	185,956	195,149	6.4%	5.8%	5.4%	4.9%

3-YEAR TREND – ESTIMATED NUMBER OF ESTABLISHMENTS

	Employee Size of Establishment									Total
Year	1-4 Emps.	5-9 Emps.	10-19 Emps.	20-49 Emps.	50-99 Emps.	100-249 Emps.	250-499 Emps.	>500 Emps.	Non-Employer	Employ-ment
2016	6,888	1,249	681	348	116	53	10	4	14,374	23,722
2017	7,273	1,318	718	367	122	56	11	5	15,176	25,046
2018	7,707	1,397	761	389	130	59	11	5	16,083	26,543

3-YEAR TREND – ESTIMATED INDUSTRY SALES ($MILLIONS)

	Employee Size of Establishment									Total
Year	1-4 Emps.	5-9 Emps.	10-19 Emps.	20-49 Emps.	50-99 Emps.	100-249 Emps.	250-499 Emps.	>500 Emps.	Non-Employer	Employ-ment
2016	2,256.5	1,075.0	1,473.4	1,991.9	1,459.5	1,795.0	1,158.5	1,083.3	1,535.9	13,828.8
2017	2,514.9	1,198.1	1,642.1	2,220.0	1,626.7	2,000.5	1,291.1	1,184.9	1,711.8	15,390.1
2018	2,801.0	1,334.4	1,829.0	2,472.5	1,811.7	2,228.1	1,438.0	1,294.4	1,906.5	17,115.8

3-YEAR TREND – ESTIMATED NUMBER OF EMPLOYEES

	Employee Size of Establishment									Total
Year	1-4 Emps.	5-9 Emps.	10-19 Emps.	20-49 Emps.	50-99 Emps.	100-249 Emps.	250-499 Emps.	>500 Emps.	Non-Employer	Employ-ment
2016	17,221	7,241	9,255	10,462	6,882	6,666	2,945	3,341	14,374	78,386
2017	18,182	7,646	9,771	11,046	7,266	7,038	3,109	3,527	15,176	82,762
2018	19,268	8,102	10,355	11,706	7,700	7,459	3,295	3,738	16,083	87,706

PUBLIC RELATIONS AGENCIES INDUSTRY
(NAICS 54182)

SUB-INDUSTRIES – 2017 ESTIMATED INDUSTRY SALES, ESTABLISHMENTS & EMPLOYMENT

Sub-Industries	Cate-gory*	Establish-ments	Sales ($Mill)	Employ-ment
Public relations services	Major1	9,904	6,016.7	36,197
Lobbyist	Minor2	1,561	990.8	4,587
Promotion service	Minor2	6,660	3,956.3	15,576
Public relations and publicity	Minor2	3,183	2,157.0	15,613
Sales promotion	Minor2	3,738	2,269.2	10,788

*Category-Major categories (Major1) are more general descriptions for companies that self-selected to capture the many functions they perform in the industry. Minor categories (Minor1, Minor2) are more specific for companies that have more detailed functions (Minor1 is a larger category than Minor2). Minor categories figures (sales, etc.) can be aggregated to larger minor categories (Minor2 sums to Minor1) and major categories overall figures.

DIRECT MAIL ADVERTISING INDUSTRY
(NAICS 54186)

NAICS 54186: Direct Mail Advertising . This industry comprises establishments primarily engaged in (1) creating and designing advertising campaigns for the purpose of distributing advertising materials (e.g., coupons, flyers, samples) or specialties (e.g., key chains, magnets, pens with customized messages imprinted) by mail or other direct distribution; and/or (2) preparing advertising materials or specialties for mailing or other direct distribution. These establishments may also compile, maintain, sell, and rent mailing lists.

INDUSTRY ESTABLISHMENTS, SALES & EMPLOYMENT TRENDS

	Year					Percent Chg. Year-to-Year			
	2014	2015	2016	2017	2018	14-15	15-16	16-17	17-18
Establishments	6,829	6,843	6,423	6,006	5,591	0.2%	-6.1%	-6.5%	-6.9%
Sales ($Millions)	7,261	7,585	7,413	7,202	6,948	4.5%	-2.3%	-2.8%	-3.5%
Employment	47,712	47,813	44,881	41,963	39,063	0.2%	-6.1%	-6.5%	-6.9%
Sales ($M)/Estab.	1.06	1.11	1.15	1.20	1.24	4.2%	4.1%	3.9%	3.6%
Sales ($)/Emp.	152,182	158,629	165,162	171,623	177,873	4.2%	4.1%	3.9%	3.6%

3-YEAR TREND – ESTIMATED NUMBER OF ESTABLISHMENTS

Year	Employee Size of Establishment									Total
	1-4 Emps.	5-9 Emps.	10-19 Emps.	20-49 Emps.	50-99 Emps.	100-249 Emps.	250-499 Emps.	>500 Emps.	Non-Employer	Employment
2016	1,357	402	312	261	112	68	14	6	3,892	6,423
2017	1,269	376	292	244	105	63	13	5	3,639	6,006
2018	1,181	350	272	227	97	59	12	5	3,388	5,591

3-YEAR TREND – ESTIMATED INDUSTRY SALES ($MILLIONS)

Year	Employee Size of Establishment									Total
	1-4 Emps.	5-9 Emps.	10-19 Emps.	20-49 Emps.	50-99 Emps.	100-249 Emps.	250-499 Emps.	>500 Emps.	Non-Employer	Employment
2016	323.4	251.5	491.8	1,086.0	1,025.6	1,672.4	1,174.3	989.0	398.7	7,412.6
2017	313.4	243.7	476.5	1,052.4	993.8	1,620.6	1,138.0	977.0	386.4	7,201.8
2018	301.4	234.4	458.4	1,012.3	956.0	1,559.0	1,094.7	960.4	371.7	6,948.3

3-YEAR TREND – ESTIMATED NUMBER OF EMPLOYEES

Year	Employee Size of Establishment									Total
	1-4 Emps.	5-9 Emps.	10-19 Emps.	20-49 Emps.	50-99 Emps.	100-249 Emps.	250-499 Emps.	>500 Emps.	Non-Employer	Employment
2016	3,393	2,330	4,247	7,843	6,649	8,540	4,105	3,881	3,892	44,881
2017	3,173	2,178	3,971	7,333	6,217	7,985	3,838	3,629	3,639	41,963
2018	2,954	2,028	3,697	6,826	5,787	7,433	3,573	3,378	3,388	39,063

DIRECT MAIL ADVERTISING INDUSTRY (NAICS 54186)

SUB-INDUSTRIES – 2017 ESTIMATED INDUSTRY SALES, ESTABLISHMENTS & EMPLOYMENT

Sub-Industries	Category*	Establishments	Sales ($Mill)	Employment
Direct mail advertising services	Major1	3,072	4,106.4	22,314
Addressing service	Minor2	86	53.7	977
Addressographing service	Minor2	2	1.4	5
Mailing list compilers	Minor2	258	198.3	1,151
Mailing service	Minor2	2,384	2,455.0	16,374
Mailing list management	Minor2	46	130.1	321
Mailing list brokers	Minor2	158	256.8	820

*Category-Major categories (Major1) are more general descriptions for companies that self-selected to capture the many functions they perform in the industry. Minor categories (Minor1, Minor2) are more specific for companies that have more detailed functions (Minor1 is a larger category than Minor2). Minor categories figures (sales, etc.) can be aggregated to larger minor categories (Minor2 sums to Minor1) and major categories overall figures.

MARKETING RESEARCH & PUBLIC OPINION POLLING (NAICS 54191)

NAICS 54191: Marketing Research & Public Opinion Polling .
This industry comprises establishments primarily engaged in systematically gathering, recording, tabulating, and presenting marketing and public opinion data.

INDUSTRY ESTABLISHMENTS, SALES & EMPLOYMENT TRENDS

	Year					Percent Chg. Year-to-Year			
	2014	2015	2016	2017	2018	14-15	15-16	16-17	17-18
Establishments	23,751	23,785	23,118	22,489	21,919	0.1%	-2.8%	-2.7%	-2.5%
Sales ($Millions)	17,246	17,937	18,088	18,219	18,333	4.0%	0.8%	0.7%	0.6%
Employment	111,793	111,955	108,812	105,854	103,172	0.1%	-2.8%	-2.7%	-2.5%
Sales ($M)/Estab.	0.73	0.75	0.78	0.81	0.84	3.9%	3.8%	3.5%	3.2%
Sales ($)/Emp.	154,265	160,218	166,234	172,117	177,697	3.9%	3.8%	3.5%	3.2%

3-YEAR TREND – ESTIMATED NUMBER OF ESTABLISHMENTS

Year	Employee Size of Establishment									Total
	1-4 Emps.	5-9 Emps.	10-19 Emps.	20-49 Emps.	50-99 Emps.	100-249 Emps.	250-499 Emps.	>500 Emps.	Non-Employer	Employ-ment
2016	3,048	652	570	529	184	133	43	21	17,937	23,118
2017	2,965	634	555	515	179	130	42	21	17,449	22,489
2018	2,890	618	541	502	174	126	41	20	17,007	21,919

3-YEAR TREND – ESTIMATED INDUSTRY SALES ($MILLIONS)

Year	Employee Size of Establishment									Total
	1-4 Emps.	5-9 Emps.	10-19 Emps.	20-49 Emps.	50-99 Emps.	100-249 Emps.	250-499 Emps.	>500 Emps.	Non-Employer	Employ-ment
2016	721.0	405.5	891.9	2,191.6	1,673.8	3,270.0	3,539.7	3,862.9	1,531.9	18,088.3
2017	724.7	407.6	896.5	2,202.8	1,682.3	3,286.7	3,557.7	3,921.2	1,539.7	18,219.2
2018	727.7	409.3	900.3	2,212.1	1,689.4	3,300.5	3,572.8	3,974.9	1,546.3	18,333.3

3-YEAR TREND – ESTIMATED NUMBER OF EMPLOYEES

Year	Employee Size of Establishment									Total
	1-4 Emps.	5-9 Emps.	10-19 Emps.	20-49 Emps.	50-99 Emps.	100-249 Emps.	250-499 Emps.	>500 Emps.	Non-Employer	Employ-ment
2016	7,619	3,782	7,757	15,938	10,927	16,815	12,458	15,579	17,937	108,812
2017	7,412	3,680	7,546	15,504	10,630	16,358	12,120	15,156	17,449	105,854
2018	7,224	3,586	7,355	15,112	10,361	15,943	11,812	14,772	17,007	103,172

SUB-INDUSTRIES — 2017 ESTIMATED INDUSTRY SALES, ESTABLISHMENTS & EMPLOYMENT

Sub-Industries	Category*	Establishments	Sales ($Mill)	Employment
Commercial nonphysical research	Major1	4,261	5,380.9	14,180
Market analysis, business, and economic research	Minor1	2,386	1,183.7	8,730
Business analysis	Minor2	517	168.5	1,675
Business economic service	Minor2	838	364.7	2,683
Business research service	Minor2	1,394	898.4	5,078
Economic research	Minor2	769	417.2	2,444
Market analysis or research	Minor2	6,089	5,477.4	39,279
Merger, acquisition, and reorganization research	Minor2	564	274.8	1,603
Opinion research	Minor2	157	67.7	1,352
Research services, except laboratory	Minor2	2,896	1,976.3	15,103
Survey service: marketing, location, etc.	Minor2	686	224.9	3,562
Commercial sociological and educational research	Minor1	166	62.8	633
Educational research	Minor2	1,558	1,544.9	8,631
Sociological research	Minor2	210	177.0	899

*Category-Major categories (Major1) are more general descriptions for companies that self-selected to capture the many functions they perform in the industry. Minor categories (Minor1, Minor2) are more specific for companies that have more detailed functions (Minor1 is a larger category than Minor2). Minor categories figures (sales, etc.) can be aggregated to larger minor categories (Minor2 sums to Minor1) and major categories overall figures.

Veterinary Services Industry
(NAICS 54194)

NAICS 54194: Veterinary Services . This industry comprises establishments of licensed veterinary practitioners primarily engaged in the practice of veterinary medicine, dentistry, or surgery for animals; and establishments primarily engaged in providing testing services for licensed veterinary practitioners.

Industry Establishments, Sales & Employment Trends

	Year					Percent Chg. Year-to-Year			
	2014	2015	2016	2017	2018	14-15	15-16	16-17	17-18
Establishments	37,840	39,939	42,023	44,301	46,881	5.5%	5.2%	5.4%	5.8%
Sales ($Millions)	24,592	27,718	30,964	34,510	38,433	12.7%	11.7%	11.5%	11.4%
Employment	331,473	349,857	368,113	388,074	410,671	5.5%	5.2%	5.4%	5.8%
Sales ($M)/Estab.	0.65	0.69	0.74	0.78	0.82	6.8%	6.2%	5.7%	5.2%
Sales ($)/Emp.	74,190	79,227	84,115	88,926	93,586	6.8%	6.2%	5.7%	5.2%

3-Year Trend — Estimated Number of Establishments

Year	Employee Size of Establishment									Total
	1-4 Emps.	5-9 Emps.	10-19 Emps.	20-49 Emps.	50-99 Emps.	100-249 Emps.	250-499 Emps.	>500 Emps.	Non-Employer	Employ-ment
2016	10,335	9,702	9,808	3,749	325	64	10	1	8,028	42,023
2017	10,895	10,228	10,340	3,952	343	68	11	1	8,463	44,301
2018	11,529	10,823	10,942	4,183	363	72	11	1	8,956	46,881

3-Year Trend — Estimated Industry Sales ($Millions)

Year	Employee Size of Establishment									Total
	1-4 Emps.	5-9 Emps.	10-19 Emps.	20-49 Emps.	50-99 Emps.	100-249 Emps.	250-499 Emps.	>500 Emps.	Non-Employer	Employ-ment
2016	1,641.5	4,050.1	10,296.9	10,418.0	1,987.6	1,060.4	554.6	185.8	769.1	30,963.9
2017	1,830.0	4,515.3	11,479.7	11,614.7	2,215.9	1,182.2	618.3	196.5	857.4	34,510.0
2018	2,038.7	5,030.2	12,788.6	12,939.1	2,468.5	1,317.0	688.8	206.9	955.2	38,433.0

3-Year Trend — Estimated Number of Employees

Year	Employee Size of Establishment									Total
	1-4 Emps.	5-9 Emps.	10-19 Emps.	20-49 Emps.	50-99 Emps.	100-249 Emps.	250-499 Emps.	>500 Emps.	Non-Employer	Employ-ment
2016	25,837	56,270	133,392	112,850	19,328	8,122	2,907	1,379	8,028	368,113
2017	27,238	59,321	140,626	118,969	20,376	8,563	3,065	1,454	8,463	388,074
2018	28,824	62,775	148,814	125,897	21,562	9,061	3,244	1,538	8,956	410,671

VETERINARY SERVICES INDUSTRY
(NAICS 54194)

SUB-INDUSTRIES — 2017 ESTIMATED INDUSTRY
SALES, ESTABLISHMENTS & EMPLOYMENT

Sub-Industries	Cate-gory*	Establish-ments	Sales ($Mill)	Employ-ment
Veterinary services, specialties	Major1	14,642	11,277.8	110,665
Animal hospital services, pets and other animal specialtie	Minor2	17,512	15,840.6	177,649
Veterinarian, animal specialties	Minor2	12,148	7,391.7	99,761

*Category-Major categories (Major1) are more general descriptions for companies that self-selected to capture the many functions they perform in the industry. Minor categories (Minor1, Minor2) are more specific for companies that have more detailed functions (Minor1 is a larger category than Minor2). Minor categories figures (sales, etc.) can be aggregated to larger minor categories (Minor2 sums to Minor1) and major categories overall figures.

TELEMARKETING SERVICES INDUSTRY
(NAICS 561422)

NAICS 561422: Telemarketing Services. This industry comprises establishments primarily engaged in providing telemarketing services on a contract or fee basis for others, such as: (1) promoting clients' products or services by telephone, (2) taking orders for clients by telephone, and (3) soliciting contributions or providing information for clients by telephone. These establishments never own the product or provide the services they are representing and generally can originate and/or receive calls for others.

INDUSTRY ESTABLISHMENTS, SALES & EMPLOYMENT TRENDS

	Year					Percent Chg. Year-to-Year			
	2014	2015	2016	2017	2018	14-15	15-16	16-17	17-18
Establishments	12,472	12,736	13,098	13,381	13,748	2.1%	2.8%	2.2%	2.7%
Sales ($Millions)	29,691	31,560	33,613	35,526	37,609	6.3%	6.5%	5.7%	5.9%
Employment	345,285	352,603	362,613	370,445	380,626	2.1%	2.8%	2.2%	2.7%
Sales ($M)/Estab.	2.38	2.48	2.57	2.66	2.74	4.1%	3.6%	3.5%	3.0%
Sales ($)/Emp.	85,988	89,505	92,697	95,901	98,807	4.1%	3.6%	3.5%	3.0%

3-YEAR TREND – ESTIMATED NUMBER OF ESTABLISHMENTS

Year	Employee Size of Establishment									Total
	1-4 Emps.	5-9 Emps.	10-19 Emps.	20-49 Emps.	50-99 Emps.	100-249 Emps.	250-499 Emps.	>500 Emps.	Non-Employer	Employ-ment
2016	1,237	380	467	634	363	401	244	242	9,129	13,098
2017	1,264	388	477	648	371	410	249	247	9,326	13,381
2018	1,299	399	491	666	381	421	256	254	9,583	13,748

3-YEAR TREND – ESTIMATED INDUSTRY SALES ($MILLIONS)

Year	Employee Size of Establishment									Total
	1-4 Emps.	5-9 Emps.	10-19 Emps.	20-49 Emps.	50-99 Emps.	100-249 Emps.	250-499 Emps.	>500 Emps.	Non-Employer	Employ-ment
2016	121.2	97.9	302.6	1,087.3	1,369.2	4,074.1	8,339.5	17,852.9	368.6	33,613.2
2017	128.6	103.9	321.2	1,154.0	1,453.1	4,323.9	8,850.8	18,799.4	391.2	35,526.1
2018	136.9	110.6	341.8	1,227.9	1,546.3	4,601.1	9,418.3	19,809.4	416.3	37,608.7

3-YEAR TREND – ESTIMATED NUMBER OF EMPLOYEES

Year	Employee Size of Establishment									Total
	1-4 Emps.	5-9 Emps.	10-19 Emps.	20-49 Emps.	50-99 Emps.	100-249 Emps.	250-499 Emps.	>500 Emps.	Non-Employer	Employ-ment
2016	3,093	2,205	6,356	19,093	21,584	50,588	70,876	179,691	9,129	362,613
2017	3,160	2,253	6,493	19,505	22,050	51,680	72,406	183,572	9,326	370,445
2018	3,246	2,315	6,671	20,041	22,656	53,101	74,396	188,617	9,583	380,626

TELEMARKETING SERVICES INDUSTRY (NAICS 561422)

SUB-INDUSTRIES – 2017 ESTIMATED INDUSTRY SALES, ESTABLISHMENTS & EMPLOYMENT

Sub-Industries	Cate-gory*	Establish-ments	Sales ($Mill)	Employ-ment
Telemarketing services	Minor2	13,381	35,526.1	370,445

*Category-Major categories (Major1) are more general descriptions for companies that self-selected to capture the many functions they perform in the industry. Minor categories (Minor1, Minor2) are more specific for companies that have more detailed functions (Minor1 is a larger category than Minor2). Minor categories figures (sales, etc.) can be aggregated to larger minor categories (Minor2 sums to Minor1) and major categories overall figures.

SECURITY GUARDS & PATROL SERVICES INDUSTRY
(NAICS 561612)

NAICS 561612: Security Guards & Patrol Services. This industry comprises establishments primarily engaged in providing detective, guard, and armored car services. Establishments primarily engaged in monitoring and maintaining security systems devices, such as burglar and fire alarms, are classified in 7382.

INDUSTRY ESTABLISHMENTS, SALES & EMPLOYMENT TRENDS

	Year					Percent Chg. Year-to-Year			
	2014	2015	2016	2017	2018	14-15	15-16	16-17	17-18
Establishments	35,303	36,901	38,328	39,696	41,384	4.5%	3.9%	3.6%	4.3%
Sales ($Millions)	42,733	44,755	46,529	48,210	50,149	4.7%	4.0%	3.6%	4.0%
Employment	600,498	627,677	651,956	675,222	703,933	4.5%	3.9%	3.6%	4.3%
Sales ($M)/Estab.	1.21	1.21	1.21	1.21	1.21	0.2%	0.1%	0.0%	-0.2%
Sales ($)/Emp.	71,163	71,302	71,368	71,398	71,241	0.2%	0.1%	0.0%	-0.2%

3-YEAR TREND – ESTIMATED NUMBER OF ESTABLISHMENTS

Year	Employee Size of Establishment									Total
	1-4 Emps.	5-9 Emps.	10-19 Emps.	20-49 Emps.	50-99 Emps.	100-249 Emps.	250-499 Emps.	>500 Emps.	Non-Employer	Employ-ment
2016	2,929	1,306	1,520	1,680	1,152	1,166	439	261	27,876	38,328
2017	3,034	1,353	1,574	1,740	1,193	1,208	454	270	28,871	39,696
2018	3,163	1,410	1,641	1,813	1,244	1,259	474	281	30,099	41,384

3-YEAR TREND – ESTIMATED INDUSTRY SALES ($MILLIONS)

Year	Employee Size of Establishment									Total
	1-4 Emps.	5-9 Emps.	10-19 Emps.	20-49 Emps.	50-99 Emps.	100-249 Emps.	250-499 Emps.	>500 Emps.	Non-Employer	Employ-ment
2016	237.5	278.4	814.7	2,382.8	3,592.4	9,800.9	12,426.0	15,803.8	1,192.3	46,528.8
2017	247.2	289.7	847.8	2,479.7	3,738.4	10,199.1	12,930.8	16,236.3	1,240.7	48,209.6
2018	258.4	302.9	886.3	2,592.3	3,908.2	10,662.4	13,518.2	16,723.4	1,297.1	50,149.1

3-YEAR TREND – ESTIMATED NUMBER OF EMPLOYEES

Year	Employee Size of Establishment									Total
	1-4 Emps.	5-9 Emps.	10-19 Emps.	20-49 Emps.	50-99 Emps.	100-249 Emps.	250-499 Emps.	>500 Emps.	Non-Employer	Employ-ment
2016	7,323	7,575	20,672	50,555	68,424	147,037	127,595	194,899	27,876	651,956
2017	7,584	7,846	21,409	52,359	70,866	152,284	132,148	201,855	28,871	675,222
2018	7,907	8,179	22,320	54,585	73,879	158,759	137,767	210,438	30,099	703,933

SUB-INDUSTRIES — 2017 ESTIMATED INDUSTRY SALES, ESTABLISHMENTS & EMPLOYMENT

Sub-Industries	Category*	Establishments	Sales ($Mill)	Employment
Detective and armored car services	Major1	4,977	3,102.3	97,208
Guard services	Minor1	11,579	8,854.8	74,388
Armored car services	Minor2	747	1,588.1	28,081
Burglary protection service	Minor2	49	34.3	706
Guard dog rental	Minor2	57	31.4	783
Protective services, guard	Minor2	1,461	10,793.1	50,852
Security guard service	Minor2	5,994	19,323.6	322,002
Detective services	Minor1	2,271	943.7	21,669
Detective agency	Minor2	1,573	741.2	20,552
Fingerprint service	Minor2	182	47.1	1,384
Lie detection service	Minor2	323	66.2	1,516
Private investigator	Minor2	10,485	2,683.9	56,080

*Category-Major categories (Major1) are more general descriptions for companies that self-selected to capture the many functions they perform in the industry. Minor categories (Minor1, Minor2) are more specific for companies that have more detailed functions (Minor1 is a larger category than Minor2). Minor categories figures (sales, etc.) can be aggregated to larger minor categories (Minor2 sums to Minor1) and major categories overall figures.

COLLEGES & UNIVERSITIES INDUSTRY (NAICS 61131)

NAICS 61131: Colleges & Universities. This industry comprises establishments primarily furnishing academic courses and granting academic degrees. The requirement for admission is at least a high school diploma or equivalent general academic training.

INDUSTRY ESTABLISHMENTS, SALES & EMPLOYMENT TRENDS

	Year					Percent Chg. Year-to-Year			
	2014	2015	2016	2017	2018	14-15	15-16	16-17	17-18
Establishments	24,741	24,998	25,308	26,112	27,008	1.0%	1.2%	3.2%	3.4%
Sales ($Millions)	213,651	222,715	231,648	242,604	253,744	4.2%	4.0%	4.7%	4.6%
Employment	972,716	982,827	995,024	1,026,647	1,061,868	1.0%	1.2%	3.2%	3.4%
Sales ($M)/Estab.	8.64	8.91	9.15	9.29	9.40	3.2%	2.7%	1.5%	1.1%
Sales ($)/Emp.	219,644	226,607	232,806	236,307	238,960	3.2%	2.7%	1.5%	1.1%

3-YEAR TREND – ESTIMATED NUMBER OF ESTABLISHMENTS

Year	Employee Size of Establishment									Total
	1-4 Emps.	5-9 Emps.	10-19 Emps.	20-49 Emps.	50-99 Emps.	100-249 Emps.	250-499 Emps.	>500 Emps.	Non-Employer	Employ-ment
2016	1,010	463	525	751	475	430	334	808	20,513	25,308
2017	1,042	478	541	775	490	443	345	834	21,165	26,112
2018	1,077	495	560	801	507	458	357	862	21,891	27,008

3-YEAR TREND – ESTIMATED INDUSTRY SALES ($MILLIONS)

Year	Employee Size of Establishment									Total
	1-4 Emps.	5-9 Emps.	10-19 Emps.	20-49 Emps.	50-99 Emps.	100-249 Emps.	250-499 Emps.	>500 Emps.	Non-Employer	Employ-ment
2016	249.2	300.6	856.0	3,241.8	4,504.9	10,990.1	28,839.4	181,746.6	919.5	231,648.0
2017	265.4	320.1	911.6	3,452.4	4,797.5	11,704.0	30,712.9	189,460.3	979.2	242,603.5
2018	282.5	340.8	970.6	3,675.7	5,107.8	12,460.9	32,699.1	197,163.8	1,042.5	253,743.7

3-YEAR TREND – ESTIMATED NUMBER OF EMPLOYEES

Year	Employee Size of Establishment									Total
	1-4 Emps.	5-9 Emps.	10-19 Emps.	20-49 Emps.	50-99 Emps.	100-249 Emps.	250-499 Emps.	>500 Emps.	Non-Employer	Employ-ment
2016	2,524	2,688	7,137	22,600	28,194	54,177	97,306	759,886	20,513	995,024
2017	2,604	2,773	7,364	23,318	29,090	55,898	100,398	784,036	21,165	1,026,647
2018	2,694	2,868	7,616	24,118	30,088	57,816	103,843	810,935	21,891	1,061,868

COLLEGES & UNIVERSITIES INDUSTRY
(NAICS 61131)

SUB-INDUSTRIES – 2017 ESTIMATED INDUSTRY
SALES, ESTABLISHMENTS & EMPLOYMENT

Sub-Industries	Category*	Establishments	Sales ($Mill)	Employment
Colleges and universities	Major1	8,015	36,078.4	233,888
Colleges and universities	Minor1	1,206	3,581.5	39,864
College, except junior	Minor2	1,765	36,648.3	106,835
University	Minor2	13,693	160,314.1	626,691
Professional schools	Minor1	965	4,849.9	11,000
Service academy	Minor2	86	153.1	1,711
Theological seminary	Minor2	382	978.2	6,659

*Category-Major categories (Major1) are more general descriptions for companies that self-selected to capture the many functions they perform in the industry. Minor categories (Minor1, Minor2) are more specific for companies that have more detailed functions (Minor1 is a larger category than Minor2). Minor categories figures (sales, etc.) can be aggregated to larger minor categories (Minor2 sums to Minor1) and major categories overall figures.

EXAM PREPARATION & TUTORING INDUSTRY (NAICS 611691)

NAICS 6111691: Exam Preparation & Tutoring. This industry comprises establishments primarily engaged in offering educational courses and services, not elsewhere classified. Includes music schools, drama schools, language schools, short-term examination preparatory schools, student exchange programs, curriculum development, and vocational counseling, except rehabilitation counseling. Dance schools are classified in 7911, and rehabilitation counseling is classified in 8331.

INDUSTRY ESTABLISHMENTS, SALES & EMPLOYMENT TRENDS

	Year					Percent Chg. Year-to-Year			
	2014	2015	2016	2017	2018	14-15	15-16	16-17	17-18
Establishments	47,534	50,318	53,767	57,302	60,606	5.9%	6.9%	6.6%	5.8%
Sales ($Millions)	6,803	7,547	8,414	9,333	10,243	10.9%	11.5%	10.9%	9.7%
Employment	143,585	151,994	162,413	173,090	183,070	5.9%	6.9%	6.6%	5.8%
Sales ($M)/Estab.	0.14	0.15	0.16	0.16	0.17	4.8%	4.3%	4.1%	3.8%
Sales ($)/Emp.	47,379	49,652	51,809	53,922	55,951	4.8%	4.3%	4.1%	3.8%

3-YEAR TREND – ESTIMATED NUMBER OF ESTABLISHMENTS

Year	Employee Size of Establishment									Total
	1-4 Emps.	5-9 Emps.	10-19 Emps.	20-49 Emps.	50-99 Emps.	100-249 Emps.	250-499 Emps.	>500 Emps.	Non-Employer	Employ-ment
2016	4,817	2,070	1,923	1,049	217	80	23	9	43,579	53,767
2017	5,134	2,206	2,049	1,117	231	86	24	10	46,444	57,302
2018	5,430	2,333	2,167	1,182	245	91	25	10	49,122	60,606

3-YEAR TREND – ESTIMATED INDUSTRY SALES ($MILLIONS)

Year	Employee Size of Establishment									Total
	1-4 Emps.	5-9 Emps.	10-19 Emps.	20-49 Emps.	50-99 Emps.	100-249 Emps.	250-499 Emps.	>500 Emps.	Non-Employer	Employ-ment
2016	423.5	478.2	1,117.2	1,612.4	734.1	731.7	694.7	622.5	2,000.3	8,414.5
2017	470.7	531.6	1,241.9	1,792.5	816.1	813.4	772.3	670.9	2,223.7	9,333.2
2018	517.6	584.5	1,365.6	1,970.9	897.4	894.4	849.1	718.6	2,445.0	10,243.0

3-YEAR TREND – ESTIMATED NUMBER OF EMPLOYEES

Year	Employee Size of Establishment									Total
	1-4 Emps.	5-9 Emps.	10-19 Emps.	20-49 Emps.	50-99 Emps.	100-249 Emps.	250-499 Emps.	>500 Emps.	Non-Employer	Employ-ment
2016	12,044	12,006	26,152	31,561	12,900	10,127	6,581	7,463	43,579	162,413
2017	12,835	12,795	27,871	33,636	13,748	10,793	7,013	7,954	46,444	173,090
2018	13,576	13,533	29,478	35,576	14,541	11,415	7,418	8,412	49,122	183,070

SUB-INDUSTRIES – 2017 ESTIMATED INDUSTRY SALES, ESTABLISHMENTS & EMPLOYMENT

Sub-Industries	Cate-gory*	Establish-ments	Sales ($Mill)	Employ-ment
Educational services	Minor1	43,163	8,024.2	142,926
Educational service, nondegree granting: continuing educ	Minor2	3,713	951.4	16,231
Tutoring school	Minor2	10,426	357.7	13,932

*Category-Major categories (Major1) are more general descriptions for companies that self-selected to capture the many functions they perform in the industry. Minor categories (Minor1, Minor2) are more specific for companies that have more detailed functions (Minor1 is a larger category than Minor2). Minor categories figures (sales, etc.) can be aggregated to larger minor categories (Minor2 sums to Minor1) and major categories overall figures.

EDUCATIONAL SUPPORT SERVICES INDUSTRY (NAICS 61171)

NAICS 61171: Educational Support Services. This industry comprises establishments primarily engaged in offering educational courses and services, not elsewhere classified. Includes music schools, drama schools, language schools, short-term examination preparatory schools, student exchange programs, curriculum development, and vocational counseling, except rehabilitation counseling. Dance schools are classified in 7911, and rehabilitation counseling is classified in 8331.

INDUSTRY ESTABLISHMENTS, SALES & EMPLOYMENT TRENDS

	Year					Percent Chg. Year-to-Year			
	2014	2015	2016	2017	2018	14-15	15-16	16-17	17-18
Establishments	40,726	41,366	42,089	43,250	44,553	1.6%	1.7%	2.8%	3.0%
Sales ($Millions)	13,091	13,610	14,137	14,798	15,491	4.0%	3.9%	4.7%	4.7%
Employment	118,666	120,529	122,636	126,021	129,816	1.6%	1.7%	2.8%	3.0%
Sales ($M)/Estab.	0.32	0.33	0.34	0.34	0.35	2.4%	2.1%	1.9%	1.6%
Sales ($)/Emp.	110,316	112,915	115,273	117,423	119,328	2.4%	2.1%	1.9%	1.6%

3-YEAR TREND – ESTIMATED NUMBER OF ESTABLISHMENTS

Year	Employee Size of Establishment									Total
	1-4 Emps.	5-9 Emps.	10-19 Emps.	20-49 Emps.	50-99 Emps.	100-249 Emps.	250-499 Emps.	>500 Emps.	Non-Employer	Employ-ment
2016	5,386	1,174	687	433	137	103	34	20	34,114	42,089
2017	5,535	1,206	706	445	141	106	35	20	35,055	43,250
2018	5,702	1,243	727	458	145	109	36	21	36,111	44,553

3-YEAR TREND – ESTIMATED INDUSTRY SALES ($MILLIONS)

Year	Employee Size of Establishment									Total
	1-4 Emps.	5-9 Emps.	10-19 Emps.	20-49 Emps.	50-99 Emps.	100-249 Emps.	250-499 Emps.	>500 Emps.	Non-Employer	Employ-ment
2016	1,072.3	614.3	904.3	1,508.2	1,052.3	2,132.5	2,371.9	2,987.6	1,493.2	14,136.6
2017	1,125.0	644.5	948.7	1,582.2	1,104.0	2,237.2	2,488.3	3,101.6	1,566.5	14,797.8
2018	1,180.4	676.2	995.4	1,660.1	1,158.4	2,347.4	2,610.9	3,218.2	1,643.7	15,490.7

3-YEAR TREND – ESTIMATED NUMBER OF EMPLOYEES

Year	Employee Size of Establishment									Total
	1-4 Emps.	5-9 Emps.	10-19 Emps.	20-49 Emps.	50-99 Emps.	100-249 Emps.	250-499 Emps.	>500 Emps.	Non-Employer	Employ-ment
2016	13,466	6,809	9,347	13,034	8,165	13,032	9,921	14,750	34,114	122,636
2017	13,838	6,997	9,605	13,394	8,390	13,392	10,195	15,157	35,055	126,021
2018	14,254	7,208	9,894	13,797	8,642	13,795	10,502	15,613	36,111	129,816

SUB-INDUSTRIES — 2017 ESTIMATED INDUSTRY SALES, ESTABLISHMENTS & EMPLOYMENT

Sub-Industries	Category*	Establishments	Sales ($Mill)	Employment
Schools and educational services, nec	Major1	9,718	1,202.5	18,145
Arts and crafts schools	Minor1	569	1,286.6	1,835
Art school, except commercial	Minor2	552	241.3	2,533
Ceramic school	Minor2	122	20.9	350
Floral arrangement instruction	Minor2	269	12.3	180
Educational services	Minor1	14,172	8,371.4	61,257
Educational service, nondegree granting: continuing educ	Minor2	1,219	992.6	6,957
Tutoring school	Minor2	3,423	373.1	5,971
Music and drama schools	Minor1	600	67.2	1,106
Dramatic school	Minor2	140	38.4	378
Music school	Minor2	1,264	280.4	3,803
Musical instrument lessons	Minor2	1,854	114.5	1,823
Voice lessons	Minor2	307	16.2	234
Vehicle driving school	Minor1	2,346	209.5	3,412
Automobile driving instruction	Minor2	567	74.4	1,207
Truck driving training	Minor2	193	36.3	573
Reading and speaking schools	Minor1	475	47.6	821
Diction school	Minor2	12	1.2	18
Language school	Minor2	1,122	215.1	3,266
Public speaking school	Minor2	264	28.4	869
Reading school, including speed reading	Minor2	162	31.7	449
Airline training	Minor2	179	103.8	745
Bartending school	Minor2	187	10.5	162
Baton instruction	Minor2	55	4.7	120
Bible school	Minor2	225	77.5	748
Cooking school	Minor2	252	57.6	771
Dressmaking school	Minor2	5	0.6	8
Finishing school, charm and modeling	Minor2	113	13.5	350
Flying instruction	Minor2	332	68.0	700
Hypnosis school	Minor2	34	5.8	69
Meditation therapy	Minor2	497	41.7	632
Personal development school	Minor2	500	95.3	1,232
Prenatal instruction	Minor2	34	5.3	86
Misc. schools	Minor2	1,486	651.8	5,211

*Category-Major categories (Major1) are more general descriptions for companies that self-selected to capture the many functions they perform in the industry. Minor categories (Minor1, Minor2) are more specific for companies that have more detailed functions (Minor1 is a larger category than Minor2). Minor categories figures (sales, etc.) can be aggregated to larger minor categories (Minor2 sums to Minor1) and major categories overall figures.

OFFICES OF PHYSICIANS INDUSTRY (NAICS 62111)

NAICS 62111: Offices of Physicians. This industry comprises establishments primarily of licensed practitioners having the degree of M.D. and engaged in the practice of general or specialized medicine and surgery. Establishments operating as clinics of physicians are included in this business. Osteopathic physicians are classified in 8031.

INDUSTRY ESTABLISHMENTS, SALES & EMPLOYMENT TRENDS

	Year					Percent Chg. Year-to-Year			
	2014	2015	2016	2017	2018	14-15	15-16	16-17	17-18
Establishments	272,970	273,380	275,756	278,899	282,098	0.2%	0.9%	1.1%	1.1%
Sales ($Millions)	311,589	327,515	345,186	363,732	382,023	5.1%	5.4%	5.4%	5.0%
Employment	2,315,935	2,319,414	2,339,568	2,366,235	2,393,378	0.2%	0.9%	1.1%	1.1%
Sales ($M)/Estab.	1.14	1.20	1.25	1.30	1.35	5.0%	4.5%	4.2%	3.8%
Sales ($)/Emp.	134,541	141,206	147,543	153,718	159,617	5.0%	4.5%	4.2%	3.8%

3-YEAR TREND – ESTIMATED NUMBER OF ESTABLISHMENTS

Year	Employee Size of Establishment									Total
	1-4 Emps.	5-9 Emps.	10-19 Emps.	20-49 Emps.	50-99 Emps.	100-249 Emps.	250-499 Emps.	>500 Emps.	Non-Employer	Employ-ment
2016	117,396	49,800	31,575	18,587	4,170	1,600	359	204	52,065	275,756
2017	118,734	50,368	31,935	18,799	4,218	1,618	363	206	52,658	278,899
2018	120,096	50,945	32,301	19,014	4,266	1,637	367	209	53,262	282,098

3-YEAR TREND – ESTIMATED INDUSTRY SALES ($MILLIONS)

Year	Employee Size of Establishment									Total
	1-4 Emps.	5-9 Emps.	10-19 Emps.	20-49 Emps.	50-99 Emps.	100-249 Emps.	250-499 Emps.	>500 Emps.	Non-Employer	Employ-ment
2016	28,338.7	31,596.5	50,378.4	78,494.6	38,712.8	40,036.7	30,242.5	39,721.4	7,664.7	345,186.3
2017	29,879.5	33,314.5	53,117.7	82,762.6	40,817.7	42,213.6	31,886.9	41,657.8	8,081.4	363,731.8
2018	31,401.3	35,011.2	55,822.9	86,977.7	42,896.5	44,363.5	33,510.9	43,545.8	8,493.0	382,022.7

3-YEAR TREND – ESTIMATED NUMBER OF EMPLOYEES

Year	Employee Size of Establishment									Total
	1-4 Emps.	5-9 Emps.	10-19 Emps.	20-49 Emps.	50-99 Emps.	100-249 Emps.	250-499 Emps.	>500 Emps.	Non-Employer	Employ-ment
2016	293,490	288,840	429,419	559,461	247,705	201,781	104,323	162,483	52,065	2,339,568
2017	296,835	292,133	434,314	565,838	250,529	204,081	105,512	164,335	52,658	2,366,235
2018	300,240	295,484	439,296	572,329	253,403	206,422	106,723	166,220	53,262	2,393,378

OFFICES OF PHYSICIANS INDUSTRY
(NAICS 62111)

SUB-INDUSTRIES — 2017 ESTIMATED INDUSTRY
SALES, ESTABLISHMENTS & EMPLOYMENT

Sub-Industries	Cate-gory*	Establish-ments	Sales ($Mill)	Employ-ment
Offices and clinics of medical doctors	Major1	182,102	182,531.7	1,225,764
Internal medicine practitioners	Minor1	5,036	5,271.2	40,145
Cardiologist and cardio-vascular specialist	Minor2	10,334	14,568.7	131,801
Endocrinologist	Minor2	1,683	1,423.5	11,023
Gastronomist	Minor2	3,270	3,716.2	29,006
Hematologist	Minor2	1,236	1,852.1	19,381
Internal medicine, physician/surgeon	Minor2	22,338	16,081.1	135,179
Nephrologist	Minor2	2,106	1,587.5	14,292
Neurologist	Minor2	6,393	5,208.4	42,648
Oncologist	Minor2	4,014	5,889.8	42,919
Pulmonary specialist, physician/surgeon	Minor2	1,940	2,853.5	18,223
Neurosurgeon	Minor2	1,189	2,124.2	9,354
Medical centers	Minor1	14,655	54,022.9	293,751
Ambulatory surgical center	Minor2	1,215	6,333.8	25,639
Clinic, operated by physicians	Minor2	16,610	47,146.2	263,858
Dispensery, operated by physicians	Minor2	158	220.6	6,219
Freestanding emergency medical center	Minor2	932	1,603.5	12,871
Primary care medical clinic	Minor2	3,688	11,296.7	44,162

*Category-Major categories (Major1) are more general descriptions for companies that self-selected to capture the many functions they perform in the industry. Minor categories (Minor1, Minor2) are more specific for companies that have more detailed functions (Minor1 is a larger category than Minor2). Minor categories figures (sales, etc.) can be aggregated to larger minor categories (Minor2 sums to Minor1) and major categories overall figures.

OFFICES OF DENTISTS INDUSTRY
(NAICS 62121)

NAICS 62121: Offices of Dentists. This industry comprises establishments primarily of licensed practitioners having the degree of D.M.D. or D.D.S. (or D.D.Sc.) and engaged in the practice of general or specialized dentistry, including dental surgery. Establishments operating as clinics of dentists are included in this business.

INDUSTRY ESTABLISHMENTS, SALES & EMPLOYMENT TRENDS

	Year					Percent Chg. Year-to-Year			
	2014	2015	2016	2017	2018	14-15	15-16	16-17	17-18
Establishments	149,176	150,122	152,144	154,913	157,743	0.6%	1.3%	1.8%	1.8%
Sales ($Millions)	96,702	101,918	107,755	114,160	120,566	5.4%	5.7%	5.9%	5.6%
Employment	911,610	917,392	929,745	946,665	963,963	0.6%	1.3%	1.8%	1.8%
Sales ($M)/Estab.	0.65	0.68	0.71	0.74	0.76	4.7%	4.3%	4.1%	3.7%
Sales ($)/Emp.	106,079	111,095	115,897	120,591	125,073	4.7%	4.3%	4.1%	3.7%

3-YEAR TREND – ESTIMATED NUMBER OF ESTABLISHMENTS

Year	Employee Size of Establishment									Total
	1-4 Emps.	5-9 Emps.	10-19 Emps.	20-49 Emps.	50-99 Emps.	100-249 Emps.	250-499 Emps.	>500 Emps.	Non-Employer	Employ-ment
2016	55,094	54,125	23,599	3,981	220	44	6	2	15,073	152,144
2017	56,096	55,110	24,029	4,053	224	45	6	2	15,347	154,913
2018	57,121	56,117	24,468	4,127	228	45	6	2	15,628	157,743

3-YEAR TREND – ESTIMATED INDUSTRY SALES ($MILLIONS)

Year	Employee Size of Establishment									Total
	1-4 Emps.	5-9 Emps.	10-19 Emps.	20-49 Emps.	50-99 Emps.	100-249 Emps.	250-499 Emps.	>500 Emps.	Non-Employer	Employ-ment
2016	13,243.1	34,195.4	37,494.2	16,739.9	2,036.5	1,092.6	513.9	435.2	2,003.9	107,754.8
2017	14,030.9	36,229.6	39,724.7	17,735.7	2,157.6	1,157.6	544.4	455.8	2,123.1	114,159.6
2018	14,819.0	38,264.4	41,955.8	18,731.8	2,278.8	1,222.7	575.0	475.9	2,242.3	120,565.7

3-YEAR TREND – ESTIMATED NUMBER OF EMPLOYEES

Year	Employee Size of Establishment									Total
	1-4 Emps.	5-9 Emps.	10-19 Emps.	20-49 Emps.	50-99 Emps.	100-249 Emps.	250-499 Emps.	>500 Emps.	Non-Employer	Employ-ment
2016	137,734	313,924	320,951	119,817	13,086	5,530	1,780	1,850	15,073	929,745
2017	140,241	319,637	326,792	121,998	13,324	5,631	1,813	1,884	15,347	946,665
2018	142,803	325,477	332,763	124,227	13,567	5,734	1,846	1,918	15,628	963,963

OFFICES OF DENTISTS INDUSTRY
(NAICS 62121)

SUB-INDUSTRIES — 2017 ESTIMATED INDUSTRY SALES, ESTABLISHMENTS & EMPLOYMENT

Sub-Industries	Category*	Establish-ments	Sales ($Mill)	Employ-ment
Offices and clinics of dentists	Major1	84,492	57,925.1	480,804
Specialized dental practitioners	Minor1	1,121	967.2	7,916
Dental surgeon	Minor2	6,301	4,569.8	38,001
Endodontist	Minor2	1,754	1,182.7	10,240
Maxillofacial specialist	Minor2	794	663.2	5,847
Oral pathologist	Minor2	586	462.5	3,927
Orthodontist	Minor2	6,869	5,004.7	48,092
Pedodontist	Minor2	569	579.7	4,915
Periodontist	Minor2	1,847	1,525.2	12,578
Prosthodontist	Minor2	799	580.3	4,714
Dental clinics and offices	Minor1	3,220	2,697.4	22,394
Dental clinic	Minor2	4,950	3,674.9	32,596
Dentists' office	Minor2	41,046	33,287.0	268,759
Dental insurance plan	Minor2	179	657.3	2,665
Group and corporate practice, dentist	Minor2	386	382.6	3,217

*Category-Major categories (Major1) are more general descriptions for companies that self-selected to capture the many functions they perform in the industry. Minor categories (Minor1, Minor2) are more specific for companies that have more detailed functions (Minor1 is a larger category than Minor2). Minor categories figures (sales, etc.) can be aggregated to larger minor categories (Minor2 sums to Minor1) and major categories overall figures.

MEDICAL LABORATORIES INDUSTRY
(NAICS 621511)

NAICS 621511: Medical Laboratories. This industry comprises establishments primarily engaged in providing professional analytic or diagnostic services to the medical profession, or to the patient on prescription of a physician.

INDUSTRY ESTABLISHMENTS, SALES & EMPLOYMENT TRENDS

	Year					Percent Chg. Year-to-Year			
	2014	2015	2016	2017	2018	14-15	15-16	16-17	17-18
Establishments	10,644	11,056	11,544	11,968	12,405	3.9%	4.4%	3.7%	3.7%
Sales ($Millions)	23,903	25,685	27,628	29,485	31,377	7.5%	7.6%	6.7%	6.4%
Employment	152,792	158,705	165,713	171,803	178,084	3.9%	4.4%	3.7%	3.7%
Sales ($M)/Estab.	2.25	2.32	2.39	2.46	2.53	3.5%	3.0%	2.9%	2.7%
Sales ($)/Emp.	156,441	161,839	166,720	171,623	176,191	3.5%	3.0%	2.9%	2.7%

3-YEAR TREND – ESTIMATED NUMBER OF ESTABLISHMENTS

Year	Employee Size of Establishment									Total
	1-4 Emps.	5-9 Emps.	10-19 Emps.	20-49 Emps.	50-99 Emps.	100-249 Emps.	250-499 Emps.	>500 Emps.	Non-Employer	Employ-ment
2016	4,466	1,015	709	598	274	193	66	73	4,149	11,544
2017	4,630	1,052	735	620	284	200	69	75	4,302	11,968
2018	4,800	1,091	762	642	295	207	71	78	4,459	12,405

3-YEAR TREND – ESTIMATED INDUSTRY SALES ($MILLIONS)

Year	Employee Size of Establishment									Total
	1-4 Emps.	5-9 Emps.	10-19 Emps.	20-49 Emps.	50-99 Emps.	100-249 Emps.	250-499 Emps.	>500 Emps.	Non-Employer	Employ-ment
2016	918.2	548.6	963.9	2,149.5	2,169.6	4,113.9	4,751.8	11,537.2	475.2	27,627.8
2017	986.3	589.2	1,035.4	2,308.9	2,330.4	4,419.0	5,104.1	12,201.6	510.4	29,485.4
2018	1,056.2	631.0	1,108.7	2,472.3	2,495.4	4,731.9	5,465.5	12,869.2	546.6	31,376.8

3-YEAR TREND – ESTIMATED NUMBER OF EMPLOYEES

Year	Employee Size of Establishment									Total
	1-4 Emps.	5-9 Emps.	10-19 Emps.	20-49 Emps.	50-99 Emps.	100-249 Emps.	250-499 Emps.	>500 Emps.	Non-Employer	Employ-ment
2016	11,166	5,888	9,647	17,988	16,299	24,344	19,246	56,988	4,149	165,713
2017	11,576	6,104	10,001	18,649	16,898	25,239	19,953	59,082	4,302	171,803
2018	11,999	6,327	10,367	19,331	17,516	26,161	20,682	61,242	4,459	178,084

MEDICAL LABORATORIES INDUSTRY
(NAICS 621511)

SUB-INDUSTRIES — 2017 ESTIMATED INDUSTRY SALES, ESTABLISHMENTS & EMPLOYMENT

Sub-Industries	Cate-gory*	Establish-ments	Sales ($Mill)	Employ-ment
Medical laboratories	Major1	8,507	9,604.7	105,219
Testing laboratories	Minor1	1,063	17,227.5	29,829
Bacteriological laboratory	Minor2	21	25.4	256
Biological laboratory	Minor2	206	484.5	4,663
Blood analysis laboratory	Minor2	193	234.9	3,614
Pathological laboratory	Minor2	587	853.4	13,021
Urinalysis laboratory	Minor2	24	25.9	189
Neurological laboratory	Minor2	82	46.4	923
Ultrasound laboratory	Minor2	383	216.5	3,142
X-ray laboratory, including dental	Minor2	903	766.3	10,946

*Category-Major categories (Major1) are more general descriptions for companies that self-selected to capture the many functions they perform in the industry. Minor categories (Minor1, Minor2) are more specific for companies that have more detailed functions (Minor1 is a larger category than Minor2). Minor categories figures (sales, etc.) can be aggregated to larger minor categories (Minor2 sums to Minor1) and major categories overall figures.

HOME HEALTH CARE SERVICES INDUSTRY
(NAICS 62161)

NAICS 62161: Home Health Care Services. This industry comprises establishments primarily engaged in providing skilled nursing or medical care in the home, under supervision of a physician. Registered or practical nurses engaged in the independent practice of their profession are classified in 8049, and nurses' registries are classified in 7361. Selling health care products for personal or household consumption is classified in retail trade and renting or leasing products for health care is classified in 7352.

INDUSTRY ESTABLISHMENTS, SALES & EMPLOYMENT TRENDS

	Year					Percent Chg. Year-to-Year			
	2014	2015	2016	2017	2018	14-15	15-16	16-17	17-18
Establishments	181,629	195,371	210,443	222,101	234,421	7.6%	7.7%	5.5%	5.5%
Sales ($Millions)	90,950	101,173	112,355	122,213	132,591	11.2%	11.1%	8.8%	8.5%
Employment	1,245,989	1,340,260	1,443,657	1,523,628	1,608,145	7.6%	7.7%	5.5%	5.5%
Sales ($M)/Estab.	0.50	0.52	0.53	0.55	0.57	3.4%	3.1%	3.1%	2.8%
Sales ($)/Emp.	72,994	75,488	77,827	80,212	82,450	3.4%	3.1%	3.1%	2.8%

3-YEAR TREND — ESTIMATED NUMBER OF ESTABLISHMENTS

Year	Employee Size of Establishment									Total
	1-4 Emps.	5-9 Emps.	10-19 Emps.	20-49 Emps.	50-99 Emps.	100-249 Emps.	250-499 Emps.	>500 Emps.	Non-Employer	Employ-ment
2016	10,169	3,953	5,621	7,903	3,983	2,415	552	263	175,584	210,443
2017	10,733	4,172	5,932	8,341	4,204	2,548	582	278	185,311	222,101
2018	11,328	4,404	6,261	8,804	4,437	2,690	614	293	195,590	234,421

3-YEAR TREND — ESTIMATED INDUSTRY SALES ($MILLIONS)

Year	Employee Size of Establishment									Total
	1-4 Emps.	5-9 Emps.	10-19 Emps.	20-49 Emps.	50-99 Emps.	100-249 Emps.	250-499 Emps.	>500 Emps.	Non-Employer	Employ-ment
2016	1,097.3	1,121.2	4,008.6	14,919.3	16,530.1	27,005.7	20,789.8	21,162.2	5,720.7	112,354.9
2017	1,198.4	1,224.5	4,377.8	16,293.3	18,052.4	29,492.7	22,704.5	22,622.2	6,247.5	122,213.3
2018	1,305.1	1,333.5	4,767.7	17,744.2	19,660.0	32,119.1	24,726.3	24,131.6	6,803.9	132,591.3

3-YEAR TREND — ESTIMATED NUMBER OF EMPLOYEES

Year	Employee Size of Establishment									Total
	1-4 Emps.	5-9 Emps.	10-19 Emps.	20-49 Emps.	50-99 Emps.	100-249 Emps.	250-499 Emps.	>500 Emps.	Non-Employer	Employ-ment
2016	25,424	22,929	76,440	237,884	236,615	304,483	160,436	203,863	175,584	1,443,657
2017	26,832	24,199	80,674	251,061	249,722	321,349	169,323	215,156	185,311	1,523,628
2018	28,320	25,542	85,149	264,988	263,574	339,175	178,715	227,091	195,590	1,608,145

SUB-INDUSTRIES — 2017 ESTIMATED INDUSTRY SALES, ESTABLISHMENTS & EMPLOYMENT

Sub-Industries	Category*	Establishments	Sales ($Mill)	Employment
Home health care services	Major1	213,744	115,648.8	1,406,911
Oxygen tent service	Minor2	725	55.0	1,351
Visiting nurse service	Minor2	7,631	6,509.6	115,365

*Category-Major categories (Major1) are more general descriptions for companies that self-selected to capture the many functions they perform in the industry. Minor categories (Minor1, Minor2) are more specific for companies that have more detailed functions (Minor1 is a larger category than Minor2). Minor categories figures (sales, etc.) can be aggregated to larger minor categories (Minor2 sums to Minor1) and major categories overall figures.

NAICS 62211: Medical & Surgical Hospital. This industry comprises establishments primarily engaged in providing general medical and surgical services and other hospital services. Specialty hospitals are classified in 8063 and 8069.

INDUSTRY ESTABLISHMENTS, SALES & EMPLOYMENT TRENDS

	Year					Percent Chg. Year-to-Year			
	2014	2015	2016	2017	2018	14-15	15-16	16-17	17-18
Establishments	16,656	16,487	16,439	16,550	16,664	-1.0%	-0.3%	0.7%	0.7%
Sales ($Millions)	836,931	901,835	967,137	1,035,139	1,101,838	7.8%	7.2%	7.0%	6.4%
Employment	3,038,478	3,007,778	2,998,897	3,019,252	3,039,965	-1.0%	-0.3%	0.7%	0.7%
Sales ($M)/Estab.	50.25	54.70	58.83	62.55	66.12	8.9%	7.6%	6.3%	5.7%
Sales ($)/Emp.	275,444	299,834	322,498	342,846	362,451	8.9%	7.6%	6.3%	5.7%

3-YEAR TREND – ESTIMATED NUMBER OF ESTABLISHMENTS

Year	Employee Size of Establishment									Total
	1-4 Emps.	5-9 Emps.	10-19 Emps.	20-49 Emps.	50-99 Emps.	100-249 Emps.	250-499 Emps.	>500 Emps.	Non-Employer	Employ-ment
2016	181	38	38	82	325	1,089	915	2,606	11,166	16,439
2017	182	39	38	82	327	1,096	921	2,623	11,242	16,550
2018	183	39	38	83	329	1,104	927	2,641	11,319	16,664

3-YEAR TREND – ESTIMATED INDUSTRY SALES ($MILLIONS)

Year	Employee Size of Establishment									Total
	1-4 Emps.	5-9 Emps.	10-19 Emps.	20-49 Emps.	50-99 Emps.	100-249 Emps.	250-499 Emps.	>500 Emps.	Non-Employer	Employ-ment
2016	58.7	32.9	80.6	465.9	4,060.0	36,685.3	103,916.1	821,108.3	729.4	967,137.1
2017	63.1	35.4	86.6	500.9	4,364.1	39,433.5	111,700.8	878,170.4	784.0	1,035,138.8
2018	67.5	37.8	92.6	535.4	4,665.5	42,156.4	119,413.7	934,031.4	838.1	1,101,838.4

3-YEAR TREND – ESTIMATED NUMBER OF EMPLOYEES

Year	Employee Size of Establishment									Total
	1-4 Emps.	5-9 Emps.	10-19 Emps.	20-49 Emps.	50-99 Emps.	100-249 Emps.	250-499 Emps.	>500 Emps.	Non-Employer	Employ-ment
2016	452	223	510	2,466	19,288	137,276	266,152	2,561,364	11,166	2,998,897
2017	455	225	514	2,482	19,419	138,208	267,958	2,578,749	11,242	3,019,252
2018	458	226	517	2,500	19,552	139,156	269,796	2,596,440	11,319	3,039,965

MEDICAL & SURGICAL HOSPITALS INDUSTRY (NAICS 62211)

SUB-INDUSTRIES — 2017 ESTIMATED INDUSTRY SALES, ESTABLISHMENTS & EMPLOYMENT

Sub-Industries	Category*	Establishments	Sales ($Mill)	Employment
General medical and surgical hospitals	Major1	15,298	899,187.6	2,653,772
Hospital, affiliated with AMA residency	Minor2	341	25,406.1	77,308
Hospital, med school affiliated with nursing and residency	Minor2	124	13,232.5	52,274
Hospital, medical school affiliated with residency	Minor2	121	14,641.0	48,334
Hospital, medical school affiliation	Minor2	343	18,171.6	86,968
Hospital, professional nursing school	Minor2	108	6,061.7	23,466
Hospital, professional nursing school with AMA residency	Minor2	49	5,434.7	12,268
Hospital, AMA approved residency	Minor2	166	53,003.5	64,861

*Category-Major categories (Major1) are more general descriptions for companies that self-selected to capture the many functions they perform in the industry. Minor categories (Minor1, Minor2) are more specific for companies that have more detailed functions (Minor1 is a larger category than Minor2). Minor categories figures (sales, etc.) can be aggregated to larger minor categories (Minor2 sums to Minor1) and major categories overall figures.

NURSING CARE FACILITIES INDUSTRY
(NAICS 62311)

NAICS 62311: Nursing Care Facilities. This industry comprises establishments primarily engaged in providing inpatient nursing and rehabilitative services, but not on a continuous basis. Staffing must include 24-hour per day personnel with a licensed nurse on duty full-time during each day shift. At least once a week, consultation from a registered nurse on the delivery of care is required. Included are facilities certified to deliver intermediate care under the Medicaid program.

INDUSTRY ESTABLISHMENTS, SALES & EMPLOYMENT TRENDS

	Year					Percent Chg. Year-to-Year			
	2014	2015	2016	2017	2018	14-15	15-16	16-17	17-18
Establishments	22,567	22,296	22,188	22,327	22,468	-1.2%	-0.5%	0.6%	0.6%
Sales ($Millions)	130,404	135,956	142,113	149,726	157,180	4.3%	4.5%	5.4%	5.0%
Employment	1,430,369	1,413,220	1,406,337	1,415,154	1,424,129	-1.2%	-0.5%	0.6%	0.6%
Sales ($M)/Estab.	5.78	6.10	6.41	6.71	7.00	5.5%	5.0%	4.7%	4.3%
Sales ($)/Emp.	91,168	96,203	101,052	105,802	110,369	5.5%	5.0%	4.7%	4.3%

3-YEAR TREND – ESTIMATED NUMBER OF ESTABLISHMENTS

Year	Employee Size of Establishment									Total
	1-4 Emps.	5-9 Emps.	10-19 Emps.	20-49 Emps.	50-99 Emps.	100-249 Emps.	250-499 Emps.	>500 Emps.	Non-Employer	Employ-ment
2016	1,687	690	771	1,555	4,448	6,797	597	62	5,581	22,188
2017	1,698	695	776	1,565	4,476	6,839	601	62	5,616	22,327
2018	1,709	699	781	1,575	4,504	6,883	604	63	5,651	22,468

3-YEAR TREND – ESTIMATED INDUSTRY SALES ($MILLIONS)

Year	Employee Size of Establishment									Total
	1-4 Emps.	5-9 Emps.	10-19 Emps.	20-49 Emps.	50-99 Emps.	100-249 Emps.	250-499 Emps.	>500 Emps.	Non-Employer	Employ-ment
2016	205.7	221.2	621.1	3,317.4	20,854.0	85,885.6	25,417.3	5,257.7	333.3	142,113.3
2017	216.7	233.0	654.4	3,495.3	21,972.0	90,490.3	26,780.0	5,533.1	351.1	149,726.0
2018	227.5	244.6	687.0	3,669.5	23,066.8	94,999.2	28,114.4	5,801.9	368.6	157,179.7

3-YEAR TREND – ESTIMATED NUMBER OF EMPLOYEES

Year	Employee Size of Establishment									Total
	1-4 Emps.	5-9 Emps.	10-19 Emps.	20-49 Emps.	50-99 Emps.	100-249 Emps.	250-499 Emps.	>500 Emps.	Non-Employer	Employ-ment
2016	4,218	4,003	10,483	46,818	264,211	857,083	173,610	40,331	5,581	1,406,337
2017	4,244	4,028	10,549	47,112	265,867	862,456	174,698	40,584	5,616	1,415,154
2018	4,271	4,054	10,616	47,410	267,553	867,926	175,806	40,841	5,651	1,424,129

NURSING CARE FACILITIES INDUSTRY
(NAICS 62311)

SUB-INDUSTRIES — 2017 ESTIMATED INDUSTRY
SALES, ESTABLISHMENTS & EMPLOYMENT

Sub-Industries	Cate-gory*	Establish-ments	Sales ($Mill)	Employ-ment
Intermediate care facilities	Major1	11,390	111,222.3	1,044,800
Home for the mentally retarded, with health care	Minor2	4,002	6,338.5	198,384
Personal care facility	Minor2	6,935	32,165.2	171,969

*Category-Major categories (Major1) are more general descriptions for companies that self-selected to capture the many functions they perform in the industry. Minor categories (Minor1, Minor2) are more specific for companies that have more detailed functions (Minor1 is a larger category than Minor2). Minor categories figures (sales, etc.) can be aggregated to larger minor categories (Minor2 sums to Minor1) and major categories overall figures.

COMMUNITY CARE FACILITIES FOR THE ELDERLY (NAICS 62331)

NAICS 62331: Community Care Facilities for the Elderly. This industry comprises establishments primarily engaged in the provision of residential social and personal care for children, the aged, and special categories of persons with some limits on ability for self-care, but where medical care is not a major element. Included are establishments providing 24-hour year-round care for children. Boarding schools providing elementary and secondary education are classified in 8211.

INDUSTRY ESTABLISHMENTS, SALES & EMPLOYMENT TRENDS

	Year					Percent Chg. Year-to-Year			
	2014	2015	2016	2017	2018	14-15	15-16	16-17	17-18
Establishments	31,369	32,136	33,130	34,200	35,308	2.4%	3.1%	3.2%	3.2%
Sales ($Millions)	66,012	70,902	76,324	82,049	87,920	7.4%	7.6%	7.5%	7.2%
Employment	784,806	803,993	828,861	855,646	883,361	2.4%	3.1%	3.2%	3.2%
Sales ($M)/Estab.	2.10	2.21	2.30	2.40	2.49	4.8%	4.4%	4.1%	3.8%
Sales ($)/Emp.	84,113	88,187	92,083	95,891	99,529	4.8%	4.4%	4.1%	3.8%

3-YEAR TREND — ESTIMATED NUMBER OF ESTABLISHMENTS

Year	Employee Size of Establishment									Total
	1-4 Emps.	5-9 Emps.	10-19 Emps.	20-49 Emps.	50-99 Emps.	100-249 Emps.	250-499 Emps.	>500 Emps.	Non-Employer	Employ-ment
2016	7,083	3,314	3,562	5,449	3,224	1,655	449	60	8,333	33,130
2017	7,312	3,421	3,677	5,625	3,329	1,708	463	62	8,602	34,200
2018	7,549	3,532	3,797	5,807	3,436	1,764	478	64	8,880	35,308

3-YEAR TREND — ESTIMATED INDUSTRY SALES ($MILLIONS)

Year	Employee Size of Establishment									Total
	1-4 Emps.	5-9 Emps.	10-19 Emps.	20-49 Emps.	50-99 Emps.	100-249 Emps.	250-499 Emps.	>500 Emps.	Non-Employer	Employ-ment
2016	853.7	1,049.8	2,837.8	11,488.6	14,945.0	20,674.1	18,898.8	5,084.5	492.0	76,324.4
2017	918.2	1,129.1	3,052.1	12,356.0	16,073.4	22,235.0	20,325.6	5,430.7	529.1	82,049.1
2018	984.3	1,210.4	3,271.9	13,246.0	17,231.2	23,836.7	21,789.8	5,782.6	567.2	87,920.2

3-YEAR TREND — ESTIMATED NUMBER OF EMPLOYEES

Year	Employee Size of Establishment									Total
	1-4 Emps.	5-9 Emps.	10-19 Emps.	20-49 Emps.	50-99 Emps.	100-249 Emps.	250-499 Emps.	>500 Emps.	Non-Employer	Employ-ment
2016	17,709	19,222	48,448	164,003	191,528	208,691	130,573	40,355	8,333	828,861
2017	18,281	19,843	50,013	169,303	197,718	215,435	134,792	41,659	8,602	855,646
2018	18,873	20,486	51,633	174,786	204,122	222,413	139,158	43,008	8,880	883,361

COMMUNITY CARE FACILITIES FOR THE ELDERLY (NAICS 62331)

SUB-INDUSTRIES — 2017 ESTIMATED INDUSTRY SALES, ESTABLISHMENTS & EMPLOYMENT

Sub-Industries	Category*	Establish-ments	Sales ($Mill)	Employ-ment
Geriatric residential care	Minor1	11,932	15,524.1	224,482
Aged home	Minor2	17,671	50,362.8	459,547
Old soldiers' home	Minor2	115	120.6	7,662
Rest home, with health care incidental	Minor2	4,483	16,041.5	163,956

*Category-Major categories (Major1) are more general descriptions for companies that self-selected to capture the many functions they perform in the industry. Minor categories (Minor1, Minor2) are more specific for companies that have more detailed functions (Minor1 is a larger category than Minor2). Minor categories figures (sales, etc.) can be aggregated to larger minor categories (Minor2 sums to Minor1) and major categories overall figures.

MUSICAL GROUPS & ARTISTS INDUSTRY (NAICS 71113)

NAICS 71113: Musical Groups and Artists . This industry comprises (1) groups primarily engaged in producing live musical entertainment (except theatrical musical or opera productions) and (2) independent (i.e., freelance) artists primarily engaged in providing live musical entertainment. Musical groups and artists may perform in front of a live audience or in a studio, and may or may not operate their own facilities for staging their shows.

INDUSTRY ESTABLISHMENTS, SALES & EMPLOYMENT TRENDS

	Year					Percent Chg. Year-to-Year			
	2014	2015	2016	2017	2018	14-15	15-16	16-17	17-18
Establishments	30,327	29,756	29,323	29,214	29,589	-1.9%	-1.5%	-0.4%	1.3%
Sales ($Millions)	5,188	5,407	5,631	5,906	6,272	4.2%	4.1%	4.9%	6.2%
Employment	63,247	62,056	61,153	60,925	61,708	-1.9%	-1.5%	-0.4%	1.3%
Sales ($M)/Estab.	0.17	0.18	0.19	0.20	0.21	6.2%	5.7%	5.3%	4.8%
Sales ($)/Emp.	82,021	87,132	92,078	96,942	101,642	6.2%	5.7%	5.3%	4.8%

5-YEAR TREND – ESTIMATED NUMBER OF ESTABLISHMENTS

Year	Employee Size of Establishment									Total
	1-4 Emps.	5-9 Emps.	10-19 Emps.	20-49 Emps.	50-99 Emps.	100-249 Emps.	250-499 Emps.	>500 Emps.	Non-Employer	Employ-ment
2016	3,180	526	276	123	81	57	14	3	25,064	29,323
2017	3,168	524	275	122	81	57	13	3	24,971	29,214
2018	3,209	531	278	124	82	58	14	3	25,291	29,589

5-YEAR TREND – ESTIMATED INDUSTRY SALES ($MILLIONS)

Year	Employee Size of Establishment									Total
	1-4 Emps.	5-9 Emps.	10-19 Emps.	20-49 Emps.	50-99 Emps.	100-249 Emps.	250-499 Emps.	>500 Emps.	Non-Employer	Employ-ment
2016	535.5	232.8	306.7	361.8	526.0	995.7	796.3	312.4	1,563.8	5,630.9
2017	561.7	244.2	321.7	379.4	551.7	1,044.4	835.2	327.6	1,640.3	5,906.2
2018	596.5	259.3	341.6	402.9	585.9	1,109.1	887.0	347.9	1,741.9	6,272.1

5-YEAR TREND – ESTIMATED NUMBER OF EMPLOYEES

Year	Employee Size of Establishment									Total
	1-4 Emps.	5-9 Emps.	10-19 Emps.	20-49 Emps.	50-99 Emps.	100-249 Emps.	250-499 Emps.	>500 Emps.	Non-Employer	Employ-ment
2016	7,950	3,051	3,748	3,696	4,824	7,194	3,938	1,689	25,064	61,153
2017	7,921	3,039	3,734	3,682	4,806	7,167	3,923	1,682	24,971	60,925
2018	8,022	3,078	3,782	3,730	4,868	7,259	3,974	1,704	25,291	61,708

MUSICAL GROUPS & ARTISTS INDUSTRY (NAICS 71113)

SUB-INDUSTRIES — 2017 ESTIMATED INDUSTRY SALES, ESTABLISHMENTS & EMPLOYMENT

Sub-Industries	Category*	Establishments	Sales ($Mill)	Employment
Entertainers and entertainment groups	Major1	15,306	1,885.4	22,531
Musical entertainers	Minor1	1,165	332.1	3,036
Chamber music groups or artists	Minor2	85	22.5	295
Classical music groups or artists	Minor2	80	44.7	332
Country music groups or artists	Minor2	45	14.4	231
Dance band	Minor2	119	21.4	360
Drum and bugle corps (drill teams)	Minor2	26	28.0	104
Gospel singers	Minor2	141	25.0	348
Jazz music group or artist	Minor2	76	18.9	210
Musician	Minor2	1,763	188.2	2,355
Orchestras or bands, nec	Minor2	960	316.3	3,539
Popular music groups or artists	Minor2	122	43.4	342
Symphony orchestra	Minor2	386	661.8	3,778
Actor	Minor2	180	24.6	265
Actress	Minor2	57	7.4	62
Disc jockey service	Minor2	2,490	283.7	3,968
Entertainers	Minor2	1,819	290.4	3,378
Entertainment group	Minor2	430	107.5	1,516
Entertainment service	Minor2	3,510	1,545.7	13,731
Magician	Minor2	415	39.5	476
Singing telegram service	Minor2	38	5.3	70

*Category-Major categories (Major1) are more general descriptions for companies that self-selected to capture the many functions they perform in the industry. Minor categories (Minor1, Minor2) are more specific for companies that have more detailed functions (Minor1 is a larger category than Minor2). Minor categories figures (sales, etc.) can be aggregated to larger minor categories (Minor2 sums to Minor1) and major categories overall figures.

SPECTATOR SPORTS INDUSTRY
(NAICS 71121)

NAICS 71121: Spectator Sports . This industry comprises (1) sports teams or clubs primarily participating in live sporting events before a paying audience; (2) establishments primarily engaged in operating racetracks; (3) independent athletes engaged in participating in live sporting or racing events before a paying audience; (4) owners of racing participants, such as cars, dogs, and horses, primarily engaged in entering them in racing events or other spectator sports events; and (5) establishments, such as sports trainers, primarily engaged in providing specialized services to support participants in sports events or competitions.

INDUSTRY ESTABLISHMENTS, SALES & EMPLOYMENT TRENDS

	Year					Percent Chg. Year-to-Year			
	2014	2015	2016	2017	2018	14-15	15-16	16-17	17-18
Establishments	124,916	122,201	120,060	118,986	119,883	-2.2%	-1.8%	-0.9%	0.8%
Sales ($Millions)	32,826	34,917	36,994	39,264	42,032	6.4%	5.9%	6.1%	7.0%
Employment	233,571	228,495	224,491	222,482	224,160	-2.2%	-1.8%	-0.9%	0.8%
Sales ($M)/Estab.	0.26	0.29	0.31	0.33	0.35	8.7%	7.8%	7.1%	6.2%
Sales ($)/Emp.	140,539	152,815	164,791	176,482	187,507	8.7%	7.8%	7.1%	6.2%

5-YEAR TREND – ESTIMATED NUMBER OF ESTABLISHMENTS

Year	Employee Size of Establishment									Total
	1-4 Emps.	5-9 Emps.	10-19 Emps.	20-49 Emps.	50-99 Emps.	100-249 Emps.	250-499 Emps.	>500 Emps.	Non-Employer	Employ-ment
2016	2,606	478	334	305	107	102	87	55	115,988	120,060
2017	2,582	473	331	302	106	101	86	54	114,950	118,986
2018	2,602	477	334	304	107	102	86	55	115,817	119,883

5-YEAR TREND – ESTIMATED INDUSTRY SALES ($MILLIONS)

Year	Employee Size of Establishment									Total
	1-4 Emps.	5-9 Emps.	10-19 Emps.	20-49 Emps.	50-99 Emps.	100-249 Emps.	250-499 Emps.	>500 Emps.	Non-Employer	Employ-ment
2016	729.5	351.5	618.9	1,492.3	1,148.7	2,956.4	8,460.4	12,063.9	9,172.4	36,994.1
2017	773.3	372.6	656.1	1,582.0	1,217.7	3,134.1	8,968.9	12,835.7	9,723.7	39,264.2
2018	828.7	399.3	703.1	1,695.2	1,304.8	3,358.4	9,610.6	13,712.2	10,419.4	42,031.7

5-YEAR TREND – ESTIMATED NUMBER OF EMPLOYEES

Year	Employee Size of Establishment									Total
	1-4 Emps.	5-9 Emps.	10-19 Emps.	20-49 Emps.	50-99 Emps.	100-249 Emps.	250-499 Emps.	>500 Emps.	Non-Employer	Employ-ment
2016	6,514	2,771	4,549	9,171	6,337	12,847	25,163	41,152	115,988	224,491
2017	6,456	2,746	4,508	9,089	6,280	12,732	24,938	40,783	114,950	222,482
2018	6,504	2,766	4,542	9,157	6,328	12,828	25,126	41,091	115,817	224,160

SPECTATOR SPORTS INDUSTRY
(NAICS 71121)

SUB-INDUSTRIES — 2017 ESTIMATED INDUSTRY SALES, ESTABLISHMENTS & EMPLOYMENT

Sub-Industries	Category*	Establishments	Sales ($Mill)	Employment
Sports clubs, managers, and promoters	Major1	28,524	15,007.1	45,895
Professional and semi-professional sports clubs	Minor1	3,233	473.4	4,306
Baseball club, professional and semi-professional	Minor2	7,511	5,357.6	37,457
Basketball club	Minor2	4,790	2,145.6	11,674
Football club	Minor2	24,838	3,223.2	22,764
Ice hockey club	Minor2	2,543	824.9	7,151
Soccer club	Minor2	13,759	1,646.5	9,900
Stadium event operator services	Minor1	4,081	1,636.1	32,330
Boxing and wrestling arena	Minor2	2,346	181.3	1,407
Sports field or stadium operator, promoting sports events	Minor2	8,358	2,937.6	31,057
Manager of individual professional athletes	Minor2	2,129	1,384.1	3,631
Sports promotion	Minor2	16,874	4,446.8	14,910

*Category-Major categories (Major1) are more general descriptions for companies that self-selected to capture the many functions they perform in the industry. Minor categories (Minor1, Minor2) are more specific for companies that have more detailed functions (Minor1 is a larger category than Minor2). Minor categories figures (sales, etc.) can be aggregated to larger minor categories (Minor2 sums to Minor1) and major categories overall figures.

AGENTS/MANAGERS FOR ARTISTS & ATHLETES (NAICS 71141)

NAICS 71141: Agents and Managers for Artists. This industry comprises establishments of agents and managers primarily engaged in representing and/or managing creative and performing artists, sports figures, entertainers, and other public figures. The representation and management includes activities, such as representing clients in contract negotiations; managing or organizing client's financial affairs; and generally promoting the careers of their clients.

INDUSTRY ESTABLISHMENTS, SALES & EMPLOYMENT TRENDS

	Year					Percent Chg. Year-to-Year			
	2014	2015	2016	2017	2018	14-15	15-16	16-17	17-18
Establishments	22,110	22,015	22,016	22,273	22,907	-0.4%	0.0%	1.2%	2.8%
Sales ($Millions)	7,621	7,991	8,380	8,861	9,493	4.9%	4.9%	5.8%	7.1%
Employment	40,441	40,266	40,270	40,738	41,898	-0.4%	0.0%	1.2%	2.8%
Sales ($M)/Estab.	0.34	0.36	0.38	0.40	0.41	5.3%	4.9%	4.5%	4.2%
Sales ($)/Emp.	188,456	198,459	208,085	217,520	226,576	5.3%	4.9%	4.5%	4.2%

5-YEAR TREND – ESTIMATED NUMBER OF ESTABLISHMENTS

Year	Employee Size of Establishment									Total
	1-4 Emps.	5-9 Emps.	10-19 Emps.	20-49 Emps.	50-99 Emps.	100-249 Emps.	250-499 Emps.	>500 Emps.	Non-Employer	Employ-ment
2016	3,130	397	183	109	23	18	5	2	18,150	22,016
2017	3,166	402	185	110	23	18	5	2	18,361	22,273
2018	3,256	413	191	113	24	19	5	2	18,884	22,907

5-YEAR TREND – ESTIMATED INDUSTRY SALES ($MILLIONS)

Year	Employee Size of Establishment									Total
	1-4 Emps.	5-9 Emps.	10-19 Emps.	20-49 Emps.	50-99 Emps.	100-249 Emps.	250-499 Emps.	>500 Emps.	Non-Employer	Employ-ment
2016	1,624.2	541.9	628.5	985.4	457.1	964.1	902.6	662.8	1,612.9	8,379.5
2017	1,717.6	573.1	664.6	1,042.1	483.4	1,019.6	954.5	700.9	1,705.7	8,861.4
2018	1,840.0	614.0	712.0	1,116.4	517.8	1,092.3	1,022.6	750.7	1,827.3	9,493.0

5-YEAR TREND – ESTIMATED NUMBER OF EMPLOYEES

Year	Employee Size of Establishment									Total
	1-4 Emps.	5-9 Emps.	10-19 Emps.	20-49 Emps.	50-99 Emps.	100-249 Emps.	250-499 Emps.	>500 Emps.	Non-Employer	Employ-ment
2016	7,824	2,304	2,492	3,267	1,360	2,260	1,448	1,163	18,150	40,270
2017	7,915	2,331	2,521	3,305	1,376	2,286	1,465	1,177	18,361	40,738
2018	8,141	2,398	2,593	3,399	1,415	2,352	1,507	1,210	18,884	41,898

SUB-INDUSTRIES — 2017 ESTIMATED INDUSTRY SALES, ESTABLISHMENTS & EMPLOYMENT

Sub-Industries	Cate-gory*	Establish-ments	Sales ($Mill)	Employ-ment
Theatrical producers and services	Major1	11,544	5,532.5	23,793
Theatrical talent and booking agencies	Minor1	2,092	537.4	2,782
Agent or manager for entertainers	Minor2	1,758	534.4	2,991
Booking agency, theatrical	Minor2	610	190.9	940
Casting bureau, theatrical	Minor2	276	47.3	233
Employment agency: theatrical, radio, and television	Minor2	231	228.3	558
Entertainment promotion	Minor2	4,450	1,459.1	6,633
Talent agent, theatrical	Minor2	1,311	331.4	2,807

*Category-Major categories (Major1) are more general descriptions for companies that self-selected to capture the many functions they perform in the industry. Minor categories (Minor1, Minor2) are more specific for companies that have more detailed functions (Minor1 is a larger category than Minor2). Minor categories figures (sales, etc.) can be aggregated to larger minor categories (Minor2 sums to Minor1) and major categories overall figures.

GOLF COURSES & COUNTRY CLUBS INDUSTRY (NAICS 71391)

NAICS 71391: Golf Courses and Country Clubs . This industry comprises (1) establishments primarily engaged in operating golf courses (except miniature) and (2) establishments primarily engaged in operating golf courses, along with dining facilities and other recreational facilities that are known as country clubs. These establishments often provide food and beverage services, equipment rental services, and golf instruction services.

INDUSTRY ESTABLISHMENTS, SALES & EMPLOYMENT TRENDS

	Year					Percent Chg. Year-to-Year			
	2014	2015	2016	2017	2018	14-15	15-16	16-17	17-18
Establishments	23,942	23,728	23,621	23,516	23,801	-0.9%	-0.5%	-0.4%	1.2%
Sales ($Millions)	22,784	23,599	24,461	25,294	26,508	3.6%	3.7%	3.4%	4.8%
Employment	282,530	280,008	278,742	277,502	280,864	-0.9%	-0.5%	-0.4%	1.2%
Sales ($M)/Estab.	0.95	0.99	1.04	1.08	1.11	4.5%	4.1%	3.9%	3.5%
Sales ($)/Emp.	80,643	84,279	87,754	91,148	94,380	4.5%	4.1%	3.9%	3.5%

5-YEAR TREND – ESTIMATED NUMBER OF ESTABLISHMENTS

Year	Employee Size of Establishment									Total
	1-4 Emps.	5-9 Emps.	10-19 Emps.	20-49 Emps.	50-99 Emps.	100-249 Emps.	250-499 Emps.	>500 Emps.	Non-Employer	Employ-ment
2016	4,076	1,525	1,533	2,215	1,327	538	36	5	12,367	23,621
2017	4,057	1,518	1,526	2,205	1,321	535	35	5	12,312	23,516
2018	4,107	1,537	1,545	2,232	1,337	542	36	5	12,461	23,801

5-YEAR TREND – ESTIMATED INDUSTRY SALES ($MILLIONS)

Year	Employee Size of Establishment									Total
	1-4 Emps.	5-9 Emps.	10-19 Emps.	20-49 Emps.	50-99 Emps.	100-249 Emps.	250-499 Emps.	>500 Emps.	Non-Employer	Employ-ment
2016	532.2	523.5	1,323.3	5,059.9	6,663.7	7,277.5	1,620.2	410.9	1,049.4	24,460.6
2017	550.3	541.3	1,368.3	5,232.2	6,890.7	7,525.3	1,675.4	424.9	1,085.2	25,293.7
2018	576.7	567.3	1,434.0	5,483.5	7,221.5	7,886.6	1,755.8	445.3	1,137.3	26,508.1

5-YEAR TREND – ESTIMATED NUMBER OF EMPLOYEES

Year	Employee Size of Establishment									Total
	1-4 Emps.	5-9 Emps.	10-19 Emps.	20-49 Emps.	50-99 Emps.	100-249 Emps.	250-499 Emps.	>500 Emps.	Non-Employer	Employ-ment
2016	10,189	8,847	20,851	66,668	78,822	67,803	10,332	2,863	12,367	278,742
2017	10,144	8,807	20,758	66,372	78,471	67,501	10,286	2,851	12,312	277,502
2018	10,267	8,914	21,010	67,176	79,422	68,319	10,411	2,885	12,461	280,864

GOLF COURSES & COUNTRY CLUBS INDUSTRY
(NAICS 71391)

SUB-INDUSTRIES — 2017 ESTIMATED INDUSTRY SALES, ESTABLISHMENTS & EMPLOYMENT

Sub-Industries	Cate-gory*	Establish-ments	Sales ($Mill)	Employ-ment
Public golf courses	Major1	11,758	12,646.8	138,751
Country club, membership	Minor2	6,170	8,061.7	85,157
Golf club, membership	Minor2	5,588	4,585.1	53,594

*Category-Major categories (Major1) are more general descriptions for companies that self-selected to capture the many functions they perform in the industry. Minor categories (Minor1, Minor2) are more specific for companies that have more detailed functions (Minor1 is a larger category than Minor2). Minor categories figures (sales, etc.) can be aggregated to larger minor categories (Minor2 sums to Minor1) and major categories overall figures.

FITNESS & RECREATIONAL SPORTS CENTERS (NAICS 71394)

NAICS 71394: Fitness and Recreational Sports Centers . This industry comprises establishments primarily engaged in operating fitness and recreational sports facilities featuring exercise and other active physical fitness conditioning or recreational sports activities, such as swimming, skating, or racquet sports.

INDUSTRY ESTABLISHMENTS, SALES & EMPLOYMENT TRENDS

	Year					Percent Chg. Year-to-Year			
	2014	2015	2016	2017	2018	14-15	15-16	16-17	17-18
Establishments	66,566	68,798	70,945	72,960	74,967	3.4%	3.1%	2.8%	2.8%
Sales ($Millions)	26,675	28,350	29,983	31,575	33,145	6.3%	5.8%	5.3%	5.0%
Employment	616,346	637,013	656,892	675,550	694,134	3.4%	3.1%	2.8%	2.8%
Sales ($M)/Estab.	0.40	0.41	0.42	0.43	0.44	2.8%	2.6%	2.4%	2.2%
Sales ($)/Emp.	43,280	44,505	45,644	46,740	47,749	2.8%	2.6%	2.4%	2.2%

5-YEAR TREND – ESTIMATED NUMBER OF ESTABLISHMENTS

Year	Employee Size of Establishment									Total
	1-4 Emps.	5-9 Emps.	10-19 Emps.	20-49 Emps.	50-99 Emps.	100-249 Emps.	250-499 Emps.	>500 Emps.	Non-Employer	Employ-ment
2016	15,760	5,141	4,557	4,760	2,131	1,267	171	15	37,144	70,945
2017	16,207	5,287	4,687	4,895	2,191	1,303	175	15	38,199	72,960
2018	16,653	5,433	4,816	5,030	2,251	1,339	180	16	39,250	74,967

5-YEAR TREND – ESTIMATED INDUSTRY SALES ($MILLIONS)

Year	Employee Size of Establishment									Total
	1-4 Emps.	5-9 Emps.	10-19 Emps.	20-49 Emps.	50-99 Emps.	100-249 Emps.	250-499 Emps.	>500 Emps.	Non-Employer	Employ-ment
2016	997.4	855.2	1,906.4	5,270.1	5,185.4	8,312.6	3,770.2	630.8	3,055.3	29,983.3
2017	1,050.4	900.7	2,007.7	5,550.3	5,461.1	8,754.6	3,970.6	662.2	3,217.7	31,575.3
2018	1,102.7	945.5	2,107.6	5,826.5	5,732.8	9,190.3	4,168.2	693.1	3,377.8	33,144.5

5-YEAR TREND – ESTIMATED NUMBER OF EMPLOYEES

Year	Employee Size of Establishment									Total
	1-4 Emps.	5-9 Emps.	10-19 Emps.	20-49 Emps.	50-99 Emps.	100-249 Emps.	250-499 Emps.	>500 Emps.	Non-Employer	Employ-ment
2016	39,399	29,820	61,979	143,270	126,552	159,796	49,606	9,326	37,144	656,892
2017	40,519	30,667	63,740	147,339	130,147	164,335	51,015	9,591	38,199	675,550
2018	41,633	31,510	65,493	151,392	133,727	168,856	52,418	9,854	39,250	694,134

SUB-INDUSTRIES – 2017 ESTIMATED INDUSTRY SALES, ESTABLISHMENTS & EMPLOYMENT

Sub-Industries	Category*	Establish-ments	Sales ($Mill)	Employ-ment
Physical fitness facilities	Major1	15,722	6,791.9	127,771
Physical fitness clubs with training equipment	Minor1	2,035	1,066.2	22,011
Athletic club and gymnasiums, membership	Minor2	2,908	2,193.4	51,664
Health club	Minor2	5,585	4,898.0	107,655
Spas	Minor2	15,574	4,271.9	98,304
Weight reducing clubs	Minor1	308	154.4	2,104
Reducing facility	Minor2	19	7.4	156
Slenderizing salon	Minor2	114	23.5	546
Exercise facilities	Minor1	1,125	322.1	7,234
Aerobic dance and exercise classes	Minor2	1,461	438.3	10,312
Exercise salon	Minor2	3,788	883.1	22,609
Membership sports and recreation clubs	Major1	24,320	10,525.1	225,183

*Category-Major categories (Major1) are more general descriptions for companies that self-selected to capture the many functions they perform in the industry. Minor categories (Minor1, Minor2) are more specific for companies that have more detailed functions (Minor1 is a larger category than Minor2). Minor categories figures (sales, etc.) can be aggregated to larger minor categories (Minor2 sums to Minor1) and major categories overall figures.

HOTELS & MOTELS INDUSTRY
(NAICS 72111)

NAICS 72111: Hotels (except Casino Hotels) and Motels . This industry comprises establishments primarily engaged in providing short-term lodging in facilities known as hotels, motor hotels, resort hotels, and motels. The establishments in this industry may offer services, such as food and beverage services, recreational services, conference rooms and convention services, laundry services, parking, and other services.

INDUSTRY ESTABLISHMENTS, SALES & EMPLOYMENT TRENDS

	Year					Percent Chg. Year-to-Year			
	2014	2015	2016	2017	2018	14-15	15-16	16-17	17-18
Establishments	60,774	59,699	59,704	60,106	60,663	-1.8%	0.0%	0.7%	0.9%
Sales ($Millions)	146,573	150,751	157,035	164,170	171,493	2.9%	4.2%	4.5%	4.5%
Employment	1,373,469	1,349,182	1,349,294	1,358,366	1,370,965	-1.8%	0.0%	0.7%	0.9%
Sales ($M)/Estab.	2.41	2.53	2.63	2.73	2.83	4.7%	4.2%	3.8%	3.5%
Sales ($)/Emp.	106,717	111,735	116,383	120,858	125,089	4.7%	4.2%	3.8%	3.5%

5-YEAR TREND – ESTIMATED NUMBER OF ESTABLISHMENTS

Year	Employee Size of Establishment									Total
	1-4 Emps.	5-9 Emps.	10-19 Emps.	20-49 Emps.	50-99 Emps.	100-249 Emps.	250-499 Emps.	>500 Emps.	Non-Employer	Employ-ment
2016	14,998	6,943	11,831	10,861	2,423	1,936	530	319	9,863	59,704
2017	15,099	6,989	11,911	10,934	2,439	1,949	533	321	9,929	60,106
2018	15,239	7,054	12,021	11,036	2,462	1,967	538	324	10,022	60,663

5-YEAR TREND – ESTIMATED INDUSTRY SALES ($MILLIONS)

Year	Employee Size of Establishment									Total
	1-4 Emps.	5-9 Emps.	10-19 Emps.	20-49 Emps.	50-99 Emps.	100-249 Emps.	250-499 Emps.	>500 Emps.	Non-Employer	Employ-ment
2016	2,286.6	2,782.0	11,922.0	28,970.0	14,204.0	30,598.0	28,202.2	36,923.1	1,147.0	157,035.0
2017	2,391.8	2,910.0	12,470.6	30,302.8	14,857.5	32,005.8	29,499.7	38,531.5	1,199.8	164,169.6
2018	2,500.4	3,042.1	13,036.7	31,678.5	15,532.0	33,458.8	30,838.9	40,151.6	1,254.3	171,493.2

5-YEAR TREND – ESTIMATED NUMBER OF EMPLOYEES

Year	Employee Size of Establishment									Total
	1-4 Emps.	5-9 Emps.	10-19 Emps.	20-49 Emps.	50-99 Emps.	100-249 Emps.	250-499 Emps.	>500 Emps.	Non-Employer	Employ-ment
2016	37,496	40,267	160,902	326,928	143,902	244,168	154,035	231,732	9,863	1,349,294
2017	37,748	40,538	161,984	329,126	144,870	245,810	155,071	233,290	9,929	1,358,366
2018	38,098	40,914	163,486	332,179	146,213	248,090	156,509	235,454	10,022	1,370,965

HOTELS & MOTELS INDUSTRY
(NAICS 72111)

SUB-INDUSTRIES – 2017 ESTIMATED INDUSTRY SALES, ESTABLISHMENTS & EMPLOYMENT

Sub-Industries	Cate-gory*	Establish-ments	Sales ($Mill)	Employ-ment
Hotels and motels	Major1	23,800	69,766.9	659,350
Motels	Minor1	12,116	5,940.0	82,595
Motel, franchised	Minor2	598	568.5	10,988
Vacation lodges	Minor1	1,163	652.0	9,020
Ski lodge	Minor2	245	1,819.1	11,009
Tourist camps, cabins, cottages, and courts	Minor2	953	361.4	5,205
Hotels	Minor1	6,489	16,167.1	229,467
Casino hotel	Minor2	664	46,028.7	134,289
Hotel, franchised	Minor2	1,207	12,465.4	35,213
Resort hotel	Minor2	2,557	5,996.7	116,310
Resort hotel, franchised	Minor2	60	399.3	4,919
Seasonal hotel	Minor2	68	124.0	1,488
YMCA/YMHA hotel	Minor2	18	41.8	1,215
YWCA/YWHA hotel	Minor2	1	8.0	70
Inns	Minor1	4,177	2,225.2	35,332
Bed and breakfast inn	Minor2	5,584	1,265.2	17,212
Motor inn	Minor2	256	185.5	2,672
Hostels	Minor2	149	154.9	2,014

*Category-Major categories (Major1) are more general descriptions for companies that self-selected to capture the many functions they perform in the industry. Minor categories (Minor1, Minor2) are more specific for companies that have more detailed functions (Minor1 is a larger category than Minor2). Minor categories figures (sales, etc.) can be aggregated to larger minor categories (Minor2 sums to Minor1) and major categories overall figures.

FULL-SERVICE RESTAURANTS INDUSTRY (NAICS 722511)

NAICS 722511: Full-Service Restaurants -- This industry comprises establishments primarily engaged in providing food services to patrons who order and are served while seated (i.e. waiter/waitress service) and pay after eating. These establishments may provide this type of food services to patrons in combination with selling alcoholic beverages, providing takeout services, or presenting live nontheatrical entertainment.

INDUSTRY ESTABLISHMENTS, SALES & EMPLOYMENT TRENDS

	Year					Percent Chg. Year-to-Year			
	2014	2015	2016	2017	2018	14-15	15-16	16-17	17-18
Establishments	253,570	253,927	256,287	260,047	264,522	0.1%	0.9%	1.5%	1.7%
Sales ($Millions)	265,896	276,440	288,732	302,556	316,960	4.0%	4.4%	4.8%	4.8%
Employment	4,818,353	4,825,139	4,869,980	4,941,425	5,026,456	0.1%	0.9%	1.5%	1.7%
Sales ($M)/Estab.	1.05	1.09	1.13	1.16	1.20	3.8%	3.5%	3.3%	3.0%
Sales ($)/Emp.	55,184	57,292	59,288	61,229	63,058	3.8%	3.5%	3.3%	3.0%

5-YEAR TREND – ESTIMATED NUMBER OF ESTABLISHMENTS

Year	Employee Size of Establishment									Total
	1-4 Emps.	5-9 Emps.	10-19 Emps.	20-49 Emps.	50-99 Emps.	100-249 Emps.	250-499 Emps.	>500 Emps.	Non-Employer	Employ-ment
2016	67,579	41,056	48,113	55,849	23,645	5,108	185	12	14,739	256,287
2017	68,571	41,659	48,819	56,668	23,992	5,183	188	12	14,955	260,047
2018	69,751	42,375	49,659	57,644	24,404	5,272	191	13	15,213	264,522

5-YEAR TREND – ESTIMATED INDUSTRY SALES ($MILLIONS)

Year	Employee Size of Establishment									Total
	1-4 Emps.	5-9 Emps.	10-19 Emps.	20-49 Emps.	50-99 Emps.	100-249 Emps.	250-499 Emps.	>500 Emps.	Non-Employer	Employ-ment
2016	6,534.6	10,434.4	30,749.9	94,478.1	87,926.0	51,196.0	6,248.0	996.8	167.9	288,731.7
2017	6,847.7	10,934.3	32,223.1	99,004.6	92,138.5	53,648.8	6,547.3	1,036.0	176.0	302,556.4
2018	7,173.9	11,455.2	33,758.3	103,721.2	96,528.0	56,204.7	6,859.2	1,075.1	184.3	316,959.8

5-YEAR TREND – ESTIMATED NUMBER OF EMPLOYEES

Year	Employee Size of Establishment									Total
	1-4 Emps.	5-9 Emps.	10-19 Emps.	20-49 Emps.	50-99 Emps.	100-249 Emps.	250-499 Emps.	>500 Emps.	Non-Employer	Employ-ment
2016	168,949	238,126	654,338	1,681,057	1,404,493	644,138	53,805	10,336	14,739	4,869,980
2017	171,427	241,620	663,937	1,705,719	1,425,098	653,588	54,594	10,487	14,955	4,941,425
2018	174,377	245,777	675,362	1,735,070	1,449,620	664,835	55,534	10,668	15,213	5,026,456

FULL-SERVICE RESTAURANTS INDUSTRY
(NAICS 722511)

SUB-INDUSTRIES – 2017 ESTIMATED INDUSTRY SALES, ESTABLISHMENTS & EMPLOYMENT

Sub-Industries	Cate-gory*	Establish-ments	Sales ($Mill)	Employ-ment
Eating places	Major1	60,477	49,055.7	791,787
Ethnic food restaurants	Minor1	3,368	2,511.7	37,767
American restaurant	Minor2	9,145	16,174.5	341,899
Cajun restaurant	Minor2	347	526.1	8,710
Chinese restaurant	Minor2	19,315	14,788.0	164,849
French restaurant	Minor2	726	1,292.6	18,858
German restaurant	Minor2	205	252.6	3,993
Greek restaurant	Minor2	766	812.2	12,786
Indian/Pakistan restaurant	Minor2	1,273	782.7	10,195
Italian restaurant	Minor2	8,395	11,983.8	228,740
Japanese restaurant	Minor2	3,773	3,623.5	45,792
Korean restaurant	Minor2	472	265.8	3,340
Lebanese restaurant	Minor2	78	81.9	810
Mexican restaurant	Minor2	16,150	11,381.4	226,724
Spanish restaurant	Minor2	398	453.7	5,892
Sushi bar	Minor2	1,767	718.7	10,576
Thai restaurant	Minor2	2,915	1,284.3	17,662
Vietnamese restaurant	Minor2	729	304.3	4,324
Pakistani restaurant	Minor2	31	12.7	138
Lunchrooms and cafeterias	Minor1	1,300	714.5	15,399
Automat (eating places)	Minor2	17	23.6	410
Cafeteria	Minor2	1,271	2,020.5	45,701
Luncheonette	Minor2	952	348.9	5,225
Lunchroom	Minor2	34	17.9	407
Restaurant, lunch counter	Minor2	337	303.5	5,440
Family restaurants	Minor1	23,370	60,758.2	955,033
Pizza restaurants	Minor1	39,931	32,460.6	660,134
Seafood restaurants	Minor1	6,009	26,957.3	257,782
Steak and barbecue restaurants	Minor1	12,578	25,264.7	332,304
Buffet (eating places)	Minor2	1,947	922.9	32,054
Cafe	Minor2	18,556	13,156.2	178,224
Caterers	Minor2	15,430	13,678.3	207,942
Chicken restaurant	Minor2	3,275	4,556.1	40,256
Misc. full-service restaurants	Minor2	4,710	5,066.9	270,271

*Category-Major categories (Major1) are more general descriptions for companies that self-selected to capture the many functions they perform in the industry. Minor categories (Minor1, Minor2) are more specific for companies that have more detailed functions (Minor1 is a larger category than Minor2). Minor categories figures (sales, etc.) can be aggregated to larger minor categories (Minor2 sums to Minor1) and major categories overall figures.

FAST FOOD RESTAURANTS INDUSTRY (NAICS 722513)

NAICS 722513: Fast Food Restaurants. This industry comprises establishments primarily engaged in the retail sale of prepared food and drinks for on-premise or immediate consumption. Caterers and industrial and institutional food service establishments are also included in this business.

INDUSTRY ESTABLISHMENTS, SALES & EMPLOYMENT TRENDS

| | Year | | | | | Percent Chg. Year-to-Year | | | |
	2014	2015	2016	2017	2018	14-15	15-16	16-17	17-18
Establishments	237,433	238,282	241,003	244,706	249,087	0.4%	1.1%	1.5%	1.8%
Sales ($Millions)	198,215	205,047	213,175	222,120	231,449	3.4%	4.0%	4.2%	4.2%
Employment	3,869,367	3,883,201	3,927,548	3,987,896	4,059,295	0.4%	1.1%	1.5%	1.8%
Sales ($M)/Estab.	0.83	0.86	0.88	0.91	0.93	3.1%	2.8%	2.6%	2.4%
Sales ($)/Emp.	51,227	52,804	54,277	55,698	57,017	3.1%	2.8%	2.6%	2.4%

5-YEAR TREND – ESTIMATED NUMBER OF ESTABLISHMENTS

| Year | Employee Size of Establishment | | | | | | | | | Total |
	1-4 Emps.	5-9 Emps.	10-19 Emps.	20-49 Emps.	50-99 Emps.	100-249 Emps.	250-499 Emps.	>500 Emps.	Non-Employer	Employ-ment
2016	63,273	35,631	54,665	65,814	11,874	808	37	14	8,888	241,003
2017	64,246	36,178	55,505	66,825	12,056	820	37	14	9,024	244,706
2018	65,396	36,826	56,498	68,022	12,272	835	38	15	9,186	249,087

5-YEAR TREND – ESTIMATED INDUSTRY SALES ($MILLIONS)

| Year | Employee Size of Establishment | | | | | | | | | Total |
	1-4 Emps.	5-9 Emps.	10-19 Emps.	20-49 Emps.	50-99 Emps.	100-249 Emps.	250-499 Emps.	>500 Emps.	Non-Employer	Employ-ment
2016	6,033.9	8,930.7	34,455.7	109,801.0	43,546.2	7,986.2	1,217.4	1,107.9	96.3	213,175.4
2017	6,287.3	9,305.8	35,902.8	114,412.4	45,375.1	8,321.6	1,268.5	1,145.7	100.4	222,119.5
2018	6,551.7	9,697.1	37,412.5	119,223.3	47,283.0	8,671.5	1,321.8	1,183.4	104.6	231,449.0

5-YEAR TREND – ESTIMATED NUMBER OF EMPLOYEES

| Year | Employee Size of Establishment | | | | | | | | | Total |
	1-4 Emps.	5-9 Emps.	10-19 Emps.	20-49 Emps.	50-99 Emps.	100-249 Emps.	250-499 Emps.	>500 Emps.	Non-Employer	Employ-ment
2016	158,183	206,659	743,441	1,981,000	705,309	101,885	10,630	11,553	8,888	3,927,548
2017	160,614	209,834	754,864	2,011,438	716,147	103,450	10,793	11,731	9,024	3,987,896
2018	163,489	213,591	768,379	2,047,451	728,969	105,303	10,986	11,941	9,186	4,059,295

Fast Food Restaurants Industry (NAICS 722513)

Sub-Industries — 2017 Estimated Industry Sales, Establishments & Employment

Sub-Industries	Category*	Establish-ments	Sales ($Mill)	Employ-ment
Eating places	Major1	87,602	32,327.7	1,034,699
Ice cream, soft drink and soda fountain stands	Minor1	1,785	432.9	15,180
Concessionaire	Minor2	1,585	5,332.9	28,810
Frozen yogurt stand	Minor2	774	228.0	6,848
Ice cream stands or dairy bars	Minor2	11,968	3,937.1	144,844
Snow cone stand	Minor2	274	33.3	950
Soda fountain	Minor2	125	26.0	817
Soft drink stand	Minor2	627	450.0	13,221
Fast food restaurants and stands	Minor1	3,478	1,134.6	41,774
Box lunch stand	Minor2	95	21.0	963
Carry-out only (except pizza) restaurant	Minor2	4,208	1,162.3	41,032
Chili stand	Minor2	124	53.0	1,748
Coffee shop	Minor2	16,987	19,243.7	212,553
Delicatessen (eating places)	Minor2	9,222	3,114.1	60,816
Drive-in restaurant	Minor2	5,691	3,371.6	126,281
Fast-food restaurant, chain	Minor2	51,734	133,754.0	1,702,984
Fast-food restaurant, independent	Minor2	3,221	1,142.7	41,781
Food bars	Minor2	327	250.1	13,024
Grills (eating places)	Minor2	14,126	7,896.9	220,308
Hamburger stand	Minor2	1,957	459.5	22,641
Hot dog stand	Minor2	1,520	210.5	8,075
Sandwiches and submarines shop	Minor2	25,896	7,270.3	236,732
Snack bar	Minor2	991	199.3	9,954
Snack shop	Minor2	389	68.1	1,860

*Category-Major categories (Major1) are more general descriptions for companies that self-selected to capture the many functions they perform in the industry. Minor categories (Minor1, Minor2) are more specific for companies that have more detailed functions (Minor1 is a larger category than Minor2). Minor categories figures (sales, etc.) can be aggregated to larger minor categories (Minor2 sums to Minor1) and major categories overall figures.

DRINKING PLACES & BARS INDUSTRY (NAICS 72241)

NAICS 72241: Drinking Places (Alcoholic Beverages) . This industry comprises establishments known as bars, taverns, nightclubs or drinking places primarily engaged in preparing and serving alcoholic beverages for immediate consumption. These establishments may also provide limited food services.

INDUSTRY ESTABLISHMENTS, SALES & EMPLOYMENT TRENDS

	Year					Percent Chg. Year-to-Year			
	2014	2015	2016	2017	2018	14-15	15-16	16-17	17-18
Establishments	49,562	47,699	46,722	46,026	45,455	-3.8%	-2.0%	-1.5%	-1.2%
Sales ($Millions)	17,502	17,794	18,327	18,921	19,511	1.7%	3.0%	3.2%	3.1%
Employment	369,214	355,337	348,054	342,870	338,619	-3.8%	-2.0%	-1.5%	-1.2%
Sales ($M)/Estab.	0.35	0.37	0.39	0.41	0.43	5.6%	5.1%	4.8%	4.4%
Sales ($)/Emp.	47,404	50,076	52,654	55,185	57,620	5.6%	5.1%	4.8%	4.4%

5-YEAR TREND – ESTIMATED NUMBER OF ESTABLISHMENTS

Year	Employee Size of Establishment									Total
	1-4 Emps.	5-9 Emps.	10-19 Emps.	20-49 Emps.	50-99 Emps.	100-249 Emps.	250-499 Emps.	>500 Emps.	Non-Employer	Employ-ment
2016	19,157	9,865	5,412	3,380	699	114	10	1	8,082	46,722
2017	18,872	9,718	5,331	3,330	689	112	10	1	7,961	46,026
2018	18,638	9,598	5,265	3,289	681	111	10	1	7,863	45,455

5-YEAR TREND – ESTIMATED INDUSTRY SALES ($MILLIONS)

Year	Employee Size of Establishment									Total
	1-4 Emps.	5-9 Emps.	10-19 Emps.	20-49 Emps.	50-99 Emps.	100-249 Emps.	250-499 Emps.	>500 Emps.	Non-Employer	Employ-ment
2016	1,915.1	2,592.1	3,576.0	5,912.2	2,689.1	1,181.9	362.1	61.1	37.0	18,326.5
2017	1,977.2	2,676.2	3,692.0	6,104.0	2,776.4	1,220.2	373.9	63.0	38.2	18,921.1
2018	2,038.9	2,759.7	3,807.1	6,294.4	2,863.0	1,258.3	385.5	65.0	39.3	19,511.2

5-YEAR TREND – ESTIMATED NUMBER OF EMPLOYEES

Year	Employee Size of Establishment									Total
	1-4 Emps.	5-9 Emps.	10-19 Emps.	20-49 Emps.	50-99 Emps.	100-249 Emps.	250-499 Emps.	>500 Emps.	Non-Employer	Employ-ment
2016	47,893	57,218	73,603	101,753	41,549	14,384	3,017	557	8,082	348,054
2017	47,180	56,366	72,507	100,237	40,930	14,169	2,972	548	7,961	342,870
2018	46,595	55,667	71,608	98,994	40,422	13,994	2,935	541	7,863	338,619

DRINKING PLACES & BARS INDUSTRY (NAICS 72241)

SUB-INDUSTRIES — 2017 ESTIMATED INDUSTRY SALES, ESTABLISHMENTS & EMPLOYMENT

Sub-Industries	Category*	Establishments	Sales ($Mill)	Employment
Drinking places	Major1	9,638	5,063.9	64,010
Bars and lounges	Minor1	3,286	1,135.4	22,324
Bar (drinking places)	Minor2	9,788	3,808.7	90,222
Beer garden (drinking places)	Minor2	95	51.0	958
Cocktail lounge	Minor2	5,594	1,991.8	38,146
Saloon	Minor2	963	272.7	5,705
Tavern (drinking places)	Minor2	12,443	4,272.4	77,980
Wine bar	Minor2	323	98.1	1,905
Night clubs	Minor1	3,664	2,093.9	38,543
Cabaret	Minor2	183	95.1	2,464
Discotheque	Minor2	48	38.1	612

*Category-Major categories (Major1) are more general descriptions for companies that self-selected to capture the many functions they perform in the industry. Minor categories (Minor1, Minor2) are more specific for companies that have more detailed functions (Minor1 is a larger category than Minor2). Minor categories figures (sales, etc.) can be aggregated to larger minor categories (Minor2 sums to Minor1) and major categories overall figures.

Definitions and Terms

Number of Establishments

General Definition

An establishment is a single physical location at which business is conducted and/or services are provided. It is not necessarily identical with a company or enterprise, which may consist of one establishment or more. Economic census figures represent a summary of reports for individual establishments rather than companies. For cases where a census report was received, separate information was obtained for each location where business was conducted. When administrative records of other Federal agencies were used instead of a census report, no information was available on the number of locations operated. Each economic census establishment was tabulated according to the physical location at which the business was conducted.

When two activities or more were carried on at a single location under a single ownership, all activities generally were grouped together as a single establishment. The entire establishment was classified on the basis of its major activity and all data for it were included in that classification. However, when distinct and separate economic activities (for which different industry classification codes were appropriate) were conducted at a single location under a single ownership, separate establishment reports for each of the different activities were obtained in the census.

Sector-Specific Information

Construction sector. Establishments are defined as a relatively permanent office or other place of business where the usual business activities related to construction are conducted. Establishments do not represent each project or construction site. Includes all establishments that were in business at any time during the year. It covers all full-year and part-year operations. Construction establishments which were inactive or idle for the entire year were not included. Establishments are based on a survey which included all large employers and a sample of the smaller ones.

Information; Professional, Scientific, and Technical Services; Administrative and Support and Waste Management and Remediation Services; Educational Services; Health Care and Social Assistance; Arts, Entertainment, and Recreation; and Other Services (Except Public Administration) sectors. An establishment is included in the census if it is an employer, the establishment has $1,000 in payroll, and was in operation at any time during 2012. Leased service departments (separately owned businesses operated as departments or concessions of other service establishments or of retail businesses, such as a separately owned shoeshine parlor in a barber shop, or a beauty shop in a department store) are treated as separate service establishments for census purposes. Leased retail departments located in service establishments (e.g., a gift shop located in a hotel) are considered separate retail establishments.

Manufacturing sector. Includes all manufacturing establishments (plants) with one employee or more and establishments in operation at any time during the year.

Mining sector. Includes all mineral establishments with one employee or more and establishments in operation at any time during the year. Establishments in the crude petroleum and natural gas and support activities for mining represent statewide operations rather than those at a single physical location.

Real Estate and Rental and Leasing sector. Data for individual properties leased or managed by property lessors or property managers are not normally considered separate establishments, but rather the permanent offices from which the properties are leased or managed are considered establishments. Data for separate automotive rental offices or concessions (e.g., airport locations) in the same metropolitan area for which a common fleet of cars is maintained are merged together and not considered as separate establishments.

Retail Trade sector. Leased departments are treated as separate establishments and are classified according to the kind of business they conduct. For example, a leased department selling shoes within a department store would be considered a separate retail establishment under the "shoe stores" classification.

Accommodation and Foodservices sector. Leased departments are treated as separate establishments and are classified according to the kind of business they conduct. For example, a leased department selling gifts/souvenirs within a hotel would be considered a separate retail establishment under the "gift, novelty, and souvenir stores" classification.

Auxiliaries sector. In the Standard Industrial Classification (SIC) system, auxiliary establishments (i.e., those establishments primarily serving other establishments of the same enterprise) were classified in the industry of the establishments served. In the North American Industry Classification System (NAICS), auxiliary establishments are classified according to the services performed rather than the industry served.

Sales, Shipments, Receipts, Revenue, or Business Done
General Definition
Includes the total sales, shipments, receipts, revenue, or business done by establishments within the scope of the economic census. The definition of each of these items is included in the information provided below.
Sector-Specific Information
Construction sector - Includes the value of construction work and other business receipts for work done by establishments during the year. Included is new construction, additions and alterations or reconstruction, and maintenance and repair construction work. Also included is the value of any construction work done by the reporting establishments for themselves.
Speculative builders were instructed to include the value of buildings and other structures built or being built for sale in the current year but not sold. They were to include the costs of such construction plus normal profit. Also included is the cost of construction work done on buildings for rent or lease.
Establishments engaged in the sale and installation of such construction components as plumbing, heating, and central air-conditioning supplies and equipment; lumber and building materials; paint, glass, and wallpaper; electrical and wiring supplies; and elevators or escalators were instructed to include both the value for the installation and the receipts covering the price of the items installed.
Excluded was the cost of industrial and other specialized machinery and equipment, which are not an integral part of a structure.
Finance and Insurance sector - Includes revenue from all business activities whether or not payment was received in the census year, including commissions and fees from all sources, rents, net investment income, interest, dividends, royalties, and net insurance premiums earned. Revenue from leasing property marketed under operating leases is included, as well as interest earned from property marketed in the census year under capital, finance, or full payout leases. Revenue also includes the total value of service contracts and amounts received for work subcontracted to others.
Revenue does not include sales and other taxes collected from customers and remitted directly by the firm to a local, state, or Federal tax agency.
Information sector - Includes receipts from customers or clients for services rendered, from the use of facilities, and from merchandise sold, whether or not payment was received. Receipts include royalties, license fees, and other payments from the marketing of intangible products (e.g., licensing the use of or granting reproduction rights for software, musical
compositions, and other intellectual property). Receipts also include the rental and leasing of vehicles, equipment, instruments, tools, etc.; total value of service contracts; market value of compensation received in lieu of cash; amounts received for work subcontracted to others; dues and assessments for members

and affiliates; this establishment's share of receipts from departments, concessions, and vending and amusement machines operated by others. Receipts from services provided to foreign customers from U.S. locations, including services preformed for foreign parent firms, subsidiaries, and branches are included. For public broadcast stations and libraries, include receipts from contributions, gifts, grants, and income from interest, rental of real estate, and dividends.

Receipts DO NOT include sales and other taxes collected directly from customers or clients and paid directly to a local, state, or Federal tax agency. Also excluded are gross receipts collected on behalf of others; gross receipts or departments or concessions operated by others; sales of used equipment previously rented or leased to customers; proceeds from the sale of real estate (land and buildings), investments, or other assets (except inventory held for resale); contributions, gifts, grants, and income from interest, rental of real estate, and dividends EXCEPT for public broadcast stations and libraries; domestic intracompany transfers; receipts of foreign subsidiaries; and other nonoperating income.

Management of Companies and Enterprises sector- For holding companies, revenue includes revenue of only the holding company establishment, including net investment income, interest, and dividends.

Manufacturing sector - Covers the received or receivable net selling values, f.o.b. plant (exclusive of freight and taxes), of all products shipped, both primary and secondary, as well as all miscellaneous receipts, such as receipts for contract work performed for others, installation and repair, sales of scrap, and sales of products bought and resold without further processing. Included are all items made by or for the establishments from materials owned by it, whether sold, transferred to other plants of the same company, or shipped on consignment. The net selling value of products made in one plant on a contract basis from materials owned by another was reported by the plant providing the materials.

In the case of multiunit companies, the manufacturer was requested to report the value of products transferred to other establishments of the same company at full economic or commercial value, including not only the direct cost of production but also a reasonable proportion of "all other costs" (including company overhead) and profit.

Mining sector - Includes the net selling values, f.o.b. mine or plant after discounts and allowances, excluding freight charges and excise taxes. Shipments includes all products physically shipped from the establishment during the year, including material withdrawn from stockpiles and products shipped on consignment, whether or not sold in the current year. Prepared material or concentrates includes preparation from ores mined at the same establishment, purchased, received from other operations of the same company, or received for milling on a custom or toll basis. For products transferred to other establishments of the same company or prepared on a custom basis, companies were requested to report the estimated value, not merely the cost of producing the items. Multiestablishment companies were asked to report value information for each establishment as if it were a separate economic unit. They were instructed to report the value of all products transferred to other plants of the company at their full economic value; to include, in addition to direct cost of production, a reasonable proportion of company overhead and profits. For all establishments classified in an industry, value of shipments and receipts includes (1) the value of all primary products of the industry; (2) the value of secondary products which are primary to other industries; (3) the receipts for contract work done for others, except custom milling; and (4) the value of products purchased and resold without further processing. Receipts for custom milling are not included to avoid duplication with the value of custom milled ores included in an industry's primary and secondary products. Some duplication exists in industry and industry group totals because of the inclusion of materials transferred from one establishment to another for mineral preparation or resale.

Professional, Scientific, and Technical Services; Administrative and Support and Waste Management and Remediation Services; Educational Services; Health Care and Social Assistance; Arts, Entertainment, and Recreation; and Other Services (Except Public Administration) sectors - TAXABLE ESTABLISHMENTS: Includes receipts from customers or clients for services rendered, from the use of facilities, and from merchandise sold whether or not payment was received. For advertising agencies, travel industries, and other service establishments operating on a commission basis, receipts include commissions, fees, and other operating income, NOT gross billings and sales. Excise taxes on gasoline, liquor, tobacco, etc., which are paid by the manufacturer or wholesaler and passed on in the cost of goods purchased by the service establishment are also included. The establishments share of receipts from departments, concessions, and vending and amusement machines operated by others are included as part of receipts. Receipts also include the total value of service contracts, market value of compensation received in lieu of cash, amounts received for work subcontracted to others, and dues and assessments from members and affiliates. Receipts from services provided to foreign customers from U.S. locations, including services preformed for foreign parent firms, subsidiaries, and branches are included.

Receipts are net after deductions for refunds and allowances for merchandise returned by customers. Receipts DO NOT include sales, occupancy, admissions, or other taxes collected from customers and remitted directly by the firm to a local, state, or Federal tax agency, nor do they include income from such sources as contributions, gifts, and grants; dividends, interest, and investments; or sale or rental of real estate. Also excluded are receipts (gross) of departments and concessions which are operated by others; sales of used equipment rented or leased to customers; domestic intracompany transfers; receipts of foreign subsidiaries; and other nonoperating income, such as royalties, franchise fees, etc. Receipts DO NOT include service receipts of manufacturers, wholesalers, retail establishments, or other businesses whose primary activity is other than service. They do, however, include receipts other than from services rendered (e.g., sale of merchandise to individuals or other businesses) by establishments primarily engaged in performing services and classified in the service industries.

TAX EXEMPT ESTABLISHMENTS: Includes revenue from customers or clients for services rendered and merchandise, whether or not payment was received, and gross sales of merchandise, minus returns and allowances. Also included are income from interest, dividends, gross rents (including display space rentals and share of receipts from departments operated by other companies), gross contributions, gifts, grants (whether or not restricted for use in operations), royalties, dues and assessments from members and affiliates, commissions earned from the sale of merchandise owned by others (including commissions from vending machine operators), and gross receipts from fundraising activities. Receipts from taxable business activities of firms exempt from Federal income tax (unrelated business income) are also included in revenue. Revenue DOES NOT include sales, admissions, or other taxes collected by the organization from customers or clients and paid directly to a local, state, or Federal tax agency; income from the sale of real estate, investments, or other assets (except inventory held for resale); gross receipts of departments, concessions, etc., that are operated by others; and amounts transferred to operating funds from capital or reserve funds.

Real Estate and Rental and Leasing sector - Includes revenue from all business activities whether or not payment was received in the census year, including commissions and fees from all sources, rents, net investment income, interest, dividends, and royalties. Revenue from leasing property marketed under operating leases is included. Revenue also includes the total value of service contracts, amounts received for work subcontracted to others, and rents from real property sublet to others.

Revenue does not include sales and other taxes collected from customers and remitted directly by the firm to a local, state, or Federal tax agency.

Retail Trade sector - Includes merchandise sold for cash or credit at retail and wholesale by establishments primarily engaged in retail trade; amounts received from customers for layaway purchases; receipts from rental of vehicles, equipment, instruments, tools, etc.; receipts for delivery, installation, maintenance, repair, alteration, storage, and other services; the total value of service contracts; and gasoline, liquor, tobacco, and other excise taxes which are paid by the manufacturer or wholesaler and passed on to the retailer. Sales are net after deductions for refunds and allowances for merchandise returned by customers. Trade-in allowances are not deducted from sales. Sales do not include carrying or other credit charges; sales (or other) taxes collected from customers and forwarded to taxing authorities; gross sales and receipts of departments or concessions operated by other companies; and commissions or receipts from the sale of government lottery tickets.

Sales do not include retail sales made by manufacturers, wholesalers, service establishments, or other businesses whose primary activity is other than retail trade. They do include receipts other than from the sale of merchandise at retail, e.g., service receipts, sales to industrial users, and sales to other retailers, by establishments primarily engaged in retail trade.

Transportation and Warehousing sector - Includes revenue from all business activities whether or not payment was received in the census year, including commissions and fees for arranging the transportation of freight. Revenue does not include sales and other taxes collected from customers and remitted directly by the firm to a local, state, or Federal tax agency.

Utilities sector - Includes revenue from all business activities whether or not payment was received in the census year.

Revenue does not include sales and other taxes collected from customers and remitted directly by the firm to a local, state, or Federal tax agency.

Accommodation and Foodservices sector - Includes sales from customers for services rendered, from the use of facilities, and from merchandise sold. Also includes dues and assessments from members and affiliates. Sales do not include carrying or other credit charges; sales (or other) taxes collected from customers and forwarded to taxing authorities; gross sales and receipts of departments or concessions operated by other companies; and commissions or receipts from the sale of government lottery tickets.

Excludes sales from civic and social organizations, amusement and recreation parks, theaters, and other recreation or entertainment facilities providing food and beverage services.

Number of Employees

General Definition

Paid employees consists of full-time and part-time employees, including salaried officers and executives of corporations. Included are employees on paid sick leave, paid holidays, and paid vacations; not included are proprietors and partners of unincorporated businesses. The definition of paid employees is the same as that used on IRS Form 941.

Sector-Specific Information

Construction and Manufacturing sectors. Comprises all full-time and part-time employees on the payrolls of establishments who worked or received pay for any part of the pay period including the 12th of March, May, August, and November, divided by 4.

Finance and Insurance sector. Includes all employees who were on the payroll during the pay period including March 12. Excludes independent (nonemployee) agents.

Information; Professional, Scientific, and Technical Services; Administrative and Support and Waste Management and Remediation Services; Educational Services; Health Care and Social Assistance; Arts, Entertainment, and Recreation; and Other Services (Except Public Administration) sectors - Includes all employees who were on the payroll during the pay period including March 12. Includes members of a professional service organization or association which operates under state professional corporation statutes and files a corporate Federal income tax return. Excludes employees of departments or concessions operated by other companies at the establishment.

Management of Companies and Enterprises sector. Includes all employees who were on the payroll during the pay period including March 12.

Mining sector. Also included are employees working for miners paid on a per ton, car, or yard basis. Excluded are employees at the mine but on the payroll of another employer (such as employees of contractors) and employees at company stores, boardinghouses, bunkhouses, and recreational centers.

Also excluded are members of the Armed Forces and pensioners carried on the active rolls but not working during the period. Includes all employees who were on the payroll during the pay period including March 12. Real Estate and Rental and Leasing sector. Includes all employees who were on the payroll during the pay period including March 12. Excludes independent (nonemployee) agents.

Retail Trade and Accommodation and Foodservices sectors. Includes all employees on the payroll during the pay period including March 12. Excludes employees of departments or concessions operated by other companies at the establishment.

Transportation and Warehousing sector. Includes all employees who were on the payroll during the pay period including March 12.

Utilities sector. Includes all employees who were on the payroll during the pay period including March 12.

www.ingramcontent.com/pod-product-compliance
Lightning Source LLC
Chambersburg PA
CBHW081717220526

45468CB00008B/1882